Tunnel
of
Mirrors

Tunnel
of
Mirrors

Ferne Arfin

First published 1st February 2022

Copyright © 2022 by Ferne Arfin
Green River Press, London

ISBN, hardback: 978-1-80227-096-9
ISBN, paperback: 978-1-80227-064-8
ISBN, ebook: 978-1-80227-065-5

Published by Green River Press, London
This book is typeset in Baskerville

For my family
across oceans and time

Contents

Part One

*I am all of my past, as every protagonist of the Mendelian law must agree.
All my previous selves have their voices, echoes, promptings in me. My every
mode of action, heat of passion, flicker of thought, is shaded...by that vast
array of other selves that preceded me and went into the making of me....*

The Star Rover, Jack London

CHAPTER ONE

Prelude

1927

Fourteenth Street is still, a stage before the actors have taken their places, before the audience has been admitted. No one sits at an open window to catch a vagrant breeze. No one lounges on a stoop for a late summer gossip about Babe Ruth's record-breaking season.

So no one sees a tall young woman, head erect, dressed all in black, making her way with prideful carriage along the sidewalk. No one wonders at how, despite the muggy August night, she shivers in her tightly clutched shawl.

The shouts emerging from the etched glass doorway of one of the small burgher brownstones - shouts of "madwoman" and "witch" - dissipate unheard on the damp, empty night. A heavy door slams.

Midway down the block, the tall young woman lifts her unfashionably long skirts and breaks into a run, running fast, like someone pursued, or in pursuit, east and south, towards the crowded, noisome immigrant quarters of the city.

If there were onlookers, persons of particularly credulous natures, they might believe they see the very air part before her; a sooty mist, parting and then swirling behind, in a wake of spinning dust devils.

But on this late Saturday night in August, the good citizens of 14th Street don't fan themselves at open windows or socialise on stoops, their trouser legs rolled to the knees. No one sees. No one hears.

∞

When Rachel was born, the midwife tied a crisp red ribbon to her blanket to ward off the attentions of the evil eye. One could never be too careful.

In those days, women knew that spirits were everywhere. They danced along Clinton Street and spun like dervishes through the tenements of Hester and Rivington. Spirits flowed along the gutters of Cherry and Henry, Broome and Delancey.

Men might accuse their wives of being superstitious, silly. But women understood things that men never saw. No one, for example, accused Rabbi Meyer's second wife of poor housekeeping when her Friday fire failed to last long enough to cook the sabbath stew, although it happened again and again. Among the congregation, the rabbi and his family were regular Saturday supper guests. Clearly, it was the rabbi's first wife, who died of the influenza, up to mischief.

And what, if not spirits, did people mean when they said that Weiss's son Schmuel took after his great uncle Emmanuel? Wasn't Manny dead of drink and bad habits a good five years before Schmuel was even born?

It was all very well for men to have their endless conversations with God, but one had only to look around to realise that God was frequently too busy to listen. Where would the world be if women didn't tend to the practical magic?

So, there were formulae to be whispered, glasses to be overturned, pinches of salt to be thrown for every piece of dropped cutlery, itchy nose, misplaced shoe. Every newborn babe wore a spot of red, a bit of yarn or a sprig of ribbon, in its bunting, to distract untoward attentions.

Once Rachel's eldest sister Sarah had taken the baby for a bit of fresh air. Sgt. O'Halloran had stopped to admire Rachel and her pretty brown eyes. He had been shocked to see Sarah slap the baby's face and spit on the ground. Even a 10-year-old child knew about the evil eye. Later, when Sarah told her mother about this unanticipated jinx, Sophie had reassured her. The evil eye does not bother about Irish policemen who don't know any better, she said. Still, she lit an extra memorial candle that night, reasoning that, amongst five thousand years of relations, it must have been someone's anniversary and it never hurt to have a little help from the other side.

It was widely understood that spirits were neither evil nor benevolent. And every household had a few; you cannot be a wandering people for millennia without taking your restless ancestors with you from one place to the next. However, as a tall tree attracts more lightening in a dense forest, some people attracted spirit company and spirit mischief more readily than others. How else to explain the blacksmith's misfortune? A gentle man who gave credit without expectation of payment and looked after his evil-tempered mother until she died; he was a mainstay of the synagogue and so soft-hearted that he gave more than he could afford to every good cause. But, when he finally married, a crowd of malice descended on his household. His pretty wife was barren and almost as foul-tempered as his mother had been. There was the fire that burned down his stable and killed two horses. And then, with his livelihood in ruins and his nagging wife telling anyone who would listen that she could have done better, six cousins from Minsk turned up on his doorstep and had to be fed.

Then again, there was the extraordinary abandon of Muttel the Shoemaker's prayers; a man so quiet and modest you could look straight at him and forget he was there. Saturday mornings in schul, the women watched him, through the lace curtain that secluded them, being tossed like a madman in every direction while the other men rocked quietly together. What legions of petitioners did his piety draw forth?

From the beginning, Rachel was one of these people, a lightning rod for spirits. Most infants give their mothers a few months of sleepless nights. As far as Sophie could tell, Rachel never learned to sleep through the night. She woke before dawn to talk. As the youngest of six children in a multilingual household, there were so many words to practice. English from her brothers and sisters, Yiddish, of course, some German that Jacob lapsed into when he was being pompous. Sophie even thought she heard a few of Rosa's incomprehensible Rumanian curses. Rosa, married to Sophie's younger brother Abie, looked after the baby when Sophie worked.

In the hours before dawn, Sophie lay awake listening to her baby's animated conversations with her toes, her fingers, the air, a stuffed toy that little Sarah had made...and others. Once, she was so certain that the baby had said, "Bubbie Ruchel wants flowers," that she woke Jacob to tell him. He groaned and rolled over, muttering that a child of eight months does not say such things. Nevertheless, later that day, Sophie took housekeeping money to buy flowers for her mother's grave. Jacob was furious. People didn't do such things, he said. Flowers were for gentiles and other pagans who worshipped their dead. But Sophie felt oddly peaceful after she had done it. Her mother had always missed her flower garden.

Poor Sophie, sleepless baby or not, she had to rise early every morning to feed her other children before going out to cook for strangers.

It couldn't be helped. Sophie's skill in the kitchen had been the salvation of the family. In the old country, perhaps, it was a great honour to be married to a scholar. Sophie's father, the gravedigger, had thought so, making room for Jacob in his home when her two brothers left to earn their passage to America.

When Jacob Isaacson, an itinerant scholar, came to town to dispute with the local rabbi, Sophie's father was the only villager who had a spare bed. He must have thought it a miracle when the scholar took a shine to his only daughter. Big, plain and without a dowry, Sophie, at 24, was well established as a spinster. And to have a respected scholar in your household, well, besides the honour of such a son-in-law, the gifts from grateful students could not be ignored.

Jacob, for his part, was ready to settle. The town was full of young boys of an age to be taught scripture and men eager to argue Talmud with someone new. Sophie was sturdy and sensible, used to living on little. If people said her mother was a little bit strange, well, what did that matter. In these small *shtetls*, unschooled people said a lot of foolish things. And Sophie could cook. A man who lives for The Law and eats well besides is truly blessed.

Life in the village was relatively peaceful. Shtetl Jews had little that anybody else wanted. As long as one kept business with one's gentile neighbours to a minimum and stayed indoors when they were drunk, a pious man could live well enough. Jacob would have been happy to stay. But the grave digger's sons were not the first to leave for America, and they wouldn't be the last. Every year, the number of students dwindled. Without students, a teacher cannot eat.

When Sophie's father died, Jacob had little choice but to pack up his family, which now included his widowed mother-in-law and his three children and join the westward march.

For Jacob, America was Sodom and Gomorrah and the Whore of Babylon, bundled up in one and spewing sin in all directions. It was a place where the people lived like *goyem*, where they forgot where they came from and what life was really for. In the old country, Jacob believed, a man worked to eat, ate to live and lived to pray. Few of his neighbours, people who had struggled for a miserable living, keeping their heads down and making no trouble, careful not to call attention to themselves, especially during Easter, shared Jacob's rosy nostalgia. Scholars, who spend their days and many nights in the scented holiness of the schul, have little contact with the hard realities. Jacob's wisdom didn't buy bread.

Here, in the new world, making money seemed to Jacob to be the whole point of life. All around him, people worked to get ahead, to be American. Whole families worked, men, women and children, to earn the mythical American Dream. And what was this American Dream? As far as he could tell, from the cheap illustrated journals he finally banned from his house, it was largely made up of white enamelled ice boxes, electrified irons, horseless carriages and scandalously immodest clothes.

In such an atmosphere, how could he persuade people that their sons should study The Law for the absolute pleasure of daily contact with the mind of God? He was too stiff-necked to do it, and few families could spare the money for such a luxury at any rate. Rabbi Meyer sent him students preparing for Bar Mitzvah. As soon as they took their turn at Torah and said their speech in the synagogue, they were gone. A few parents paid him to teach their children to read Hebrew so they could read the socialist *Forward*, which you read backward because it was printed in Yiddish. There was no living for a family man in these things.

In fact, for Jacob, there was no living of any kind in America. He was too frail and soft for labour. Sophie's brother tried to get him a job at the Post Office but, even after several years, his English was too poor. When he tried to speak to Americans, he could feel the scorn of eyes that saw him as an ignorant fool. This was too much for Jacob's dignity. Eventually, he stopped trying.

In the end, it was Sophie's strudels and dumplings and fragrant stews that saved them all.

Just up Rivington Street, a Bialystoker named Kandel ran a small delicatessen. He sold salamis and meats that he spiced and cured himself. His wife made marinated herrings and, in the back, he kept a wooden barrel of sour pickles in garlicky brine. Sophie loved the smell of the place. She noticed, too, that people often ate what they bought before they took it home. "Wait a *bissel*, Kandel," they'd say as he wrapped their purchase in crisp waxed paper. "Leave me a piece out, so I'll see if it has any taste."

"My grandmother's taste, I'll give you," he would snap. But then he would throw in a bit extra for the sampling.

One side of the shop was lined with shelves of cans and bottles. A travelling salesman from Battle Creek had persuaded Kandel that every modern grocer was stocking these convenient foods. The wave of the future, he said. But nobody wanted expensive *goyesha* food they couldn't examine and smell. The cans were dusty and their labels were beginning to fade. Sophie convinced Kandel that if he pulled out the shelves, he could set up a nice little counter and people would come for a snack, maybe even a meal. She also convinced him, with a plate of her stuffed cabbage, to give her a job.

Within a year, the little counter had turned into a cafe. Sophie fed workmen, peddlers and schmoozers all day and then went home to feed her own.

Now pride is a great waster of time and energy, but Sophie was no fool. She understood that for her husband, pride and self-respect were inseparable. She also understood the value of a peaceful household. Whatever she did in the world outside, in their home, Jacob was king. And, as might be expected of the king of such a diminished kingdom, he ruled like a tyrant. If outside his door the world was on its way to the Wrath of God, he, like Lot, would be the One Just Man. Under his roof, Tradition and The Law would be observed to the letter. It never crossed his mind that after a while it was more Sophie's roof than his. To be fair, such a radical idea never occurred to Sophie either.

By the time Rachel arrived, Sophie had borne eight children, one still at birth and a second taken by whooping cough when he was six months old. Rachel came into a world only recently saddened by the death of Sophie's mother, Ruchel. Still, a birth so soon after a death was meant to be a *mitzvah*, a blessing. The child was named for her grandmother, as Tradition dictated, and welcomed into an extended family of sisters, brothers, cousins, aunts and uncles. She was the youngest and the last, the pet of them all.

∞

On Third Avenue, a fashionable young couple amble, hand in hand. They have been to an open-air dance in Washington Square and their festive clothes glow in the yellow orange wash of the street lights. The young man swings his cream linen jacket carelessly over his shoulder. The girl shakes her head when she laughs, a deliberate mannerism to make her cream and yellow hair ribbons bounce and rustle.

For some blocks now, the young man has been trying to steal a kiss, but every time he thinks he might, the girl pulls away and skips ahead.

When Rachel rounds the corner, they can hardly ignore her. Even in New York, a woman holding up her skirts and sprinting through the streets is an odd sight. But a shabbily dressed woman running through this district at such a late hour is probably a matter best left alone. Besides, the boy has eyes only for his flirtatious companion. And as for the girl, she is pressed by more amusing concerns. It is a fine summer night; she has been to a party; she is wearing the most perfect yellow kid dancing slippers in New York, and she has been teasing her young man mercilessly for the better part of five city blocks.

They step aside to make way for the madwoman and, as they do so, Rachel and the girl look each other full in the face. The glance is merely passing but the young girl cannot help being moved, astonishingly so. Quickly, she looks away, embarrassed and stricken. For just that instant, she believes she has seen the purest, most profound loneliness imaginable; hungry loneliness, endless, dark and insatiable. It pulls at her, draws her remorselessly, the way a dream phantom tears you from the safety of your bed to wake you in a crumpled heap on the floor, unable to give voice to your night terrors. The girl imagines she must break away or be consumed.

Searching for a rescuer, or perhaps merely a distraction, her eyes settle upon the puzzled, still eager, young man. She throws herself into his arms, clings to him, buries her face in his chest. Her delicate arms grip him like a drowner.

The young man can scarcely believe his luck.

CHAPTER TWO

Menscher's wolf

1907

Voices, faces, words, sounds, stories. From the very first moment. From the very first time you open your eyes, they are all talking at you, singing, whispering, shouting, laughing, clapping, squealing.

The little ones that peer at you between milk-coloured slats, face to face, alongside. The big ones that lean down over you and fill the whole world with themselves. The ones that you can only see sometimes when the light is just around the corner. The ones that you can only hear. The ones that never come near and fly away if you reach for them and sing the same little tune to you again and again.

Sometimes they give you things. A red ball that does nothing but roll away. A soft, blankety thing that looks like them but has eyes that never blink and a mouth that never opens. An egg on a stick with something inside that sounds like rain when you shake it.

Sometimes they tell you things. Words, sounds, faces, voices. Sweet whispers with touching on your face. Gruff barks so you jump and wail. Slow music that makes you sleepy. Quiet moans from wet faces. Scary words that make their eyes go wide. Secrets.

Who's Mama's good girl?... She has eyes just like your mother. Your mother always had such pretty eyes...Why is she so tiny, Mama? ...Listen, she's singing with the fiddler...Can't you quiet that child? I have pupils to teach! ...These are your fingers and these are your toes...In the deep dark forest there are wolves... Watermelons, ripe and sweet, wau-di-muhlowns!...*B'ruch atah Adonai*...Give it to me; it's mine! Give it back to me or I'll tell Mama what you did!...and they carry naughty children to the mountains and EAT THEM...Rosa, stop already with the stories! ...You smoked a cigarette with Mayer, I'm gonna tell...So, your Bubbie Ruchel had a garden and she loved her flowers so very much...Now Mama's going to sew. Don't tell Papa because it's *Shabbas*...I'm the prettiest, Mama said so ...*and when my Papa's cows ate the flowers, they were all sick. But they were hungry, you see.* Is Mama's little girl hungry? ...*The soldiers came and they took all my brothers into the Tsar's army*...We danced at my wedding, just like this...Sha, your sister is sleeping, at last...But Mama, Duvi took my... Sha!

Stories, voices, words, sounds. They talk to each other.

Well, she tells everyone that he died on the boat, but I heard from my brother Berel that he took up with an Irish shiksa he met in immigration. If my Jacob knew!...and so, if I tell you, he didn't know how to work the heaters in the hen house. I mean, what does a blacksmith from Cracow know about chickens? The first winter, all the eggs boiled. *Nu?*...so what do you think of that? ...For that one? A good match? With that *gulyah* on her nose? She should live so long...She never did; she never went around with a *Kulak*. Not her...So how come, when he's so dark, the oldest boy is blond? You tell me...Two weeks at the immigration and then they sent them both back!...*Aleph beh's gimel*...I'm telling you. What he gets for a chicken! It's a miracle anyone can make *Shabbas*.

You can hear when they are happy or angry. You can hear when they are afraid. You know who is sly and who is vain. Don't tell Papa. You know when someone is bad because you are never bad. There are whines and giggles and whispers, and you can hear the true things even when the words are false.

If you laugh and wave your arms and legs, you can make them talk to you. You can make them play music and clap and talk in rhymes. Nine ten the big fat HEN! And what you hear, voices, words, sounds, stories, is better than what they give you...a ball that rolls away, a doll that doesn't blink or move its mouth...because when you are all alone, you can close your eyes and bring everything back. You can hear it all over again, all by yourself. You can see the words, just like things. You can smell the stories, just like Mama. And all the people are there whenever you want them. Company. In the dancing sunlight. In the mirror. Beside you to soothe you in the dark. And always, *always* behind your eyelids. To tell you everything. To sing you all the songs. Clap hands, clap hands till Papa comes home. Bubbie Ruchel gives you flowers. *Don't tell Papa.* And the man with the fiddle plays all night at Mama's wedding. Uncle Berel had a farm, Ee-aye, ee-aye...Five six pick up sticks.

From the very first time you open your eyes, they are all talking, telling stories, telling secrets, telling memories. So why, when at last you can make them understand you, are they so surprised that you remember, that you know?

∞

Rachel told everyone who would listen about the flower that Uncle Shoe was going to bring her.

Shoe was Sophie's older brother Berel. Like his mother before him, he had a green thumb. He had put the money he saved from working as a presser in Vienna into a small farm in Connecticut where he grew seasonal vegetables and tended a few apple trees.

Whenever he visited, Sophie hollered at him to take off his dirty farm shoes before he spoiled her freshly mopped floor. As no one takes the trouble to make formal introductions to an infant, Rachel thought this regularly repeated greeting was his name. Soon everyone but Jacob called him Shoe as well. Jacob said, how would his account be written in the Book of Life if you didn't use the name he was given before God?

Before her third birthday, Shoe asked Rachel what kind of a present she would like. She asked for a flower. Sophie thought it was an odd request. What did the child know about flowers? Had she ever even seen one? Perhaps at Kandel's daughter's wedding. But she was only six months old then. Shoe promised to bring her a flower she could look after all by herself.

For weeks Rachel talked of nothing else. This child talked sooner and more often than any of the others. Even though Sophie was in the habit of ignoring the constant chatter most of the time, she could not fail to notice. Rachel told Kandel. Then she told Kandel's wife. She made sure that all the cafe's regulars heard the news. She talked to herself about it. Sophie even overheard her telling Menscher the janitor's dog—from a safe distance, of course.

Menscher kept a big yellow mongrel tied to a rope at the bottom of the stairs. Rachel called it Menscher's wolf and never got closer than the full stretch of its tether. It was no use, Sophie's explaining that it was not a wolf, just a tired old dog. Didn't all the other children shout, "Wolf, Wolf," whenever it barked? There is no arguing with such logic.

"How will the flower stay a long time?"
"We'll give it water, little one."

"Will it be very thirsty?"

"Flowers are always very thirsty."

"What colour is a flower?"

"Well, I don't know. Flowers are all different colours, you know. Red, yellow, white. We'll see."

"Not red!"

"Yes, sometimes flowers are red. We'll have to wait and see."

Sophie hoped that Berel had not forgotten.

"Not red!"

But on the day, a bright warm Sunday in June, the flower that Berel brought was red, a big healthy geranium in a wooden box, with three heavy heads of dark red blooms.

After the weeks of excitement, Rachel's disappointment surprised everyone. She refused to thank Shoe. She refused, even, to talk to him, though she sat by the window, whispering to the empty air as she sometimes did, nodding and gesturing, her eyes clearly focused on some creation of her imagination.

"Rachel, be a good girl and say thank you to Uncle Shoe."

"No. Bad flower. Ugly bad flower."

This response earned her a sharp smack and she was sent to the bedroom to think about her naughtiness.

Later, when Sophie tried to get to the bottom of things, Rachel insisted, "You know. Red is for blood. You know. Bloody flowers."

What an idea. "Who told you that? Did Tanta Rosa tell you such nonsense?"

Rachel shook her head.

"Who then?"

"The lady."

"What lady, Rachel? What are you talking about?"

"You know. The lady," she whined. "She tells me. The soldiers took the boys and there was blood on the flowers. You know. Red is for blood."

Sophie was dumbstruck. When her mother was a girl in Russia, the Cossacks razed her village and impressed all the young men, including Sophie's uncles, into the Tsar's army. In the fighting, her grandfather's livestock was butchered in the yard. The eglantine, the only flowering thing they had because it was quick, wild and free, was turned red with cow's blood. Sophie could still remember her mother's own garden in Austria. Yellow, white, pink, but never red.

Who would tell a child such a terrible story? Ruchel would not have told the older children; Sophie was sure of that. It must have been Rosa, with her childish love of fantastic tales. Did the woman have no sense at all?

But Rosa had never even heard the story.

The next day, Sophie found all the flower heads broken off, the petals scattered and crushed on the floor.

∞

Menscher's wolf has eyes that flash like candle flames and long yellow teeth and a slobbering mouth. *Mensher's wolf is crying because he is hungry.* But no one has been naughty, no matter what they say. *They don't know, but we do.* No one has been naughty so Menscher's wolf is crying for his empty belly.

...And Menscher's wolf will get you if you don't watch out!

"When the moon is full..."

"What is 'moon is full' Tanta Rosa?"

"When the moon is all round in the sky, like a big cracked plate. When that happens, all the people lock their doors and shut their windows tight. Because even if their children are naughty, no one wants the wolf to carry them off to the mountains."

"Does the wolf ever get the children?"

"Sometimes, Mamaleh, sometimes. Once, in my village, two little boys. They were very, very bad boys. They ran away to follow the gypsies with the dancing bear..."

"What is gypsies?"

"That's a different story, Mamaleh. Another time...They ran away and their father had to travel for two whole days and nights to find them and bring them home."

"Did he punish them?"

"Oh yes, little one. He shaved their heads so all the village would know how naughty they were. That's how the wolf found out. And then, one night, they disappeared, and no one ever saw them again."

"The wolf?"

"Absolutely, Mamaleh. Eat your noodles."

"Did the Papa lock the doors and shut the windows tight?"

"Well, of course he did. But it was too late. Because the wolf brought a *golem* to open the doors."

"A golem? ...I don't like the white pieces."

"All right, leave the cheese, just eat the plain noodles...A golem looks just like a man, but it's not a man at all."

"What is it?"

"Well, swallow first and then I'll tell you...Some people say that a golem is magic that looks just like a *mensch*, a person, but it has no soul..."

"What's that?"

"Oy, that also is a long story...Let me see...A soul is what God puts inside of you so you know who you are. *Vershtay*?"

"Doesn't a golem know who it is?"

"Oh, it knows, it knows only too well, Mamaleh. Because you see, a golem is a soul that has no friends, no spirits to keep it company."

"I have friends. Mrs Kandel gave me a pickle. And the lady who gives me flowers..."

"What lady?"

"The lady...and the man who plays the fiddle...and..."

"Stop talking and eat up. Everybody's soul has friends to talk to them when they sleep and so they're not afraid of the dark and so they sing inside when they hear music. And all the people who live with God can come and be with your soul whenever they like."

"I know."

"But the golem is all alone. Always. And he searches all over the world for spirits to keep him from being so lonely."

"Is he very sad?"

"No, Mamaleh, he's very angry because it isn't fair."

"What is 'fair'?"

"Oy, *vey'ss mir*, so many questions. Eat up and I'll tell you later."

...And Menscher's wolf will get you if you don't watch out.

CHAPTER THREE

Lessons

Everyone has a song. Every word. Every thing. The spirits sing and the music goes where it will. *Follow it. This song is yours. Listen.* If you do not find it here, you will find it there; if not now, then later. If I am not for myself, then who will be for me? *Follow us. We sing for you. We will be heard.*

No one guessed at the spirits that sang in Rachel as she sat with the women and children, severed by a lace curtain from the worshippers at schul. Or that, sitting on the kitchen floor while Mama and Sarah made the supper, she chanted along with Jacob's Bar Mitzvah boys. Rachel understood Papa would be angry if he knew she shared the special music for talking with God. But she could not help herself.

Since before memory gave names to the world, she had watched Papa teach the boys; three days a week after American school for the paying pupils, every night after supper for her two brothers. She listened as they practiced, some with great fervour but most with reluctance, the ancient, familiar melodic patterns. Girls were not permitted to join in by singing aloud. But inside Rachel, it was never silent.

Rachel's father drew the Hebrew letters on a small chalkboard propped on a kitchen chair. The six boys copied. Every letter had a proper way to be written; first down then up and across...or up, through and down. And every letter meant something more than the sound it made when you said it. *Beth,* or beh's as her father said it, meant a place. *"Beh's El",* her father explained, "Place of God." *Chai* for blessing. Rachel knew this one particularly because when her mother showed her a locket that belonged to Bubbie Ruchel, she said, "Someday, when you're older, you can wear it. It's a Chai, for luck."

"Blessings are not luck," Papa had corrected.

Rachel believed that the way the boys made the letters must have had something to do with the magic that was in them because as her father circled the six boys, clustered on the floor at the end of the room, correcting their work, he took their hands to guide them through the proper motions. These, she solemnly believed, must be very important.

The letters fit together to make words that were only for men and boys. They sang them. Papa and the boys stood up to sing them. Rachel had noticed that when Mama or Tanta Rosa talked to God, which they did all the time, or to Bubbie Ruchel and to other spirits who Rachel didn't know, they did not sing. But the spirits came crowding round to listen anyway.

When Mama cried - Rachel didn't know why - and talked to her mama, Bubbie Ruchel comforted her. Sometimes her hands on Mama's shoulders were red with blood from her Papa's cows. Often there were others too, all nodding and murmuring.

Rachel wondered if God was there when the men sang to him with their special music. As she didn't know what He looked like, she could not be sure. Once she asked Papa about this. He said that it was a sinful question, that even the true name of God could not be spoken. How, then, does He know when you are talking to Him? How do you know that He comes? She wished she could join in just to see.

But on one late afternoon in October, everyone was too busy to think about what wishes or wonders passed through the mind of an infant girl child. Rachel, who was three and some, drew pictures with a piece of charcoal on cardboard Sarah brought home from the shirt factory. Mama and Sarah were cooking a stew of meat and vegetables and fruit, a *tzimmes*. If she was quiet, Rachel knew, she would be rewarded with a carrot or a black, sticky prune.

Mendel, Rachel's oldest brother, was still at work, at the warehouse on the docks. When he came home now, always barely in time to wash for supper, he brought the smell of the waterfront with him. And the dreaming rhythms of the ships.

At the kitchen table, Bea bent over a school book. Immune to the repetitive chant of Papa's six boys at the far end of the room, that served as kitchen, parlour and, at night, bedroom for Mama and Papa, she chewed her pencil and traced the inscrutable lines in her book with her index finger. Bea had begged Papa to allow her to stay on at school. An American lady in a dark shirtwaist dress, wearing a hat with daisies, even came to the house to talk to him about it. But Papa said it was a waste of time to fill Bea's head with dreams that would be no use in life and that would make her a disobedient wife. So next year, when she would be twelve, she would join Sarah at the shirt factory until she was old enough to have a husband.

None of them would go to American school if Papa had his way. But school was the law and there was never enough money for Yeshiva. Besides, Yeshiva was only for boys. And in this foolish, wicked place, Papa said, even girls must go to school.

Rachel loved the peaceful kitchen, wood-warmed at this time of day. Mama opened the stove door to stir the fire and a glowing plank of firelight spread across the room. Then the door clanged shut and the grey wash of late afternoon flooded back. Papa did not allow the electric light to be turned on until it was fully dark, to save the light bulb, he said. All the boys squinted over their lessons.

Papa was in a temper because of Duvi's mistakes. At ten, Duvi, the younger of Rachel's two older brothers, prepared with the Bar Mitzvah boys. Although he was the youngest and the smallest of the class, Papa demanded perfection. He was, after all, the scholar's son. But Duvi was a dreamer and he was always elsewhere. He played stickball in the gutter, all the other boys cheering him on. 'Run Davey, run.' He hid in the alley behind the pawnbroker's shop, watching, with Schmuel Weiss, the pawnbroker's son; watching the big boys shoot craps for money. He stole an orange from a pushcart on Orchard Street. Run Davey, run.

"Duvi! Pay attention."

Papa didn't shout, but Rachel could hear the rising of his anger. Soon someone would be sorry.

"Watch," Papa said. "Like this. Down, across, up. Down, up, down, through." He lowered over Duvi, watching him write. "Again."

Rachel wrote too. With her charcoal, she followed the lesson on her cardboard, squeezing the words around the pictures she had already drawn. Down, across, up. Down, up, down, through. Soon every available space was covered with the song. *Shema Yisrael*, between the sun and a cloud, Hear O Israel. *Adonai Elohenu*, along the dark, straight line of rooftops, The Lord our

God. *Adonai echad*, on the ground, beside Menscher's sleeping wolf, The Lord is one.

Rachel could not stop writing the song. The words ran sideways along slanting lines of raindrops. They filled the boxy panes of childish windows; they piled up the chimneys and bounced among the cobblestones. Everyone was singing. So many voices. And suddenly, Rachel sang aloud as she wrote. Her tiny, soprano piping across the companionable orchestration; like a flute among the cellos, it commanded and silenced them all.

A Bar Mitzvah pupil giggled. Sophie paused over her stew and stiffened to be chastised for her blaspheming child. Bea looked up from her studies and five-year-old Ruth, attracted by the quiet from her game of Jacks on the landing, clung, half-hidden, to the door frame.

Jacob the patriarch crossed the room in two strides while Rachel still, sweetly, called the people to witness in the ancient way. Scribbling and singing, the child, as ever, in the happy world of her own making. Only when Jacob snatched the cardboard did she remember the sting of punishment. The song, and the singers, trickled away. Yet she smiled. She had trapped the music in her drawing. Look. It is everywhere. Can't you hear it?

Jacob, especially in anger, was a man of few words and those he would not deign to waste on a creature who had not arrived at the age of reason. A girl child. Would this man, who every morning thanked God for not being born a woman, rail at an ape? Would he spend his breath disputing with wild beasts?

"Woman," he hissed at Sophie. Although his voice was low, Rachel could see her mother cringe. "Can you not govern your child? Has God sent you to try me? You have filled my home with your daughters; you have made my sons worldly, wilful and lazy. Must you now allow your child to mock God's holy instruction? Look," he growled. He shoved the cardboard in Sophie's face. "A sacred mystery scribbled by a monkey. Is this possible in my own home? Gravedigger's daughter," he spat, "have you no sense of piety?"

These questions had no answers. Sophie dared not offer any and Jacob would never tolerate justification where none could possibly exist. But Rachel winced at the ringing of Mama's painful obedience.

Jacob fed the lyrical drawing to the wood-burning stove. Rachel covered her ears with her hands as, licked by flame, the music shrieked.

The lesson in ruins, the boys were dismissed. From then on, Rachel was banished to the landing, or in warmer weather, the stoop, during Jacob's classes.

For little girls and monkeys, a tinkling game of Jacks, a rag dolls' party, a browse through the pictures in Tanta Rosa's magazines. Upstairs, the intimate sanctity of the afternoon kitchen belonged to boys, God and the deaf. Rachel had learned she was none of these.

Wait. There is music. You will find it. We will find you. The wandering of days, weeks, months. Seasons. The endless tedium of being trapped in childhood. From the stoop, Rachel puzzles over the urgent rhythms of the street, of life being lived in a thousand different ways. In the kitchen, she listens to the liquid counterpoint of Sarah and the rabbi's son, courting under watchful eyes. On the landing, she hears the shuffling dirge of Menscher's footsteps, now pausing, forgetfully, to pat his slobbering yellow dog, long since gone. Soon Menscher will join him in tender meadows of memory.

∞

"She is such a solemn child," Kandel said. "Always so far away."

Rachel dipped a ladle into the briny barrel in the back of his shop, poking for pickles, fat and not too dark, to bring up to Tanta Rosa. It was too early for the café customers; the little delicatessen was quiet.

"Solemn?" Sophie laughed. "You should see her talking to the sparrows that come to the fire escape. Whole conversations. Jokes even. You would think they answered her back. Full of talk that one...when she wants to be."

"No, not solemn," said Sophie. "Patient. It's like she waits."

"For what?"

"Ah, God knows."

Rachel lifted a plump, dripping half-sour from the barrel and arranged it on the piece of waxy, white paper Kandel gave her.

"She listens to everything," Sophie said, "and stores it away, inside. Sometimes she tells me what my mother, she should rest in peace, would think. And do you know, she is most of the time right?"

Rachel put her choice on the counter, along with two pennies. While Kandel wrapped the purchase, Sophie, who was slicing the strudel for display, patted Rachel's head absently. "All right, little one?" she said. Rachel nodded. She watched Kandel deftly tie the packet with string and wondered what surprise he would give her. Sometimes he was too busy. But not today.

"Here, maydeleh," he said. "For you." And he handed her a bow-shaped egg *kichel*, crisp with sugar.

"What do you say?" Sophie prompted.

"Thank you, Mr Kandel."

Sophie watched Rachel trundle out of the shop, thinking, all the while, that perhaps her youngest child had a very old soul. She almost said so to Kandel.

Another winter. Rachel writes forbidden words in forbidden letters in the window frost. No one sings. No one comes. She scratches the icy glass clear. Cabbage leaves and onion skins freeze in the puddles below, then disappear under a layer of white.

∞

That winter was a silent dream of falling skies. The street lights haloed yellow in lavender twilights of snow. People said they couldn't remember the like since the old country. Tanta Rosa told Rachel that when the North Wind grew angry and restless with the world, he howled and blew and conjured up great mountains of snow to bury it. But when the people saw it, they said how beautiful it was, sparkling in the moonlight. And when the children woke, they were delighted. They laughed and danced and built snow palaces in the sunlight. Then the North Wind blushed with pride and he was so sorry for his anger that he slipped away.

"And do you know what? The snow went with him."

"Why?"

"Because that is the way of things, little one. And do you know what else?"

Rachel held her breath. Tanta Rosa's stories quivered with old, remembered tunes.

"Well, when the South Wind saw that nobody would stop her, she laid a soft green path right to the doorsteps of the village so that the spring could wake up the flowers and bring the world back to life all over again."

When spring came, the snow gave up a hidden cargo of rotted vegetables, broken eggs, wet rags, fish heads, cigar butts, newspapers and horse manure. The drains clogged and sewers overflowed. For days the air stank. But a primal descant larked above the strident stench. It hinted, in breezes that crossed the water, of grassy days which, although never to be seen in Rivington Street, raised smiles in winter sullen faces. Even Yossel, the rabbi's dour son, was touched by it, bringing Sarah a courting gift of greenhouse parsley when he came to call.

For Rachel, the warm, long days were filled with other reasons for excitement and anticipation. Mama poked through boxes of hand-me-downs at the Settlement House for a pair of proper, black high button shoes that would fit her. Lisle stockings were darned. The hems of two of Ruth's plain dresses, with sashes that tied in the back, were let down. Already, Rachel was growing taller and more slender than her sisters. Tanta Rosa gave Rachel a hardboard covered book with clean, piney smelling, lined pages and a new yellow *Ticonderoga* pencil. She taught Rachel how to write her own name in American letters and helped her to mark it in the white square on the book's black and white marbled cover.

One afternoon, just before Papa's class, Rachel took one of Ruth's school books to the stoop and entertained herself by picking out the letters that she knew. It pleased her that bits of her name were embedded in mysterious combinations on every page. This, too, was a kind of magic.

As the boys began arriving, Rachel slid across the stoop to let them pass without looking up from the book. She did not, at first, notice that one of them, a pale, thin-lipped child, had stopped and was staring down at her.

"It's a *shandeh*," he said, "a shame."

Surprised, she looked up at him.

"It's a shandeh for a girl to be reading in the street, so everyone can see," he sneered. "And in English, yet. If you cannot hide yourself, at least you should be reading Hebrew. Shame on you," he said, and he stroked one index finger with the other in the universal gesture of censure that all children know.

Turning back to her book, Rachel tried to ignore him. Angry tears burned her eyes, but she bit her lip to prevent them from spilling onto her cheeks. If she lacked fluency and eloquence - and perhaps because she did - she understood injustice. She was also beginning to understand pride.

But the little princeling, a skinny, raggedy boy, scarcely bigger than she, remained, casting his shadow over her.

"I will tell your Papa," he said. "You are making a scandal. He will stop it."

Slowly, Rachel raised her eyes to his. Her face was blank, her brown eyes huge. All she said was, "No, you won't". But it seemed to the boy that the whole late afternoon hubbub of Rivington Street rose in a crescendo of defiance. Whinnying horses, laughter, argument, the wooden wheels of a pushcart on cobbles, the distant clang of a trolley. Doors slamming, children shouting, somewhere a flute. A pandemonium of life that pushed all thoughts of tattling from his mind.

Terrified, he fled up the stairs.

Rachel rested her hands on the pages of the open book and let the humming promises flow through her.

Do you know that David, the greatest king of all, was a holy fool who sang for God? Or that his arid, barren wife was tone deaf? The music goes where it will. It seeks itself. It finds its home.

CHAPTER FOUR

A crossing

Boundaries, limits, ends, beginnings. Doors are for opening, streets for crossing, walls for climbing over. *Push out, push on, push beyond. Come, imagine, see.* The spirits have no limits. *We have danced in the sky.* They have no conscience. One day, you will go too far.

A pebble plunged towards the East River, unimaginably distant. Rachel, pressing her face against the cast-iron railing, waited to see it splash and sink. The pebble, the last one in her apron pocket, disappeared, swallowed by the lively air beneath the Williamsburg Bridge. Her decision was made.

Duvi, who went everywhere and knew most everything now that he was a runner for Tammany, said the bridge was so high and the currents beneath so fierce that if you dropped a rock the size of your fist, you'd never see it hit the water. Rachel had decided to use this amazing information as a test. If she saw just one of the pebbles she had gathered at the foot of the bridge hit the brown water, it would be a sign and she would go home. But two pockets full of the biggest she could find had now vanished.

Breathing deep, she turned towards Brooklyn, committed to serious adventure and her first deliberate act of disobedience. It was the spring of course. It could not be helped.

Spring astonishes the city. All at once, the crabbed sycamores of pocket parks are feathered yellow-green. Overnight, tamaracks push up tenement air shafts and tangle in clotheslines. Where the sidewalk is cracked, new sumacs and locusts force out the iron-coloured winter weeds.

And the smell, so insistent and pleased, riding in across the East River on the backs of gulls.

Over the pushcarts and underneath the *El*, conversations lengthen with the days. Coatless children play *potsie* and *skellie* in the streets, scattering like startled sparrows and gathering again around the passing trolley cars.

Life moves out of doors. Sticky windows are forced open, sending cheap muslin curtains fluttering like checkered flags. On the fire escapes, women flushed with kitchen heat refresh themselves with glasses of lemon tea, their stockings rolled down to their ankles.

The inner life of the tenements, seething all winter behind windows steamed with human breath, boils over into the streets. The Lower East Side turns inside out, like a peeled orange.

For weeks, Rachel, seven-years-old in the late spring of 1914, had been tormented with the scent of restlessness.

"What smells, Mama? Can you smell it?"

"Can I smell it? Who can *not* smell it when Rosa stuffs cabbage?"

"No Mama, not that one, the other one..."

Sophie straightened, letting Jacob's shirt slide off the scrubbing board into the tepid suds. Dramatically, she sniffed the air.

"Child, I can smell washing soda and oilcloth...and your Tanta Rosa's terrible cooking. *That* is what I can smell."

Rachel looked for spring in vain among the frail trees of Jackson and Seward parks. She followed her nose, eyes closed, to the far end of Delancey Street, where the road swept up onto the Williamsburg Bridge.

May called, unmistakably, from the other side, a wilderness of almost remembered fields and woods. The bridge was the gateway. But the Williamsburg Bridge, with its trolley cars and subway tracks, its pedestrian ramp crowded with colourful, hurrying people, was forbidden by Papa. The bridge end of Delancey Street was the end of the world.

Fancy women from Allen Street took the air on the Williamsburg Bridge. Irish gangsters, Italians and atheists. Rowdy gentiles of every sort.

"What are fancy women, Papa? Atheists?"

"May God forgive you for asking."

With the rest of Miss Keogh's second grade class, Rachel cut paper flowers

34

for Mothers' Day. Miss Keogh said they should think about all the things their mothers did for them so they could thank them on this new special day that Mrs Jarvis had begun in Philadelphia. Rachel drew Roses of Sharon and listened to the names of faraway places. *Philadelphia. Alasehir. Rabbah.* Bubbie Ruchel watched with some interest. From the top of the coat cupboard, she scowled. On the way home, Rachel tore up the paper flowers and threw them in the gutter.

She knew what Papa would say if she asked for a penny to buy real ones.

"What holy day? In school they teach you to celebrate gentile holy days?"

"But Papa, it's not a gentile holiday. It's an American holiday."

"American shamerican. There are Jewish holy days and there are *goyesha* holy days. I have no pennies for pagan stories."

Which is why, on the Sabbath, when she should have been playing quietly or thinking about serious things, Rachel, all by herself, was crossing the Williamsburg Bridge to Brooklyn.

This was the most wicked thing she had ever done. Before this Saturday in May, misbehaviour had almost always been an accident. The grown-up world was full of rules you never knew about until you had broken one. This was a real plan. And if Papa found out, there would be real punishment, maybe even the strap.

It was going to be worth it. She was sure she could see Brooklyn already. It had open, rolling hills covered with nodding blooms. How glad Mama would be to have real, alive flowers for Mothers' Day. In Brooklyn, people sat on the backs of horses that didn't pull carts; horses that bent low and tore the long soft grass with their yellow teeth. When the Levitzes from upstairs moved to Brooklyn, Sonia Levitz told Mama that she would have a big back yard with room for chickens to scratch.

"But Sonia, so far from the schul," Mama said.

"Herschel says there is a minyan already for schul in the Rabbi's house. So, we will build a new schul. My Herschel says we came to America to be pioneers. So, *schon*, I will be *eine richtige* pioneer!"

Pioneers. Open spaces. Cowboys and Indians. Like the pictures in the soft covered books that Duvi hid under his mattress. So, it was with more than a little disappointment that Rachel skipped off the bridge into rows of tenements just like her own. Perhaps they were newer, perhaps a little bigger, but they were much the same. The only chickens scratching were in wire crates outside a poultry store.

Crushed, she sank onto a curbstone and stared at her scuffed shoes. How could this be? She had been so certain. If she hurried back across the bridge, no one would ever know she had been gone. But what kind of adventure was that? She was thus deep in thought, considering what to do next, when a thickening presence made her look up.

A man was standing over her. He wore a long black coat although it was summery warm. His flat black hat had fur around the edge of its wide brim and his beard was much longer than Papa's trim whiskers. Rachel thought he looked like the men arriving every day now from Poland and Russia, where Bubbie Ruchel was born. She had heard Mr Kandel tell Mama that these new people were running ahead of a war. When she asked about that, no one but Duvi would tell her anything and all he wanted to talk about was soldiers and blood. There had already been too many soldiers and too much blood.

"Maydeleh, are you lost?" The man's voice was gruff but friendly.

Rachel shook her head. "I wanted to pick flowers. For Mothers' Day. But there are none."

"Ah, but of course there are. There are always flowers somewhere. That way," he said, and he pointed just beside the sun.

Rachel followed the direction of his arm with her eyes. As far as she could see, flat, paved streets, lined with sidewalks and tenements, ran to neat, square corners. She wanted to ask him how far but when she turned he was gone, vanished among the pushcarts and storefronts near the base of the bridge.

Come. Walk now until your shadow races ahead into the darkening day. Come. The city thins but never ends.

Rachel had no idea how long she had been walking. After the paving ended, she followed the telegraph poles, crunching down streets of crushed rock. Now the wooden poles and power lines marched along empty dirt roads, the advanced creepers of a strong, delicate vine that would soon drag the city behind. If she squinted, she could see it shimmer on the alien landscape of tilled fields and sandy hills. Here the houses were only big enough for one or two families. They clustered in little groups, surrounded by pale yellow waste ground and tough, coarse grass. Stands of *sukki* weed waved their seedy heads above her and sang wind songs that drew her on.

It was so quiet. Rachel had never been alone in her whole short life. She was not alone now. A peddler with a stout black stick tramped along up ahead of her. He bent forward under the weight of his sack and sometimes she could hear the familiar clattering of his pots and pans. If she stopped to lace her shoe, the peddler stopped too, apparently waiting for her. Sometimes he seemed to be waving her on, but though she ran, she could not catch up with his steady, burdened gait. In the few settlements they passed, small knots of people went about their own business, paying them no attention. The peddler never stopped to sell anything. Once a farmer trundled by on a flat-backed wagon loaded with sacks. Like Uncle Shoe, he wore overalls and big, dirty boots. He called to her.

"Hey kiddo, you lost or something?"

Rachel shook her head. Behind her, the road pointed straight to the sun and home. She waved at the farmer, who shrugged and drove on.

Only the big sky was crowded, populated with greedy mobs of seagulls who tilted and screamed. Now and then, they settled on a field, scaring up clouds of iridescent starlings.

By now, Rachel had forgotten her reason for setting off. So filled was she with sounds and scents and sunlight that the journey was its own reward. She spread her arms wide and danced slow circles, listening with the tips of her fingers. She would have passed the little pond behind a screen of scrub pines had not the call of fine sweet water surprised her with an urgent thirst. Suddenly, nothing was more important. Heedless of her Sabbath clothes, she pushed through the stunted trees and bramble, scrambled and slid down steep, soft banks and, plunging her face into the dark surface of the water, drank like an animal. Only when she sat back, dripping, muddy and dazed, did she notice the riot of Spring wildflowers at the water's edge.

Daisies, dandelions, clover, water iris, buttercups, lady slippers, purple loosestrife. Queen Anne's Lace smelling of sweet carrots. Sturdy black-eyed susans. The names would come later. Now there were only colours and a swelling hubbub of strutting, preening, wheedling.

Unable to choose, Rachel grabbed for anything that would give up its hold of the black slime. The cattails refused to let go, but a bunch of sweet flags came up in a slick suck of roots and mud. She yanked and tore and snapped until, her arms full and her chin yellow with buttercup pollen, she sat back, panting.

If Rachel had started for home, she might have arrived with the last of the daylight. Instead, she took off her squishy shoes and waded into the pond. Her tired feet sank into cool mud. She wiggled her toes and watched the play of sky on water, smiled and thought of nothing at all.

A solitary gull swooped and tore at the pond. It rose and hovered low, barely as high as the twisted scrub pines. It sat on the air so close to Rachel that she could see the drops of water on its sharp smiling beak, shiver at the wisdom in its dense, unblinking eye. It invited as before it had welcomed, *balanced in our windy wake while we crossed the pitching night under a million stars.*

When I would not part for you again, you cleft me with your sharp keels. If I let you, you can ride me like a lover. If I want you, I will keep you for my own. You are on me but I am in you. You are scattered as the stars in the firmament. Everywhere. And where you are, so also am I, rocking in the rhythm of your blood. Always. We are a drawing apart. We are a coming together. Forever.

Rachel ran; her wet shoes and a few woody-stemmed black-eyed susans crammed in her apron pocket. The packed dirt road disappeared and she ran across a shifting pan of white sand, gritty, glowing and warm. Ahead of her, dunes, held by a silver tracery of *dusty miller*, hid the source of the now thunderous chaos of voices. Laughing, sighing, shouting. *Come. Hurry. See.* Or was it the reply of her own rushing blood as she struggled upward, the soft sand sliding away underfoot?

She crested the dune and stopped, stunned before the living water. More water than she had ever seen. More than she, or anyone, could understand. It rose in swells of glassy green that broke with a roar then teased and nibbled the shore. It stroked the gentle slope of beach with sinuous, vanishing fingers.

And where it ended, there was only sky. Rachel had never before seen a horizon uninterrupted by the works of man. She held her breath. When she released it, her long sigh was taken and entwined in the throbbing song of the Atlantic. Something was growing; something enormous. It spread out in every direction, curving across the face of the water and beyond. Exhausted and nearly fainting with hunger, Rachel sat back into the sand and slept.

She dreams of swimming in a blood warm sea. Is this swimming, this weightless dancing on the thick green sky? She dreams of beautiful creatures with silky coats of dense brown fur, whiskery faces and warm, dark eyes. They breach then dive and roll, looking back up at her through swarming phosphorescence. One of them swims beside her. His eyes are not dark like the others, but clear and light, as though they have trapped the sky. She wants to touch him, but he is always just beyond her reach. Again and again he darts away from her outstretched hand. Perhaps it is a game, but it is tinged with hungry sadness. And cold. Now she is shivering under the blinding stars. With each juddering gasp, her mouth fills with the bitter, salty taste of the cold. The creature with the sky in his eyes dives and rises beneath her. He is warm in the cold green sea. He is harnessed with water weeds. She rides on his back to the shore.

Rachel awoke, shivering, into a cloudshadowed moonrise. Two fishermen with long poles and strings of flat brown fish knelt by her in the sand. One of them spoke.

"*Piccolina, cosa fai qui da sola?*"

She stared at him, searching her memory in vain for understanding.

The fisherman took off his sweater and wrapped it around her shoulders. "Little girl, what you do here all by you self?"

Still, she did not reply.

His companion raised his hands in a gesture of helplessness. "Maybe she doan speak no English, you think?"

But, though his accent was strange, Rachel did understand his question. She simply had no idea how to answer it.

In my cold, wet arms, I will rock you warm. I am restless in your blood. Forever.

CHAPTER FIVE

Advent

We are a drawing apart. We are a coming together. We have watched each other through so many eyes. When I was a wandering beggar, you gave me sweet wine. You have dreamt me awake in a northern sea. You are my peculiar treasure. Comfort me with apples.

It would have been so easy to lie. Who could believe a child of seven would walk nearly ten miles? For no reason at all. At the stationhouse, the policemen fed Rachel sandwiches and milk while, in another room, they questioned the two Italian waiters for more than an hour before they accepted their story. That they had gone fishing between shifts at the Sheepshead Bay Inn. That they had been on their way back to work, loaded down with a good catch of bluefish and flounder, when they found Rachel sleeping in the sand on Brighton Beach.

A policeman questioned Rachel as well. Had she taken a ride from a stranger? Did someone, some man, offer her sweets? Where had she been when she was snatched from the street?

Rachel could have colluded. She could have constructed an elaborate scenario from these puzzling questions that continued during the long ride back to Rivington Street. If she had, she would not have been punished.

Instead, she might have been bundled off to bed, consoled by Mama's tears, sweet warm milk and *mandelbrot* for dunking. Tanta Rosa and Uncle Abie might have come down from upstairs with all her cousins, Uncle Abie bringing his flute to cheer her up and Cousin Chaia singing all her favourite songs. Of course, Tanta Rosa would have told her a good story. Her sisters and brothers would have treated her with the awe and respect due an invalid. She might even have enjoyed a night alone in the bed she shared with Ruth and Bea. These comforts had a certain appeal.

But Rachel wanted to be at the centre of a different kind of fuss. She was the prodigal returned and she wanted a prodigality of admiration. She wanted Ruth to hang on to her every word; even her older brothers and sisters to be impressed. She had crossed the Williamsburg Bridge and felt the subway trains shiver the world between water and sky. She had studied the faces of strangers, godless and pious, listened to their incomprehensible tongues and eaten their forbidden food. Hadn't she walked across Brooklyn all the way to the Atlantic Ocean? Hadn't she listened to its songs and dreamed sea dreams, seen the moon rise from the water? Best of all, hadn't she ridden all the way home in the front seat of a real gasoline buggy?

Naturally, Papa would be very angry, but that prospect was thrilling too. At last, she would feel the strap he never used to punish the girls. How she had envied Duvi when he raised his shirt to show off the red welts on his back; when Mama soothed him with cool water and honey cake. Surely, now she had earned the strap. Her palms itched where they had clung for hours to Mama's flowers, the few damp, wilted black-eyed susans that she had stuffed in her apron pocket. Mama said itchy palms meant riches to come. Rachel felt protected by an aura of special distinction. She insisted, in the face of disbelief all round, that she had walked all the way, without help.

Eventually, the evidence could not be denied. Yossel, Sarah's young man, pointed out the holes in the soles of Rachel's shoes and stockings, the matching blisters on her feet.

Papa, scowling and silent, stalked out of the bedroom. Mama, already swollen eyed from weeping, fell sobbing into the arms of Tanta Rosa and Uncle Abie, who led her away. It was left to Sarah, tight and prim, to paint a picture of the commotion Rachel had caused.

When Rachel missed lunch, Mama had sent them all over the neighbourhood looking for her. After she failed to appear for supper, Ruth had to be put to bed in tears, worrying that Rachel might never return and alternately hoping that she would stay away to avoid Papa's wrath. Papa, Mendel and Uncle Abie had gone off with a policeman and a posse of neighbours to search for her. And Duvi's friend, Councilman Tierney, had sent firemen to scour the sewers and conduits near the docks. "Now everybody knows our business," Sarah said.

"Even the *goyem*." By nightfall, Mama was so hysterical, she nearly fainted. Twice. "And to be so wicked on *Shabbas*. God forgive you."

Rachel knew this last was for the benefit of Yossel, who wore his habitual deathwatch expression. She tried to mimic his mournful face to create a semblance of remorse. But the fiddler plays a wicked tune and Rachel was not sorry. There was a mysterious, peaceful pleasure, a calm in the eye of this hurricane. She had been the least and now she was the greatest. She sat back and waited for the inevitable. But the punishment, when at last it came, was not what she expected

The wooden chest, under the kitchen window, had come with Rachel's parents from the old country. Rachel didn't know much about what was in it other than the sabbath candlesticks and Papa's extra *tallis*, the prayer shawl he was saving to be buried in. The chest was locked with a big metal padlock. The authority of this lock was purely symbolic. Jacob kept the key hanging on a nail by the sink in plain sight. But no one dared touch it. Even Sophie had to ask Jacob to open the chest when she needed the brass candlesticks to make *Shabbas*.

Now, Jacob sent everyone but Rachel upstairs to Rosa and Abie's. He sat before the chest, fingering the key. Rachel stood before him, still, curious.

"Rachel," Jacob said. If you had not known him, you might have imagined he spoke gently. "Do you know that you are not allowed to go on the bridge?"

She nodded.

"Why?"

Rachel thought about all the things she had been told. About the gangsters and hooligans and gentiles; the crowds who could push a little girl off the platforms onto the subway tracks or into the path of a trolley; the ladies who wore shiny dresses, the ladies Mama always crossed the street to avoid. She was about to list these dangers when Jacob, as was his habit, answered his own question.

"Because," he said quietly, "I have forbidden it."

"But..."

"This is not a discussion!"

Jacob looked down at his laced fingers. Slow seconds hauled the moon across the night. On the fire escape, a blue jay chuckled throatily. Rachel wondered why so many things were forbidden. But she did not ask. From across the street, another blue jay answered the first.

Jacob was still looking at his fingers when he said, "I want your solemn promise that you will not go on the bridge again."

Rachel said nothing. She listened to the birds and wondered about their particular, chattering voices. They were laughing. She stared at her father until he had to look up at her. His eyes were dull, a faded blue. Outside, an evening breeze gossiped in someone's snapping laundry. Why had she never before noticed how watery and weak his eyes were?

"Do I have your word before God?"

Still, she was silent. Spittle glistened in her father's whiskers and a piece of slimy whitefish, the remains of his breakfast, clung near the corner of his mouth. How small and stooped he looked. His *yarmulka* didn't fit. It rested at an odd angle, pointing peculiarly on his skull.

"I will have your word," he demanded, but he seemed to falter under Rachel's steady gaze. He had to look away to continue.

"Since you are so disobedient," he said, "and wander where I have forbidden you to go, you will not leave this house until I have your word...Take off your clothes."

Rachel heard him speak as though from a great distance. Because it did not seem to matter, she obeyed. She untied her muddy apron and handed it to Jacob. Then she undid the buttons and hooks of her cotton dress and pulled it over her head. Jacob waited. She wriggled out of her petticoat and gave him that as well.

"*All* of them," he said. But, although he watched the pile of clothes grow on the floor, once again he looked away.

She pulled off her lisle stockings. Beach sand hissed to the floor when she slipped out of her cotton bloomers. How easy this was. How silly.

For the first time, Jacob seemed to notice that the kitchen windows were uncovered. He closed the flimsy curtains, then went into the bedroom and emerged carrying Rachel's other dress and nightclothes.

He put all the clothes into the wooden chest, locked it and hung the key on the nail by the sink, all this without once looking at Rachel's hairless, naked little body.

Was that it? Where was the strap? Rachel shivered, but it was only because of the cold.

Now Jacob stood up, his back to Rachel. Light from the bare kitchen bulb made his jacket shine. When he spoke, his voice was flat. She could hardly hear him over the gossip and laughter that had been growing until it bounced off the walls in all directions.

"There they will stay, until I have your solemn promise," he said. "Now, go to bed."

Rachel did not hurry to the bedroom. She took her time, listening, trying to understand the clarifying refrain of the murmuring voices. It was an old song. So old. It was about power. It was about fear. It was about the smallest seed at the heart of the world. *The least will become the greatest.*

And it was why her father was ashamed to look at the smooth ribs of her chest, her round belly, the warm little triangle between her legs. Ashamed. He was *ashamed*. Rachel wrapped this new knowledge around herself with the bedsheet. She hugged her shoulders, enjoying the cool, warm, firm softness of her flesh. *Restless, restless in your blood.* She smiled.

A week later, while Jacob, Rabbi Meyer and a delegation of men from the schul discussed charity for the refugees, she was still in the bedroom. Still hugging her secret. Still smiling.

∞

Miss Keogh had been a young woman when she first visited the cold water flat at 75 Rivington Street. In the spring of 1917, she was no longer young, but she still wore a shirtwaist dress and a hat with daisies on it. She had never succeeded in her mission to persuade Jacob Isaacson to allow his children the freedom of a complete education - as complete, at any rate, as the New York City Board of Education could provide - but she continued to try.

He was an odd one, she reflected, as she climbed the four flights of stairs. So rigid and old fashioned when so many others were taking up every opportunity with relish. Not only for their children but for themselves as well. Her heart swelled with the patriotism that only an immigrant can feel - for Miss Keogh was an immigrant too - when she thought of the enthusiasm of her night school classes at the Settlement House. People old enough to be her grandparents struggled with English and Citizenship and Geometry to earn diplomas. Didn't he realise that here his bright children could do almost anything, become almost anything they chose, if only he allowed them to be taught?

Miss Keogh believed she had good reason to equate education with freedom. As one of the youngest of twelve children, and sure to be lacking a dowry, she might have been locked up, like three of her sisters, with the Poor Clares or the Ursulines, had not a scholarship to the State Normal School at New Paltz given her the freedom to make her own way.

She had first visited Isaacson with the enthusiasm of a young teacher enchanted by an eager pupil. That had been little Bea, who at ten had been so hungry for history that it broke Miss Keogh's heart to see her dragged from school. She had come again for Davey, then Ruth and now Rachel, the youngest.

Miss Keogh's visits were unofficial. It was Isaacson's right to take his children out of school when they reached eleven. If he had complained, she might have even received a reprimand from the School Board. But Miss Keogh was a generous and childless woman who lived to help her students get on in the world. Although she knew he would greet her with the same stiff-necked scorn as before, she prepared herself to face Jacob Isaacson for the last time.

She took some comfort in the knowledge that without his cooperation, his children seemed to find their own paths anyway. All except slow, shy Ruth, who would add little to the world but expect little from it in return. Perhaps, she reflected, it was the place that gave the freedom and not the schooling after all. Perhaps that was it. The right sort of spirit could flourish in this place.

Look at Bea, soaking up the history of European socialism wherever she could find it. At the Settlement House, at the Ethical Culture Society, at the East Side Socialist Club. Miss Keogh was proud of Bea, at 19, a leader of her union local. She had campaigned to get New York women the vote. Soon women would have the national vote, Miss Keogh was sure, and when that happened, who could guess how far Bea and her colleagues at the International Ladies Garment Workers Union might go?

Then there was Davey. Miss Keogh was less sanguine about his prospects, but certainly he had achieved freedom of a sort. The local political machine had been quick to spot the advantages of his agile mind and fast legs. She wondered whether Isaacson, when he sat across the Sabbath table from the son he called Duvi, knew what being a cadet for Miss Harriet Klein's Dance Academy and Social Club really meant. Two of Hattie's "ladies" were taking math classes at the Settlement House because Hattie couldn't find a bookkeeper who could keep his mind, and his hands, on the books.

And what would happen to Rachel? Miss Keogh stopped to catch her breath at the third-floor landing. She was a puzzling child. Although Miss

46

Keogh would not have called her bookish, she was sure that Rachel had gone through every book in the grade school library. Like Davey, she was quick with numbers as well. But there was something else about her. Something penetrating and still. From remarks overheard in the schoolyard, Miss Keogh concluded that some children thought Rachel had the evil eye and were a bit afraid of her.

Of course, Miss Keogh reassured herself, that was nonsense. But she could not deny that Rachel's independence was striking and unusual in one so young, especially, among these people, in a girl. Rachel never wanted help with her school work, preferring to puzzle through on her own. And, unless she believed she deserved it, she rejected the praise and encouragement that other children seemed to demand.

Miss Keogh remembered, now, the first time she had seen Rachel's spirit manifest. It had happened three years before. Rachel, who was seven at the time, had been absent from school for a week. Miss Keogh visited to investigate, to see if, perhaps, a nurse from the Settlement House should call.

When she arrived, Isaacson and a group of men were holding a meeting. Rabbi Meyer was there and several others. Rachel, it seemed, was being punished. Miss Keogh vaguely remembered that she, herself, might have been involved in the cause. Something about Mothers' Day. She was explaining to Isaacson that keeping a child out of school for such a reason was against the laws of the State of New York when the bedroom door opened and Rachel appeared, completely naked. She stood for a moment in the doorway, smiling at Miss Keogh while the men gasped and shielded their eyes with their hands. The rabbi actually put his hat in front of his face.

Isaacson jumped up, his body shaping itself into a shout that seemed to wither in the rays of the child's sweet smile. He sank back into his chair.

At the time, Miss Keogh had been dismayed. She found the men's modesty ridiculous and somewhat disturbing. What could be more harmless, more beautiful, really, than the nakedness of a child?

While the men cowered, Rachel had crossed the room. She had taken a large key from a nail beside the sink and had used it to open a wooden chest that sat under the kitchen window. The chest seemed to contain a collection of garments. Miss Keogh watched Rachel pick through them, considering first one, then another, like a young woman choosing for a party. A striped, fringed shawl, one of those shawls the men wore in their synagogues, slipped from the edge of the chest to the floor. Absently, Rachel bunched it up and tossed it back in. At the time, Miss Keogh remembered thinking how peculiar it was to keep a child's clothing under lock and key. But she supposed there must be some reason for it.

Eventually, Rachel had selected a nightdress. She started for the bedroom, then stopped in the middle of the kitchen near the men. She shook out the nightdress, gathered it and lifted it over her head.

Once again, Isaacson sprang from his seat. But before he could collect himself for action, Rachel had shrugged into her nightdress and disappeared into the bedroom.

It had all happened so quickly that thinking of it now, three years later, Miss Keogh was not sure she trusted her memory. But at the time, she believed she understood why the men covered their faces in fearful, shocked modesty, one of them muttering a prayer.

For as she turned to go, Rachel had glanced at Miss Keogh. Her round, brown eyes glowed with a look Miss Keogh would never forget. Now, her hand raised to knock, for the last time, on this door, Miss Keogh saw it once again, full of knowing satisfaction. For the merest fraction of a second, before her native common sense reasserted itself, she had been certain that she was looking into something more than the eyes of a child.

Part Two

Where night by night she dreams herself awake
And gathers to her breast a dreaming man

The Dreaming of the Bones, W.B. Yeats

CHAPTER SIX

The essence

On the Northeast corner of 118th and First, on the back of a 1927 flatbed Ford with Massachusetts plates, six bushel baskets of the choicest Concord grapes ferment. On Monday, the tiny purple fruit was perfect, so tight and round with juice that the slightest pressure from the tongue made it explode in the mouth. This year, with his brand new truck, the farmer cut a whole day off the trip, so the delicate grapes arrived in prime condition. Now, he eyes his fly-blown crop sadly and scans the dwindling crowd for the tall young woman who comes every year to buy his Concord harvest.

It is Friday afternoon, the last day of the October grape market. A few Italians pick over the bargains. Soon it will be dark and once the Jewish sabbath begins the market will be over.

For eight years, he has brought his wine grapes to the annual New York market. Since prohibition, it is the only way to get a fair price for the fruit that God never intended for eating.

She came from the start, a tall, slim girl in a bustle of brothers and sisters, all older than she. They let her choose and, her lips already purple from tasting, she picked the best. Then the oldest, a young man in his twenties, paid for six bushels, enough to make a modest supply of kosher wine. It was nearly the entire harvest from one, sun-washed hill that overlooked the Sudbury River.

She always bought the same. Just when he began saving them for her, he could not be sure. Or why. Although he has seen her change from an adolescent into a striking young woman, he knows nothing about her. They have never talked about anything but the grapes. He is not even sure if the little boy she brought, last year and the year before, was her own.

Now it is dark. She will not come. Even if she did, her grapes are no longer fit for use. It is only curiosity that keeps him watching for her.

This year, his wife insisted on making the trip to New York to see the talking picture. He promised to take her tonight so he cannot wait much longer. Perhaps one of the other market men saw the woman with the boy. Perhaps she bought from somebody else. He would like to ask but he doesn't even know her name.

∞

Asleep and awake in the dance of time.
We wandered warm in a reddening vineyard.
Remember.
Broad leaves whispered and poured sun sugar into the drying fruit.
I climbed the highest branches of the carob tree to watch the sea.
You were afraid.
Did you know that they would steal me in their long boat?
Untell the days; you cannot call back yesterday.
But only remember.

A kitchen full of women. Bursts of laughter and gossip. The slap of wet hands on joints of lamb and fowl flesh. Knife and block, spoon and bowl sing timeless, sacramental music. Rachel listened, daydreaming, as she seeded raisins for a noodle *kugel*.

It was the Festival of *Rosh Hashonah*, the New Year, and behind the protection of steamy windows, all the Isaacson women, joined by Tanta Rosa and Cousin Chaia, prepared the feast. Only Sarah was missing. As befitting a *rebbitzen* to be, she was in schul with Yossel, the rabbinical student and her intended of long standing.

Rachel plumped the raisins in hot water, a trick of Bubbie Ruchel's that made the seeds easier to loosen. She licked the Adriatic sweetness from her sticky fingers and thought about a golden boy who spoke in song of islands.

It amused her to watch Mama shadowing Tanta Rosa. If Rosa added a pinch of spice to a dish, Sophie tasted it and added a pinch of something else. And she kept a hawk's eye on the box of salt. Holidays were the only occasions when Sophie allowed Rosa near her cooking. She did it for the sake of family, but she tried to steer her toward the easier jobs. This was not always simple.

One year she had given Rosa twenty pounds of potatoes to peel and by the time she had finished, there were barely enough for five people, let alone the fourteen who had to be fed.

Rosa's gift was not for cooking. It was for talk. Today she was encouraged by Bea, who was collecting what she called "testimonies" for a City College project. In the absence of the men, especially Jacob, who had chastised her more than once for her foolish tongue, Rosa entertained them with one far-fetched story after another.

"So, did you ever see a demon, Tanta Rosa?" Bea asked.

"And would I be standing here in front of you if I did? What a question! Not me...no, never...But my father...He did."

The conversation had drifted to ghosts and spirits because, instead of staying in schul with the rest of the men and boys, Sophie's brothers, Abie and Shoe, were somewhere by the East River, emptying crumbs from their pockets to rid themselves of sin for the New Year. The ritual was called *tashlich* and Jacob disapproved of it. He said it was barbaric, a pagan rite to appease demons who were said to live in bodies of water. The dispute over this custom was almost as old as the Jews themselves. But the men in Sophie's family had always done it. Shoe, who had never married, came down from Connecticut especially for the day.

"Enough already, Rosa." Sophie didn't like this kind of talk. You could never tell what might be listening.

But there was no stopping Rosa. Sophie glanced at Rachel, reassured that her youngest, now 15 and a beauty, seemed to be thoroughly absorbed in cleaning the raisins.

"He was the tenth man at an exorcism, so he saw."

"And he told you?" Bea was a stickler for details.

"Why would he tell me? Wasn't I only a child at the time?"

"So how did you hear about it?"

"*Vey iss mir*, do I have to draw you a picture? I was listening at the door when he told my mother. It was a boy who was possessed...about my age. I knew him and I was curious. So that's how I heard."

"But what made them think he was possessed?" Bea asked.

"Well, first of all, his father caught him trying on his sister's clothes. And he used to walk in his sleep. Twice they found him near the well in the middle of the night. Everybody knows going near still water at night is a bad practice."

53

"Oy Rosa, such nonsense you talk," Sophie said. She was stirring balls of dough in boiling honey and her irritation was tempered by concentration.

"Well, it's true all the same. Everybody knows that." Chastened, Rosa kept still for a while and the talk turned to practical kitchen matters.

"How much oil, Mama?"

"Enough...Like this, so it feels right."

Bea waited for Rosa to take up the story again. At night school, her history professor had advised the class to let people tell their stories in their own time. She was eager for more, but she was a conscientious student.

"Maybe he was just funny in his head," Rachel prompted.

Sophie looked up at her.

"Maybe," said Rosa. "But they said he talked in his sleep too. And when he did, a woman's voice came out of his mouth."

"What did he say?"

"Well, I don't know that part. I told you, I was only little...So anyway, the parents asked the rabbi for advice and he sent for a *tzaddik*, a famous righteous man, who came all the way over the mountains, from Bucharest. People said he could make miracles."

"Now I know you're making this up," Sophie sighed.

"I'm telling you. It was a famous story in my village."

"I thought you heard it from your father who was there."

"I did. He was. But you ask anybody from near Brasov and they'll tell you just the same."

"I can see I can't stop you, so you might as well finish." It had occurred to Sophie that if her sister-in-law lost herself in a story, she would forget about the cooking and everybody's digestion would be the better for it.

"So where was I?"

"They sent for a *tzaddik*..." Rachel reminded her.

"Right...So then, they all went to the boy's house...the ten men and the *tzaddik*. And the *tzaddik* began to shout at the *dybbuk*, the ghost, to tell its name and what it wanted...You know, that's how they do it...and it turned out it was Chana, the milkman's wife, who died of the smallpox twenty years before."

"What did she want?"

"Nothing."

"Nothing?"

Rosa began to chuckle. "You see, she didn't even know she was dead, the stupid woman. She fell asleep with a fever and when she woke up, she was in a strange bed. She couldn't find her husband...which, I should tell you, didn't surprise her at all. But the worst of it, all her old friends looked so tired and unhealthy. You see, she didn't know they were twenty years older. She thought they all had the same fever that she had."

"For a story you heard through a door, when you were little, you know plenty," Sophie interrupted.

"Sha...I'm not finished...Anyway, nobody seemed to know her. Naturally, she knew them all and she called them by their names. 'Herzl, *vey iss mir*, you look terrible,' she said to the tailor. She didn't know he was twenty years older."

"You said already."

This time, Rosa ignored Sophie.

" 'Doesn't your wife feed you good?' she asked him. 'Get some sleep, Herzl. Drink some milk. God forbid, you'll have a stroke if you don't take care. And where is that no good husband of mine? Already the milk is turning sour'."

Sophie couldn't help chuckling too, though she tried to conceal it with a cough.

"So then, the *tzaddik* yelled, 'Nobody knows you here. You have no friends,'... because of what the sages say."

"What do they say?" Bea asked.

"If you have no friends then life is not worth living, is what they say...'*Either friendship or death*'...You can read it in the Talmud...So she looked around, and sure enough, no one in the room wanted to be her friend...My father said he saw the soul come right up, out of the boy's mouth then. It touched them all..."

"Rosa!"

"I'm *telling* you...and they could hear it crying 'Where are my friends...I have no friends. Don't you know me? I am Chana, the milkman's wife'... Why it even settled on the shoulders of one young man and said, 'Don't you remember? I nursed your wife when she had a fever.'...But the young man said, 'I am only 20 and I have no wife. It was my mother you nursed.'"

Now Rosa was still.

"So what then?" Bea said.

"So what then? So what do *you* think? It vanished like a puff of smoke...and when it was gone, all their faces were wet with its tears."

Rosa smiled and sat back, evidently satisfied with the reception her performance had received. Outside it was beginning to get dark. Soon the men would be home and they would expect the meal to be ready.

Rachel wiped the serving dishes with a cloth while Bea and Ruth laid the table. *Either friendship or death.* She seemed as quiet and peaceful as the evening. But the singing boy was licking raisin juice from his fingers and he looked so thoughtful it made her sad. She could have found new friends, Rachel thought. She could have waited for them to find her. And when the boy began to sing, she joined him, humming softly.

∞

Bessie Costello was 17 years old. Her parents had died of the Spanish flu in 1918 so she lived on her own in a rooming house on The Bowery. Bessie had yellow curls and the kind of curves that never go out of fashion with the boys. "Boys don't never dance with girls who wear corsets," Bessie said. She wore rouge on her lips and smoked cigarettes in the street. She could dance the Black Bottom and the Fox Trot like nobody's business. People said she was going to hell.

Bessie Costello was Rachel's best friend.

"What did they have on?"

Bessie and Rachel sprawled on Bessie's frayed carpet. While Bessie coloured her fingernails, Rachel read the papers aloud.

"I don't know...It doesn't say," Rachel said. She ran her finger along the column. "Wait a minute...wait a minute...Here, it says, 'The Reverend Mr. Hall and Mrs. Mills were found locked in a death embrace behind the abandoned farmhouse in New Brunswick'...it doesn't say."

It was 1922. Mussolini had marched on Rome to set up the world's first Fascist government. In Ireland, the Free State was declared and civil war broke out. Warren G. Harding and his cronies were using the White House as a get-rich-quick scheme while, in California, a man named Kalmus invented Technicolor. Neils Bohr won the Nobel Prize for describing the atom and three Canadians extracted insulin from a cow's pancreas.

But for Rachel and Bessie, whether Theda Bara wore underwear was much more important. And what really mattered was whatever made the front page of the New York Daily News.

"Maybe they was naked as jay birds."

"Oh, for heaven's sake, Bessie!" Rachel shook her head. Bessie may have been older, but Rachel liked to think that she herself was the one with more sense. "He was a minister. From a church...and she was the choir leader."

"Well, you know...in the heat of their passion and all."

The heat of passion was the subject of some serious speculation ever since the girls had become regulars at the Sunday matinees. They had sighed over *The Sheik* and *Blood and Sand*, although Rachel was less impressed than Bessie because she was sure that Valentino painted his face.

In Bessie's rooms, the girls read *"Indolent Kisses"* and *"What I Told My Daughter the Night Before Her Marriage,"* and wondered whether Mae Busch opened her mouth for all her screen kisses or only the close ups. Together with Bessie, Rachel had begun leading a life that no one at home, except Duvi, knew anything about.

Every morning, on the way to work, Rachel stopped at Bessie's to change from the modest cotton dresses her father allowed into one of the swingy, short frocks that she and Bessie made during their lunch breaks. Then, their hemlines a daring nine inches above the ground, the two girls swanked uptown to their jobs at Mishkin's, Theatrical Costumiers to the Trade.

Mishkin's son, Arthur, managed the sewing rooms. He was sweet on Bessie and any friend of Bessie's was a friend of his, so both girls could count on extra break time for their own sewing. They could count on remnants of fabric, from time to time, as well.

Mishkin allowed his trimmers to keep the beads and feathers swept up at the end of the day. Lately, Arthur, who Bessie kept on a very long leash, had begun passing on the full boxes of beads that were often left over when a show was dressed. These were supposed to go back into stock but Arthur said, "What the heck. They're paid for. If my old man asks, you got them from the sweepings."

"You're a real prince, Arty," Bessie would say and he would glow for a week. Sometimes she even gave him a peck on the cheek. It was a small price to pay for the very same sequins and beads the showgirls wore when they danced for Ziegfeld and Minsky.

Rachel and Bessie were making special dresses. They had big plans. It was no use knowing all the latest steps, if you couldn't show them off at the *landsmannschaft* socials, where bearded old men and everybody's mother prowled the dance floor. And most of the boys at Corkery's Shamrock Dancehall thought a good time was slipping a double bathtub gin into a girl's Moxie and seeing how far you could get her to go. If you went to Corkery's too often, the regulars started thinking you were a *charity girl* who would do just about anything for the price of a bottle of pop. Drunken boys were always staggering out of there whistling the tune to *I'll Say She Does*. Even though Corkery made his payments, the place got raided at least once a month. Duvi said it was part of Corkery's arrangement with Tierney, who was the local boss, because it kept the neighbours off the councilman's back. Duvi always knew about the raids in advance, so the girls never got into trouble.

But now Rachel and Bessie were ready for better things. In the right place, a girl could meet big spenders who were hot steppers and who carried real Canadian whiskey in silver hip flasks. But for high-class dancehalls like Roseland or Dreamworld or Feldman's Coney Island Palace, they needed real dance dresses.

Bessie thought Rachel should bob her hair. But some things couldn't be left behind in Bessie's rooms and Rachel was careful to protect her new double life. "You said you wasn't afraid of your old man," Bessie insisted. Rachel couldn't make Bessie, who never did anything by half, understand that some arguments were not worth the trouble. Or that most of the trouble would land on her mother. Bessie hadn't had a mother in such a long time.

Rachel weighed a heavy hank of glass beads across the palm of her hand. Bugles. The most delicate cylinders of crystal blue and green, threaded on lengths of fine silk. They sparked like a shoal of moon-chased minnows. There were enough to finish.

"And about time too," Bessie said. Bessie had grown impatient with Rachel's fussy particularity. Anything that glittered made Bessie happy. While Rachel waited for just the right colours, Bessie had finished her dress and was stringing a boa of pink dyed marabou feathers. She waved it under Rachel's nose. "Ain't these just *dee*-vine?" she said. "Ain't they just the cat's pyjamas?"

Rachel didn't have the heart to tell her she looked like an explosion at bead factory; Bessie was so eager to make what she imagined would be a very grand entrance at Roseland. "Look out fellas, here I come."

Rachel had planned more carefully, making sure Arty found just what she needed. If Arty ever wondered why he took so much trouble for a skinny

Jewish girl, when he was already married to one and when it was her Irish shiksa friend he was after, Rachel did not let him wonder for long. Still the dress had taken months to finish. It was covered with beaded fringe and scattered with iridescent sequins, flashes of silver and the smallest seed pearls that Arty could finagle. From its pure white hemline, it rose in a narrow column through all the greens and blues to a deep cobalt at the shoulders. When Rachel put it on, she looked like a creature risen from the bottom of the ocean, seafoam still clinging about her knees.

"Geez, you look like a million, kiddo." Bessie said. "Who'd ever guess you was jail-bait."

But only...
Woman child never child
   ...remember...
Sister mother daughter bride
   ...remember...
Swimmer climber helix diver
   ...remember...
But only remember who you are.

CHAPTER SEVEN

Jazz Babies

Chaos confounding where no night can hide us
Watch for the play of the words of the singer
Look for the song of the hands of the piper
Shine for me mermaid, nobody's baby
Put on your glad rags and light up the dark.

Ice coated the cast iron balcony as Rachel eased herself out of the bedroom window. Her foot slipped sideways and she sat down, hard. Six storeys of fire escape rang in metallic sympathy. A shiver of icicles clattered to the street.

"Damn."

"Why'ncha wake up the whole building, why dontcha?" Duvi whispered from the landing below.

"I didn't notice you were so quiet. I heard you all the way up."

"That's 'cause you were listening out for me...You better make sure."

Rachel crouched and slid across the landing to the kitchen window. It was open a crack. All winter the whole family slept with cold noses because Jacob said fresh night air was healthy. They also sneezed and coughed from November to March, which proved, Sophie insisted, that the night air was full of poisons and demons. It was one of the few family arguments that Rachel was glad her father always won. His victory made it easier for her to come and go as she pleased.

She peered in, satisfied but not surprised that Jacob and Sophie were sound asleep on the folding bed. Very little could wake her father on a Saturday night after he'd finished toasting the Sabbath Queen with plenty of homemade *slivovitz*. Looking down through the slippery gratings, she wondered whether she could just walk out the door. That might rouse Sophie but Rachel could always tell her mother she was going to the toilet at the end of the hallway. Would she be alert enough to notice that Rachel was carrying a dress and shoes in a brown paper bag?

"Hurry up. I'm freezing."

Duvi leaned back on the railings below, hugging himself for warmth.

Rachel looked into the shadowy kitchen again. Mischief disputed with itself in the corner and her mother was dreaming of *mohn* cakes. No, it was all too complicated. And the risk of Jacob putting an end to these night-time sorties was far too great. Anyway, the fire escape was more of an adventure.

She crawled back to the bedroom window, hooked her fingers on the cold sill and pulled herself up to look in. Bea was snoring, a loose black curl dancing gently across her face with every breath. The big lump of eiderdown, rising and falling with the rhythm of sleep, was Ruth, hunkered down under the covers for warmth. Only Sarah was awake. She sat up on her elbow hissing and fizzing. Rachel could not make out what she was saying although she assumed "God" and "punishment" were part of the message. They always were. In the moonlight, Sarah's angry eyes glittered. Rachel winked at her and waved. Then, softly, she pulled the window down.

There was no way Sarah would tell. Her betrothal to Yossel had already lasted almost ten years, what with Yossel having to take time off from rabbinical college to look after his widowed mother. Now he was nearly finished and once he had his own congregation, he could count on a good living and a comfortable apartment. The Widow Meyer never tired of telling people what a good catch her son was; how lucky Sarah would be. She had only reluctantly agreed to the engagement in the first place. Ten years or not, she would break it off at the slightest hint of any more scandal.

Sarah was twenty-five, a whole year older than Sophie had been when she married. "And everyone was so surprised, because I was an old maid already," Sophie often told them. Who would have Sarah now if Yossel changed his mind? There was no way Sarah would tell.

Rachel and Duvi felt their way down the spidery railings. They traversed the face of the building in darkness, grateful for the cold that kept anyone still awake at 10 o'clock safely indoors. Duvi watched the customers coming and going from the coffee house on the corner, tugging Rachel's skirt whenever the coast was clear. Several times Rachel had to stop to rub life back into her numbing fingers.

Across the street, a figure, bundled in brown fur, crouched for warmth in the shadows on the stoop of number 86 and whistled against the cold. From its bulk, Rachel judged the figure to be a man. Either Duvi didn't notice or else he wasn't worried about being seen by him.

Duvi didn't wait at the bottom. Rachel tossed her paper bag to the street, braced herself and jumped the last few feet. The whistling man was melting the air with summer songs. He turned his face into the light, smiled and seemed to salute Rachel with a nod.

"Is he a friend of yours?" she said. Duvi was already halfway down the block.

"What?"

"Do you know him?"

"Who? Come on, Rachel. Shake a leg." Duvi grabbed her hand and pulled her around the corner.

A shiny Pierce-Arrow sedan, with the engine running, waited midway up Ludlow. In the driver's seat, Schmuel "Call-me-Sammy" Weiss tapped his manicured nails on the steering wheel and bounced with nervous energy. "Let's go, let's go."

Duvi shoved Rachel into the back seat, jumped on the running board and swung himself in next to Schmuel. He ran his fingers over the dashboard. "Nice," he said. "New?"

"Yeah. The Man says that a person in my situation has to be making what you might call a big impression all'atime. Otherwise, some wise guys would not get the message that business is business."

Duvi laughed.

Schmuel's "situation" was the kind it wasn't smart to ask questions about; any more than it was wise to ask about the business of *The Man*, whom Schmuel never mentioned by name. In the neighbourhood, some people called Schmuel "the driver", but whether that referred to his job or his flash cars, Rachel was never sure. The Man's Duesie was often parked outside Schmuel's father's pawnshop.

Schmuel reached back to give Rachel a flask of gin. "Have some of this, doll."

"No thanks." Rachel didn't like gin. She imagined that cologne tasted about the same. At Dreamworld they could buy near-beer and plenty of boys would be carrying brandy or whiskey. She could wait.

"Go on," Duvi said. "It'll warm you up. Your teeth are givin' me a headache."

"No thanks."

"Suit yourself," Schmuel said. He pulled away from the curb and they headed off to pick up Bessie on the way to Dreamworld.

Dreamworld was the place to be on Saturday night. On other nights, during the week, the halls near the garment district were popular for a few hours after work. Girls in pairs practiced the new steps to the music of a solitary piano man or a ragtime trio. They flirted experimentally with the boys who congregated around the edge of the dance floor waiting for a chance to break in, and generally polished up their Saturday night skills. Most people had to get up for work and would drift away early.

Monday nights, when his wife visited her cousins in The Bronx, Arty took Rachel and Bessie to Roseland on 42nd. He and Bessie did the lovers' two-step and Bessie would let him hold her tight, the two of them turning in the smallest possible circles. Rachel saved her smiles for the boys who liked fast dances. If there was never anyone special, it was still a good time for a couple of hours.

But Saturday night at Dreamworld was magic.

Hundreds of people came from all over town, dressed to the nines, each trailing a wake of spirits set free to play. Under the coloured lights and slowly turning mirrored globes, an otherworldly buzz and chatter mingled with the laughter of shop girls and the bravado of labourers, who re-invented themselves for every new encounter. They had the glamour, revealing their possibilities instead of themselves. Everyone was beautiful. Anything could happen.

There was a real orchestra - with violins, a ragtime trio and a jazz band, taking turns so the music never stopped. At Dreamworld, you could dance till dawn, or until the speakeasies and jazz cellars and gambling clubs woke up in the early hours of the morning.

The balcony at Dreamworld was famous for smooching. If a boy said, "Do you want a smoke?" or "How 'bout we watch for a while", he was really asking you to sit on his lap up there in the dark. A lot of girls only danced until they were invited to the balcony. Rachel had not yet met the special boy upon whose lap she wanted to sit, although she'd been asked plenty of times. The really insistent boys were easy enough to discourage. "I'm only 15 and my big brother will be looking for me."

When she met the right boy, she wouldn't bother to mention her age. Or her brother.

Once she thought she had. He was a man, really; probably at least 25. They'd been thrown together in the eliminations of a dance-off. When Rachel did the shimmy in her mermaid dress, no one else stood a chance. And he danced with an abandoned passion that would have been terrifying if it were not somehow familiar. The band could barely keep up with them. Rachel liked his glossy curls and his lively blue eyes. His tie was undone and his shirt collar open. When Rachel shimmied, he threw his head back and laughed, a galloping earthy music. She noticed that his throat was beautiful, that she wanted to touch it. She had never had such a feeling before.

They'd won ten dollars each. Amid the excitement and applause, he had lifted her in a sweeping hug, spinning her around. His shirt was damp; his sweat smelled spicy and male. When he led her off the dance floor, Rachel was sure he would take her to the balcony but he'd only thanked her, said, "See you later", and disappeared into the crowd.

Rachel had watched for him many times after that, but she had never seen him again.

"Forget it," Bessie advised. "Them pretty Irish fellas is charmers but you can't count on 'em for nothin'."

Bessie also advised her to be less choosy. "How you gonna know if you got a special one if you ain't never had no practice to know the difference?"

"We'll just find each other, I guess."

Bessie stared at her. "Boy, you sure got some funny ideas...Okay, okay...so you just find each other...Geez...Then what?"

"What do you mean?"

"Well, how you gonna know what to do...what the boys like and all?"

Rachel blushed. "We'll learn together...the way people do...you know."

"I'm sure I don't know no such thing. If it was all that easy, there wouldn't be so many guys like Arty chasing after girls like me."

Rachel was silent.

"Listen kiddo, I'm gonna give you the best piece of advice you ever got. I ain't never yet met a boy who knew what he liked until I showed him. And if a boy don't know what he likes, he sure enough ain't gonna know what you like."

"But I don't know what I like."

"That's what I'm sayin'."

Rachel was beginning to think that Bessie was right and that, perhaps, tonight was the night to find out.

∞

Shalimar and Jicky, tobacco, bay rum and eau de cologne. The perfume of the dance floor rose from solid base notes of wax and booze. Rachel enjoyed it as she leaned on the shoulder of a lanky young man who walked her through a listless two-step.

Bessie and Schmuel had disappeared to the balcony hours ago. Unlike other places, Dreamworld charged full price for girls. And you had to have an escort. Arty couldn't come out on Saturday nights so Rachel had suggested going with Duvi and his friend Schmuel who were already regulars. It was just meant to be a way to get in. Of course, Schmuel thought Bessie was hot stuff. That was no surprise. But who would have guessed that Bessie would take a shine to Schmuel? Rachel couldn't figure it.

Duvi liked to dance with tall girls so he could press his face against their bosoms. He had just danced by with a redhaired giantess. His expression as he inhaled her lingerie made Rachel laugh out loud.

"Something funny?" the young man said.

"No...I was just thinking."

"It must have been good if it made you laugh."

"Yeah...well...I thought I saw somebody I know."

"What's funny about that?"

It really wasn't worth the time it would take to explain. Duvi had already propelled his partner across the floor and out of sight. Rachel shrugged. "I'm thirsty," she told her partner. "What have you got?"

The young man gave her a flask of brandy, rough, new and grapey. She sipped, ignoring the bitter taste, waiting instead for the clear space it would open inside her.

Funny how people said strong drink warmed you up and made you fuzzy. Rachel had never found it so. It was more like a cool wind that blew the clouds away so you could see the stars and hear the ringing sky.

She drank again and then returned the flask, hoping the young man had exhausted his attempts at conversation. It was nice, sometimes, to shuffle about with an undemanding partner, to watch the other dancers or follow the loopy thread of a clarinet weaving pictures in the air. Tonight, it scrawled lazy golden circles around the brasses and strings. It darted about the drummer, scribbling jokey, bubbly filigrees. It climbed to the ceiling, hovered, then swooped down and wrapped itself around the walking bass, pulling so tight the bass had to pluck itself free in a jumpy fit of pizzicato. The clarinet player said "Yeah" and laughed. He caught Rachel's eye and she knew he had been watching too.

Soon the rhythm would change. Rachel cast about the room for a new partner. She realised the lanky young man was probably doing the same, but etiquette demanded that he dance with her until somebody else cut in. Not far away, a delicate looking Italian boy with untouchably brilliantined hair seemed to be making the most of the music. He had a gentleness about him that, just at that moment, appealed to her. By the time the band broke into the bunny hug, she was dancing with him.

He said his name was Vinnie. He worked as a mail clerk in the Flat Iron Building, a job that took him all the way to the twenty-second floor several times a day. "My boss says I waste too much time looking out the windows." On clear days, he said, from the top floor, you could see the cargo ships anchored twelve miles out along "Rum Row", and the Coast Guard cutters buzzing back and forth just inside the limit. After the tango, Rachel followed him to the balcony.

He was a nervous talker. Rachel leaned against a column and listened, nodding and smiling from time to time. He rooted for the New York Giants because he always stood up for the underdogs; he was saving for the down payment on a used Model-T but his father thought he should wait and buy a Buick Six, it being built more solid and all; his parents came from Agrigento but he was born on Mott Street; he liked opera better than the pictures; he had five brothers and two sisters; his oldest brother was a priest, but he could take it or leave it if you want to know the truth. Rachel didn't much care either way; she wished he would get on with it and kiss her. She watched the reflections of coloured lights on his patent leather shoes and wondered what to do next.

She could, she supposed, just kiss him first. That was probably what Bessie would do. Such direct action did not appeal to her. Often, if she listened to her own stillness, a course of action would compose itself. But the buzzing in her head refused to resolve itself into a theme. Vinnie droned on and on, his voice putting her into a kind of trance where Douglas Fairbanks swings down from the rigging. With his trusty cutlass, he swashbuckles his way across the heaving deck.

The organist goes berserk.

Lon Chaney, his eyes aflame, his face contorted with evil lust, pins a struggling Mary Pickford against a cannon. *Ah ha, my pretty, at last you are mine.*

Vinnie put one hand on the column behind her and offered her a cigarette.

"No thanks, I don't smoke," Rachel said.

"Do you mind?"

"No. Smoke if you like."

He lit a Camel, showing off by blowing rings. Sour tobacco smoke tickled Rachel's nose. The deck is ablaze. Holding a lacy handkerchief to his face, Douglas Fairbanks squints through the haze, then leaps to the rescue.

One quick thrust and he dispatches the villain overboard. He lifts Mary Pickford in a one-armed embrace. With the other arm, his cutlass gripped between his teeth, he grabs some rigging that, handily, is within reach and, gently cradling Mary Pickford, who has fainted dead away, he flies through the air to the safety of his waiting corsair.

Now the organ is subdued.

"You still with me?"

"Hmm?"

"You looked like you were...you know...thinking...or something."

"Did I? Oh...sorry...I was...uh..."

"So anyway, like I was saying, you gotta understand that when Dempsey gets in the ring, he's like an artist with his fists. And footwork? Hey, when it comes to footwork, there's nobody who can..."

Vinnie's eyes looked over Rachel's shoulder watching Jack Dempsey's fancy footwork in the middle distance of nowhere while Douglas Fairbanks gazes at the swooning Mary Pickford. His eyes gleam with desire. The tips of his moustachios quiver. She opens her eyes...*My hero!* and looks shyly away. He turns her face towards his. In a burst of ecstatic crescendos, they kiss.

"So then I said, if the Yankees didn't have Ruth they'd still be in the cellar, and he said St. Louis had the sluggers to beat next season so I said..."

Rachel stifled a yawn. She looked down at the floor, tilted her head, gazed up at Vinnie through her long, brown lashes and waited. In a few seconds, he lost track of his he-said-I-saids and stumbled to a halt. He lifted Rachel's chin, searching her eyes for a sign of permission. Apparently finding it, he kissed her.

His lips were warm and dry, sort of firm and soft at the same time. They were nice. She kissed him back. Nice, though lots of other things were nicer. Her mouth slightly open, she touched his lower lip and, more out of curiosity than desire, explored it with the tip of her tongue. He seemed to shiver and she felt his warm sigh on the back of her throat. How interesting.

She wanted to watch but when she opened her eyes she couldn't see anything closer than his perfectly ordinary ears so she closed them again. Besides, she realised, she didn't need to see to understand the message of his ragged gasps. He seemed to like some things more than others. If she nibbled his lips or ran her tongue into the corner of his mouth, he purred and squirmed. She could feel his whole body moving tensely as he pressed her against the column.

She rested in the music, determined to concentrate on sensations which, while not as electrifying as she had imagined, were, in the cadent darkness, becoming more exciting.

Below them, in the circle of light, the quickening heartbeat of the drums stirs the dancers. They are shouting. He covers her ears with his hands but she can still sense them in his trembling. Blind navigator, he maps her face with his lips, his teeth, his velvet tongue. Coarsened fingers scrape her neck. Resting his sweet soft head in the hollow of her throat, he strokes the skin between her breasts until she arches her back, crying out. Oh, best beloved. When he silences her with his hand, she tastes the blood from his chains. The fevered *cithara* goads the whirling dancers and cymbals gild the air. Soon the *syrinx* will wail and they will come, with their blackened faces, to take him into the circle and worship the fire in his eyes. He smells them coming. Run, he whispers, run away. But she will not let him go. She wraps herself around him, digs her fingers into his back. And when they tear them apart, she leaves a trail of bloody scratches along his golden arms.

"Hey...hey...take it easy sweetie."

Rachel stared at the Italian boy. She could see his face but the parts of it didn't seem to fit together. His lips moved, inches from hers, but she had to strain to hear him through the dying fall of music and voices.

"Wow," he said. He shook his head. *"Madonne."* There was blood on his cheek.

She pushed him away, trying hold on to a current of impressions that was running off like water from an open palm. *Chaos confounding, cold and dark*

Nothing was left but confusion and dream sadness. Someone's desperate grief. *Oh shine.*

"...I...I...my big brother will be looking for me. I have to go."

"Listen...You're really something...Maybe you wanna...you know...go somewhere else?"

"I have to go."

"Wait a minute, don't be a tease. We were just..." He grabbed her wrist.

"What do you want? I can't...I...I'm only 15. Let go of me."

"Look baby, don't get so excited. It's nothing to cry about."

What an odd thing for him to say. Rachel touched her cheek and felt there alien tears.

Chaos confounding, cold and dark
Where is the beacon flame?
Who lights the fires?
Shine for me mermaid, shine for me fair maid
Shine for me, shine for me, shine.

CHAPTER EIGHT

States of grace

On silent wings
Across the hungry nights
Above the vagrant seas
Come home
On silent wings
Beyond the clamorous days
Beneath the vacant skies
Come home
On silent wings
Come home

Sunday morning. Rachel sprawled on her stomach, watching the windows across the street through a sunfall of feathers. From this position, propped on her elbows across the bed, her chin in her hands, Rachel could look into half a city block of third and fourth floor tenement flats.

No one else was home. Once Sophie was satisfied that Rachel's "headache" was a mood and not a fever, she left for work. All the others were out making their Sunday lives in the freedom of the Christians' day of rest.

Rachel rolled back the left sleeve of her nightgown and examined her wrist. It didn't hurt much, but the Italian boy's fingers were clearly marked in purple turning yellow around the edges. Why had he grabbed at her like that? She had lain awake through the predawn hours thinking about it. Shouldn't she feel frightened? Or angry? The longer she considered these questions, the more questions they raised. Why, for example, hadn't she told Bessie about it? Bessie would have had something to say about anything that involved boys. Instead, she had told Duvi that she was tired and he had sent her home in a taxicab.

Now, as she watched her neighbours through the mesmerising veil of snow, imagining stories for the silent pictures that played across dozens of screens, her thoughts wandered. She let her mind reach out across the empty spaces and touch the different lives and souls that might populate a gloomy tenement on a late morning in winter. Whether what she saw and heard was real or imagined, even Rachel could not have said. It was merely her way of knowing whatever needed to be known.

She had stopped talking about such ideas and feelings long ago. Once, when she was small, she and three playmates had watched birds gorging themselves on red berries from the schoolyard hedges and had considered tasting them.

"Everyone says they'll make you sick," Rachel said.

"Who says?"

"They do." And she pointed to the people perched on the branches of the elm tree that overlooked the yard, all of them, in their dove-coloured coats, shaking their heads, gesturing and twittering.

"The pigeons say so?" The other children laughed. "That's because they want them all for themselves."

Everyone but Rachel ate the berries. Two of the girls burned their lips on the peppery fruit and spat them out. One girl, who had eaten the most on a dare, was sick in bed for days.

That was when the other children began to whisper about the evil eye. That was when Rachel began keeping most things to herself.

Lazy flakes, rose and fell on the whim of air currents. Rachel picked one that drifted across her view. It almost landed on the fire escape when a gust caught it and took it dancing circles back toward the sky. Then it settled in a downward spiral. She craned her neck to follow it all the way to the street.

The knife grinder's wagon turned into Rivington Street. He rang his bell and stopped. In a few minutes, a small group of people gathered round him with their knives and scissors. The knife grinder's Palomino pony shook his head and exhaled warm clouds. The pony's patience was aristocratic. He held his head high and never snorted or pawed the road, even when the knife grinder's whetstone screamed and threw sparks that melted holes in the snow. His bearing and his liquid brown eyes held generations of grace. Rachel closed her eyes and settled on the pony's back. She pressed her face against his milky neck. His tangled, dirty mane turned to creamy, hay scented silk and she felt the warmth of his heart.

The wind blew a shutter of snow.

At an open fourth floor window, far to the right, the woman who made sweaters for a contractor was knitting with brown yarn. She was always there, the window open whatever the weather. In Sarah's opinion, she kept the window open because "All that ugly brown wool stinks." Jacob said, "Some people know the value of fresh air." "She keeps the window open so an angel can bring her dreams," was Tanta Rosa's explanation. Rachel liked that one best.

A rhythmical song of stitches ran through the knitting woman's mind like a magical incantation. Sometimes she moved her lips slightly in time with the recital. *knitone-purltwo-knittwotogether-slipone-knitone-passtheslipstitchover.* While she worked, she hardly looked at the knitting. Her eyes rested on the middle distance, as though waiting for visions. At the end of every row, she put down the knitting, sighed and looked at the sky. She almost never put the work down before the end of the row. Today she did. She leaned over her windowsill and looked down into the street. Rachel followed her gaze to the knife grinder's pony.

Then the knitting woman shook out the piece she had been working on. It wasn't a sweater at all, but a big, soft cloak that she threw out the open window. It spread and rippled, floating down to cover the beautiful Palomino, which instantly became a handsome young man. He rubbed his eyes. Then, wrapped in his new brown cloak, he rushed upstairs to the knitting woman and shut her window to make her warm. Nobody but the knife grinder noticed. He stared for a moment at the limp traces in his hand, then went back about his business.

Two across to the left and one down, the shade was drawn. The newlyweds. Rachel remembered when they arrived, the whole street turning out to cheer them and throw rice and nuts. Later, a procession of visitors brought gifts of bread and salt.

The husband was smaller than his darkly ample wife and given to sharp, awkward gestures. He seemed always to be dressed for office work, even at night, when he played the fiddle and she sat, her hands folded in her lap, listening respectfully. Rachel wanted to see them and, as the thought occurred to her, the young wife raised the shade. The husband was at the table. The wife placed food in front of him. She stood back and watched him eat, her face wistful with defeated optimism.

The husband jabbed at his food, chewed twenty times, counting off as he did so, and swallowed with a great galumph of his Adam's apple. Then he jabbed again.

She was so tentative toward him, like a stranger. This puzzled Rachel. Even arranged couples got to know each other first, were given time to accept or reject the matchmaker's proposals. Rachel decided she must be a picture bride, shipped by her family from a poor but sunny Croatian village to this drab life in a cold water, third floor walk-up on Rivington Street. She had sailed down the Adriatic, across the Mediterranean and through the Straits of Gibraltar, where the sea changed from the colour of heaven to the murky green of the winter Atlantic. She carried all her possessions in a small leather-strapped trunk; a few linens, some warm clothing, the brass candlesticks that were a present from her whole village.

Although she had seen his picture when the matchmaker brought it, she was still disappointed to find him so frail and nervous. But along with her belongings, she carried the hope of her family. So she would make the best of it and give him no cause for complaint.

Sarah's prolonged engagement spared Rachel and her sisters such dilemmas. Jacob was too much of a traditionalist to consider proposals for his younger daughters before his eldest was safely wed. Rachel was glad of this. She was in no hurry to leave a tyranny she understood and had learned to tolerate, for the mysterious and unpredictable world of married life. Once you got married, you didn't belong to yourself anymore. That's what Jacob believed. When Rabbi Meyer was still alive, he and Jacob had discussed the graceless state of families nowadays while Rachel served them glasses of tea and slices of Sophie's strudel; the two of them acting as if she didn't have ears to hear.

"It's the politics I'm blaming," Jacob said. "Votes, rights...it makes the women *meshugga*, puts too many ideas in their heads."

The Rabbi sucked his tea through a sugar cube. His own wife, God bless her, had been making him *meshugga* for years.

"Look at my Bea..."

"A *sheyna maydel*, she should live and be well."

"All the time she is busy with politics. Meetings, petitions, unions...you shouldn't know from it. And what will happen in the end...No husband...that is what will happen."

"Now Jacob, you shouldn't say such things. I have heard of young men who would value a clever wife. There is no accounting for taste."

Jacob ignored him. "And if I forbade it, God forbid, she is old enough, in this godless country, to move right out of her own father's house. What chance of a respectable match then, I'm asking you?"

"But Jacob," Rabbi Meyer soothed, "do you not think that when a woman is a *mensch* she makes a better helpmeet for her husband?"

"A *mensch*? A person?" Jacob snorted.

"All the same, obedience is only..."

"It's impossible," Jacob said. "A married woman cannot be a person on her own. Didn't *Hashem*, blessed be, make the woman from Adam's rib?"

The Rabbi disagreed. "Yes, yes, of course. But he always meant for there to be two, not one."

"So now, you are not only a mind reader, but you can read the mind of the Almighty as well? How can you say such a thing?"

"Jacob, open your eyes. It is right there in front of you. First...before He made her... He said, 'It is not good that the man should be alone.' Not good for what?... Not good for *His* plan, blessed be, that's what. He always meant for there to be two. Two separate...the man and the woman, two separate."

Jacob scowled. He always grew irritable when someone could quote scripture to win a point away from him. Even the Rabbi.

"Tell me Rabbi, since you are so smart that *Hashem* Himself lets you in on His secret plans...so tell me, why didn't he make her from the clay? Why did he make her from Adam's rib?"

Rabbi Meyer sat back and smiled. He sipped his tea and gathered up crumbs of pastry with his fingers. "Ah, you see my friend, the Lord Almighty is a poet and an artist. In the merest brushstroke of His will he puts so many meanings...so we can puzzle over it forever."

"So tell me...you have solved this puzzle?"

"I'm telling...I'm telling."

Rachel, pouring the men fresh glasses of tea, thought Rabbi Meyer's stories were almost as good as Tanta Rosa's.

"Because later," the Rabbi said, "when they had troubles...you shouldn't know from such troubles..."

"*Kinahora*," Jacob agreed. "It shouldn't happen to a dog."

"So when He sent them troubles, He wanted them to solve them together, to be a family. And how better?... I'm asking you...How better than if they always remembered they came from one flesh? So, *schon*...forever they would be two from one...And *Hashem*, blessed be, He made them so they would never forget. You know the saying, that when you are born, the Almighty chooses for you a spouse in heaven."

"Maybe, my friend, you are a little too much the poet yourself," Jacob laughed. "Well, I hope that when the time comes for my daughters, He will give me a clue about these heavenly choices."

They agreed to disagree by moving on to talk of other things. That was the trouble with The Law. Two men could dispute for hours, shifting from one point to another and, in the end, each could still feel justified in his own interpretation.

When her father was ready to make her a match, he would give her away to someone who thought as he did. *He* would find the one heaven had named. Rachel wanted to do her own finding. And she did not want to belong to anyone. At least, not yet. She knew that even Jacob would not force her to go with a husband she disliked. But how could you tell what kind of a husband a boy would turn out to be? Some husbands beat their wives. Some, like Jacob, scowled all the time and almost never laughed. If a nervous, gentle Italian boy could grab you and leave bruises all over your wrist for no reason, who could tell what might happen with a man who believed God meant him to correct his wife?

Rachel had never seen Jacob strike Sophie, but she knew many people would not think less of him if he did. Three across and one up from the newlyweds, there was a man who struck his wife almost every day. Once it was because she oversalted the chicken. Right now, he was waving his arms about and shouting because she dared to touch him before she had visited the *mikvah*, the ritual bath, to purify herself after her time of month. He regarded her with such loathing that in his mind Rachel saw her covered with weeping, leprous sores. Furious that he couldn't strike her because touching her again would compound the sin, he picked up a milk bottle and threw it at the wall. Milk and glass exploded against the plaster. The woman cringed. Rachel had felt her mother cringe, in just the same way, at her father's passionate anger. There were many different kinds of violence.

Were there different kinds of passion too? Rachel's only knowledge of passion came from the movies. In the movies, passion was a kind of sweet pain that bubbled up out of nothing. And as soon as you felt it, the screen went dark. The movies always ended when the passion began. Rachel was never satisfied with this.

"What do you think happens next?"

"They live happily ever after," Bessie would say.

"But what if...?" There were always *what ifs*. What if he didn't like her cooking? What if he drank too much? What if they got bored? What if he had a temper? What if they were always poor?

"Raaachel! It's just a movie. People in the movies always live happily ever after. They make wild, passionate love and they live happily ever after. That's what happens in the movies."

"Aren't they embarrassed?"

"For what?"

"Well, after they make wild, passionate love...how do they...you know...eat breakfast together and all?"

Bessie would not be drawn. "People in the movies don't eat breakfast."

Rachel wanted to ask her if she and Schmuel made wild, passionate love. She was desperately curious to know what happened after. But she didn't have the nerve.

A cushion of light, dry snow built up, filling all the spaces in the grating. While she watched, a sea gull emerged from the sun storm and settled on the fire escape, its feathers almost perfectly camouflaged in the cloud of flakes that puffed up around it. Another appeared, balanced on the railing. Then another. They were blocking the view. Rachel tapped the glass to scare them off. They ruffled and started but would not fly away. She had to shift her position to see beyond them.

Directly above the newlyweds, two children, a boy and a girl, played a card game. The little girl had silky yellow braids, fastened with white ribbon bows. The little boy's shirt had a collar.

The mother, who was wearing a flowered apron, came to watch them. She said something and the children responded. The father joined them, putting his arm around the mother, and all four smiled not, it seemed, with happiness but with distracted contentment.

These people seemed to have no passion at all. Rachel had never seen them argue. Or laugh. Or shout. No one ever played a musical instrument. And when visitors came, they never came in crowds. Try as she might, Rachel could not hear a single thought pass through their heads or imagine a story for the lives these people led.

She had named them The Perfect Family after she realised that they looked just like the pictures in her grade school reader. She had never seen them in the street and nobody she knew lived in such bovine serenity.

They probably ate boiled chicken sandwiches on white bread spread with margarine, grey boiled peas and plain mashed potatoes without even chicken fat to give them taste. The boy and the girl probably had their own beds, their own separate rooms. So there was never anyone to gossip and giggle with after the lights were turned out; no one to roll up against for warmth, nobody else's cold feet to tangle with in the night.

Rachel sensed that The Perfect Family were lacking something important. If she could have discovered precisely what it was, she might have understood why they made her so sad. In the end, it hardly mattered. Rachel had long ago decided that they were simply a trick of the light and didn't exist at all.

Way across on the right, the last third floor apartment was empty. Rachel liked to populate it herself, setting little dramas in motion on the darkened glass, then watching to see how they turned out. But now two more sea gulls joined the three already settled on the fire escape, completely blocking the view. Rachel was annoyed because, for a just a second, she thought she had seen someone by the window. She closed her eyes to remember the image. Was it a man with flute? No amount of rapping on the window would budge the stupid, fearless birds, so she couldn't be sure. She considered opening it to chase them away, but the snow that had collected against the glass would have melted all over the bed if she did.

Instead, she rolled onto her back and stared up at the stained ceiling. Her wrist throbbed. Dispassionately, she examined it. If it were true, what the Rabbi said, about heaven's choice, then surely the chosen one wouldn't cover you with bruises. She remembered the inexplicable grief; not her own, but someone else's. "If God's got a fella for me, I sure hope he ain't the jealous type," Bessie said when Rachel told her the Rabbi's story. Maybe that was it. Maybe she had betrayed someone without even knowing.

It wouldn't happen again. The next time she kissed a boy, it would be because she wanted the boy, not the kiss. She would know what wanting the boy should feel like when it happened; she would hear the music, see the future in his eyes. *It will be like coming home.*

In the meantime, she would follow her will where it led. Bessie knew a lot of things, but Bessie was running to a different destiny. Rachel understood that, to find her own, she must stay free. She wished she were as old and as clever and as brave as Bea, who already did exactly as she pleased, without pretending. Bea would never marry and she didn't even care. She wished she were as quick-witted as Duvi, who could scheme his way around anyone.

The only freedom she really understood she found in the dancehalls, when she could re-create herself for the night, surrounded by hundreds of others who were doing the same. No silly Italian boy with rough manners would scare her away.

The bedroom was warm. Rachel took off her nightgown and slid under the covers. She hugged herself, running her fingers along the soft down of her arms until her hands met and she clasped one within the other like a lover. Examining her wrist, she noticed, without surprise, that the bruises were gone. Settling back on her pillow, her eyes closed, she rode the knife grinder's Palomino pony dreamily into the storm white sky.

By ones and twos, people trudging through the snow on Rivington Street stopped to join a small group looking up at one fourth floor window at number 75. No one, they all agreed, had ever seen anything like it. Some of the women wondered, aloud, what it could mean.

"It's just the weather," the knife grinder said. "All this sunshine and snow mixed together. They're just confused, that's all there is to it. Nothing peculiar about it at all."

Most of the men grunted in agreement, but still they watched as, by ones and twos, sea gulls came from every direction to settle on the fire escape outside one window at number 75. They flapped and preened as new arrivals hovered before squeezing in. The press of birds cleared the balcony of snow, which scintillated down, dry iridescent clouds, on the heads and shoulders of the people below. At least a hundred pure white gulls had already massed and they were still arriving. No one, everyone agreed, had ever seen such pure white gulls. They balanced on the railing, filled the floor of the balcony, lined up along the windowsill. The late comers settled on the backs of the others. They didn't make a single sound.

It will be like coming home.

CHAPTER NINE

Rope enough

Don't know, don't care
We can take you anywhere
We can turn your soul to ice
Burn you bare for paradise
Don't know, don't care
We can take you everywhere
Play with us, ignore the price
Come on in, the water's nice

"I am the Queen of the Night. Onward, Charioteer! Take me to my city of stars." Rachel waved her arms and settled back on a sack of potatoes, giggling.

"Chrissakes doll, where do you get all that crap?" Schmuel snorted. "You're crazy."

"No she ain't," Bessie hiccupped. "She's blotto."

They all were. Schmuel's friend Stinko, Rachel's "escort", had passed out affectionately embracing 100 pounds of Long Island Best, US Grade A bakers. The farmer, a dour Dutch Calvinist from Hardscrabble, perched in his open cab, pretending to ignore the goings on in the back of his truck. Four sorry specimens; three sheenies and an Irish tart, by the look of them, fancy clothes or not. The farmer, a man of spotless soul and dry politics, had a nose for such things. He hoped none of them vomited on his load.

He would not have given them a lift at all but for the twenty dollars that Schmuel and Stinko gave him - twice as much as the potatoes would fetch at the market. The one waving her arms about and declaiming at the moon was just a baby. He wondered what her parents thought about what she got up to. Whose idea was it, anyway, to drag a kid like that all the way out here in the middle of the night?

The fact that her parents knew nothing at all about what she got up to would have irritated but not surprised him. Those people had no morals anyway. They bred like rabbits. Small wonder they couldn't keep track of where all their kids were. Still, it was a shame. Sheeny or not, she looked such an innocent little thing.

In fact, the entire escapade was Rachel's idea. Success had bred contempt for the rules. The easier it became for Rachel to slip out from under her father's thumb, the more daring her adventures had to be. Tonight, after the dancing had paled, and after Schmuel had gotten as far as Bessie would allow him to go on the balcony, Rachel had talked him into driving them all out to Long Island.

"Whaddya wanna go there for. There is not nothing out there but farms and cows."

"And cow lovers," Stinko had snickered.

"We could see the Milky Way. We could take our shoes off and walk on the beach."

"For cryin' out loud. It is goddam February."

"Yeah...well...if we go to the beach, we might see some bootleggers."

"Lemme give you the low down on this. These bootleggers, which you are so hot to see...and who, I am not saying there are any of them out there to be seen...would not be appreciating being seen by the likes of you."

"Oh come on, Sammy, let's go," Bessie said. "It'll be fun."

So they had piled into Schmuel's Pierce Arrow at one o'clock in the morning, crossed the Brooklyn Bridge and headed east. Unfortunately, Schmuel, who Rachel was convinced had *mamaliggah* for brains, didn't carry any extra fuel. They had run out of gasoline in the middle of nowhere, in the middle of the night. Sometime later, they had run out of whiskey too.

They spent hours shivering in the car before a farmer, taking his storage potatoes to the wholesale market in Lower Manhattan, passed at about 4 am. He wasn't all that willing to have them sprawling on his produce, but Schmuel and Stinko had flashed money and a deal was struck. They might just make it before the neighbourhood woke up.

Then again, they might not. The risk excited Rachel, especially as she was the only one of them who really risked anything. Schmuel's father was strict too, but boys could get away with more and Schmuel was the only son he had left. She didn't have to wonder what her father would do if she sashayed in just as the family was settling down to breakfast. She would probably end up locked in the bedroom for the rest of her life. The idea made her giggle again.

They huddled against each other like puppies in a litter; Stinko snoring, Bessie and Schmuel cuddling and whispering, and Rachel crammed in the middle, trying to get comfortable on the lumpy sacks. Stinko turned over in his sleep and his arm fell across her. She turned her face away from his juicy, whisky scented snorts. She didn't like his sleazy moustache or the way he kept calling her "Toots" but she let him rest against her, for the warmth, until his limp weight made her breathless. Struggling out from under him, she eased herself up and looked over the side panel of the truck. It was nearly daybreak. Already the eastern sky had paled to a chalkboard grey and some of the stars were winking out.

They were near the shore. Rachel could smell the ocean, although a rise of land hid the beach and deadened the sound of it. A beacon, its source blocked by the hill, washed circles of light across the sky. Bootleggers, Rachel thought. She waited and watched, but nothing happened.

"What's that?" she called to the driver. He didn't answer. Perhaps he couldn't hear her over the sound of the motor. "What's that?" she shouted again. She crawled over the sacks of potatoes to the front of the truck. It never crossed her mind that he was ignoring her deliberately. She never even considered that he had any reason not to answer her until she tapped his shoulder and he shrank from her touch. His eyes were cold and dead. It was a look she had never seen, close up, but she had been raised to recognise it. It didn't matter. Just another man trying to make the world a smaller place. They were in his truck, weren't they? He took their money. She pressed on. "What's that?" She had to shout over the wail of the engine. "Bootleggers?"

The farmer snickered. Stupid too. "No, girlie. It's the lightship," he said. "The what?"

"The lightship...the lightship...so ships don't run aground on the sandbars." Rachel was silent. Despite himself, the farmer felt compelled to explain. "It stays out there."

"You mean like a lighthouse?"

"Yeah...like a lighthouse."

"Is there anyone on it?"

"Of course there's someone on it. Howdya think the light keeps burning?"

"Who?"

"I don't know...the Coast Guard...somebody."

As adventures went, this one had been pretty tame so far. The others were all asleep. Rachel settled back on the potatoes and watched the sky, lulled by the music of the sweeping light, as it plucked arpeggios of shooting stars from the Milky Way. People said that in February the water was warmer than the air. She tried to imagine what it might feel like to dive up from the warm bath of the Gulf Stream into the frigid night.

On the lightship, a sailor pulls up the collar of his blue wool pea coat and scans the choppy black water. The sea is quiet. To the West, the lights of the coast gather and multiply around the city. He thinks about his leave, two days away, and smiles. This time he'll have pockets full of money to do the town up right. The freeloading pelican, that has been hanging around for a week, breaks up from the surface of the water and alights in the lifeboat. The sailor salutes the bird. "Too late for supper, pal." He puts a cigarette between his lips. He doesn't light it but remains, holding a box of matches in his hand, watching, listening.

The pelican hears the sound of the outboard motor first. It lifts its head from under its wing and flaps about.

"Ssh...settle down."

The sailor strikes a match. It flares up for a second before the breeze extinguishes it. He drops it in the water and lights another. The motor cuts out. Now he can hear the splash of oars and the gentle creak of oarlocks. He strikes another match and drops it. Then, unconsciously touching his wallet, he turns his back on the sea, smiles and lights his cigarette. After a few minutes, he hears the outboard come to life again.

The truck bumped along a dirt road. The glow of the city was just visible but they were still miles out. The engine coughed, whined and died. "What the...?" the farmer said. The truck grumbled to a halt. "Damn." He lit a kerosene lantern, climbed down from the cab and raised the hood.

Rachel leaned over the side panel. They had broken down near a quiet bay somewhere along the South Shore. With the engine silenced, the water was just audible. Bessie and Schmuel stirred and woke. Stinko sat up and rubbed his eyes. "Where the hell are we? Pardon my French, Toots." While he slept, Rachel had almost forgotten what a jerk he was.

"I think there's something the matter with the truck," Rachel said.

Bessie poked Schmuel. "You better go help or the 'queen of the night' here could end up engaged to your stupid friend."

Both boys scrambled off the back of the truck. The driver handed Schmuel the lantern and bent under the hood. "I'll be darned if I can find anything wrong with the darn thing," he said.

"Let me," Schmuel said. "Motors are whatcha might call my speciality."

In the back of the truck, Rachel and Bessie built a windbreak from potato sacks.

A black Olds taxicab crosses the city line near a back road in Queens. Tar paving ends and the road changes to packed, rutted dirt. The driver worries about his under carriage. "You gonna pay me for the damage to my cab?"

"Don't worry about nothing," his passenger says. "You just drive."

"Much further?" the driver says. He turns to look over his shoulder at the man in the back seat.

"Just keep your eyes on the road and button up, okay. I'll tell you when we're there."

The driver likes to have a chat, now and again. The man in the back seat makes him nervous and when he's nervous he likes to talk. But he turns around and buttons up. A hundred dollars buys more than three trips back and forth to the city. It buys a lot of silence.

Bessie hugged her knees and yawned. "What a night, eh kiddo?"

Rachel nodded. Right now, hunkered down in her potato fortress, her mind was elsewhere.

"Ain't you scared of getting caught?"

"Ssh...listen. Do you hear that?"

"What?" Bessie heard the murmur of male voices as the boys and the farmer studied the engine. "I don't hear nothin'."

"Can't you? There's a boat on the bay...Can't you hear it?"

Rachel squeezed her eyes shut.

A big dinghy, with an outboard, is overloaded and riding low. Two men perch on top of dozens of wooden crates, trying to stay clear of the water that washes over the gunwales.

"We're gonna fuckin' sink," one of the men says. "I told ya we shoulda made two trips."

"Shut up and pay attention," the other man says. He sees a kerosene lantern swinging up ahead. "We're nearly there. The hack's already on the beach...And I don't want to tell you no more to watch your lip."

Somewhere near the Queens-Nassau boundary, a black Olds taxicab bounces up off a rutted dirt road onto smooth tar paving. Thank God, civilisation, the cabbie thinks, but his passenger sits bolt upright and smacks him on the back of the head.

"Whaddya some kinda wise guy? This ain't the right way."

"Look, Mister," the cabbie says, "I don't want no trouble. I just go where you tell me."

"Well, I sure as hell didn't tell you to turn back to the city. Did you turn left at that fork, like a told you?"

"Yeah, sure Mister. I don't want no trouble."

"Stop the cab...Stop!"

The nervous cabbie slams on his breaks, throwing his passenger to the floor.

"Jesus, Mary and Joseph! You wait here. And leave the engine running."

The passenger gets out of the cab. He kneels into the glow of the headlights, unfolds a map, and studies it. "Did you go right at that fork, like I told you?" he shouts.

"Left, Mister. You said left." Now the cabbie is getting the shakes. "I don't want no trouble, Mister."

"You keep sayin'."

"Left...you said left."

"Yeah, yeah." The passenger looks at his pocket watch. "Shit."

Bessie heard the outboard motor just as it sputtered out. After a few minutes, three coney rabbits scrambled over the dunes. Two dove for cover in the scrub. The third sat up on its haunches and looked around. Then it too dove into the scrub.

"Someone's on the beach," Bessie whispered.

Rachel nodded. She was grinning.

"What you so pleased about?"

"Ssh."

The girls heard the two men arguing before they saw them, panting and puffing as they crossed the soft sand near the road.

"I thought you said the hack was on the beach. He's fuckin' miles away."

"And how's he gonna load all the crates on the sand without gettin' stuck, genius? Use your brains."

"Yeah, well...I ain't draggin' all them fuckin' crates ten fuckin' miles up this fuckin' beach."

"I ain't gonna tell you again...Watch your mouth. Next time, I'll shut it for you personally."

"Talk, talk."

Two big men in navy blue overcoats heaved themselves to the top of the dune. One of the men was wearing a Homberg. The other man kept reaching up to adjust a hat that must have blown away on the water. The bottoms of their coats and their trouser legs were wet. They seemed to be making straight for the truck.

The farmer, Schmuel and Stinko were too busy tinkering to notice. Schmuel had made Stinko slide underneath on the road.

"They didn't say nothin' about no fu...friggin' truck."

The farmer pulled his head out from under the hood and eyed the two strangers who had appeared, apparently, out of nowhere. He didn't say a word.

"Who the hell are *you*?" the hatless man said.

Stinko tried to sit up and hit his head on the undercarriage. "Aw, Cripes."

"Who's askin'?" Schmuel said. An aura of adrenaline heat enveloped him.

"Oh...a wise guy." The hatless man put his hand in his pocket, hoping to suggest a gun. While the men sniffed each other out, Bessie and Rachel crouched out of sight. It was soon clear that the hatless man was not where he thought he ought to be.

He pointed to the kerosene lamp. "How long you been burning that?"

"Fifteen, twenty minutes maybe."

"The hack's on the beach....the hack's on the beach," the Homberg taunted.

"You are really askin' for it...Where is this place anyway?"

The farmer, who hadn't said much, turned slowly and looked at the small clusters of lights to the North, the orange glow to the West. "Hard to say exactly. Could be near Freeport...Oceanside, maybe."

The hatless man kicked the bumper. "Shit" He stuck his nose under the hood. "So, whatsa matter with your truck?"

"Dunno...Up and died on me."

"Geez Boss, they got rats here," the Homberg squealed. Something small and furry poked its head out of the scrub and twitched its whiskers, transfixed by the pool of light around the kerosene lamp. The hatless man jumped and pulled his hand out of his pocket, so everyone could see he didn't have a gun.

"Chrissake...it's a fuckin' rabbit, Einstein.!" The Homberg smirked at his boss's new vocabulary. "Wipe that grin off your face and go and start this pile of junk."

"I told you...it's dead."

"Yeah...well, my associate here's got the touch."

The Homberg climbed up into the cab. "Crank it up," he shouted.

The farmer turned the crank and the engine wheezed. But after two tries, it coughed and turned over. Both Rachel and the hatless man smiled. "You see," the hatless man said. "Magic."

"How'd he do that?" the farmer sputtered.

"I told you...he's got the touch."

The hatless man ran his hand along one of the side panels. "Nice truck, you got here, Mister."

"I thought you said it was a pile of junk." In the absence of guns, the farmer's sullen nerve had returned.

"Figure of speech...figure of speech...I am thinking, you got this nice big truck and my associate and me, we got this...situation...Now, the way I see it, we got you going... so now, you owe us a favour."

"What kind of situation's that?"

"Well, we got this...this merchandise...on the beach, you understand...and it looks like our transportation is not going to show."

"We ain't in the right place, Boss."

"Can it...Anyway...It would not do us no good to leave this...merchandise lyin' around on the beach all day, we got to get it to the city."

"Merchandise?"

During this conversation, Schmuel and Stinko had casually strolled across the dune. Now Stinko came running back and answered the farmer's question.

"Christ, Mac, how're ya gonna get all that hootch outta here?"

In the back of the truck, Rachel jumped and nearly clapped her hands together.

"Wuzzat?"

"Relax, hare brain. It was probably another rat."

"That's a helluva lotta booze sittin' in the sand," Schmuel said.

"Me and my friend here was just discussin' that very question."

The farmer straightened up. "I won't have anything to do with hard liquor."

"I ain't askin' you to have anything to do with it. I'm just asking you to help me get it to the people to which it belongs."

"I'm sorry...I won't carry alcohol in my truck."

"I could make it worth your while."

The farmer hesitated. "No...I'm sorry. I'm full up. I've got a load of potatoes."

"What if I paid you to dump the spuds." The hatless man took out a fat billfold.

The farmer, the man of spotless soul and dry politics, eyed the wad. "How much?"

"Say fifty."

"Say a hundred."

"That truckload of potatoes? Do me a favour."

"I'd be breaking the law."

"Sixty?"

The farmer considered.

"Sixty-five," the hatless man said. "...I can't do better than sixty-five."

"You got yourself a pickup, Mister."

Schmuel, Stinko and the farmer disappeared onto the beach with the two men. While they were gone, Rachel and Bessie rocked with laughter and shoved sacks of potatoes off the truck. By the time the Homberg appeared with the first crate of Trinidad rum, the road was littered with them.

"What the...? Hey boss, there's a couple of skirts back here."

The hatless man came round the back. "Well, I'll be...Having a good time, ladies?"

"Could be better if you'd crack open one of them crates," Bessie said.

Rachel kept silent. The smile faded from her face. As she looked into the eyes of the hatless man, she felt cold sand in her shoes.

"Sweetheart, I would love to oblige. But this here's a paid consignment. I'm afraid you're gonna have to come down from there so's we can load up."

While the men loaded the crates, Rachel watched with a growing sense of unease. The farmer kicked a sack of potatoes and wondered how six people were going to ride on top of his new cargo. Somehow, in the course of his regular market run, he had become the Union Pacific.

"Where we gonna sit?" Bessie said. Rachel had said nothing for some time. Being locked in the bedroom for the rest of her life was beginning to look like a real possibility.

"Well now, Blondie, that's a problem...But you and your friends look pretty healthy to me...I figure, come daylight, you'll get a lift."

Bessie looked to Schmuel for help, but it had come down to a matter of money; Schmuel and Stinko had been outbid.

Meanwhile, Rachel was staring at the man with the Homberg.

"Hey Boss," he said. "Maybe we got room for the skinny one."

"You got ideas, Romeo?"

"Geez Boss...she's just a kid...I got a sister looks just like her."

The hatless man studied Rachel. "How old are you, kiddo?"

"Fifteen."

He whistled. Then he walked around to the back of the truck and studied the load.

"Okay...okay," he said to the Homberg. "But she rides up in the cab with me. You can sit on the booze."

They squeezed on board, Rachel between the farmer and the hatless man. Rachel could feel the farmer grow rigid with a distaste that even money could not soften.

In the kitchen, Sophie boiled water for the coffee and set out smoked white fish and bagels for breakfast. Jacob was still snoring. She heard the girls stirring in the bedroom but when she opened the door, to call them to the table, she found them all fast asleep. Rachel, who was clutching her eiderdown tightly under her chin, looked flushed. Sophie touched her forehead. Anticipating a fever, she was astonished that the child was ice cold. She leaned over and slammed the window shut. Jacob and his fresh air. As she left the room, Sophie noticed the unmistakable tang of the sea. A storm must be coming.

Rachel waited to make sure her mother was once again puttering about in the kitchen. Then slowly, gently, so as not to wake Ruth who was curled up beside her, she eased herself out of her coat and dress and pushed them, between the bed and the wall, down to the floor.

A storm must be coming.

CHAPTER TEN

The Seánachie

On the day that Rachel was born, in another place...

"...four...five...six...seven...eight...Good on you man...Not even a broken one ...And in this evil weather. Good on you man."

Ciaran McMurrough took another pale egg from his pocket and placed it on the table. "Nine," he grinned. "And when is the weather not evil, this time of the year?"

The young man dropped a heavy coil of rope from his shoulder, shrugged out of his jacket and settled by a corner of the fire. Four other men, all older by at least a generation, shifted in their seats to make room for him.

"I near had herself and all...and a fine, fat one she was...but for what I saw put my mind off of chasing birds."

"Oh, aye?" one of the older men said. "Orla, bring this man a pint...Go on lad. Tell us what it was you seen."

They were all fond of him, Flora McMurrough's fatherless son. The four men, Tommy Kiernan, Fergus McQuaid, Mickey Joe Thomas and Bertie MacDoon had been there for the rescue on the day he was born. One of them might even have been his father, though Flora never said.

That day, although it was close to her time, Flora had climbed down to the shingle, with Tommy Kiernan's sister Mary, to gather bladder wrack for the kelp kilns. Mary said Flora was singing while she worked, as she always did, with the seals gathered round on the rocks about, listening, when the babe decided to come into the world. Mary had scrambled up for help. But Flora must have thought to make it back on her own. By the time the four men arrived with their rope ladders and a sling, Flora was halfway up the cliff. There she was, lying on a *creeshin*, a narrow ledge where stubborn sheep would get themselves stuck from time to time. And at her breast was the hungry boy she had birthed herself.

She had wrapped him in the sealskin she wore to stay dry, the one old McMurrough had got off the bull that drowned in his nets. Tommy Kiernan and Bertie MacDoon went over the edge to lash the mother and babe to the sling, while the other two men tended to the ropes and the hauling. By then, some women, arriving with a cart and blankets and broth in a pot, had set up a great commotion, as women do, about the state of poor Flora and the child. But when they'd heaved them over the edge, they were both as fit as if the canniest handywoman had been there to preside over the labours in the usual way.

And what a boy he had been. Some dark curls already on him and eyes the colour of a summer sky.

McMurrough, Flora's father, was too old to teach him much but stories and fiddling, so the neighbouring men of the *clachan*, Kiernan, McQuaid, Thomas and MacDoon, had taken him in hand. All of them had, at one time and another, courted Flora. Each wondered who might the father be; each knew Flora would say if and when she had a mind to. In the meanwhile, there were things an island man had need of knowing.

From Tommy Kiernan, he learned to lay the nets across the mouth of the bay and haul them in, flapping full of fish. Fergus McQuaid taught him how to read the tides, the swells and weathers and where the sunken wrecks and reefs could turn the calmest seas to killers. Mickey Joe Thomas showed him how to make lobster pots from the ling heather and where the choicest secret places were to lower them in. It was Bertie MacDoon who took him climbing the cliffs and rock stacks off the western end. He showed him the best caves for bird eggs and how to know if rats had settled in the puffin hollows before you stuck in your hand and found out the hard way. He often said the boy was a natural, fearless where it was steepest. He warned him off the dangerous places, knowing, soon or late the boy would test them. "Is it any wonder, with him being near skyborn himself?"

He was a singing child. Before he could properly stand, he would join in the *ceilidhs*, mimicking the sounds of the instruments, bouncing and kicking in time to the music. It was useless, Flora's trying to soothe him with a lullaby. He would simply clap and sing along, his enormous eyes flashing and alert. But he was slow to talk. He waited so long to comment on the world, they worried, at first, that he might be simple. When, at last, he spoke, it was clear he had his share of the McMurrough family gifts.

"We caught a mermaid in the nets today, Mam. But I set her free when Da Tommy wasna lookin'."

"Did ya now? And what did she look like, this mermaid?"

"She was lovely, she was."

"Indeed?"

"She had long, curly hair. Pretty green, like the sea grass we gathered over by Cooraghy."

"Hmm?"

"And she was covered all over in scales. Shiny they were, all blue and green and silver...And Mam...?"

"Yes?"

The boy's eyes glittered with such innocence, Flora thought, it could near break your heart.

"She didna have nothing on her...to cover her boobies."

"Ach! You wicked, wicked boy! Be off with ya now and wash your hands for tea."

"Yes, Mam."

"And when you're sayin' grace, you best mind to ask Our Lord to forgive you for making up such naughty tales."

"Yes, Mam."

"You ask Our Lady and all."

"Whatever took you to the cliffs on such a day as this, lad?" Fergus McQuaid asked.

"It is not such a bad one as all that...I've climbed in worse when there was need."

"Or when there was Duigan's Cathleen lookin' on, eh son?" Tommy Kiernan said and the others laughed.

Ciaran's eyes darkened. "I've done with her...She'd have me in an apron, stood behind a counter in her father's shop."

"Surely not," said Fergus.

"Aye...that way or not at all."

"You have to set her straight. Show her who's boss."

"There's them who'll have you anyway you like," the barmaid said.

"Plenty more fish," said Tommy Kiernan.

"Ah, be quiet, the lot of you," said Bertie MacDoon. "Give the man leave to talk."

Ciaran stared into his glass. "She weren't the one and all," he said.

The barmaid left off the drying of her glasses and leant over to pat Ciaran's head. "Don't you worry about that bit of a madam. *I'll* be the one. You name the place and I'll teach you a thing or two."

Embarrassed, he smiled and ducked away. At eighteen, Ciaran was still young enough to blush.

"A thing or three, more like," joked Bertie MacDoon. "Let the man be. He's time enough for the likes of you, Orla O'Rahilly."

The cloud passed. Ciaran laughed, wet this throat with bitter and remembered.

Once again, he swung across the face of the cliffs over Altachuile Bay, lashed, above, to the rocks they call *The Weeping Marys*. The sea foam cast lethal lace on jagged stone needles below. The men listened, rapt. Even without his fanciful embellishments, the young man's exploits on the cliffs were legendary.

"Such a wind there was," he said. "When I went over, it took me up and carried me fifty, maybe a hundred feet across before I found a hold. Ah...it was like flying...I near lost the hand rope but at the while it was grand."

"Where did you cast over, man?"

"The end of Cleary's pasture...over by the Marys."

Tommy Kiernan whistled. "It is a sheer wall to the sea." The others nodded.

"No, it canna be so sheer as all that...The birds build their nests aplenty. And where a gull can roost, so can my fingers and my toes find a place.

"So, it was alright, you know...and straightaway I find a nest with three eggs. Still warm they were. And I'm thinking how pleased me Mam will be with the surprise. Just the other day she was saying, now the sea birds were back, as it would be a nice change from hen's eggs soon enough.

"But the she-bird, she's a fierce one. She's squawkin' and pokin'...and me holding on to the rope with the one hand and covering my face with the other... and I'm thinking to leave her be and find me one less brave...When out of the sky comes another and the two of them are flappin' and squawkin' together.

"It's the Da, I thinks...and I can't be goin' on with this. There's plenty more is easier...Then, I seen that he was a blackback...one of them that harries every other bird living...and quick as you please, he's sent the she-bird packing. He finds himself a wee ledge above and settles himself, watching me...So, it was alright, and I took the eggs.

"So, there I am, lying out, my feet against the cliff, looking this way and that, to see which way would be the best, you know, when it commences to rain. Now, down below me, maybe ten feet, there's two more nests. One is to the left and one is to the right. But the rain is drivin' powerful hard. So, I says to myself, Ciaran says I, you got in your pocket three fine gull eggs."

"Aye...and the first three of the year," said Bertie MacDoon.

"That and all. So, I says you done it man. Go home and get some drink into ya. But now, this bird...the one that come from out of the sky...he dives off his perch, like he seen a fish, dives straight down at the she-bird below me, to the left, and sets up a mighty flap and squawk with *her*...sends her right away. In the nest, two more beauties, just waitin' for the taking and him setting on the edge, looking up at me like an invitation...You wee bugger, I thinks. What *are* you about then? And away I go to get them."

The other men laughed.

"Now, it come to me that this blackback gull is looking for some wee'uns, just hatched out, to make a meal of. Or maybe it's clearin' out the place to make room for its own."

"Maybe," said Bertie MacDoon. "Those blackbacks is a quarrelsome lot."

"Aye." Ciaran paused to drain his glass. He wiped beer suds from his mouth with his sleeve and leaned back into the warmth of the fire. He closed his eyes and a contented smile spread across his face.

Mickey Joe Thomas, who always said the least but was the most impatient, leaned across the table. "Don't keep us hangin' man...What was it you saw?"

"I'm gettin' to it, I'm gettin' to it; I'm picturing in my mind the way it was."

Ciaran sat forward. Behind him, a sod fizzed into flame on the fire. As night was falling, Orla brought a candle to the table. In the light of fire and candle flame, Ciaran's eyes glowed pale against his weather burnished skin.

"Well now," he said, "rain or no, it seemed a waste of all that climbing not to follow the fellow where he's leading, emptying one nest after another and me filling my pockets. Now and again, he's stopping for a meal of razorbill eggs... you know, they're particular for those. And I'm thinking, fair enough, help yourself...I've had my share of nasty bites from that lot...when I look around and I'm near as far as I can go; just by the cave, with my rope near played out."

"What cave would that be?"

"The one they call *Moira's Sorrow.* You know the one."

"Aye and I do," said Bertie MacDoon. "In that place I told you never to climb alone."

"I've climbed alone there many a time...and so haven't you and all."

Bertie shook his head. "Maybe...maybe...But am I my mother's only son?"

"Ach, Bertie...you'll be knittin' me socks like an old woman soon," Ciaran laughed.

"The man's right," Tommy Kiernan said. "Isn't he here and all, and his pockets full of eggs? Go on, son."

Ciaran took a deep breath. "So, it was alright, and I commence to haul up on the body rope when I see this eider in her nest, just off to the side. Such a fat one, the likes of which you'd not soon see this time of the year. And, you know how an eider duck will lie right on the eggs and stay put when you come up on her. Many a time I've lifted one off the eggs and put her back down again, no trouble at all."

"Sure and she'll bite you if she's a mind to."

"Oh, they'll not do you much harm. You can lift them right up and put them in your pocket."

"You best wring their necks first," said Mickey Joe Thomas and the others all shot him evil looks and told him to hush himself.

Now Ciaran looked from one man to the next. When he was certain of his audience, he began again.

"I says to myself, she's a good one for the pot I says and the feathers won't go to waste neither. So I reach across to grab her and as I done it, a gust of wind come out the west and damned if it doesn't blow me clear off my feet in the one direction and send my hand rope flying in the other."

Each man understood the danger of swinging free against a cliff, and no one to help. They bent closer in silence. All except Bertie MacDoon, who clucked his tongue and grumbled.

"So, now I'm spinning round and my hand rope is twisting into my body rope and my legs is tangling up with the lot and the wind is after makin' me into a wee'un's kite."

"Were you not scared, son?"

"Ach, aye, of course I was. But Bertie taught me that's when you must keep your wits about you the most and look sharpish."

"Would that you minded better what I taught you of climbing alone."

"So I was thinking at the time...and that's when I seen her." Ciaran looked to his empty glass and reached into his pocket for coins. "Parched, I am, just thinkin' on it...Would yous be wanting another?"

"Seen what, man?"

"Over on the rock stack...the big one...the place where the cormorants dry their wings in the wind...I seen a white cormorant, big as life...For now the rain is stopped and she's spreading out her feathers for drying."

"You never seen a white cormorant," said Fergus McQuaid. "The thing doesn't exist."

"I did...clear as I'm setting here to tell it. White all over, in every part of it. And I was sure amazed...so that I near forgot my situation...me turning there at the end of the rope and the cliff face below dipping in, away from my feet.

"So now, I'm in a powerful predicament. My ropes is in a mess and me annoyed to distraction by the look of this bird, when round I come again and the bird is gone..."

"You never seen it in the first part," Fergus interrupted.

"...and where she was, there's a woman standing...her hair flying behind her...and..."

"You seen a woman on the stack?" said Tommy Kiernan.

"Aye, and I did...Her skirts, white and fine, blowing about her...So lovely she was it put the heart across me...and she pointing at something...like she's wantin' to show me...but when I look again, she's gone altogether. And where she was, there's nothing at all...but a tune, the likes of which you'd be hearing and you waking from a dream."

The four men relaxed back into their seats. Clearly, the tale had moved into the realm of the fantastic. Even Bertie MacDoon chanced a smile.

"Ach, lad you're *seánachie*, if ever there was one...a natural storyteller born," said Mickey Joe Thomas.

"It runs in the McMurrough's," laughed Tommy Kiernan. "Your grand-da, Donal, was the best born liar I ever met."

"How did you raise yourself out of there?" Bertie asked.

"Well, I commence to think, what was it at all the woman was pointing to; for though she's gone, in my heart I can feel her still. And that's when I see the spar of rock…just past my reach but I'm thinking that, if I get to swinging on the next gust of wind, maybe I might just grab it. Did you know there was a spar, juts out just the top of *Moira's Sorrow*, Bertie? You never showed me such a thing."

"I never seen it, myself. What I showed you was not to go in that place by yourself."

"Aye and mind I won't be goin' soon again. But it was there all the same… So I says to myself, Ciaran I says, you have got yourself into a fine lot of trouble, but now man, you must wait a wee while and maybe on the next big gust you might just grab that spar of rock. And so I done it.

"So it was alright. And once I had a hold it was no trouble at all to set my ropes to right and climb back up. Then, you see, a powerful thirst come on me, so I come here, fast as I could, to tell you." He tilted his head back and emptied his glass.

"Ya do have a way with a story," said Tommy Kiernan.

"Even if it is mostly a load of oul' baloney," laughed Bertie MacDoon.

"You never seen a white cormorant," said Fergus McQuaid. "No such a thing was ever livin'."

"It is the truth, every word. The truth and all."

"Aye, lad…aye…and so your grand-da always said, the same." Bertie put his arm around Ciaran's shoulders. "You best be bringin' them eggs to your Mam now. She'll not be well pleased with us sending you home full of anymore drink."

"Will yous be coming round later? I've a mind to pick up the fiddle for a while tonight."

"If your Mam will have us, we'll be there," said Bertie MacDoon.

Carefully, Ciaran slipped the nine eggs back into his pockets. He said his goodbyes and made his way into the salty night. The wind had blown the clouds away and rare stars peppered the sky; the veil of the Milky Way fine and white, like the woman's billowing skirts. As he climbed the rough track to the western end of the island and home, he listened again to the woman's music, his fingers, unconsciously, finding the tune on the fiddle strings.

He was pleased his story had been a success. He loved to talk by the light of the fire, to feel the men's rapt attention, to raise their gasps and laughter. But he wondered, as he often did, if ever they would believe him.

CHAPTER ELEVEN

A monkey fur coat

When a schul grew big enough to call itself a synagogue and needed velvet and silver for its Torah scrolls, a committee of men would be delegated to visit Moses Weiss. If a *landsmann* lacked the money to deck his daughter's wedding canopy in flowers, the flowers would arrive anonymously, white roses, gardenias and ivy, and everyone would know they came from Moses Weiss.

Moses Weiss courted social approbation like a suitor chasing an expensive mistress. In a community where everyone's life was marked by poverty and most people were, at one time or another, customers of his pawn shop and money lending business on East Broadway, Moses Weiss's generosity bought him respect, if not respectability.

In his younger days, Moses Weiss had been a frequent visitor to a certain house on Allen Street known for its particularly exotic ladies. He liked his whiskey and a good game of pinochle and what he didn't know about the trotters you could scribble on the inside of a match book.

But from the day his wife Rivka died, of a prolonged and harrowing bout of diphtheria, leaving him with two small sons and a daughter, he became a reformed character. People said Rivka, God rest her, must have visited his dreams, dripping and feverish, to warn him of retribution in the world to come. Such visitations were not unheard of. Whatever the cause, he was a changed man. He gave up drinking and gambling and never crossed the threshold of the house on Allen Street again. His only vice was an occasional Havana, which he smoked in silence at the end of the Sabbath, after a day of contemplation. All that remained of his former life was a number of slightly shady customers who still came to pawn the family treasures to pay off their poker debts. Business was business.

After he repented, Moses Weiss devoted himself to the correct Jewish upbringing of his children. Because he had been inattentive to such matters in the past, he often sought rabbinical advice and his reputation as a man of rigidly orthodox principles grew. Next to Jacob Isaacson, no one knew anyone more devoted to The Law than Moses Weiss.

Moses had no doubt that Nathan, his older son, would take over the business and be the joy of his old age. In his safe, he kept a box full of money that was going to pay for Nathan to go to a fancy, private business college because he was such a smart boy. But, when America joined the war, a recruiting officer filled Nathan's head with nonsense. He never returned from the battlefields of France.

Schmuel, his remaining son, tormented Moses with memories of his own wilder days. By the time Schmuel was twelve-years-old he was running pocket money craps games. In no time at all, he had learned to gamble on the horses, the prize fights, the baseball. Now that he was a young man, he drank. That was not a worry. In New York, in those days, no one paid attention to the law. Even housewives bought pure spirit, from a man who came door-to-door, to make plum brandy for their husbands. And you had to be a big-time bootlegger to interest the FBI. But that he often drank too much, was disrespectful and chased after fancy women was, Moses's believed, a punishment sent to try him for his own evil days.

Moses hoped, now that Schmuel had regular job driving cars for a rich man, he would soon settle down. Mr. Stein, *The Man*, was a frequent customer in Moses Weiss's pawn shop. The pieces he brought were always best quality and he never pawned them but sold them outright. He didn't haggle over prices, although sometimes he made curious requests.

"My wife, she's always changing her mind, so do me a favour and don't put this on the counter for a couple of weeks."

"Listen, Mr. Stein, maybe you shouldn't sell. Give it to me for pawn. Then, two, maybe three weeks, you come back...it will still be here."

"No, Mr. Weiss. It is better that it is out of my hands...to teach my wife a lesson."

Another time he said, "Mr. Weiss...we can have a discussion? Man to man?"

"But of course, Mr. Stein...So what can I do for you?"

"Well, you know...a man like me...sometimes my wife, she doesn't understand what I need. She is a respectable woman; you know what I am saying?"

Moses Weiss may have been a reformed character, but business was business.

"Yes, yes, of course."

"So, I bought this for...my...friend."

"It is a beautiful piece, Mr. Stein. From you, always the best."

"Yes, but my…friend...she doesn't like it, so..."

"I can give you a very good price."

"Schon, don't I know? Why else I am coming to you all the time? But now, I need from you a special favour."

"So tell me."

"Well, I wouldn't want my wife she should know I am buying and selling for...you know...someone not family. People come in...they see...they talk. It could get back to my wife. So, I can count on your discretion?"

"Absolutely."

Moses Weiss was not a stupid man. Like most people, he simply knew how to look the other way. Anyway, wasn't The Man a big time pal of the police commissioner? Besides, it wasn't a good idea to upset such a good customer, who was also his son's employer, just when Schmuel was, at last, showing signs of becoming a *mensch*.

So, if he sowed a few wild oats, what was the harm? Now he was earning a decent salary, he would find himself a nice Jewish girl from the neighbourhood and she would straighten him out. In fact, Moses Weiss was so sure that a Jewish girl from a strict, observant family was exactly what Schmuel needed that he had already asked Rabinovitz, the matchmaker, to begin making enquiries.

At about the same time that his father summoned the matchmaker, Schmuel was busy being reeled in by Bessie Costello. By March, he was so besotted with her that she could make him do just about anything. He let her drag him around the ladies' lingerie department at Lord & Taylor's. He spent his poker winnings on crocodile handbags, striped silk dresses and hats made of exotic feathers. He gave her a cameo brooch with a diamond eye, which he warned her not to wear out of doors for a couple of months. He nearly lost his job because The Man found out that instead of polishing the Duesie, he let Bessie talk him into taking her for a ride in it around Central Park. Once, though nearly stupefied with boredom, he spent a whole Sunday sailing back and forth on the Staten Island Ferry because Bessie and Rachel wanted to see the Statue of Liberty up close.

Bessie could get Schmuel to do just about anything except tell his father he was keeping serious company with a *shiksa*.

It was simple. Schmuel wanted the pawn shop. His father might be impressed with his regular job, but Schmuel knew that until he had something big to offer, he would never be more than an errand boy. The Man had told him so himself the day Schmuel tried to join up.

"Listen kid," he said, dropping his *landsmann* accent the minute he stepped out of Moses Weiss's pawn shop, "Muscles you ain't got. Nerve you got plenty, but guts? Who knows. Brains? Face it, you're *strickly*, not your average genius. I already got enough dopes who are of the opinion that they are your genuine-article-genius on my payroll to give me a headache. Bums like these I do not need any more of.

"What you got kid...*maybe* what you got...is connections. Your old man has got a nice little business. Respectable. Could be, maybe, it'll be yours one day. In my line of occupation, a friend with such a business could become a very important friend of mine...if you see what I mean.

"But in the meanwhile, another no-talent *schlepper* I need like a hole in the head."

Schmuel assumed he was being dismissed. He started to get up.

"Siddown kid. I'm thinking."

The Man settled into himself and thought. He had a baby face and when he thought he looked like he was filling up his diaper. Schmuel had to stifle a nervous impulse to laugh.

"So, tell me Sammy...I can call you Sammy?"

Schmuel nodded.

"You know cars, kid?"

Schmuel knew cars.

The Man went to the window and pointed to an immaculate Duesenberg parked by a fire hydrant. "Whaddya think of that?"

"It's a real humdinger, Mr. Stein."

"I'll tell you something. That baby did not cost me no small change. Forty thousand smackers. But I been thinking. It ain't whatyacall behoving for a man like me, who spends forty thousand bucks on a car, to be driving it myself."

"No sir, Mr. Stein."

"Yeah...well...you can call me Boss, kid."

Schmuel had just enough brains to know he didn't need brains to run the pawn shop if he was on The Man's payroll. Moses Weiss was already 75 years old and, teetotal or not, not so healthy. All Schmuel had to do was wait. He tried to explain to Bessie that she had to wait too. Moses Weiss could tolerate a lot of things from his son, but since he'd seen the light, a serious carrying on with a *shiksa* was out of the question. If it came to that, he'd leave the business to his spinster daughter Dinah - "God bless her, the living image of her mother, she should rest in peace. And what a head on her shoulders." - and Schmuel would be an errand boy for the rest of his life.

Bessie was not a waiting kind of girl.

It was not that Bessie minded taking Rachel - *a nice Jewish girl from the neighbourhood* - along everywhere they went. Rachel always disappeared as soon as they got wherever they were going; the dancehalls, a nightclub, Steeplechase Park at Coney Island. Bessie often wondered what she got up to. When she asked, Rachel never made a lot of sense.

"Ain't you lonesome, all on your own?"

"I'm not all on my own. Look at all the people."

"So, did you meet anybody?"

"I don't think so."

"Kiddo, this ain't a trick question. Either you meet somebody or you don't. So did you?"

"I don't think so."

Sometimes Bessie took another tack. "So what you been doing all this time? Smooching under the boardwalk?"

"No."

"So what then?"

"You know...looking around...and that."

"Yeah? What's to see around here?"

"Oh things....the beach...the water...the boys."

Bessie smelled an angle. "Boys, huh? Anybody good?"

"Hmm. Well, there was this really beautiful boy fishing off the footbridge by the bay. The sun was in his hair. He was just like a picture in a book."

"Yeah. And?"

"And what?"

"Rachel! Geez....what was he like?"

"He was lovely."

"So what did he say? Are you gonna see him?"

"I didn't *talk* to him."

"Why not? He was with someone? What?"

"No, He was all on his own. He didn't see me."

"Don't you know nothing? You see a cutie all on his own and you don't know how to make him see you? What's wrong with you Rachel?"

"I didn't want to."

"Why?" Bessie wailed in frustration.

"He didn't see me."

In the end, it didn't matter. Rachel left Bessie and Schmuel to themselves. At Dreamworld, she always had plenty of partners. Wherever else they went, she didn't seem to mind being on her own. She told Bessie she had company.

And it was not that Bessie minded the intrigue and secrecy. There was a whole network of streets on the Lower East Side where, if Bessie ran into Schmuel, she had to pretend she didn't even know him. Bessie liked this game so much she told Schmuel, "Tonight at Dreamworld, you pretend like you're a married stranger and we have to hide from your old lady. Put your head down on my shoulder, like that, so's nobody will know who you are. There...ain't that good?" Bessie loved anything that made real life more like the pictures.

No, what was beginning to worry Bessie was that by the time his old man kicked the bucket, Schmuel would be tired of her and go after somebody younger and prettier. Bessie had just turned eighteen and, as she frequently told Rachel, "Girls like me don't keep forever."

Bessie was not about to let a free-spending, good time like Schmuel slip through her fingers just because his father might not approve. She figured that, while she still had her looks, you understand, she could worm her way into Schmuel's father's affections. He was a man, wasn't he?

Bessie didn't know Moses Weiss.

She hadn't worked out exactly how she would go about it, so things could have gone along pretty much the same for a long time.

Moses Weiss thought Schmuel was seeing *that Jewish girl from around the corner.* She was a little odd, but her father was very respectable and her sister, Moses had heard, was engaged to a rabbinical student. That couldn't be bad.

Jacob Isaacson still had no idea that Rachel slipped out, night after night - although Sarah was bursting to tell him - or that most Saturdays, when he was in schul, she was riding the loop-the-loop at Coney Island. Sundays she went off with some girlfriend from work. Although he didn't know the girl, as long as Rachel didn't shame him, he felt he didn't need to know.

Just when Jacob had assumed this practical blindness about his youngest child, he could not be sure. Thinking about her disturbed him, which annoyed him because she was only a girl. And why she disturbed him was a mystery. Around the house, she was obedient and respectful. She gave her mother most of her earnings. She helped Sophie with the cooking - though Sophie complained, "Such help I could live without. Like Rosa she cooks."

Whenever Jacob tried to fathom his unease, whenever he tried to pin this background of discomfort on some specific incident, his mind filled with a kind of fragrant fog. Instead of his daughter's childhood, he remembered his own. He chased rabbits in the sun-dappled Bohemian forest near Pilsen and listened to birds make dream music that lulled him to sleep. Such ramblings troubled him. *I am getting fashimelt in my head, like an old man.* His solution was to think about Rachel as little as possible. If there was need for his concern, Sophie, no doubt, would tell him.

The spirits' freedom is a mirror trick - *Play with us if you dare. We are easily bored with waiting games, with turns at blind man's bluff* - and fathers are never as simple as their children believe.

Bessie lifted the cameo brooch out of its blue velvet box. The diamond eye loosed dancing multi-coloured sparks on the walls and ceiling. She was irked that she couldn't wear the brooch outside of her rooms. She knew better than to ask Sammy where it came from, but she wondered about it, nevertheless. She held the brooch against her shoulder and studied it in the mirror. The diamond was so pretty and sparkly; it must be real. Sammy wouldn't tell her it was real if it wasn't. Would he?

Slowly, an idea began to form in Bessie's mind and slowly, a smile spread across her face. She thought, carefully, about exactly what Sammy had said.

He never said she couldn't show it to anyone. She'd already shown it to Rachel. No, what he said was, she shouldn't wear it. *"Don't wear the ice until I say so."* That was not the same thing at all.

Bessie put the brooch back in its box and snapped the lid shut. She stroked the blue velvet, thinking it was time she got Sammy to buy her a velvet dress. She had made up her mind. After all, a smart girl's gotta know the value of the gifts she accepts.

A yellow-haired girl in a monkey fur coat slid a cameo with a diamond eye across the counter to Moses Weiss.

He tried to assume a professional air, as he examined the brooch, but the girl's perfume made him dizzy and her fingers whispered through the fur of her coat. He felt queasy and the sound of his own heart pounded in his ears. He balanced the brooch on the palm of his hand, assessing the weight. Then, pressing a jeweller's lupe to his eye, he studied it more closely. "Very good carving," he said. He spoke so softly that the girl was forced to lean toward him, enveloping him in another cloud of scent. She knew she was unnerving him; he could feel it. He reminded himself that he was a reformed character and that she was the sort of little tart who must be accustomed to unnerving men.

"Excellent," he choked, "...and the diamond...at least two points...maybe three...From your mother you said?"

"Yeah. She left it to me," she said.

"I could make you a very nice offer...if you changed your mind."

"No, I couldn't never sell it. I was just interested Just in case, you know. I couldn't never sell it." The girl sniffed loudly and dabbed her eye with a perfumed lace hankie. "It's all I have left of her," she said.

Moses was not impressed. He was polite, trying to appear impassive. He knew enough about peroxide blondes who reeked of perfume to know they didn't have the kind of mothers who left expensive cameos. But where she got the cameo was her own business. He was more interested, and more disturbed, by the young woman's monkey fur coat.

Although he took little interest in women's fashions, how could a man who ran a pawn shop not know a thing or two about fur coats? This one was old fashioned; longer than the current style. The glossy fur was a natural reddish brown instead of the black that most were dyed nowadays.

"The fur coat too, she left you?" he said.

"What this? Oh, no...My boyfriend give it to me. Pretty swell huh?"

The yellow haired girl held the lapels wide and turned to show off the coat. Moses noticed the scalloped hem where the narrow animal skins were seamed together.

"Very nice...May I?" He reached for the coat.

She stepped away, clutching the coat close to her body. "I ain't sellin' this," she said.

"No, no, of course. I wasn't suggesting...I am just wanting to admire. Your boyfriend, he must be generous." Moses did not want to seem over eager but he was having some difficulty moderating his tone of voice.

"Such quality you don't see every day. I can have a closer look?"

"Yeah, well, I guess so." Moses watched the silk satin lining slide cooly down her arms. When she gave him the coat, his fingers disappeared in the floppy fur. He turned it over and stroked the lining with the palm of his hand. When he pressed his face into the collar, all he could smell was the young woman's perfume. He could hardly breathe.

"Something the matter with you, Mister?"

"What...Oh, no...I...I." He was nearly choking. "Such a beautiful coat," he said, holding it against his face. The girl snatched the coat away from him. "I gotta be goin' now," she said.

Moses simply nodded. "...such a beautiful coat," he muttered.

"Yeah, well...toodeloo," said the yellow haired girl and she swept out of the shop.

When the young woman was gone, Moses closed the shop and locked the door. He pulled down the manila paper shade, turning the afternoon sunlight to a rusty glow. All around him, precious objects shimmered in glass cases. Gold watches, strings of pearls, garnet and diamond rings, silver spoons, flutes and fiddles and brass candlesticks, crystal bowls, a model of a ship with mother of pearl sails; they swam in his vision like treasure scattered on the bottom of a turbid lake. He rubbed the back of his hand across his eyes. Then he climbed the stairs to Dinah's room, the front bedroom, over the shop.

Moses had not entered this room for years. Once he had shared it with his wife. Shortly after she died, he had moved his things to the storage room behind the shop. Now, only his children slept upstairs. Sometimes, when Dinah nagged, he took supper in the upstairs kitchen, but most of the time he preferred to remain downstairs, eating his meals from a tray, surrounded by boxes of old clothes, stuffed birds under glass bells, gramophones with polished brass horns, boxes of wedding rings sorted by size, artefacts of other people's failures.

He turned the doorknob and entered the front bedroom. The brass bed Rivka had died in was Dinah's now. The maple chest of drawers, the bedside table, the big wooden wardrobe in the corner, were all remnants of his days as a heedless, married man. Dinah was too sensible a girl to worry about sentiment and superstition. "A bed is a bed," she said, "and I am too old to be sharing one with my little brothers." She had been equally matter of fact about her mother's clothes, tying them in a bundle for the rag man before Moses had a chance to stop her.

The few things he had managed to save, he had draped with canvas and hung in the back of the wardrobe. He pushed Dinah's dresses to one side, raised the canvas and ran his hands across all that remained of his late wife. A wedding dress, crumbling and yellowed; the blue silk shirtwaist that had always been his favourite; the coat of thin brown tweed in which she had shivered across the Atlantic, its elbows rubbed bare long before they landed on Ellis Island. "When I make my fortune in America," he had told her then, "I will wrap you in furs and you will never be cold again."

Once America went to his head, he had not been a good husband. Some said that, with his gambling and womanising, he had been one of the worst. But he had kept that promise. For their tenth anniversary, he had given her a fur. Now, even before he held the empty wooden hanger in his hand, he knew the coat was gone. He had suspected as much as soon as the yellow haired girl walked into his shop. He had known for certain the moment she let him hold her red brown monkey fur coat.

For the first time in ten years, Moses Weiss sat on his marriage bed. Tears filled his eyes. Not only was his son, *his only son*, a wastrel; he was a liar and a thief. Would this punishment never end? What must I do, he asked, to make him a *mensch*?

A breeze ruffled Dinah's lace curtains and a shadow crossed the sun. The room became very still. Moses Weiss felt cold and afraid. He began to tremble. "Do something useful for once in your life, you stupid man," said Rivka. She was standing by the window, her red eyes glazed with fever. When she opened her mouth, the whole room filled with her voice.

"What must I do?"

"Stop shaking like an idiot and marry him to a Jewish girl before it is too late."

"Who should I marry him to? Tell me who?"

But she was gone. The sky echoed with piercing laughter that only some people heard.

That afternoon, Moses Weiss walked across town to the little storefront office of Rabinovitz the matchmaker. The very next day, Rabinovitz called upon Rachel's father.

CHAPTER TWELVE

Smoke and fire

Trouble first, trouble after
Dancing in the shadows
That fall between us

They met, the three of them, under a canopy of gossamer and feathers, green lamé and gold chains glowing darkly in the shadows and the quivering resonance of crystal. But it was not like old times in the dancehalls. They were crammed in an upstairs storeroom and Mishkin's interpretation of *Winged Victory*, which was going to be the showstopper of the 1923 Follies, spread her giant, spangled wings over their heads. The airborne bits of marabou and excelsior made Schmuel sneeze.

In the aftermath of Rabinovitz's visit, finding a place and a time to meet took a certain amount of guile. Of the three of them, Rachel was the only one who had any. But Rachel's activities were now also the most circumscribed. Sarah chaperoned her everywhere, accompanying her back and forth to work, snatching her pay envelop from her on Friday afternoons. Except for the hours she spent at Mishkin's, Rachel was never far from Sarah's watchful eye. The key to the newly fitted bedroom window lock hung on a chain around Jacob's neck.

"Papa only lets you go out to work because I need a trousseau." Sarah buzzed with smug self-satisfaction.

Schmuel's father had also laid down the law and now Schmuel spent most evenings drinking tea with desperately eligible Jewish girls whose parents were in as much of a hurry as Moses Weiss to marry their children off. Once Jacob Isaacson had turned down his proposition, with a rudeness he considered shocking and unforgivable, Moses had set Rabinovitz the task of finding someone with an urgent desire for marriage. "What a parade of *meeskeits*," Duvi told Rachel. "You wouldn't believe there were so many ugly old maids in New York."

Duvi, who enjoyed the freedom of a hall bedroom, with its own entrance, carried messages back and forth when he could. Schmuel told him about Bessie's ill-considered visit to the pawnshop. "Dames," Schmuel said, shaking his head. "I thought Bessie was a smart cookie. Who can figure?"

It took Rachel a while longer to discover why, with so many Jewish girls looking for husbands, Rabinovitz had come seeking *her* hand for Schmuel Weiss.

"Papa was outraged," Sarah gleefully reported. "He said you were only a child...and besides, he had other daughters to think about first. He said that you didn't know anything about boys yet, Poor Papa...'I should marry her to a man of the world like Schmuel Weiss?' Papa said. He didn't say a worthless, no good like Schmuel Weiss, but that's what he meant."

For once, Rachel found herself in agreement with Jacob and Sarah.

"So then, Mr. Rabinovitz got insulted. He said, 'Forgive me, Mr. Isaacson, you shouldn't think I am presumptuous...but in this business I have a long time been...My business I know. And it is always a better match when the couple have already shown their intentions. It is not as if they are not keeping company. Every Sunday, Mr. Weiss tells me...and Saturday nights too, I hear.'

" 'You are mistaken,' Papa said...'Rachel is a decent girl. On Saturday nights, she is in bed where she belongs.' Poor Papa. So, then Mr. Rabinovitz said that maybe he was mistaken after all, but that Mr. Weiss was in a hurry to marry Schmuel to a decent Jewish girl, and *since* he was spending so much time with you, he thought...That's when Papa threw him out."

In the end, it was Bessie who gave the game away. Nearly a week had passed since Rabinovitz's visit and the strain of missing Schmuel told in dark circles under Bessie's eyes.

"I didn't think it would do no harm," she said. "How was I supposed to know he gave me his mother's fur coat?"

They were sorting through a box of blue paillettes, the big sequins made of fish scales.

"Why did you go there in the first place?"

Bessie didn't answer. She paused to study her face in the mirror-like scales. "My eyes is all red," she said.

"Bessie?"

She began to snivel. "I didn't think it would do no harm. I just wanted to see him up close...to see if I could...you know..."

"If you could what?"

"...oh...well...I just thought..."

"No, you didn't...You didn't think at all."

"Yeah...well, maybe...But, I mean...he didn't know me from Adam...and anyway, Sammy told him he was going around with y...with...with..."

"Bessie?"

"...with...you know...a Jewish girl."

Bessie hiccupped loudly and blew her nose into the Belgian lace hankie that Schmuel had given her. Was it possible to want someone so much; to do something so stupid and not even think about the consequences?

Rachel watched her wring the damp handkerchief, smeared with rouge and tears. She wanted to be angry with Bessie but how could she? Hadn't she done the same thing? Hadn't she been doing it all along? She had never once wondered that Bessie and Schmuel dragged her along everywhere. Why? She had never questioned her own urgent desire for freedom. Where did it come from? What was it for?

Rachel, who often understood the motives of others, was unaccustomed to examining her own. Now, as she tried, dozens of voices argued, wailed, and screeched in her head. Dozens of pairs of eyes, staring back at her from the box of paillettes, entranced her. Sad, beseeching eyes, scornful eyes, mocking eyes, eyes full of love and eyes full of pain. She felt dizzy, insubstantial, as if letting go, she would become a reflection and vanish into the box of shining blue eyes. She squeezed her fist. The sharp sting of a fish scale cut through her dream and into her palm. The moment gone, nothing remained but the singing of a single string.

Rachel shook her head to stop the ringing in her ears. Bessie and Schmuel had used her. No, that wasn't fair. She knew they had all used each other. *Why* was not important. *Why* had never mattered to Rachel as much as *how*. She had always chafed under the restrictions of her father's house, but now, having flown, she could not bear being caged. Something must be done.

An idea began to form in Rachel's mind. They could use each other still. Bessie was moaning and sobbing. Though it beggared belief, the girl was really in love with Schmuel Weiss. "Be quiet," Rachel snapped." I'm thinking." Her hardness shocked them both.

An icy voice whispered in Rachel's ear. "Stop snivelling," she said to Bessie. "I have a plan."

"Marry *you*? Whadda you nuts!?" Schmuel's astonishment set *Winged Victory* trembling, loosing a cloud of marabou lint. Rachel waited until he finished sneezing.

"Think about it," she said.

"I *am* thinking about it. And it gives me the shakes. No offence, doll, but you are not no way the girl of my dreams, you know what I mean?"

"The feeling is mutual, I'm sure."

"So what kind of a cockamamie plan is this? Bessie...whatsa matter with you? You think this is a smart idea? How'd I get myself mixed up with such a pair of brainless dames?"

"Let her tell it," Bessie said.

Rachel, who had worked it all out in her mind and had then painstakingly sold it to Bessie, was tired of explaining what seemed to her a perfectly obvious solution. "Schmuel," she said, "you're not interested in me...not even a little bit, right?"

"No offence, babe...I'm not sayin' you're not a looker or nothing like that... But me, I go for a little more meat on a broad." He patted Bessie's thigh and she giggled. Rachel could barely conceal her distaste.

"Well, this may surprise you, but if you laid a finger on me, I just might throw up...No offence."

Schmuel squirmed. He started to say something, but Bessie put a hand on his shoulder and he just glared at Rachel.

As Rachel saw it, the matter was cut and dried. Bessie wanted Schmuel. Schmuel wanted Bessie but he also wanted the pawnshop.

"And whadda you want, doll?"

"I want a place to live. Out of the neighbourhood. A place where my father can't boss me around. I want to be a married woman, so I can do what I want."

"In my book, a husband's got a lotta say in what his wife gets up to."

"A real husband."

"Look babe, this here is all goin' miles over my head. You wanna spell it out, what you're sayin'?"

"What I'm saying is, we get married and get an apartment somewhere else; uptown, Brooklyn...somewhere the whole world doesn't know our business. Then, you just leave me alone. I don't care how much time you spend with Bessie. You don't even have to come home at night. You just never touch me."

Schmuel, who usually had a wisecrack for every situation, didn't know what to say.

"It's called a marriage of convenience," Rachel said, pleased to find a use for the expression she had seen in *A Bintel Brief*, the advice column in the Yiddish newspaper. "Refugees do it all the time."

"I ain't no refugee."

"No, but you might end up married to one."

Schmuel considered the prospect. He turned to Bessie. "This idea...you like this idea?"

Bessie nodded. "It wouldn't be forever, Sammy. After a while, you could just get a divorce...and then..."

"Yeah?"

"Your father's an old man," Rachel said. "He can't live forever." Although she had imagined she would have to harden herself to say such things, the words flowed like ice water. "We wouldn't have any children...so it wouldn't be that hard to get a divorce...People do it all the time nowadays."

"Well, this is all a swell idea ladies. But the way I see it, we got one big problem. Your old man already said no."

"Then we have to change his mind."

Schmuel studied Rachel with a new respect. "I ain't sayin' yes and I ain't sayin' no...but I gotta say, you got *chutzpah* for a kid."

The baker's fat little son was the apple of his mother's eye. Every day, when he came home from school, she fed him milk and frosted butter cookies, Neapolitans oozing with French custard and scribbled with chocolate, juicy purple hunks of huckleberry pie.

When customers came into the bakery, the baker's wife would brag about her fat little son. Such good manners, such rosy cheeks, and what a scholar, you shouldn't know from it. Because the baker's crumb cakes were the best to be had for blocks, people tolerated her endless boasting, which was peppered with cautious *kinahoras* just in case the evil eye was lurking. But sometimes, to stop her mouth, they offered a titbit of news, a nibble of gossip, a tangy morsel of information. As a result, what the baker's wife didn't know was not worth knowing.

Because of his mother's attentions, and when he was not protected by them, the baker's son was tormented by other children. They teased him for his sissy clothes, for his waddling gait, and for his complexion, as sleek and as pale as a cream fed pig. Crossing Delancey, where his torturers were joined by packs of Irish and Italian hooligans, was an ordeal beyond his endurance. So twice a week, when he had to cross Delancey to visit Jacob Isaacson for Bar Mitzvah lessons, his mother accompanied him, holding his hand so he wouldn't be accosted by riff raff.

During the lessons, she waited upstairs at Rosa's, drinking coffee and eating strudel with Sophie and Rosa. Rosa enjoyed her company, but Sophie, who didn't like to speculate about other people's business, tolerated her only because Jacob said she had to. Sensing this, the baker's wife tried to ingratiate herself with Sophie.

"If my husband, he should live and be well, could make strudel like yours, already we'd be millionaires."

Sophie would smile politely and cut her another slice.

About a week after the meeting in Mishkin's storeroom, the baker's wife arrived carrying a bottle of real Canadian whiskey and a bunch of flowers. Jacob thanked her for her generosity. "Oh," she laughed, "it is not from me. Where would I get such a thing as a bottle of whiskey? The young man downstairs asked me to give it to you. He said to thank you; that you would understand. The flowers, he said, you should be so kind, to give to Rachel."

Jacob rushed to the window. Schmuel, downstairs polishing the Duesenberg, waved up at him. He snapped the window shade so hard he nearly tore the waxed canvas from the pole. "Isn't he the pawnbroker's son?" the baker's wife said smiling slyly at Sophie. "A handsome young man, *nu*? But *some* handful, I hear. And Rachel, such a beauty. She is what now, fourteen, fifteen?"

The next day, every bakery customer took home a tasty crumb of news, tied up with their parcels of danish pastry and *mohn* cakes. "You don't have to take my word for it. Walk over to Rivington Street and see for yourself."

Sure enough, anybody who took the trouble - and plenty did - saw Schmuel's Pierce Arrow, or the Duesie, parked in front of 75 Rivington Street day and night. Thursday, when people were out early, shopping for Shabbas, Schmuel was there as well, leaning against the car, a white carnation boutonniere in his lapel, his fedora tilted at a jaunty angle. When Sarah and Rachel emerged, he snapped to attention, opening the car door.

"Would you ladies like a ride in this fine automobile?"

Sarah grabbed Rachel's hand and dragged her to the trolley stop.

Once a week, on Sunday nights, the Pilsener Mutual Aid Society met in the café on the corner. They exchanged news of the people left behind, managed the burial funds, sponsored widows and orphans, drank coffee and *slivovitz* until closing time and generally enjoyed the sound of Yiddish spoken in the Pilsener way. Although Jacob had wandered out of Pilsen as a very young man, his fondest memories were still connected to the place and he liked the company of his countrymen. He went, without fail, every week.

At ten o'clock, one Sunday night in late April, as the men of the Pilsener Mutual Aid Society drifted out of the café, their lively conversations tailing off as they said their goodbyes, they were confronted by a shocking sight.

Under the streetlight across the road, a pair of lovers were twined in each other's arms. The young man gripped the young woman's body. In the yellow pool of light, the men could clearly see him touch her bosom, run his hand down her back and squeeze her bottom through her modest green cotton dress. The young woman squirmed and pressed herself against the young man in a way that no respectable woman ever would.

"Oy, a *shandeh*, an outrage," one of the men said. "To see such a shameful thing in a public place. Young people nowadays."

"What is the world coming to, I would like to know," said another.

Just then, the slender young woman laughed with pleasure. She threw her head back and shook out her unmistakable long chestnut curls. Three of the men stopped talking and looked at Jacob Isaacson, who was turning purple with embarrassment and rage.

Suddenly, perhaps aware that they were being watched with such disapproval, the young couple parted, running as fast as they could, in opposite directions.

Jacob did not waste time with pleasantries; he entered with a roar.

"Where is your daughter?"

Even if her other daughters weren't sitting around the kitchen table, doing the mending, Sophie would not have had to ask which daughter Jacob meant.

"She went to the toilet. She'll be back in a minute."

Jacob stormed out of the apartment and took up watch outside the water closet on the landing. The door was closed. He knocked and was surprised to hear Rachel reply, "I'm coming...Just a minute."

In a little while, the sound of flushing water still echoing behind her, Rachel emerged. She was breathless and pink, but her hair was neatly braided, bound with a red wool tie. She was wearing the brown bombazine dress that had belonged to Sophie's mother.

Jacob looked over her shoulder. There was no place to hide anything in the little room. "What?" Rachel said. "...what?" But Jacob had slammed and locked the door behind him. He never noticed the snugness of Bubbie Ruchel's dress, or that a tiny strip of green cotton peeked from below the hem.

Jacob felt powerless. Could he stop Schmuel Weiss from parking his car where he pleased? It was a free country, everybody kept telling him; free enough for a no good bum to harass decent people and what could they do? And could he lock up his daughter? In this free country, that was not allowed either and there were busybodies from the Settlement House ready to make sure it didn't happen.

Besides, had she really done anything to warrant such a punishment? As far as he could tell, the child was innocent. She went to work with Sarah, came home and did chores, visited with her cousins upstairs. He had even convinced himself that he was mistaken about the scene outside the café. What his *landsmen* thought they saw was their own business. Justice demanded better proof.

Mendel, his oldest son, was summoned from Brooklyn for a family conference. There was talk of sending Rachel to stay with him and his wife. But Mendel's wife was expecting a child soon and she did not want the burden of her sister-in-law. Maybe after, when the baby was born. Maybe then Rachel could come and help. Jacob told Sophie that by the time his grandson arrived, it would be too late.

"Maybe it will be a granddaughter," Sophie said.

"God forbid," said Jacob, "that my son should be visited with the misery of daughters."

Meanwhile, with the whole neighbourhood already buzzing, Rachel disappeared.

On a Wednesday evening, at the beginning of May, Sarah waited for Rachel, as usual, outside Mishkin's Theatrical Costumiers to the Trade. It was a fine, soft evening and spring birds sliced across the midtown granite with colour and song. Because, in his business, he used so many feathers, Mishkin had a fondness for the creatures and he scattered seed on the window ledges of his building to attract them .

Sarah watched a bluebird build a nest in the ornamental stonework above the door. She spotted a robin and a bright red oriole that had not yet left for its cooler summer home. Perhaps, because she was thus engaged, Sarah did not notice the passage of time. People, in small chattering groups began to come out, but Sarah was fascinated by the ingenuity of the bluebird, as it stuffed bits of newspaper and dead leaves into the cranny above the door.

Eventually, when the bluebird flew off, Sarah noticed stripes of pink and orange in the sky. The streets had turned quiet. She looked at the watch she wore on a chain around her neck, an engagement present from Yossel. Eight o'clock and no sign of Rachel.

Perhaps she was working late, finishing a garment. Mishkin sometimes paid the girls for extra hours when a deadline was near. The door was locked. Sarah banged on the glass and squinted into the darkened lobby. Soon the janitor appeared. "Closed," he said. "Go away...closed."

"Is anybody working upstairs?" Sarah shouted through the glass.

"Nobody home," the janitor said. "You come back tomorrow. Closed now."

Sarah raced to the trolley stop. Rachel was not waiting for her there. Her only option was to go home. She did not find Rachel there when she arrived. Schmuel's car was gone as well.

"Will you have another? It's good for you, all that lovely fruit."

Mrs. O'Grady, Bessie's landlady, ladled a cupful of sweet, alcoholic syrup from an earthenware crock of fermenting fruit and sugar she kept in the corner of her kitchen. Nowadays, everybody made do with whatever was at hand and Mrs. O'Grady's tipple was a recipe a German lodger had given her, one week, in lieu of rent.

"Ah girls," Mrs. O'Grady said. "In the old days, a woman of property, such as myself, could enjoy a glass of port by her own hearth and nobody to trouble her. Them days is gone forever."

As Bessie had hoped, Mrs. O'Grady, who had been nipping into her *rumtopf* throughout the day, was squiffy.

Earlier, after Bessie and Rachel had leafed through all Bessie's copies of *Silver Screen*, eating popcorn and drinking Moxie, and after Bessie had painted Rachel's fingernails magenta, the night was still young. Bessie offered to tweeze Rachel's eyebrows into the thin arcs of surprise that were all the rage, but after one or two minutes of exquisite pain, Rachel decided her eyebrows were fine the way they were.

"You suppose they got a search party out lookin' for you?"

"No. My father's really mad and everybody is keeping out of his way. And my sister Sarah is probably crying, because it's all her fault and she should have told ages ago."

"Yeah?"

"Something like that."

"They've eloped," Sophie wailed. "*Gott in Himmel*, they've run away to get married. And it's your fault. You are to blame. You couldn't let nature take its course? No...not you...you had to turn my house into a prison for your own child. And now look what you have done."

Jacob was too stunned by Sophie's courage to respond. She had never berated him for anything. It was not her place. But now was not the time to chastise his wife. He had other things on his mind. He paced the kitchen, looking out the window now and then, trying to decide what to do.

"If she does not come home in the next hour, she is not welcome in this house."

"So where should she go? In the street she should go?"

"Let her stay with your sister-in-law who all these years is filling her head with foolishness. She can stay with your brother, the farmer, who lives with the *goyem* in Connecticut. She will not stay under my roof another night!"

"It is *my* roof too," Sophie said.

"Woman, you would try the patience of a *tzaddik*. All of a sudden you have found your tongue? Remember who you are! And where is the supper? Are we to starve while we wait for this...this...*Jezebel?*"

Now it was Sophie's turn to be shocked by her own forwardness. Cowed, she busied herself at the stove.

"Let's go see my landlady...she's a scream."

"My fingernails are still wet."

"Well blow on them...Come on, let's go. If she's stiff, she might even tell your fortune. She's better than a gypsy."

"What'll it be girls...the cards or the tea leaves?"

"Which is better?" Rachel asked.

"Well, my mother, God rest her, she was one for the cards. Never failed, my mother said. And you could take them out of your pocket any old place and know just what was happening round the next bend, so to speak. But then my Granny...now her people were tinkers and travellers in Mayo in the old days... my Granny, she said that with the tea you put a little bit of yourself into it, you see, and you left a little bit behind for the wee folk, the gentle people, you know...so that made it better...That's what my Granny said."

"What do you think?"

"Just now, what I think is that fruit syrup makes me pretty thirsty, so let's do the tea leaves."

Mrs. O'Grady lit a candle. She spooned tea from a metal box, printed with red and black and gold to look like lacquer, and brewed it strong and dark. She drank hers with milk and sugar both. Rachel had never seen anybody put milk in tea. She tried some and discovered that she liked the velvety texture.

"Don't gulp it, dearie. Just drink it natural and slow so's it's got time to tell."

When Mrs. O'Grady reached for Bessie's cup, Bessie pushed her hand away. "No," she said. "Do Rachel tonight...She ain't never done it before."

"Rightie ho...give us your cup dearie...Cross my palm with silver."

"What?"

"Cross my palm with silver." Mrs. O'Grady held out her palm and waited. Rachel had no idea what she was waiting for.

"Give her some money, Rachel...otherwise it don't work."

Rachel found a nickel in her pocket and gave it to Mrs. O'Grady, who shook her head.

"Geez Rachel...silver...you need silver. Don't you got a dime or a quarter or something?"

She didn't so Bessie had to give her one. "You give it to her, from your hand, otherwise it don't work."

Once the finances had been settled, Mrs. O'Grady poured a little water into Rachel's cup. She swirled it around, poured it into a pot on the table and then turned the cup upside down. She crossed her hands over the upturned cup, closed her eyes and muttered something that Rachel couldn't make out, although she thought several saints were mentioned. She wondered if God would punish her for participating in such mumbo jumbo, but she had long ago stopped trying to second guess God.

Mrs. O'Grady turned the cup and stared into it. Rachel stared too. A few wet leaves clung to the bottom and sides. Then Mrs. O'Grady began to speak.

"I see a tall, dark stranger."

Bessie poked Rachel and the two girls giggled.

"Be quiet girls...or the leaves won't tell."

Rachel bit her lip and Mrs. O'Grady continued.

"...a tall dark stranger...no, not so tall as all that...but a fine figure of a man. What lovely strong shoulders on him...and, oh my goodness, such beautiful eyes...This man loves you...He will give you children...a child? I can't be sure."

Mrs. O'Grady closed her eyes. "You made him unhappy," she said.

"How did I make him unhappy?" Rachel whispered to Bessie. "I haven't even met him yet."

"Ssh!"

One of Mrs. O'Grady's lodgers slammed the front door, sending a gust of night air through the house. The candle flame grew bright and tall. Suddenly, Mrs. O'Grady sat bolt upright and opened her eyes wide. When she spoke again, her voice was distant and full of echo.

"Trouble and sorrow," Mrs. O'Grady said. Rachel heard dozens of other voices, each with a music of its own, whispering and singing. *Sorrow, sorrow, sorrow.*

"What kind of trouble," Rachel said.

"Hush!" Bessie snapped.

"Trouble first...trouble after...You are too proud." The voices echoed *proud proud proud.* "You are impatient for the one who comes in his time. You must be patient."

Mrs. O'Grady sighed. The candle flame silvered her eyes. When she looked at Rachel, someone else looked with her. "You will know me," she said.

"You have always known my song. Swimming in the darkness. You will know me. Trouble first...trouble after...Only you can break the circle."

Now Mrs. O'Grady fell silent. After a moment, she looked up at Rachel. "Well dearie, how was that?"

"I don't know...what did it mean?"

"Oh, I never know what any of it means. It's mostly a load of nonsense to me. But it means something, you take my word. It always means something."

"That was creepy," Bessie said later when they were back in her rooms.

"Is it always like that?" Rachel asked. "Is that the way she does it for you?"

"Geez no. She mostly says how I'm gonna have lots of money, break lots of hearts, have plenty of kids...you know, that kind of stuff. I ain't never seen her say nothing like that before. Wasn't you scared?"

"Why would I be scared? It was just a lot of silly hocus pocus."

But Mrs. O'Grady's performance had pushed Rachel toward a decision. She had spent long enough causing minor upsets at Rivington Street. It was time to bring matters to a head.

"Can I sleep over?" she said.

"You sure, kiddo?"

"Yes, I'm sure."

"Hey, what the hell," Bessie laughed. "It's now or never, right kiddo?"

"Right."

When Schmuel brought Rachel home at 10 o'clock the next morning, the whole street turned out to watch. Sophie had apparently won the struggle over Rachel's domicile, but Jacob sent her straight to the bedroom and locked the door. She never even had time for the excuse that she had rehearsed; that she had taken ill at work, that she had gone to a friend's house with a bad stomach ache, that if they only had a telephone she would have called. Jacob was not interested in excuses. Social workers and busybodies be damned. She would stay locked in that room until her spirit was broken.

Later that afternoon, Sarah was summoned to tea with the Widow Meyer. When she returned, her eyes were red and swollen. "Let them get married," she said.

"This carrying on I should reward with a wedding? Absolutely out of the question."

"Papa, please," Sarah wailed. "Let them get married or I will be a spinster for the rest of my life."

Trouble first, trouble after
And the shadows
Fall between us

CHAPTER THIRTEEN

Shipwrecked

We are the castaways
The promise never broken
Our hungry sea roots
Search for anchorage.
And you are landlost.

Bubbie Ruchel wore black and Rivka Weiss complained that the pickled herrings were too salty. They eyed each other warily from opposite sides of the hall. Schmuel's Uncle Manny kissed all the pretty girls and, although the vices that finished him had also wasted him away, he danced a sprightly *kazatsky*, leapfrogging right over Schmuel into the centre of the circle. With both The Man and Councilman Tierney in attendance, the drink flowed freely. And wherever there is music, dancing and wine, so also there are spirits. The uninvited guests were many and their mood was mixed. They swelled the ranks of the musicians, snaked between the *hora* dancers, gossiped about the quality of the catering, which Sophie had quickly organised with the help of Mr. Kandel.

They had married on the third Tuesday in June; Tuesday because it was the day that God blessed twice; June, not because of fashion, but because, until Rachel turned sixteen, the State of New York would not have allowed it, with or without parental permission.

Rachel, behind her thick veiling, was dry eyed, as were most of the guests. Only Sophie and Rosa wept. Bessie watched with the crowd of passers-by who had gathered outside to see the bride.

All the men danced with the bride, as was the custom, and Schmuel made sure there were no wallflowers, not prompted by gallantry but simply because that was also the custom. What with being introduced to relatives and being whirled about the dance floor, the bride and groom had little time for each other. So, if there was anything less than loving devotion between them, it was lost on the revellers.

Uncle Abie, his flute specially polished for the occasion, had assembled a rag tag orchestra of his musical cronies. Now and again, they were joined by a guest who had consumed sufficient wine to contribute a Yiddish song or to fiddle a tune, its essence almost buried in Levantine ornamentation.

A young man with a fiddle hovered near them, apparently too shy to join in. No one invited him up to the platform. He sat on a bench near the players, hugging his instrument close to his body, his chin resting on its shoulder. Rachel, certain that she had seen him before, thought he might be somebody's cousin. Schmuel had so many relations and, even among her own family, there were cousins thrice-removed who only appeared at weddings and, Rachel supposed, at funerals, although she had never been to one.

He was nice looking, though rather pale. Listening to the music, he had closed his eyes so that Rachel was able to admire him frankly. He was not very tall, but he filled the space he occupied with a muscular grace. Rachel found herself stirred by unfamiliar feelings that, in other circumstances, might have been reserved for the groom. The young man tilted his head to one side and the fingers of his right hand moved subtly in time with the song, picking out the melody along his arm.

He wanted to play. She would talk to him. He looked lonely. One mustn't be lonely at a wedding; even a sham of a wedding like this one. She would ask him where they'd met. She would tell him that anyone with an instrument could join the players. But just at that moment, Uncle Shoe appeared to claim his dance with the bride.

Was there ever a stranger honeymoon?

The bride, in a yellow rain slicker, bobbed along on *The Maid of the Mist*, as close to the falls as its captain dared; stared unbelieving, in the wax museum, at dioramas of daredevils who rode barrels over the torrent and sometimes lived to tell it; ate chopped egg sandwiches in her room, not knowing that the guest house had been chosen because it was kosher, not understanding that the ring on her finger excused her from the omnipresent signs. *Unaccompanied single ladies will not be seated.*

The groom, wearing a straw hat, drank iced tea on a sunny porch under a roof of Victorian gingerbread; played poker with men in cutaway suits who wore gold watches and bet with ten-dollar chips; strolled among the paddocks, appraising the odds and admiring the horseflesh.

They had boarded the overnight train, the New York Central *Honeymoon Special* for Niagara Falls, at Pennsylvania Station, right after the wedding party. Both fathers objected on the grounds of Tradition, but Schmuel and Rachel insisted. They had already proven that they knew how to get their own way, so Schmuel's father relented and gave them Pullman tickets. Sophie, sensibly, pointed out, that even if the couple had been willing, she and Jacob couldn't afford to wine and dine a *minyan* of ten praying men for seven days.

Schmuel left the train at Dobbs Ferry. He gave Rachel a fistful of bills and said, "Have a good time and don't do nothin' I wouldn't do." He met Bessie, who waited on the illuminated platform. Rachel watched them kiss as the train pulled out of the station. They were off for ten days of racing at Saratoga, where they would register as Mr. and Mrs. Samuel White of Murray Hill, so they could stay at a fashionable, restricted, hotel with no questions asked.

Rachel, who had once walked to the ocean but who had never since ventured more than a few city blocks on her own, went on alone. After Schmuel had gone, she sat on the lower berth, too nervous and excited to sleep and, she noticed with some confusion, too afraid. When the porter made up the berths, Rachel, in embarrassment, told him Schmuel was stretching his legs in the corridors. After he left, Rachel stripped down to her underclothes and climbed to the top one. The sheets were linen and the blanket satin edged. The pillow was lofty with fresh feathers. She put her arms around it, resting her face against the cool pillowcase.

The train rumbled northward through the dark but, before she could settle into its steady motion, the natural consequence of the wine and salty food consumed at the wedding party made her so thirsty she had to climb down for a drink. Beside the basin, she found a small glass jar, with a tumbler for a cover. Guessing that it probably fit into the mysterious, bent wire contraption on the wall beside the berth, she filled it and carried it back up. Now, once again, she curled up in the unaccustomed luxury of the bedclothes and tried to rise into sleep on the rhythm of the rails.

The iron wheels release a many throated music. Labourers and schoolteachers, thinkers and adventurers, lovers, pilgrims, gamblers, journeymen and rogues have sung their dreams and left their voices along these tracks.

A delicate theme shines in the foreground. Someone, close by, is playing a violin and humming. Perhaps in the next compartment. Sliding over the strings, the strange lament coaxes out a tense melancholy that, all day, has been waiting just outside the celebrations. Rachel hugs herself and breathes deeply to chase it off but the air is saturated with sorrow. And the mood, once invited, grows in confidence and strength. The humming voice croons into a sob. The first tears of her wedding day surprise Rachel's eyes. She turns her face into the pillow to dry them. The music vibrates there, and in her blood, a restless, tidal rise and fall. The musician is below her. She leans over the edge of her berth and looks for him in the shadows but all she can see is the silvery trace of his song.

Now she is beside the wedding guest. His eyes are closed and his dark lashes are pendent with tears. How sadly his bow rides the strings, as he draws the music from some terrible corner of his soul. She wants to comfort him. She wants to hold him and whisper to him. *Nothing is as sad as this song.* But, without knowing why, she knows this is not true. And there is such dignity in his beautiful face that she dares not touch him.

The song ends. He puts the fiddle in his lap and raises his head. His eyes, unearthly bright, are crowded with life. He is crowned with water weeds. He doesn't seem to see her. "Who are you?" she says but he is looking beyond her and he does not respond. He extends his arm, pressing his palm forward. Is he reaching for her, or pushing her away? His sigh chills the compartment.

"Why are you so unhappy?" She tries to take his hand, but although he is beside her, she must stretch with all her strength to touch it. And when at last she succeeds, it is not a hand she feels at all but cold, rank sea slime. Sea wrack and oozy weeds twine around his arms, spreading, as she watches, to cover his shoulders and chest. His coronet is a moving mass of sandworms, snails, scuttling scavengers. He has limpets for rings on his fingers and bloodless pink hermit crabs devour his eyes.

Ropes of eel grass slither between their hands. She struggles to hold on but they are pulling him away. *They are always pulling him away.* "I'm sorry," she cries, "...forgive me...I didn't know...Please...I ...Oh, please, don't..." He answers, but the sea washes over the sand of his voice.

"*Forgive me...Forgive me...Forgive me...*Forgive me...." The sound of her own words startled Rachel awake, soaked and tangled in wet sheets. Thrashing in the distress of her dream, she had tipped the jar, spilling cold water all over herself and the bedding. She changed and sat up, shivering, in the lower berth, for the rest of the journey.

The unsettled mood, that had overtaken Rachel on the train, stayed with her. Niagara Falls was a place for lovers so there was nothing much to do. The shriek of falling water was inescapable, the bone chilling mist ubiquitous. It was the season of the Rose Festival, posters proudly declared, and all the public places were dripping with bloody roses. Rachel bought a ticket for a day trip on a paddlewheel steamer and rode across Lake Erie.

It smells of kerosene and garbage. Schools of rotting fish belly up from the dark, sickly flowers of corruption scattered before the bride. Does no one else feel the bleak evil of this landlocked water? But all around her, couples hold hands and gaze into each other's eyes. No one else watches the floating timbers and dead birds. No one else listens to the whispering dead.

Rachel had not thought much about what she would do with her freedom once she had won it. Being miserable had never been part of the plan. Was freedom only worth having when it was stolen?

When, at last, she boarded the New York Central back to Manhattan, she was glad to look forward to something new. Schmuel had rented the top half of a house on West 12th Street. It was barely a mile from Rivington Street but it was a million miles from the Lower East Side. Once ensconced in four rooms of her own, practically in Greenwich Village, she could decide what to do. She could create a life that nobody could take away from her. By the time the train passed Peekskill, where the Hudson carried the smell of the sea, her spirit had revived. She was even pleased to see Schmuel when he boarded at Dobbs Ferry.

"So, didja have a good time?"

"Yeah...it was okay...You?"

"Swell, kiddo...When those snooty goyem put on the dog, they do it in style, lemme tell ya...I would not have no trouble getting used to it. No trouble at all...you know what I mean?"

"Hmm...I suppose."

"...No trouble at all." Schmuel smiled and leaned back in his seat. "So, these big waterfalls...they really something or what? 'cause now Bessie wants me to take her."

"Bessie would like Niagara Falls."

"Yeah...so...anyway..." Schmuel's voice trailed into discomfort. The etiquette of their situation eluded him. Clearly, he thought they ought to make conversation, but small talk had never been one of his strengths. "I guess you ain't gonna be so pleased to see the inside of Mishkin's after this ritzy trip you just had, eh?" he said.

"Mishkin's? I'm not going back there. I quit."

At the same moment, they both realised that this was probably the first of many things they had never bothered to consider.

"Whaddya mean *I quit*...Just like that? You do not even discuss with me, your *married* husband, about a thing like this?"

"Schmuel, married women don't work unless their husbands are poor. You're not poor. What would your father think if I went out to work?"

"I gotta support *you* too? Christ."

"What do you mean, me *too*?"

"Now Bessie wants a place of her own. She don't think it's right I should be callin' on her at Mrs. O'Grady's no more...seein' as I am a married man and all. And I cannot *exackly* bring her home to my *wife* now, can I?"

"I didn't think about that."

"Guess not... I may not be poor now but it sure looks like I'm *gonna* be poor."

They rode together in silence. Schmuel's brow creased as he tried to work out how much would be left for the horses once he'd paid for his harem.

Just after Yonkers, the train traversed a series of ever longer tunnels, each slab of shadow resounding with a sudden slap of dread. Dark, light, dark, light, dark, light. When the train swept into the shrieking darkness for the final approach to the station, panic pressed on Rachel's ears and forced the breath back into her mouth. She squeezed her eyes shut and was, at once, dazzled by scattered shards of vision.

A mirror breaks into a hundred pieces, each fragment reflecting those puzzled, reproachful eyes. *What have I done?* No one answers. The eyes rush away, receding into an oblivion of slivered glass until, just when she thinks they are gone, they appear again, bright and full of fear. And the heartbreaking noise of the screams. All night long, she has listened to the screams. "They will see the fire. It will guide them home," the headman said. But how would they see it, and the fog as thick as cream? And how would they know the beacon from the lights the seawives set to lure the men into their watery beds? She can hear him, far below, where the path is hid and the rescuers cannot go for fear of being lost also. All night long she has listened to him call her name. She can feel him, clinging to the rocks with the others, the women and the children too, while the sea nibbles their number and their cries grow weary and faint. "It is only the seals, after crying to the mist, in the way that they do," the headman says. "Would they put to the boats on a night such as this?" But she knows that *he* would. They all know it. And now the sea will have them. Because of the promise she forced him to make. The fire will not warm the hall, the pipers and the drums cannot drown the pitiful cries of the ones they cannot save. The mothers, the wives, the husbands and the brothers accuse her with eyes that will never forgive. But no one has lost what she has lost. *Oh, what have I done?* She covers her ears with her hands.

"Pretty noisy, eh doll?" Schmuel's shout cut across the chaos. His face was still twisted with the unaccustomed effort of thought and it was a moment before Rachel recognised him. "You okay? You look like maybe you're gonna be sick or something."

"It's just the train," Rachel told him, and by the time she said it, that was what she believed.

"Listen," he said. "I been thinkin'...I don't never wanna hear no more of this *Schmuel* crap. From now on, you call me Sammy...you got it? If I'm gonna be a meal ticket for the both of you gold digging broads, I got a right to some respect."

I am the promise never broken
You are the anchor and the bride
...And you are landlost

CHAPTER FOURTEEN

Married love

The chains that bind us
You unknowing forge
The fires that burn us
You unwitting feed
Beloved friend
It turns again

"So then she saw it and she screamed, 'My mother never told me it would look like *that*! It's such an ugly little thing.' And I'm telling you, the poor man, God bless him, he just wilted away. Just like that."

Women's laughter bounced and echoed off the tiled walls of the bathhouse pool. Now that Rachel was a married woman, she accompanied Tanta Rosa to the mikvah, the ritual bath every Friday after dark.

But before you could dip a toe into the living water, you had to be spotless. So first they joined Tanta Rosa's friends in the Baruch baths at the river end of Rivington. There, a whole new world of bawdy female conversation opened up to her.

"Just like that? How do you know such a thing? You were there?"

"How do I know? Because she told me, that's how. Six weeks they were married, she wouldn't let him near her...'such an ugly little thing'...*Gott in Himmel*."

"So what happened?"

"So what happened? So what always happens? One night, he drank a lot of whiskey and then he forced her. I'm telling you. And after that, I suppose, she must have learned to look the other way because now she's carrying the eighth. So, schon. That was that. But you know what I think? It's a good thing they're stronger than us. Because what virgin would touch it if she never saw it before?"

"Oy, if they would only hear us," the second woman laughed. "But it's true. My husband, he should live and be well, a beauty contest he wouldn't win with it. But God forbid he should know I said so."

" 'It's such an ugly little thing!'...Oy, vey..." the first woman hiccupped.

"And *so* sensitive! Worse than children they are. One cross word and *pfft*, nothing."

"Enough already," Rosa laughed. "You're embarrassing my niece. Look, you're making her blush."

"What's to be embarrassed?" the first woman said. "She's a married woman. She doesn't know what I am talking about? I am embarrassing you, Rucheleh?"

Rachel drew her arms through the warm water. "No, it's okay," she said. In fact, after two months of married life, she had yet to see a naked man. The women's conversation fascinated her. There were things she wished she could ask, but then they would know the truth about her marriage to Schmuel.

"Wait till you have babies. Then nothing will embarrass you."

"Do you remember Chava Moscowitz?" the second woman asked.

"The one who moved to Chicago?"

"That's the one. They used to run the hardware store on the corner of Clinton Street?"

"Yeah? So?"

"So every time she got pregnant, she cursed him for the whole nine months."

"I remember...I remember..." the first woman chuckled. "Right in the store, in front of the customers."

"And such curses, you shouldn't know from it; that he should get a boil, right on the end; that it should itch with prickly heat for a hundred years and then maybe he would cut it off and leave her in peace."

"Oy, I remember...I remember...And such a little one he had too."

"*Vey iss mir*, is there nothing you don't know? You saw it?"

"Me...How would I see it; I'm a decent married woman. *She* told me once. She said, 'Every time he comes near me, he makes a baby. Who would think such a little *pipkeh* could make so much trouble?' That's what she said, I swear."

"Oy, stop already," the second woman gasped. "I'm laughing so hard, I'll pee in the water yet."

"God forbid."

The women settled into a companionable silence. Rachel raised herself out of the pool and sat on the edge, adjusting the scratchy wet skirt of her swimming costume. Later, at the mikvah, she would be able to enjoy moment of pure contact between herself and the tepid water, nakedness, rare and brief. She wondered what the women would think if they knew she really had no need to join them there. The *mikvah* was for purification, to make a woman fit to be touched by her husband. The Law said women were unclean until they'd visited the *mikvah* seven days after their time of month.

Tanta Rosa's Rumanian friends turned the ritual into a social occasion. It was their custom to prepare for every Sabbath with a gossip at the public baths followed by a proper, holy immersion at the mikvah. Rachel guessed, from the things they said, it was because most of them lay with their husbands on Friday nights.

The first woman was not the sort who could stay quiet for long. "But you know something?" she said. "I think she must have found a nice big one...more to her liking."

"*Oy gevalt*, your mind is in the gutter...What are you talking about?"

"Well, you know...the last child she had...the blond boy...He didn't look like her and he didn't look like him. So where did he come from?"

"She said she saw an angel when she was in labour."

"*Balt*...and my mother was a hundred-year-old virgin when I was born. I think that's why they moved to Chicago, you know."

"It could be true," Rosa said. "It happens. Didn't it happen to Sarah, in the Bible? And she was such an old woman that when the angel told her, she laughed."

"Rosa, Rosa, the *things* you believe. Those days are dead and gone, take it from me."

"Maybe yes, maybe no."

"So, Rucheleh," the second woman said, "You have for us some news in that department yet?"

"Please," Rosa interrupted. "What's the matter with you? You don't think about anything else? It's only two months they're married. Leave her alone."

"What? Two months isn't long enough?"

It was the first time Rachel had been asked this question, but soon enough she knew it was on everyone's mind. After all, wasn't that why women got married; what they were made for? Even the affectionate term for little girls, *mamaleh*, meant little mother. Parents could be so greedy. No sooner had Schmuel brought his father the Jewish bride he demanded, than the old man was asking for a grandson. None of this bothered Rachel. It would be a long time before jovial interest turned to concern. And it would mean less family argument when it was time for the divorce.

Keeping up appearances was more of a bother. Once she'd spent the wedding presents decorating the four rooms on West 12th, scouring the downtown stores to match the pictures she cut out of *The Ladies Home Journal*, everyone wanted to visit. "So where is Schmuel?" Sophie asked. "He's never here when I come to see you."

"He's playing pinochle."

"All the time he plays pinochle? Every time I come? What's the matter, he thinks I will be too critical?"

"Mama, please. He likes to go out with his friends."

"Yes, all right, they all do. But Rachel, he's a married man now. He has responsibilities."

"He knows."

"I hope he does...I just want you should be happy." Sophie put her arm around Rachel's shoulders. "So tell me, Rucheleh, everything is all right? He looks after you good?"

"Everything is fine, Mama."

"Schon...Good...That's what I like to hear."

Sophie looked through the door of the second bedroom. It was simply furnished with a single bed, a chest of drawers and a chair. Schmuel almost never used it, but Rachel had arranged it for the odd occasions when he had to work too late to go to Bessie's. "So who is this room for? You are getting a boarder?"

"It's a guest room."

"A guest room? Fancy schmantzy. You have so many guests?"

"Well...you know...sometimes the men play cards late. And Schmuel has relatives in New Jersey; Uncle Shoe could stay when he comes down; you could stay over," Rachel lied.

"Better first I should see you make it into a baby's room."

"Mama, please."

"All right, all right. It's none of my business."

"What is it like...when you're married?" Ruth asked. Although eighteen months older than Rachel, she was just beginning to notice boys.

"What is *what* like? You live with someone; you eat together; you sleep together. You know. Like Mama and Papa."

"No, that's not what I mean."

"Well, what *do* you mean?"

"You know...when you're younger than Mama and Papa...it's different... isn't it? When you...Oh, you know. Do you wear clothes when you sleep?"

"Of course I do. I wear a nightgown, just like Mama."

Ruth was not satisfied. She was having some difficulty framing her questions and Rachel, who was afraid she knew exactly what Ruth meant, was being deliberately obtuse.

"Does he kiss you?"

"Of course he does. He's my husband."

"What does it feel like when he kisses you?"

"It feels um nice."

"Nice how?"

Although Schmuel had kissed Rachel repeatedly, and flamboyantly, in front of their wedding guests, he hadn't touched her since. She could barely remember that day, let alone what Schmuel's kisses felt like. Still, she sensed that this was the sort of thing a young girl talked about with her married sister. She didn't want to disappoint Ruth. She closed her eyes and imagined the taste of a kiss.

So soft and smooth. His lashes feather my cheek. And his tongue is like silk. I rest my face in the warm hollow of his throat, where his skin is so fine I can feel his heartbeat against my eyelids. He is damp and salty, smelling of nectarines. I hold his head in my hands, my fingers combing his curly hair. And he kisses my neck, my shoulders, my breasts. His breath surprises the tender skin behind my knees. His cheek is cool and sandy where my legs are warm and smooth. There is no part of me his lips do not visit, no part of me his tongue does not taste. And I do the same. His body is a great mystery. For though it is hard and muscled, it is as soft as his touch. His arms, his thighs, his buttocks are furred and downy. The soles of his feet are like warm velvet. All over him, there are secret, fragrant places alive with the rhythm of his heart. Gently, he strokes my thighs until I open to him and when he enters, I am a sheath, fashioned only to hold him, golden and glowing, hot and silken as his tongue. Soon there is no place but the place where we are joined, no part of me but the parts where we touch, where I struggle to cross the barrier of our skins. If I hold him tightly, I will vanish into his flesh, disappear like a drop in the sea, a breath on the sky. I cannot bear to be so separate. I growl and tear and shout his name. Then, he stops my voice with his own, a long, sweet shuddering cry. And suddenly we *are* the sea; we *are* the sky. There is nothing else beneath the stars but what we are. We lie with each other in waves of light that spread like ripples on a pond until they cover us with sleep.

"Schmuel doesn't have curly hair."

Rachel looked at Ruth and realised, with a start, that she had actually uttered all she had imagined. Ruth's eyes were wide and her mouth was hanging open. Rachel could feel the heat of a scarlet blush creeping up her neck.

"Anyway," she said, "you don't need to know about things like that. You're just a baby."

"I'm older than you."

"Don't you ever tell anybody what I told you. It was just something I...I read in a book. I made it up."

But Rachel, still virginal after months of marriage, was wet and spent. She had no idea where the vision, which she had seen and felt with the conviction of memory, had come from. She had not made it up. Not one word.

They stopped going to Dreamworld. "Married people don't do that," Schmuel said. And now that Bessie spent all day at Mishkin's and most nights with Schmuel, Rachel never saw her. Except for Friday nights, Schmuel and Bessie spent most of their time in Bessie's new apartment.

142

On Friday nights, Rachel and Schmuel fulfilled their mutual bargain by pretending to be a couple celebrating sabbath with the in-laws.

Once Rachel invited both families for Shabbas at West 12th Street, because she thought it was a married sort of thing to do. The evening was not a great success. Even though Sophie had written careful instructions for the simple meal, and even though Rachel followed them to the letter, the chicken tasted like softened wood, the carrots and potatoes were hard in the middle. Everyone was excessively polite. What with all the effort and concentration of chewing, nobody had time to ask nosey questions. While she and Ruth cleared the dishes, Rachel overheard her father-in-law reassure Schmuel. "Don't worry, she'll learn. Your mother too could burn water at the beginning." After that they alternated Friday nights between the families.

When they went to East Broadway, Schmuel's older sister cooked. Dinah was sensible and straightforward. She had lost her own chance of marriage while looking after her father and brother but the sacrifice did not seem to have embittered her; she had few illusions, but she was not hard. If the situation were different, Rachel would have enjoyed having Dinah as a confidante and friend.

Rachel missed the intimacy of friendship. Without Bessie, there was no one to tell about the changes taking place in Schmuel. They began just a few weeks after the wedding. She had been ironing his shirts - *For all you're costing me, you could at least do my laundry* - when she forgot and called him Schmuel.

"I told you, I am Sammy to you," he growled.

"I'm sorry...I forgot."

"Yeah?" he said. And he hit her face so hard her nose bled. "Maybe now you'll remember."

Another time he hit her because she spent seventy-five dollars of the wedding present money on a couch for the parlour.

"Whaddya need that for? Seventy-five bucks! What, so your mother can sit like a queen when she comes to complain about me?"

"My mother doesn't complain about you."

"Oh yeah? You think I don't hear from my father how she worries I play cards too much? Ain't you got enough brains to make up some other excuse when I'm not here?"

"I'll try."

"You do that...Seventy-five bucks. Geez, you stupid broad...I had plans for that dough." And he stormed out.

Perhaps it was not Schmuel, but only the situation that had changed. After all, Rachel had given him so little thought before they married, she had no real idea of him. Or of what he was like under pressure. And as is usually the case, money, or the lack of it, caused pressure almost from the start.

Schmuel had expected a raise now that he was married. "What for?" The Man said. "I pay you plenty enough to keep a wife very comfortable. You wanna keep a chicky on the side, that is not my problem. Maybe you should have been so smart as to wait until you got promoted to take up with another dame. Then you could afford to cheat on your wife."

Bessie didn't consider Schmuel's lack of money her problem either. With the sort of twisted logic that only Bessie could sustain, she figured that, as Schmuel's kept woman, she was entitled to the kind of presents she could buy for herself with the money she earned at Mishkin's. The fact that she could afford to be free with her earnings because Schmuel paid her rent did not enter into it.

And Bessie was bored. "All we ever do anymore is eat and screw...You don't buy me nothing...You don't never take me no place. I'm sick of stew," - Bessie's skills in the kitchen were only marginally better than Rachel's - "I wanna go to Delmonico's."

All Schmuel wanted was what he figured men have always wanted. Good sex, a few laughs, peace and quiet. Almost at once, he began to lose the very things he had married to acquire.

When Bessie didn't get her way, Bessie crossed her legs.

"This is the third day in a row you give me the same crap. Ain't there nothing else to eat in this house?" Schmuel picked over a plate of noodles and pot cheese.

On a Monday night, during the dog days, Schmuel had moved into the spare room at West 12th Street. He and Bessie, he said, had had words. He didn't say what about. "Ah, she'll get over it. She's probably on the rag." But she was taking her time. Whatever was bothering Bessie on Monday was still bothering her when Saturday rolled in with a layer of humidity that sat on the city like grease.

Rachel didn't like having Schmuel around. She would have liked to strip down to her shift to cool off. When Schmuel was annoyed with Bessie, he became sullen and the August heat did not improve his temperament.

"I could make you some eggs," she said.

"Yeah, you do that." He poured himself a whiskey. "Don't you have no place to go?" he said.

"It's too hot and muggy to go out."

Rachel felt him watching as she moved between the icebox and the stove.

"That a new dress?"

"No, I made it from an old one."

"Glad to hear somebody knows how to save money."

He stretched back in his chair and half closed his eyes.

"Why don't you go apologize to Bessie."

"I ain't got nothing to apologize for."

"Oh."

She wet a cloth at the sink and ran it over her face. Then she broke the eggs into a bowl and beat them with a fork. She poured them onto sizzling butter in a skillet. Hot air shimmered over the black surface of the stove. The eggs snapped and bubbled. While she watched them, Rachel reached back and unfastened the top two buttons of her dress, lifted her heavy braid and wet the nape of her neck with the cool cloth. She thought about the cold bath she was going to take as soon as she finished in the kitchen.

After she put the eggs on the table, Rachel turned to go, but almost immediately Schmuel grabbed her by the wrist and pulled her back. "Christ almighty...can't you even crack an egg? Jesus, I'm bleeding."

Perhaps it was the heat. Perhaps it was the week of his constant, unwanted company. Or perhaps it was the memory of an Italian boy who had once left his purple fingerprints on her arm. Suddenly, Rachel crackled with anger. "Let go of me," she snapped, pulling her hand away.

Schmuel lunged and caught the back of her skirt. She felt a staccato ripple as the fabric gave way. He spun her around, snatching her flailing arms. His gums bled, cut by a shard of eggshell that had slipped between his teeth. "Look what you done to me, you useless bitch," he snarled and spat a mouthful of bloody eggs onto the table.

He was standing. The strength of his grip astonished her. She struggled to free herself but his fingers burned like knotted rope. Then he let go of her right wrist and wrenched her head back by her braided hair. "Here," he said, "taste your cooking." And he pressed his dripping, feral mouth against hers, leaving a smear of bloody saliva on her lips and chin. She spat at him and, with her free hand, scratched at his face, his ears. "Jesus...Bitch," he said, and he punched her in the stomach. As she doubled over, he threw her down. She was aware of a cupboard door grazing her forehead and the sharp crack of her head hitting the floor.

Now he was on top of her, on the floor. With his left hand, he held both of hers, pushing them against her throat with the weight of his body so that she could hardly breathe. He was using his right hand to tear at her clothes and his own. She pressed her legs together and tried to raise her knees to push him off, but he was sitting on them. He dug his fingernails into her thighs to prise them apart and fell on her. She could feel his belt buckle cutting into her side. The rhythmic jab of its metal tongue punctuated the dull pounding as he beat himself against her. He stank of eggs and sweat. Weak, from lack of air, Rachel gave up her silent struggle and waited for Schmuel to finish. She let her mind float free, watching from somewhere above, so that even the startled gasp that accompanied the knifelike shock of penetration, seemed to come from someone else, some poor, bruised woman crumpled on the floor below.

But she cannot so easily escape awareness. *The fires that burn us...you...The chains that bind us...you...* When she closes her eyes, another, the one who is always at the edge of awareness, stares back. *Oh, my beloved friend.* Her eyes burn with his tears of frustrated rage. His mouth is stretched in a roar that thunders through time, rivers of guilt and shame in her rushing pulse.

A cold, numbing pain spread across her belly. Schmuel thrust against her, grunted and rolled off. For a moment, she lay on the kitchen floor, unable to move. Then she gathered her torn clothes around herself and limped to the bathroom.

She took a rough towel and tried to scrape away the filth between her legs. She wanted to scrub away every trace of him. To scorch him off her skin. But she was too sore and swollen to touch herself, to make herself feel clean. She looked at the towel. There was blood and a fetid, marshy smelling sap that turned her stomach. She tasted bile at the back of her throat and leaned over the bathtub to wretch.

She flinched when Schmuel came to the bathroom door. "Don't worry. I ain't gonna hurt you," he said.

Rachel answered him with her wide, brown eyes. As others had before him, Schmuel shivered in their stillness. He became defensive. "Come on, it wasn't so bad," he said. "You might even get to like it. Lotsa women do."

Although Schmuel was not of an imaginative bent, the hatred and vengence in her gaze was eternal. It passed through him, beyond him, as deep and infinite as the reflection in a pair of facing mirrors.

He tried to chase away the feeling with words. "Anyway...I got the right," he said. "Who you gonna complain to? Who's gonna blame me for schtupping my wife." His sneering laughter died in his throat. "You ain't thinking of telling Bessie now are you?"

Rachel didn't answer. She turned her back to him and continued washing her thighs. He crossed the bathroom and grabbed her shoulder. "Don't you get no wise ideas about telling Bessie, I'm warning you. Don't you get no ideas about telling Bessie."

He stalked out of the bathroom.

Rachel didn't plan to tell Bessie. Or anyone else. But about a month later she woke up nauseous. And not long after that, everybody knew.

It turns again

∞

Droplets of clear water sparkled along the fibres of the webby membrane. As the midwife held up the caul to examine it in the sun, water filmed into lenses across its honeycomb cells, scattering spots of light on her arms. The thing was nearly intact; a miracle after she'd had to fish it out of the garbage. But then a caul itself was something of a miracle. After twenty years of midwifery, she could no longer count the number of babies she'd helped into the world, yet she could recall only half a dozen born with this magical veil over their faces. She could remember each one of them, each with its face squeezed tight behind a mask of film; the way each one had taken its first gasping breath when the caul was lifted away, as though it was being born all over again.

She had known what it was, of course. And what to do with it. Her own mother had taught her how to scrub it with coarse salt and wash it in three changes of water. Now she spread it to dry in the May sunlight, creamy white and fresh smelling, on a clean linen cloth.

When it was dry, she would wrap it in the same linen and give it to Rachel in secret. The poor girl abandoned months before this birth of a son, barely more than a child herself, needed as much good fortune as she could get.

The gift of the caul had a special poignancy for the midwife. Nearly seventeen years before, she had delivered Rachel, who was now the first of her own to bear a child. She remembered Isaacson's disappointment when she told him his wife had given him a healthy girl. "Another one?" he sighed and poured himself a glass of plum brandy. He had not even been interested in looking at her.

Although the midwife knew Jacob Isaacson, since, by reputation only, as far as she could determine, he had not changed. The way he had muttered and grumbled; you would have thought he was about to become the grandfather of a bastard. After all, it wasn't the poor child's fault that her husband had run off with some shiksa floozie to God knows where. Hadn't Isaacson allowed the wedding in the first place? When everyone knew what kind of a reputation Schmuel Weiss had?

The baker's wife told the midwife, and everybody else, that they'd already filed the papers for a divorce at City Hall. "For abandonment, and adultery," the baker's wife said, clucking her tongue. "I heard also that he was knocking her around...but what else is new?"

"So an American divorce...that is enough nowadays? What about the rabbis?" the midwife had asked.

"Do I know? A new husband she is not going to find so fast without a *get*."

The midwife blotted the caul with another piece of cloth and thought about how, even in the new world, men did as they pleased while women still had to look after each other. Yiddish vaudevillians could make jokes about Jewish divorce; *She gets me, I told the rabbi. So the rabbi said, you have to get a get. So, I got a get. And what did that get me?* It was no joke for a woman like Rachel. Her baby would need a father. Under other circumstances, plenty of young widowers would marry a woman with a baby. She was so pretty, even a bachelor might take her with another man's child. But without a *get*, a Jewish divorce from a rabbinical court, no one would have her. And without Schmuel to ask for one, there would be no Jewish divorce.

"I heard," the baker's wife said, "That the brother in Brooklyn is taking the baby to raise with his own...Isaacson is insisting... because it's a boy."

"Why?" the midwife said.

"You're asking me?... Why do they ever do anything, men? To make *tsuris*, aggravation. To get their own way, why else?"

"So how do you know this?"

"Mrs. Lieberman told me. You know, she lives downstairs from them... So, yesterday she heard them arguing through the air shaft; that a boy needs a father to teach him God's Law."

"Isaacson can't teach him?"

The baker's wife had shrugged. "Do I know what goes on in a head like that? Maybe he thinks he's too old Anyway, as soon as it's weaned, they're sending it away for its own good. That's what Sadie Lieberman told me."

The midwife pictured Rachel, smiling and whispering to her new born son the way all new mothers did, and wondered how it must feel to have a child torn away after you had laboured to bring it into the world. Since she, herself, was a virgin, she could only imagine it.

There was no irony in this. Her profession was often the respectable resort of ugly women who knew, from an early age, they would have to fend for themselves. The immigration doctor on Ellis Island had written *dark facial strawberry mark* on her papers. But the men in her home village, considered it a mark of Cain. After all, wasn't her own mother well past her bloom when she was born? Surely, some spirit mischief, perhaps Lilith herself, must have been involved.

Sometimes the midwife thanked God for the deformity that had made her unmarriageable and thus independent of the stupid, thoughtless cruelty she had seen men practice in the name of God's Law.

Once again, the midwife examined the caul, marvelling at its intricacy. She knew that this was where God did his work, whatever men like Jacob Isaacson thought.

After she had separated it from the remains of the birth that were being prepared for burial, as was the custom, the midwife had told Rachel that someday it would protect a loved one from drowning and accidents at sea. Isaacson overheard her and became furious.

"Throw the evil, filthy thing away," he growled. "This is a God-fearing home. I will have no superstitious nonsense under my roof."

The midwife, whose years of spinsterhood had empowered her tongue, told him to throw it away himself. But he would not touch it; would not even look at it. In the end it was Sarah, the daughter who most resembled him, who had gathered it up and tossed it in a pail with the kitchen scraps, from whence the midwife had rescued it.

God's Law. As if God had anything to do with it. They made it up to suit themselves, the men; sat in dark little schuls arguing and twisting logic until it supported their own convenience and their childish squeamishness. The midwife had seen enough of life and death to know that God demonstrated his creation through the cycle of a woman's body. And yet, men had made of it a thing unclean, requiring purification before it was fit to be touched.

She had spent her life watching God quicken in women's bellies. There was nothing unclean or impure about it. Nothing that would wilt flowers, collapse cakes, turn wine to vinegar, soil men with the sin of Eve.

So many rules. And all because they were afraid, all because they would rather contort themselves into intellectual knots over the mind of God than look, with eyes that really saw, at the way He brought life and death together in women's blood.

Part Three

If the sea demands it, you must let it go.

Irish folk saying

CHAPTER FIFTEEN

Another country

"Do you think there will be guns on the Sound tonight?" The young woman shivered. As the night was mild for April, Ciaran guessed it was the excitement. Women, he had noticed, found the war thrilling when they were not touched by it. But he hugged her for warmth and she leaned back against him.

"If not this night, then another soon enough."

She was the new Gaelic schoolteacher, over from Tyrone, and her name was Gráinne. She was a hearty girl, big and solid. Ciaran felt the thickness of her through her coat. Ah, but her masses of coppery curls were lovely. While he fiddled the reels, he had watched her, the coils of her hair bouncing in time with the music. In between the dances she told him she was a great admirer of the old tunes. Her Irish was soft, precise, learned. After a while, he invited her to walk with him .

"Will ya come with me, then?"

"And where might it be that you've a mind to go?"

"Up by the East Lighthouse...It is fine for walkin'. If Tom Fergus is on the watch, I will show you the rocket."

"Are you after taking me to the moon then, Ciaran McMurrough?" she laughed.

"Ach no...it is for the lifesaving, for the shipwrecks and all."

"Would there be many of those?"

"Aye. Myself I seen a brave few...So will ya come wi' me?"

Briefly, she had considered. Then she had smiled at him. She had a fine looking face when she smiled.

"It is a soft night. Aye and why not?" she said. He supposed she knew it was a courting place when she agreed.

The moon hung big and yellow over Church Bay as they climbed the track behind the village. It turned the dry stone walls into the bleached bones of fantastical creatures. Giants and heroes and phantom steeds. These walls had marked the way long before anyone living could remember. He wanted to hold her hand, to tell her the stories of the places they passed through. But she was talking politics and waving her arms about, all caught up she was in the Easter news from down in the South.

"Do you think they will hang the lot?" she said.

Ciaran shrugged. In truth, he did not bother to think about such things. If Dublin folk would slaughter each other over politics when the Hun was after trying to starve them all, it was sure no business of his. It never came to ought but heartache for the women and the children. A man had only to think on the gruesome landmarks all around him to know the truth of that.

He interrupted her chatter.

"Have you heard the name of that rise just yonder?"

She shook her head.

"It is called *Crock-na-screedlin.*"

"Hill of screaming?"

"Aye, that is what they call it...after the screaming of the McDonnell women; them that watched the Campbells slaughter their menfolk from that very place."

"Why did they do that?"

"Ah, it was a long time ago. Likely it was over which lot would be the king's men and which would not, some such foolishness. If you are wanting to know, Father Rafferty can tell you about all the massacres. You must ask him to show you in his book."

"*All* the massacres?"

"Gráinne girl, do you not know this place is soaked in blood? For a thousand years and more. There is places on Rathlin would take the heart out of you, to hear the things they done, one lot and another. By them rocks they call the Castle? That is where the Queen's men threw women from the clifftops, the fine-lookin' ones, when they had done with them, you see. In that time they killed everything living. Hundreds and hundreds. On a winter's night, you can hear them still, the poor souls crying out for the ones they lost."

"Can you?"

"Aye and you can. It is a pitiful sound. Terrible. Many's the time I heard it myself, when the wind was after chasing its tail down the glens; callin' out the names and all."

He could tell from her look that the past had touched her, though she was not certain she believed him. It was all right. Sometimes, he was not sure himself he believed half the things he thought he knew. She let him take her hand and they walked on.

They sat against a wall beneath the war-darkened lighthouse watching drifters ply the Straits of Moyle. The drifters too were darkened but, in the clear night, their silhouettes were strong and black on the moon bright water.

She didn't complain when he put his arm around her shoulders. Now, he looked down at her, admiring the pale slope of her nose and the way some curls, too lively to be restrained by pins, took up the moonlight around her broad forehead. Perhaps he would kiss her soon. If she were not still for talking, perhaps he would.

"Look you, there's another," she said, sitting up and pointing.

Ciaran looked out to sea. A drifter, about halfway across to Kintyre, shadowed the surface of the sea, tending one of the barrage nets that crisscrossed the channel. Once he and Tom Fergus, who was called after his father Fergus McQuaid, spotted twelve on a single watch. Some said there were forty of them between Kintyre and Fair Head over on Ireland. But if MacNeill, the Coast Guardsman, knew, he was not saying.

"Do you think you will join up?" she asked.

Although some had already gone, Ciaran did not see the sense of fishermen and seafaring boys leaving to fight in holes in the ground with the coastal shipping and all the fishing grounds being harried by U boats. But it was not a choice he would likely have to make.

"I'm thinkin' I will not," he said. "I canna leave me Mam to be all on her own in such times as these."

Sensitive over obligations that kept him still at home, a man of twenty-seven, he added, "I keep the watch and man the rocket in my turn, along with the others. I have a grand uniform to wear and all."

Gráinne nodded and rested back against his shoulder. He felt the weight of her against him and shifted to press his nose into her nettle scented hair. She let him take her hand and he stroked her fingers, each in turn. Soft little hands she had, for such a strapping girl.

"Will you stay here when it is done, then?"

Ciaran sighed. She was still for talking after all. He would have to try another way.

"Well," he said, "I'll not go far...when there is paradise to be had just there, no further than a man can shout and it be a fair wind." And he pointed west across the water.

"So, it is for Antrim you're bound when the war is over?"

"And why would I go to that quarrelsome place? No it is not to Ireland I will go, but to the Green Island, when next it comes."

"The Green Island?"

"Aye, do you not know the stories?"

She shook her head.

"It is an island that rises from the sea but once every seven years. Green and lovely it is, all the year around, with skirts of fine white sand, washed by water warm as milk and it steaming in the bucket. Why the people thereabouts swim in it. Just for their pleasure. Can you imagine?

"This sea is leaping with fishes, every colour and kind, so that you need but dip in your nets to pull out a feast. And the trees is dripping with sweet grapes - green, in bunches - and apples...and oranges...the like you might be lucky to get from the Manor if you done some work for them at Christmas time."

"It is a fine gift for blatherskite you have yourself."

"You may say so, but haven't I seen it myself and me runnin' before the tides, right there, beyond the whirlpool, *Slough-na-morra*?"

"Did you now?"

"Aye...and when I seen it, I says to myself, Ciaran I says, when next it comes, you mind to be ready...with stones of home in your pocket. For you see, that is how you can make it stay. But, if you've no mind for such stories, girl..."

He settled back against the wall and waited; his quiet smile hidden by the darkness.

"It is a fine moon tonight; do you not think so?" she said.

"Maybe."

"And soft for this time of the year."

"Aye...for this time of the year."

"Oh, go on then," she said, "and tell me."

He laughed softly. "All right, all right. But you must hush and listen close." He slid his hand up her back until it rested beneath her curls, on the warm nape of her neck.

"Well, the people of this island, beautiful they are, every one; the men fit and strong. And the women, ah, the women...Well, almost as pretty as you they are, with eyes on them the colour of emeralds...or," he paused to look at her, "...or dark brown as oak wood that has been lying in a bog.

"They have no need of other jewels, with such eyes as those, I can tell you. Still, they do be decked with ornaments of silver and gold, the men and women both, for they find it all about, though none knows from where it comes. Myself, I'm thinking it is the seals bring it up from their cities at the bottom of the sea."

"Aye?"

"Mmm."

Ciaran felt her soften. She was smiling her pretty smile. He kissed her forehead, but she pulled away.

"Is there no more to it then?"

Now it was she who was teasing. But the game was sweet. For a while longer, he would play.

"More?...There is everything...Did I not tell you of the music?...Why, aren't they singing all the day long...and playing on their harps and fiddles and such like...when they are not reaching into the sea for a bit of fish or catching the fruit falling out of the trees...And the trees...so tall and full of leaf they be a wonder to see...and to hear also...for the sea breezes play music in their branches...so that the place itself has a kind of song, the which you can hear," he was whispering now, their faces almost touching, "and you being so very still."

"It sounds a grand place," she sighed just before he kissed her.

Almost at once, the night was full of light and the urgent sibilance of phosphorous flares. Ciaran jumped up, dragging Gráinne to her feet.

"What is it?" she cried. "Are they fighting from the boats?"

But Ciaran was running towards the rocket house.

"No," he shouted back. "It is a submarine has broke the nets. You must go from here now."

The gentle musician who, moments before, had wooed her with fairy stories and whispers, was gone. She wanted to stay, to watch the pyrotechnics that paled the moon. But she obeyed the command in Ciaran's voice and scurried down to the village, the maroon that summoned the rocket crew shaking the hills behind her.

Nine men watched the sea. The night had gone quiet. After the commotion of the muster, the business of making the equipment ready and the taking of positions for action, they had only to wait. For a while, their eyes followed the U boat's passage, her course marked by underwater flares on the bit of barrage net she carried away. Four drifters converged at the break and gave chase as best they could, joined by a faster gun boat out of Portrush. But the glow worm trail soon disappeared and it was clear to the men on the cliffs that the warships had lost their quarry.

"She's found the deep channel," Ciaran said. "We'll see no more of her tonight."

"They'll be late watching on the North, sure," Tom Fergus said.

Ciaran nodded. He would not have admitted, not even to himself, that he was disappointed. In the year since the volunteer companies had formed, the U boat commanders had proven their skill at running under the nets to make mischief north of the island. The only action the East crew had seen was on the exercise ground. No doubt the Coast Guard Officer, in charge of all the volunteer companies, would soon gallop up to tell them to stand down.

Ciaran and Tom Fergus, rested against the wagon, watching the others. Fergus McQuaid, who was volunteer-in-charge, manned the rocket machine, every now and then checking the legs of the tripod, though the need had long passed. Father Rafferty and the altar boy, who was called Eamonn, passed around big, cork covered jugs of tea they had carried all the way up from the village. When he realised that Eamonn had forgotten the mugs, Father Rafferty cuffed him behind the ear. Poor Eamonn was always being cuffed by the good father.

"Ah, let the lad be, Father," said Bertie MacDoon. He paced the clifftops, kicking the pegs that held the furled cliff ladders in readiness. "Isn't it a war we're having and not a tea party after all?"

"And if Our Lord is wanting to send us tea parties instead of fighting, you'd best be thankful for it," said Father Rafferty.

Ciaran smiled. "It isna tea, but a wee drop and my bed that I'm wanting," he said to Tom Fergus. "I've a powerful lot of ploughing in the morning."

158

"Myself and all," Tom Fergus said. Then he laughed. "I'll warrant it wasna sleep you was after getting when I seen you before."

"What are you on about, man?"

"Didn't I see you with the new schoolteacher, and she hurrying down the hill when I come out to signal the others?"

"Aye...And what of it? What is the harm of a bit of kissing in the moonlight?"

"No harm in it at all," Tom Fergus said. "But the women wouldna say so."

"Would they not? I'm thinking they like it well enough when they are at it."

Tom Fergus raised his eyebrow and shook his head.

"What?" Ciaran said. "Say what it is you're after saying, man."

"Nothing," Tom Fergus said. "I am after saying nothing...only that there are them that are askin' when at all you will be choosing a wife at last and settling down."

Ciaran knew it was Tom Fergus's Cathleen, that was Duigan the shopkeeper's daughter, who was doing the asking. Poor Tom Fergus, three days a week measuring lengths of twine and weighing lumps of cheese in his father-in-law's store, an apron tied round him and all. Himself, he'd had a near escape.

"Tell your Cathleen, that maybe I've a mind to stay a bachelor for a wee while. Could be I will be like Bertie and never take me a wife and all."

"I was just after wondering," Tom Fergus said.

"That's as may be, but there is all kinds of women and myself I like the..."

"It is MacNeill...MacNeill is coming!" An east island man, who had been watching from a rise, shouted across their talk. Ciaran was glad of the interruption. This conversation with Tom Fergus was an old one. How was he to settle down when there was such a lot of pretty women? And every one of them grand in her own way.

Soon they heard a horse on the rocky path and the Coast Guard officer came over the hill. "It is all over for tonight, men," he said. "You may stow the gear and stand down." And, wasting no more words, he rode off to the north.

After, there was little time for talk. The stowage was careful work and each man had his own task. Ciaran checked the coils of the rocket line. Once sure it was properly faked back and forth across the wooden pegs, he and Bertie carried the big wooden box to the front of the wagon. Then he made fast the clips that held the heaving canes to the sides. Tom Fergus and his father dismantled the tripod and the rocket machine itself while others saw to the hawsers, the pulleys and rigs that made up the apparatus. They worked in silence, exchanging only those words that were needed.

When they were done, Tom Fergus clapped a hand on Ciaran's shoulder. "I must watch a wee while longer," he said. "Wait for me, man, and we will walk up west together."

"Ach, but I cannot. I'm thinking it is a short way to morning and a long walk to my bed and all."

"It is that."

"And I must first fetch my fiddle that was left in the kelp house after the dancing. Could be you'll catch me up along the path."

"Could be I will...Safe home then, man."

"And you and all. God bless."

Home smells. Peat smoke and fish oil from the lamp that Flora put by the window. The damp animal stink of wool; his pullover and socks drying by the fire. She'd set out whiskey and a glass and gone to bed.

Ciaran threw a sod on the fire. He pulled his boots off and stood them by the hearth. Then he poured himself a drink and settled by the table. He closed his eyes, savouring the silence and the way the whiskey lit a warm path all the way to his belly.

So, there were them that was asking when he would choose a wife. Ah well, let them. For wasn't the world a mad place in the meanwhile to be having such thoughts? What had he need of a wife when there was girls willing; when there was work to be done, and his Mam still fit to look after him and glad to do it? And where would he put her, and the wee'uns that would come after and all? No, there was time later for all of that. When the war was over and there was hours in the day and men to spare to build a wee house. Maybe then he would look for a wife, a quiet woman with a song about her. A woman who could look into his eyes and understand what it was that was in his heart. Without so much talking.

He stretched his tired legs and yawned. The wind was quickening. There would be weather in the morning, sure. He listened to it hustle round the chimney. It rattled the door, setting the strings of his fiddle, that hung beside it, humming. His mother turned in her sleep and began to snore, the sound of her muffled by the feather bed that hid her form.

He and Bertie had made the bed and the quilt, from feathers they had climbed for when he was still a boy. Bertie's cousin Fionula, who worked at the Manor, helped them piece together the covering from torn sheets and petticoats she had managed to spirit away. That year, so many linens were destroyed by the mangle in the Manor House laundry that the landlord made his wife send to Derry for a new one. Ciaran poured himself another whiskey and laughed to remember that there was even a piece of the English rector's surplice got sewn up in the thing.

One morning, while Flora milked the cows, he and Bertie had replaced her straw filled pallet, and the bit of torn tweed she used for a blanket, with the wonderful feather bed.

When she saw it, a bed as fine as if she had been a bride itself, she dropped the bucket, the milk running everywhere.

"I made it for you, Mam. Myself and Bertie, we done it," he said.

"The boy climbed the feathers himself," said Bertie.

For a while she was speechless. She hugged them both, smiling and teary all together. Then she sat on the bed and stroked it.

"Wherever did you get such fine linen? With bits of lace and all."

Neither he nor Bertie could tell her.

"Ah," she said. "Is it that I'd best not be showing it off to her ladyship then?"

"Best not, Mam."

Flora laughed. She gathered up a corner of the feather bed and held it against her face.

"Well," she said, surveying the puddles now soaking into the earthen floor. "I see I will be sleeping like a queen and all, but we'll not a drop of milk for our tea. Will you stay and eat with us Bertie? It is only a bit of mackerel we have. But there is cabbage still and some carrots in the ground."

Ciaran wondered then, as he had often wondered since, why his mother and Bertie had never married. Sure and they were fond of each other. That had been plain to him from the time he was old enough to take heed of such things.

Once, when he was seven or eight, he had asked her.

"Ach, child, the things you are after saying. Where is it at all that you have got such ideas?"

He was afraid to tell her the thoughts that troubled him. That it was a fine thing to have four "fathers" to teach him all they knew, but that he wished he had just one like other boys.

"Why do you call my Da 'Da Fergus'," Tom Fergus had asked him, "when he is not your Da? My Mam says he is your Mam's cousin only. My Mam says that you have not a Da of your own at all."

He was afraid to tell her for fear that it would make her cry. So he had fallen silent.

Perhaps she had guessed. "You are a lucky lad to have so many good men looking out for you," she said. "Bertie is like a brother to me, and he loves you like his own. So you do be glad of it and count your blessings. And we will have no more such silly talk."

She had her secrets, Flora did, and that was that.

Ciaran stretched and yawned again. Well, perhaps she was right. There were other things that were more important. And right now, sleep was the firstmost, with the ground to break for barley and oats in the morning. He banked the ashes to keep the fire, extinguished the lamp and went to bed.

CHAPTER SIXTEEN

Communion

It was a good field and it would give a good harvest. The undisturbed earth was heavy yet it was dark and it turned easily under the plough. Ciaran pulled the horse to and looked back at the furrows behind him. The mare was well trained. The rows ran straight, but for the detours round the hillocks that stood out, shaggy and pale, against the damp black soil.

Already, in late April, the five mounds were showing signs of the meadow flowers that would cover them by June. Wild orchids, eyebright, dog roses, mallow and clover. Vetch, that cursed weed, was that thick, he would have a job of keeping it from the grain all the summer long. There was no help for it. He had promised Flora he would not disturb the dead.

She was not well pleased to hear that this year he would turn the *Ouig* to barley. "Your Grand-Da Donal, God rest him, never ploughed that field," she said, "...never once in all his days. I have it in my head he said no good would come of it."

"Ach, Mam, you know it is only stories. It is a grand growing place. Yourself, you're always after saying how the beasts give sweeter milk and them grazing on it for a wee while only."

"Aye...maybe...but it is not the immortal souls of them dumb creatures I have a care for."

"It is a good field, Mam. I'm thinking it will be a hungry winter with the war keeping the steamers from the bay and chasing the fish from the Sound. How can we leave it idle at all, and it be good enough for barley or corn itself?"

She had no answer. But when he left the cottage that morning, she held his face in both her hands. "You do be careful...and say a prayer for the poor unbaptised sinners who do be sleeping in that place."

It was called the *Ouig*, the place of graves, for the mounds that were scattered over it. But the name was legend only, for no one knew who made the mounds or if they were graves at all. They had been there long before the Christian days. Father Rafferty said the saintly monks who first brought the word of God to the island had written of them. The mounds were ancient even then.

Ciaran's Grand-Da Donal had told him that when he was a boy a professor had come over from Scotland to look at them. He brought notebooks and drawing pads, measuring tools, tiny wee spades and brushes.

"He was full of book learning," Donal said, "but I mind he had no sense in him at all. He give me a shilling for one of them blue stone axe heads, the ones that any fool can find. Older than the Good Book itself he said it was. Imagine. And them lying by the dozens on the ground up to Brockley." Grand-Da Donal had liked the story and had told it often.

The professor, Donal said, was in a fever of excitement after he dug into one of the mounds. "Beside himself, he was. You wouldn't credit it, when all he was after finding was some round stones, beads he said they was, and a bit of a broken pot and a leg bone...though if you was to look at it, you'd say it was the bone of some beast that folks was throwing into the field after they had eaten of it, in olden times."

"Why do you not plough the *Ouig* then, Grand-Da?"

"Ah well...You know that your Mam, she's fond of the purple flowers that come in the springtime of the year...and your Grand-Mam before her, God rest her. And isn't it powerful work to break it straight, there being no need of it at all, with them lumps sticking out of the ground."

There was need of it now. If the war didn't end soon, they would use every scrap of food they could grow themselves come winter. No one was talking of an end by Christmas anymore. But if it chanced to stop, the barley would be welcome over to Islay. He could get cash money for it, maybe some whiskey too.

Still, before he put the plough to the field, Ciaran said a *Pater Noster* and asked the Mother of God to pray for any who might be waiting for Judgement under that ground.

It was a peaceful kind of work, alone on the *Ouig*. With no one to stop him from whistling a tune or singing if it came into his head. He listened to the soft scrape of earth against the ploughshare, the *thunk-a-thunk* of the mare's heavy hooves on the meadow grass. Under it all, the steady give and take of the sea. For, though the field finished in cliff tops, as most did, a chimney of rock brought up the sound of it, as clear as if he were standing at the waters' edge.

He had been right about the weather. But it was only a freshening wind, with no storm to it at all. The day was clear and fine. From high up on the *Ouig* he could just see Inishowen Head on Donegal. Shrouded in mist it was, beyond the green of Antrim. When the horse turned the plough, the Mull of Kintyre hove into sight, sky mountains behind it that were likely clouds or maybe Scotland itself. Ah, it was enough to give a man comfort and he being hard at it all the while.

So lost was he, admiring the Lord's handiwork, that he might have missed the find had not a clatter against the ploughshare caught his ear. He stopped and looked at the ground he and the mare had just opened. There was nothing but the lumps of earth, riddled with roots. He bent down and broke a clod in his hands. The cool soil ran between his fingers. Good it was, but new as well. He would have to harrow the field before he could sow.

He stood to the plough, but the odd sound echoed in his mind. The earth was always throwing up flint arrow heads and axes round these parts. But he had heard of more valuable things coming up with the slice of the plough. Over to Knockans a fellow found twelve silver coins that the postmaster sent to the museum in Belfast. They said they were of the Danes and paid him eight pounds for the lot. A bit of money was always welcome. He stopped again and walked back to the spot where he had first heard the noise on the share.

Kneeling, he slowly worked the clods with his bare hands. He ran his open palms over the surface, his brow creased in concentration. Black dirt limned the cracks and calluses of his fingers. He found nothing. Sitting back on his haunches, he rubbed his chin, leaving a gritty smear. Ah well, if others would be pulling money up out of the ground, good luck to them and all. He was about to give up when three whitish pebbles caught his eye, the way they lay, one beside the other...and all of them the same size and shape. He scrambled to the spot and dug his fingers around one of them. It was as big as a twist of barley sugar. When he tried to lift it, he realised that it was attached to the two he could see and to others, still buried.

As he scratched at the earth, Ciaran felt his heart quicken. He tried to still his rising excitement. Likely it only was a few links of a chain that might be put to use if it were not rusted through. If it were that, it were a good length. He could feel it with his fingers, a foot and more.

Unearthed, at last, and spread before him, it gave few clues. It was a chain of some kind, of that he was certain, though some of the links were fused into rigid lengths. But whether it was for work or ornament he could not see, for it was crusted over with lime and minerals carried down by the rain. He scraped at the crust. It stuck tight. He would need more than his fingernails to shift it.

Well, it would have to wait. The sun had already passed midday. There was still half the field to plough if he were to harrow tomorrow before handing the mare on to Mickey Joe. He dropped the chain into his pocket where it rubbed against his thigh and niggled at his mind for the rest of the day.

"That was good, Mam."

Ciaran wiped the last of the eggs from his plate with a piece of wheaten bread and stuffed it into his mouth.

"How did you taste it at all, and you eatin' like the devil himself was after snatching it from you?"

He burped and smiled.

"I'm thinking your belly will make a powerful complaint tonight for haven't you filled it like you was in a race." She shook her head and took her shawl from the peg. "Will you be bringing your fiddle to the *eesha gawnil?*"

She was off to a gathering at the church hall where the women were making a quilt for Mickey Joe's Bridget and her young man that would be married in the summer.

"Could be I'll be coming later, Mam. There's the plough needs mending."

"Are you after blinding yourself with working in the dark?"

"It is bright enough and it only evening time."

"You best put some paraffin in the lamp, then, for I'm thinking myself it makes a better light than the oil from the wee fishes."

Ciaran had already thought of that, filling the Talley lamp when he had come home from ploughing. "I will, Mam," he said.

He watched her cross the yard and disappear down the lane. When he was certain she would not return, he took the chain from his pocket and spread it on the table. He laid his pocketknife and two long iron nails beside it. When he

166

lit the Talley lamp, which, with its lenses and reflectors, cast a white hot light, he saw something he had not noticed before. The crust that covered his find was not lime or minerals at all. It was made of bones and shells, the leavings of wee barnacles and the like. He turned it over in his hands. He had seen such deposits on the flotsam that washed into the tide caves at the bottoms of the cliffs. The thing had lain in the sea, for years perhaps, before someone had carried it up to the *Ouig*.

He picked up a nail and, using the handle of his knife as a mallet, began to chisel away at the stuff. He had barely begun to work on the first link of the chain when the nail found a purchase. The crust fell away in two pieces, like the shell of a walnut.

Gold. There was no mistaking it. Hadn't he seen and touched it often enough when he helped the priest serve the Mass as a boy. Sure and it was gold, for nothing sticks to gold, but only the sea creatures had hidden it by living and dying all around it. It was a kind of a bead. The dull yellow sheen took his breath away. Thick and heavy it was and about as long as his index finger from the tip to the first knuckle. It was only one, but by itself it was a fortune. He put his tools to the next and the crust came away easily.

The second was much the same as the first, to which it was linked. The beads were narrow in the middle and wider at the ends, smooth on one side, the surface only so unsteady as the hand of the man who had made them. There were channels carved in the tops. The channels of the second bead were filled with blue stone, flecked with white. He touched the stone. It was not as smooth as the gold but it had been polished once.

These channels made a familiar pattern. Ciaran turned the beads in the light until he recognised it. Knots. They were made to look like reef knots, the channels joined and crossing in the middle like a couple holding hands and them swinging face to face in the dance.

His hands were trembling. He found the whiskey and took a mouthful, straight from the bottle. He sat and stared at the two golden beads, holding the edge of the table and breathing deeply. Then he set about freeing the others.

The room disappeared and the hours passed. There was only now. There were only his two hands in the dazzling beam of light and the growing chain of thick gold beads. Beautiful they were, wonderful. Some held their blue stones; some gave up the stones to the calcified shells. It didn't matter. What mattered were the beads themselves, glowing and warm and humming with the years.

By the time he heard Bertie and Flora on the path below, he had cleaned the lot. Now, what he did next he could never explain, to himself nor anyone. Not then nor ever after. For Ciaran was not a man to keep a story to himself. And sure, if ever he had a story to tell, he had one that night.

He doused the Talley lamp and set it outside the door, hoping all the while that Flora and Bertie had not rounded the bend and seen its light. Then he lit the *glashin* oil lamp and set it in the window. The table was littered with bits of petrified shell. These he gathered up. Finding no likely place to discard them, he stirred them into the fire and threw on a fresh sod.

He had just time to climb under the covers, his clothes still on him, when they entered the house.

Flora knocked gently on the bedroom door. Then she opened it and looked in.

"Fast asleep he is," she told Bertie.

"And no wonder," said Bertie. "for doesn't he work all the hours the Lord sends."

"Aye, poor lad."

"Ach, Flora, you need not trouble yourself. It is a fit young man and not a lad he is. A bit of toil will do him no harm at all."

Flora closed the door muffling their conversation. In a little while, Ciaran heard Bertie leave. He waited, listening, the golden chain clutched in his fist under the pillow.

At last, she was asleep. Ciaran cracked open the bedroom door, reassured by the sound of his mother's snoring. He lit the candle by his bedside and spread the chain across his lap. He counted the links. They were not links precisely. More like they were beads that were joined together, all the same. There were twenty-two. The thing was too heavy to be worn by a woman, and she being less than a giant. No, it was made for a man. A prince maybe. Sure and there was that much gold to it. He could scarce imagine what price such a thing would fetch. He considered what to do.

Quickly, he discarded the notion of bringing it to the postmaster, the only government official on the island. It was one thing to send a handful of silver coins through the post, but the chain was in another class of treasures all together. He must take it, himself, to Ireland. But where? Could be he would have to go all the way to Belfast, or maybe even Dublin. He didn't relish the notion. Ballymena was the biggest town he'd ever visited, in the time of the Lammas Fair. There, even in the company of Bertie and Mickey Joe and Tom Fergus, he had felt befuddled by the crowds and the noise. And he had come across city folk on the Causeway, where he went to sell birds and eggs. They were sharp tongued and impatient, full of irritation and consternation all together. The thought of wandering, a stranger, among such people, the gold chain in his pocket, filled him with dread. Besides, there was plenty more farm work still to be done.

He could ask Father Rafferty what to do. The priest would know. For hadn't he been to the priests' school at Maynooth that was that close to Dublin and all. Father Rafferty knew many worldly things besides the saving of folks immortal souls.

He made up his mind. In the morning, he would show the chain to Flora and after, he would pay a call on Father Rafferty.

Now he ran the nugget-like beads through his fingers. Truly, they were a marvel. And it was not the gold only that made them so. For the art of the craftsman was alive in them, though, himself, he be long dead and buried in a pagan's grave. Even the clasp, a thick hook on the one end that fitted an eyelet on the other, was skilfully wrought. He lifted the chain and watched the beads swing in the candlelight. Then, with some difficulty, for he had never done such a thing before, he fastened it around his neck and let it slide under his pullover.

It was not so heavy as he had supposed. It rested so easily against him, sitting just below his collarbone, that he could barely feel it. He had to touch it with his fingers to be sure it was still there. It was as warm as his own skin, almost like a part of him.

He pulled his knitted shirt over his head. Then, taking up the candle, he went to the window and examined his reflection against the night dark glass. Though he was not a vain man, he was not displeased with what he saw. The golden collar might have been made for him. A vagrant thought entered his mind. *Why not keep it?* It was an idle notion and all, for what need had he, an ordinary man, of a golden collar the likes of this? Or any like at all? But once the idea had gained entry, he could not send it away. He blew out the candle and sat on his bed in the dark.

How could he sleep with this strange idea singing restless in his brain, in his blood? *Keep it*, it crooned. *It is yours*, it insisted. *Made for you.* Finally, unable to settle, he dressed and, quietly, so as not to wake Flora, he crept out of the house.

For as long as he could remember, Ciaran had soothed his troubles by the sea. If it could be wild and dangerous, it could be steady and comforting also. For wasn't it everlasting, the sea. Forever itself. Like the stars in the sky. But a man couldn't touch the stars, nor ride them at all.

And wasn't it everywhere as well. Why right now, somewhere, the sun was shining on it. Every kind of folk were working and playing upon it, beside it, even, God have mercy on us all, beneath it. At this very moment. The arms of the sea embraced them all. To be with the sea was, for Ciaran, a kind of communion with all the souls and saints that had ever lived or were waiting to be born. It was a communion, he was ashamed to admit, he had never felt as strongly at the Mass, the wafer melting on his tongue. Likely Father Rafferty would have said it was the will and not the feeling that mattered for the blessing of it to be given. But, he believed, this feeling was a blessing too, for didn't it restore a man's tired spirit?

He made his way down the steep path in the cleft between two cliffs, to where the *clachan* boat was beached. A flat rock, on the edge of the shingle, was his special place. There he sat now, eyes closed, mind as blank as he could make it, listening to the sea with his heart.

How long he sat thus, he could not have said. Nor what thoughts may have passed through his head. When he opened his eyes, he was only aware that the gentle ebb and flow had washed him calm. He touched his chest with the palm of his hand and the merest shadow of a smile warmed his face.

There was the Ouig to be finished. In the morning he would pull on his clothes and go about his work in the usual way.

He reached under his pullover and touched the collar, already comfortable and familiar against his skin. *I am meant to wear it. I was chosen to have it.* How ever could a payment from some government office replace this strange and remarkable feeling?

"It is mine," he said aloud, for he knew, as sure as he had ever known anything, that it was.

CHAPTER SEVENTEEN

The Feis

Cushendall was singing and dancing for the *Feis*. The streets were crowded with music makers. A troupe of Islay sword dancers, the women in their shiny white shirts and high black boots, practiced under a tree in the town square. There were pipers from Ballymena, a tattoo of *bodhrans* and tin whistlers by the hundreds. Ciaran had heard some fine singing; he'd watched a woman from Dungannon play a magical harp, her fingers flying invisibly across the strings, and he'd won a medal for his fiddling. It had been the choicest kind of a day and now he was thirsty.

Somehow, he had lost Bertie and Tom Fergus in the crush. He hoped that Bertie wouldn't tell Flora that they had been separated. She had not wanted him to go. July, she said, was ever a bad time for peace loving folk in Antrim. It was the marching season. In Flora's imagination, every town in Ulster was, at this very moment, being ruined by the men of the Orange Lodges. "Them with their bowler hats and sashes, their banners flying," she would say. "And after in the taverns, full of drink and cursing Papists. No good can come of it... you mark me."

It was no good him saying it was different at the *Feis*. "Didn't your Grand-Da Donal bring home scraped knuckles or a bloody nose, every year, along with his medal? It is a bad time for an Irishman in that place. And this year, with all the troubles, it will be worse."

Ciaran touched his medal and smiled. She would be pleased enough to see he'd upheld the tradition, for it was the McMurroughs who always brought the honours back to the *clachan*. This year there had been more challengers than ever before. And after the hardships of the winter, the worst he could remember, the *Feis* was just what he needed.

The familiar sign of *The Fisherman's Return* swung into view. Bertie and Tom Fergus would find him there, soon enough. In the meanwhile, he would slake his thirst and find a pretty girl to listen to his stories.

The winter of 1917 had been brutal and hungry. There was no spare barley from the *Ouig*, for money *or* whiskey. It was eaten, but for one sack of seed, by February. They ate seaweed, the way, it was said, people did in the famine times, and nettle soup, salted mackerel and the eggs Flora pickled from Ciaran's summer climbing.

In December, a sheep went over near Bull Point and though the cliffs were glazed with ice sharp enough to slice rope, Ciaran and Bertie climbed down to fetch it, grateful for the Christmas mutton. They brought back limpets from the rocks. Flora was ashamed of such scavenger's fare.

"It may be a beggar's feast," Bertie told her, "but it is a beggar's winter we are having. Over on the east end, I hear they are eatin' the seals that wash up dead after the depth bombs."

Flora was horrified. "Ach, they are no better than savages over there," she said, "to be feasting on them poor creatures that could be their own lads come home from the war." After that, she boiled the limpets for tea without complaint. Sometimes, when there was nothing to burn but cow dung, they ate them raw.

By a miracle of the war, there was plenty of bread. Early in the winter, a food convoy, going through the straits under escort, had been attacked by German torpedoes. The fighting ships took a beating; one of them towed off for repairs and the HMS Drake going down right in Church Bay. She was a big one, a heavy cruiser, 14,000 tons MacNeill said. She wallowed about a bit before she capsized at anchor. And while the lifeboat men raced to save the crew and complement, there wasn't an islander watching from the shore who didn't enjoy the irony. For wasn't it Sir Francis brought the soldiers to massacre the McDonnells for the Queen, Sorley Boy himself watching and weeping from across on Fair Head.

Later, that same day, the U boats chased the convoy round the western end and sank a flour carrier. When her cargo floated ashore, there was fine white flour, still usable, in the centre of the sacks.

With the first cold winds of October, Ciaran hid the gold collar, which he now thought of as *the treasure*. He had kept it a secret but sensed it was not fit to be wearing a fortune of gold around his neck in such hard times. If someone had seen it, if it were to slip out from under his pullover, what would people think? It would be all very well to say that it was the blockade and not want of money that plagued them all. But how could he explain that he was breaking the law to keep a thing that could make them rich? How could he tell anyone, especially Flora, when he did not understand, himself, why he could not part with it?

Maybe that was the reason he hid the treasure. Maybe it was something else entirely. For he had noticed, too, that it seemed to disturb his sleep. Night after night, he woke from dreams he could not remember, soaked and anguished, filled with sorrow and a fleeting sense of struggle and of flight. Sometimes his skin was tender and pink where the treasure rested, as though it came alive and burned him while he slept. Once, in the half sleep of morning, he was convinced that someone soft and fragrant lay beside him in his bed. Sweet fingers curled in the hair of his chest; hands so small they disappeared in his. He awoke to find himself caressing the golden beads.

Whatever the reason, the treasure now lay under his clothes in the wooden chest at the foot of his bed. Though he no longer wore it, hardly a day passed when he didn't look at it, or hold it, as though, by touching it, he might understand.

For months, the news from France had been bloody. Though the fight at the Somme finished in November, the grieving had only begun. That winter, the banshee wailed and the keening of women was heard all over Ireland. None of the island boys who went to the battle ever returned.

Perhaps Flora thought Ciaran was restless for the fight. For what seemed to him the hundredth time, she made him promise not to go.

"There is not a time that you go in the boats that I do not fret."

"Ach, Mam, you know this is idle talk. For what way at all would an island man live and him not goin' in the boats."

"You must swear that you will not go in the boats to the fight, for how would I live, all on my own and you lost to the sea before ever you got there."

He would swear and then she would make him swear again, sometimes adding oddly, "And you must promise me that you will not take your boots off in the boats or put your naked foot into the sea."

"Why, Mam?"

"It is a fear that I have...Promise me."

"It is an easy promise, for isn't the sea bitterly cold for a man's naked foot."

"You may laugh...but I know more than you of the old ways...and those folk were wise enough who made them."

"Yes Mam."

"And you must eat ought that swims until you are safe on solid land."

"Yes Mam."

If the warm weather brought lambs to the pasture and flowers to the moors, it brought little hope to Flora's heart. "I'll warrant there will be graves enough for all that blooms," she said.

You would have thought those poor souls, drifting home from the western front had seen enough of killing. But now it was politics and broken English promises that twisted their spirits and gave some of them a taste for more. In the harbour, every boat brought violent news from Ireland. Beatings and blood. Policemen down in the South, feckless Catholic boys closer to home.

In May, Ciaran sold a calf to a man from Ballycastle on condition he bring it across himself. He left Flora on her knees saying the Rosary and when he returned, a few hours later, she was still at her beads.

Island bound in June, Ciaran was restless, and so reckless on the cliffs that Bertie scolded him.

"Be you easy, Bertie...do you not know that I can fly?" he laughed. "And what harm can come to me with you to watch and the mare on the ropes?"

"You must let the man be," Bertie told Flora, "for he is trapped in your worries and careless with it."

"He'll not come to grief on the cliffs," Flora said.

Then came July, and the time of the *Feis*. Flora would not have a minute's rest until Ciaran was safe at home, but she knew there was nothing she could do or say to keep him from going.

∞

The smell of flowers. A thundering head and stinging lips. Ciaran opened his eyes under a strange ceiling, a strange soft pillow under his head. A blurred but definitely female shape bent over him, dabbing his cut lip with a brandy-soaked cloth.

"Ow."

"Ah, you've decided to join the livin' have you? Well, you may be sorry for it soon enough and you bruised all over as a windfallen apple."

Before he could properly see, an image of her coalesced around the throaty scrape of her voice. Raven hair, a painted mouth and soft round bosoms. She was the girl from *The Fisherman's Return* who had admired his blue riband and his medal from the *Feis*.

He blinked. "...Is it Tilly?"

"So, you remember my name. It is a good beginnin'. Your friend was sure and certain you was dead and buried."

He squinted to take in the rest of the room. Behind the girl, Tom Fergus leaned against a chest of drawers. "Your Mam will slaughter us both," he said.

"Ach, the boat." As Ciaran sat up, the roaring in his head was joined by a chorus of complaint from every part of his body. And, realising that he was naked he snatched at the bedcovers.

Tilly laughed. "Are you shy, man? You need not trouble yourself on my account...and anyway, wasn't it your friend put you in my bed and all?"

"You need not trouble yourself about the boat, neither," Tom Fergus said. "It left us behind, hours ago. Bertie has gone ahead to spin a yarn for Flora and my Cathleen. Though I'm bound if I know what all he will say. When your Mam casts her eye on the state you are in, she will slaughter us both."

Ciaran relaxed into the soft bedding. So it was Tilly's bed he was lying in. And nothing for it but to wait till morning. Through throbbing lips, he chanced a smile.

"Mind you keep a drop of that brandy for myself and all, for I am feeling still dizzy in my head."

"Oh aye? Myself I'd scarce believe it when you've stones only for brains. Whatever were you thinking of at all; yourself and three of them, and them soldiers in uniform?"

It was coming back to him now. "Ah, it was only a bit of a brawl...and weren't they the worse for a drop too much taken? The one of them that had one arm only and all?"

"One maybe, but desperate strong it was, for wasn't he holding you up and the other two pounding away?" Tom Fergus said. "You may thank the saintly protectors of drunken fools that Bertie and me come along. Else they would have killed you sure."

Ciaran was less clear about how the fight had ended than he was about how it had begun.

"I wasna drunk, man," he said.

"Were you not? A fool only, then."

"Nor that neither. I didna choose to quarrel with that lot."

"Myself, I maybe believe you...for wasn't Bertie only just saying that their like are all over the town this year; drinking to King Billy and spoiling for a fight with an Irishman, and him being a Catholic."

"Ah, it were never none of that, man. How would it be at all?"

"It is you must tell me; for myself, I was only at the finish."

"It was my prize, man. It was the medal that riled them." Ciaran touched his chest, then looked around the room.

"It is safe in my pocket," Tom Fergus said. "Well, safe enough after the trampling it took...and the riband in shreds."

"Where is my fiddle?"

"Bertie has taken it with him on the boat. It was Tilly that saved it from destruction. You were tellin' how it started, man."

"Aye, so I was." He closed his eyes.

"Well?"

"Mmm hmm." Ciaran's natural instincts never deserted him. Within his aching head, he sorted the details, of which he could remember few enough, to make a story of them. Tom Fergus, who had witnessed such a performance many times before, knew it was no use rushing him. At last, he began.

"I mind I was singing for Tilly all the songs I fiddled at the *Feis*, and telling her how it was for my Grand-Da's wedding song...the one that he made himself...that they give me the prize over all the others."

"You were after making me believe it was the wee folk give it to him," Tilly laughed.

"So my Grand-Da always said."

"His Grand-Da said a powerful lot of blether in his day."

"Well, God bless his soul and all."

"All right, then. But it is not your Grand-Da we are waiting on."

"Tom Fergus, man, you have, yourself, the soul of a greengrocer...with no patience in it at all." He grinned at Tilly and continued.

" So, it was all right, you know. And Tilly laughing and smiling. Do you know you have a pretty smile, girl? And I'm whistling the tunes and all, when these three fellows come up to me and one of them says, all friendly like, 'I see that you are a decorated man, though you haven't the uniform of a soldier. Was it for the Somme they hung that round your neck or somewhere else at all?'

"No, says I, it is not a fighting man that I am...more's the pity...for you are brave lads all.

" 'Well then,' says he, 'in what way are you wearin' a medal around your neck?'

"Isn't it only for fiddling at the *Feis* that they have given it me? says I.

" 'Is it the truth and all?' says he. 'I'm thinking you would not be so full of boasts and medals if Jimmy had been there. For wasn't he the finest man for the fiddle was ever seen in Antrim?'

"And is that so, I'm thinking; for you know Tom Fergus, there is not a man has beat me for five years and more. So, I asks the fellow, who is this Jimmy? And if he is such a fine fiddler, where was he at all?"

Tom Fergus sighed.

"Well then, here comes this one-armed boyo. 'I be that Jimmy and all,' says he, 'and I would have beat you sure, but for that I left my fiddling arm to feed the flowers in Picardy.'

"So...well...you know Tom Fergus, I was right sorry for the fellow. It is a bleak day and a tragedy for a man to lose his fiddling arm. So, I says to myself, Ciaran I says, you must give this man a bit of heart, for isn't it troubles he has and plenty. I am that sorry for you, man, I says. But you must thank the Lord that you didna leave your life and all, for thousands did; and them poor souls having to go with the story they had, and no confession at all."

"Ach, man. You didna say that."

"Aye and I did...for it is the truth and all; so what would be the harm in it? So it was all right, and I commenced to talk to Tilly again when this fellow pushes me on the shoulder. 'Are you after mocking me?' says he. Not at all, says I. What way would I be doing that? 'I am thinking that you are,' says he, 'or else it is my comrades you are mocking'...and he shoves me again."

Ciaran winced as Tilly touched his right eye with a wet cloth. "Merciful God, have a care girl. It is that sore that I am."

"Not half so sore as you will be tomorrow," Tom Fergus said.

"Mmm." Ciaran sank back on the pillow. "You must go easy Tilly girl, and me a broken man all together."

Tom Fergus snorted. "You've time enough for that, man, when you have told it all."

"There is scarce more to tell, for it went quickly after that. I have no quarrel with you man, says I.

" 'More like you have no belly for a quarrel and all,' says the first fellow. Then he takes Tilly by the arm. 'You will not drink with a coward such as himself, when there is heroes all around have need of your comfort,' he says.

"So...didn't I tell him to let the girl be? But he has his hands on her now. Rough he was and all. And so I hit him."

"You hit a one-armed man?"

"Ach, no. I mind it were one of the others. I took him on the chin, I did."

"But it were you that threw the first punch?"

Ciaran thought for a moment. "Could be that it was...maybe."

"Well, wasn't I right, then? You are that big a fool and all."

Ciaran laughed. "Ah, it were a right good barney, and didn't I do some damage myself?"

"How would I know that, when it was yourself was carried out, and you bloody all together?"

"You did, darlin'," Tilly said. "You gave them what for, blow for blow, until that one-armed devil of a fellow grabbed onto you from behind. Then, I was that scared, I will tell you, for weren't they after making a corpse of you. And such a good-lookin' blue-eyed fellow as yourself and all." She patted his hand.

Tom Fergus rolled his eyes heavenward. "If you be fit enough, man, we best be on our way. It is night already and the town full of fiddlers and singers and such, and them all wanting a place to sleep."

Ciaran groaned noisily.

"Ah, the poor man," Tilly said. "You must not make him wander the town and him in such a parlous condition. You are welcome to stay dearie, and I will give you comfort...for didn't you save me from that rowdy lot and all?"

Tom Fergus shrugged. "You must please yourself, man. But mind you meet the morning boat. I've not the stomach to face your Mam without you."

When Tom Fergus had gone, Tilly sat on the bed and toyed with Ciaran's hair. "Now," she said, "I'd be guessin' that you've come to your senses at last." Her voice had a gravely catch. He remembered it was the sound that had first drawn him to her in the tavern. He sighed.

"Are you still dizzy in your head, darlin' ?"

"No...I am not."

"Do you not care for me at all?"

"Aye and I do...Of course I like you girl. And why wouldn't I?"

"I don't know. What is it then? Sure and you've got a heart in there." She put her ear to his chest. When she laughed, he felt warm gusts of breath in his hair.

"Ah, Tilly," he said. "My mouth is that sore. I fear I am not much use for kissin'."

By now her hand had vanished under the covers and was wandering down his belly to his groin. "Is that all that is troubling you, sweetheart? Myself, I think you are well lively enough for a bit of fun. And do you think it is your kissin' I am after?"

∞

They crossed with the morning post. Tom Fergus had slept in a byre. He was sullen and he spent most of the voyage picking bits of straw from his clothes and hair.

"You may wipe that grin from your face," he said, "for there are some of us who canna buy a soft night for the price of a smile and a wink."

"Tom Fergus, you must learn to be more contented."

"And how must I do that?"

"Ah man, it is more easy than you know. You see, you must enjoy what is given, *when* it is given you. For isn't the day soft and all, the sunlight at play on the water and nary a swell on the sea?"

"It is the tongue lashing I will suffer for your sake that I am thinking of."

"For that, I am truly sorry. But you know, a woman's tongue is a paltry weapon and all and I'm thinking you will likely live to see another day."

"Could be you are right." Tom Fergus laughed and Ciaran knew there was peace between them. He listened to the slap of the oars and the argument of the gulls.

In mid channel, a pair of seals came alongside. They circled the boat, diving, then surfacing and rolling onto their backs. Tiring of the game, they soon swam off together, toward their basking rocks on the western end. Ciaran watched them until they disappeared. He closed his eyes and dove with them, breaking the thin membrane of cold between the water and the air. Weightless and warm. The slanting rays of sunlight cut like threads of honey through a world of green skies and silence.

It was always the silence that broke the spell and brought him back to his senses, for Ciaran lived in a singing world. He could not long tolerate the deathlike emptiness of silence. Gasping, he opened his eyes and was, at once, refreshed by wind song and water music.

Flora poured a bowl of soup and set it on the table before him. She sat in her chair by the window and took up her knitting.

"You are home at last," she said when he came through the door. "Well, God be praised for that. You'll be wanting your broth I suppose."

She had said nothing since.

He listened to the wooden needles click and shifted uncomfortably. She would have her say, soon or late, and he wanted to be done with it. But she would not be hurried.

"I'm thinking to climb Ruecallen before the tide returns," he said.

"Oh aye?"

"Mickey Joe was only just saying that the sea is all afloat with bits of the Drake. Could be some useful thing has washed into the tide cave below."

"Could be."

"Maybe I will see if Bertie will tend the ropes. Or else, I will take the mare."

"Mmm."

He knew she was angry for she was not even singing in the way that she did when she knitted, the tune that told the stitches.

"Have you no words for me, Mam?" he said at last.

"And what words would those be? You are a man grown. And though you are my son and all, if you will be as much a fool as the rest of them when you've a bit of drink in you, it is beyond my words to change you."

"It were not the drink and all. Did Bertie not tell you?"

"You must not credit Bertie for a good liar...nor me for a fool enough to believe him. And when ever have you come home from the *Feis* without a blackened eye or a blooded nose? Your Grand-Da was the same. I am only glad that you have come home alive at all, for you would not hear me that times have changed."

"They have that."

"So now you know."

CHAPTER EIGHTEEN

The MacNamara

"Give us another...give us another...*please* Ciaran."

"Soon...soon...First you must all settle down."

Four of Tom Fergus's brood huddled against Ciaran. Bridget and Padraic, the twins, clung to his legs. Two-year-old Jimmy drowsed against his shoulder. Tommy, as close as his nine-year-old's dignity would allow, poked the fire with a stick. Mary Catherine, at ten the eldest, helped her mother tidy the kitchen, stopping, from time to time, to listen.

A killing gale, with January snow on its back, beat against the windows, but inside, the cottage was warm and peaty. Tom Fergus knocked his white clay pipe against the hearthstone. "Myself, I'm thinkin' we got her roofed in the nick of time," he said. They had spent the day finishing the lean-to that would make room for Tom Fergus's still growing family. Cathleen was heavy with their sixth.

"Aye," Ciaran said. "That we did." He closed his eyes and rested his cheek against Jimmy's baby-fine hair. His arms and shoulders still held the pleasant ache of hard work.

Padraic tugged Ciaran's trouser leg. "I havna' had me turn at all," he wheedled.

"Enough," Cathleen said. She mopped the table with a damp cloth, stopping now and again to scrape at a stubborn bit with her fingernail. "Your Da and Ciaran have earned themselves a bit of quiet, and it is time you were in your beds."

"Aw, please Mam...I havna' had me turn. Give us the *Big Black Dog* Ciaran; tell us that one."

Cathleen paused at her work. "It is too late to be goin' on with devil stories the likes of that one," she said, "and the wind tearing down the hills lookin' for souls. You'll not get a minute's sleep with fears."

"But I havna' had me turn..."

"You'll have your turn soon enough," Cathleen said. "Poor Ciaran will be runnin' out of stories with all this clamouring for more."

"It is all right Cathleen," Ciaran said. "Come, rest yourself a while and I will tell them one other."

"Just one is all," she yielded, "while I ease my feet...and then it is off to bed, the lot of you." She pulled up a stool next to Tom Fergus. Mary Catherine settled on the floor beside her.

"So now, Padraic lad, what kind of a story are you wanting?"

"The cat that was the devil."

Ciaran laughed. "No, your Mam is right," he said. "Do you want to be fillin' your head with fearsome dreams and it near bedtime itself?"

"Aye, I do and all."

"No," Ciaran said. "You must have a care for wee Jimmy and your sisters for they are not as big and as brave as you are."

"A true one then."

"Do you think that I would tell you one that was not?"

Tom Fergus chuckled and winked at Ciaran.

"Could be I mind a good one, that my Grand-Da used to be tellin' us of a winter's night. Do you know of Mary Keenan and her *currach*?"

"It is a story for girls you're after tellin' me," Padraic scowled.

"Ah, but it is not. It is a story about Rathlin itself and the people who do be livin' here to this very day."

"Is it a true one and all?"

"As I am setting here beside you myself. The truth and all."

"And are there wee folk in it?"

"Padraic, lad, how will you know if you will not keep still and listen?"

Ciaran waited while Bridget and Padraic arranged themselves against his legs. Then he began.

"It were a long time ago, so long that no one livin' minds her still, that Mary Keenan lived in Rathlin with her Mam and Da and brothers and sisters. Just like yourself. And they lived right here abouts, up to Kinramher way.

"Now, this Mary, she had a *currach* of her very own. And in it she went round the island, to gather the sea plants and mushrooms that grow in cool dark places at the bottoms of the cliffs...for you see, her Mam, that was a handywoman, had the need of such things."

"All by herself, she went?" Bridget said.

"Aye, that she did, for she were powerful brave herself...and her Da made her the currach from wicker and calico and tar, in the old way."

"Me Da made me a wee one the likes of that for the model races at Ushet," Padraic said.

"I mind he did...for didn't I help him make it and all? But Mary Keenan's *currach* was never a plaything. It were a proper boat for going over the water... Of course, she only ever went in it when the seas were quiet with no shores on them at all.

"Well, one fine day...I mind it were near midsummer or could be it were in the Lammas tides that rise in August... this Mary is after gathering sea plants, as always. But while she's about it, a swell comes upon the shingle and sweeps her *currach* right away...and there's poor Mary Keenan, left all alone on the rocks by Altachuile." Ciaran paused.

"Me Da says it is the tallest place, four hundred feet and more, with no way there but by the sea." Tommy, as the oldest boy, collected facts and liked to show them off.

"Does he now? Aye, it is a fearsome high place and all. But it can be climbed by them that knows the way. Myself I done it more than once. Bertie and me together."

Cathleen clucked her tongue.

"But Mary, she were not a climber like myself. So, there was nothing for it but to scramble to a dry place and wait to see what might happen next. So, it was all right, and three whole days and nights she waited."

"Did they not look for her?" said Bridget.

"Aye, they did. Her father and her brothers too. But on the second night, her *currach* floated into the harbour without her. And in them days, the people used to say, 'If the sea demands it, you must let it go.' So after that they weren't lookin' for poor Mary anymore."

"Why?"

"Well, wasn't it what they believed and all? That if the sea were after having something, or someone, and they took it back, then it would be changed

183

altogether. So, if a man were peaceful and gentle and him near drowned, then after, he would be quarrelsome and fierce. Such like was what the folk believed, you see."

"Was she not afraid?"

"Not first off, she were not, for didn't I tell you that Mary Keenan was a brave lass? So, it was all right and wasn't it a bit of an adventure and all? In the day she's eating sea weeds and limpets from the rocks and drinking water from a freshet spring that's runnin' down the cliffs. But come the third night, it were powerful cold...and she's missing her Mam and Da, her sisters and her brothers and all. That night she wept and sobbed the like would break your heart to hear, until she fell asleep."

Ciaran paused and cleared his throat. The chiming clock, in its pride of place on the mantle, struck eight. Cathleen stood up. "Ach, isn't it long past bedtime," she said, "and the lot of you nodding off already. Tomorrow will be time enough for the ending."

This was greeted with a universal chorus of protests. *Aw Mam, please Mam, it is the best part, Ciaran hasna' finished me turn.* Cathleen looked to Tom Fergus for help that was not forthcoming.

"Bring us the jug and some glasses," he said, "We've need of a wee drop to warm us. And then they may have the ending; for a story once begun must be finished, do you not see that woman?"

"All right. But into your night shirts, first, all of you. And mind you wash your faces. Behind your ears and all, Padraic!

"Well, here is one who'll not complain over bedtime," she said as she lifted Jimmy from Ciaran's arms. Tom Fergus watched him stroke the sleeping child's head. He poured two glasses of fiery, white liquor. "It is time you were makin' a few of your own," he smiled.

"Maybe...maybe."

Behind them, at the basin, the children finished their washing amid a commotion of splashing and squealing. Once again, they gathered between the two men.

"Did you keep mind of where I was, Padraic?"

"She was bawlin' and shiverin' on the rocks, and missin' her Mam and Da."

"Ah, right, that would be the place. So, it was all right, and fast asleep she goes. But when she wakes, well isn't she warm and snug and all? For she's wrapped in a sealskin...'Now where at all did this come from?' says she, 'and me all alone on the rocks?' Ah, it were lovely. All soft and deep and furry it was. Did you ever put your hand on such a thing, Bridget, the skin from off a seal?"

"Ach...no." Bridget wrinkled her nose.

"I did and all, for my Grand-Da took one from a drowned creature that my Mam had for an apron when I was wee like yourselves."

"A seal canna be drownded and it swimmin' with the fishes," Padraic snorted.

"Aye they can," said Tommy. "Just like ourselves they are, for the needin' of air to breathe. Where did Mary's come from, Ciaran?"

"Wait now and you will hear. 'Where at all is this lovely thing coming from?' says Mary Keenan...and she opens her eyes and sees, right there on the rocks beside her, the handsomest fellow she'd ever chanced to gaze upon. It put the heart across her to look on him and, straight away, she fell in love."

"What did he look like?" Mary Catherine said.

"You must picture him in your mind's eye, girl, for my words cannot describe him, such a fine lookin' fellow he was. 'Who are you?' says Mary Keenan, 'and where is it that you are comin' from?'

" 'I heard you weepin', Mary Keenan,' says he, '...and drinkin' from my freshet spring. And now you must come with me, for haven't you stole my heart and all?'

"Well, didn't she commence to weeping and wailing all over again. 'I cannot leave me Mam and Da,' says she, ' and me only a bit of a girl. But sure you have took my heart...How ever can I choose at all?'

" 'Now Mary Keenan,' says he, 'I will not have you weepin' on my account, for haven't I waited long enough to find you? And I can wait till you are a woman grown. You have my promise given, that I will come again. Now give me back my coat and climb upon my back,' says he, ' and I will bring you safe home.'

"So Mary Keenan gives him back his coat of fur and well maybe she blinked her eye, for when she looks again, isn't there a shining young seal up there on the rocks beside her. She's wondering, herself, wherever has that handsome young fellow gone to when the seal speaks to her as clear as can be. 'Climb on, Mary Keenan,' says he, 'and we'll be away.'...and so, she done it."

Bridget sighed. "He was a selkie."

"Could be that you are right, for wasn't he magic and all."

"Did he take her home straight away?"

"Aye. Right back to her Mam and Da and brothers and sisters, safe and dry. You can imagine, they were that pleased and surprised to see her. But when she tells them how she's come to be saved, her Mam was sore annoyed. You see, she had the knowing of magical creatures, because she was a handywoman. 'No good will come of this,' says she, 'for that sort will be wanting its payment, one way and another.' "

"Why?" said Tommy.

"Well, there's them that believes it is a curse to be favoured by the faery folk and them with no loyalty or sense of mortal cares but all them spells and powers just the same."

"But he promised to come back," said Bridget.

"That he did...but who can know the truth of their sort? For aren't they fickle and them glamouring themselves into any shape that takes their fancy."

While the children considered this, Ciaran pulled off his boots, hung his damp socks by the fire and slipped his feet back into the boots. "The fire will warm them," he said,"...the way they'll comfort my toes for the journey home."

"Will you comfort your belly with another of these?" Tom Fergus said, lifting the jug.

"Could be that I might. But a wee one only, for the ride home and all. Would yous be wanting a song before I go?"

"But you havna' told the ending," Padraic squealed.

"Did he come back? You must say, Ciaran...*please*," said Bridget.

Tommy and Mary Catherine, being older and wiser, held their tongues. Ciaran's stories always had endings.

"Well of course he did for didn't he promise that he would, in the time that Mary Keenan had grown to be a young woman with a fine look about her so that all the lads were courting her and all. He came a stranger, from a ship that was wrecked on the rocks by Altachuile, and him, only, alive to tell of it. He were fit and strong, though he were but small. Full of songs and stories he was, enough to charm them all who met him...and Mary Keenan herself...all over again."

"Didn't she know him straight off?"

"Sure and she did. But this Mary Keenan had her pick of fellows, now she was grown into a beauty. So he went about his wooing of her and soon enough they went to the priest to be married.

186

"So, it was all right, you know. And didn't they build themselves a little house, over by St. Bridget's Well. It is standing still, though no one lives there anymore. And by and by, their children come, boys and girls, one after the other. And they all took his special name, MacNamara, that was Mac Con Mara in olden times."

"Did the selkie take the wee'uns to the sea?" said Bridget.

"You must not run before me, for isn't it my own story I am tellin' and I will tell it in the way that it goes."

"But did he?" Padraic said.

"By and by you will know."

Ciaran went to the window and stretched. "I am that weary in my bones," he said. "It is a desperate storm tonight. I'm thinking I best be goin' or I'll not fall in with the path for all the snow and wind."

Tom Fergus winked and the children knew Ciaran was toying with them. "Did you wash all them potatoes from behind your ears, Padraic lad?" Ciaran said. Padraic nodded his head vigorously.

"I suppose a wee while longer then won't make the devil's difference, and the mare not troubled by a bit of snow." He sat on the edge of the table staring past them all into the fire.

"So," he continued, "they lived a happy life, Mary Keenan and her MacNamara and their brood. Three sons, fine and dark, they had and two blue eyed girls and all. In the tenth year, MacNamara says to Mary, 'It is long past time I was goin' woman and that sorry I am to say it, for haven't you been a good wife to me and all. But I am aching for my home now so I must leave you. And you know, Mary, that it is my sons must come wi' me.' "

The children grinned and poked each other.

"Well can you imagine it?...Poor Mary, she was annoyed to distraction. Destroyed she was with the news...to lose her handsome MacNamara and her sons as well. Oceans of tears she wept, so that she near broke his heart and didn't he relent at last, in the end."

"He didn't take the wee'uns?"

"No, he did not. 'Ah Mary,' says he, 'don't I love you truly, and I would not see you in misery. The bairns may stay. But we must make a pact between us, for that is the way of it, and it is you must come with me.' "

" ' But how will they live, and them only wee?' says Mary...So the selkie told her that when they were grown into strong men and women, he would come to take her to his home beneath the sea and there they would live forever. Now he gave her a token of the bond between them. 'You must keep this safe,' says he, 'and when the time is come, you must throw it in the sea, by Altachuile...in the place where first we met...and it will be a signal between us. Then I will come.' "

"What was it at all?"

"What was what?"

"The token, that he was after givin' her?"

"Well, it were some precious thing, you can be sure of it."

Bridget was not satisfied. "But what was it, itself," she demanded.

"I canna be sure I mind it, for wasn't I but wee when my Grand-Da told me."

"Ach, Ciaran!"

It is the way of secrets that they are forever wanting to be told. Truly, he could not remember whether his Grand-Da had described the magic gift at all. Perhaps it was only his desire to satisfy the curious child that now inspired him. But as he said, "It were a jewel I suppose," he felt an irresistible desire to say more. "I have it in my head it were a necklace. Aye, that was it, a necklace of gold, the like she had never seen. Fat beads it was made of, shaped in knots of rope they were." The rush of words left him so breathless and light-headed he had to collect himself to continue.

" 'You must throw it in the sea,' says he, 'and I will come. This our bargain, Mary, and if you do not keep it, the sea itself will rise to claim my sons.' So she promised. Then he took his beautiful fur coat and he was gone.

"Well Mary did as she was told. She hid the golden collar in a chest under the linens. And after a while, when all the children were big and fit, she knew that it was time, so she went to find the treasure. But when she looked for it, under the linens, it was vanished altogether."

"Where did it go?"

"I'm getting to that part. Did I tell you Mary's mother was a handywoman?"

"You did."

"Well, she had the knowin' of all secret spells and such like. One day, when she was snooping and prying about the house...for that was the sort she was... she found the necklace. Of course, she knew at once just what it was. So she took it to a special field and buried it in the ground where no one would ever think to look for it.

188

"Poor Mary was beside herself. She searched the house, high and low, in every nook and cranny. But there was never a sign of it to be found. She went in her *currach*, that was old now but sound with it, for in them days that was how they made them, and she went to the rocks by Altachuile. Day after day she went, and her sitting on the rocks and calling out his name. But there was never a bit of a word of him. Not ever again."

Ciaran stopped. He closed his eyes and let his head fall back. Finally, Mary Catherine, who had remained quiet through most of the telling, spoke. "What happened to them?"

"Didn't she die of a broken heart and all, and him still waiting for her in the cold, dark sea?"

"Still?"

"Oh aye. You may listen for him, his pitiful, lonely cry, at midsummer or in the Lammas tides or when the fog is heavy and cold; for sure she was the true love of his life and he is the promise unbroken that can never rest without he finds her."

Wind scoured the cottage, shuddered the chimney and hissed in the licking flames. Tommy pushed a fresh sod into the heart of the fire. It was he who broke the spell.

"It were a good story, Ciaran," he said, "but it canna be a true one at all."

"So you may say, but I will tell you that there is always truth in stories, every one. And there is MacNamaras on this island livin' who would not step into the sea at all, to this very day, for fear himself will come to claim them. Why, doesn't the name mean *son of the sea* and all? My Grand-Da's mam was a MacNamara itself. And every one of us, of that ilk, still walk with the mark of the sea hound upon us. I will show you."

Tom Fergus and Cathleen exchanged grins as Ciaran wriggled out of his boot. When he spread his bare toes, a thin web of skin seemed to stretch between them, but he jammed his foot back into his boot so quickly that the children were not sure what they had seen.

"Show us again."

"....again Ciaran."

"I didna see..."

Ciaran savoured the commotion, enjoying, in particular, the gasps of the ever sceptical Tommy.

"That is enough for now," he said. "You best be getting to your beds, or, if I know your Mam at all, there will be the devil to pay."

CHAPTER NINETEEN

Flora

She fed the seals. After she cured the mackerel, she filled a bucket with the guts and trimmings for the seals. If a catch had been good, she threw in a wheen of *glashins* or a few *lythe*.

When he was a boy, she took him with her. "You must share with them when there is plenty," she said, "for isn't it themselves are after warning the fishermen of the storms and fogs with their merciful cries."

They would stand at the top of the path until they were seen; *waitin' for the welcome*, his mother called it. First a solitary creature would appear, perhaps a hundred yards from the beach. It would rise, head and shoulders from the water, then roll and dive. When next it surfaced, it would be surrounded by five or six companions. Once Ciaran had counted eleven.

"It is their nature...they are *made* curious," Flora said. "Come on then... hurry up now. They will be wanting to see what we have got for them." Together, they would scramble down the scree to the shingle beside Cooraghy Bay. By the time they reached the beach, the young ones would be splashing in the shallows, too timid to come ashore, too greedy to swim away.

In summer, after a spell of dry weather, she would give him a wee pail and send him to gather lumps of crystal salt from the leathery wrack. He preferred to sit beside her watching them, their faces childlike and wise both together, while she coaxed them onto the beach with wordless song.

It was hard to believe there were those who would shoot the seals for little more than sport. But Ciaran had heard such stories. Tommy Kiernan knew a man on Arran who killed a seal by accident. "He was only after scarin' it away from the nets, you see," Tommy said. "But I mind he never had a bit of luck on land or sea ever after." Once, at the Lammas Fair, Ciaran had seen a Scotsman wearing a sealskin waistcoat. "Aye, they do be killing them in those parts...for they say they steal the salmon that are after coming home to spawn," Bertie explained.

"I am destroyed with the hearin' of such things," said Flora. "For aren't they but harmless and wantin' to trust us? Well, more fools them, is what I say... for you know it is the truth that when they do not come, the fishes do not come neither."

There were one or two would take the fish right out of her hand; and an old grey spotted bull that let her touch him from time to time. Flora would never admit to this, nor speak of it at all, but Ciaran had seen it happen, more than once, when he was climbing.

He had feared for her life the first time, him perched on the face and helpless, two hundred feet and more above the beach. Even from that height, he had recognised the big, scarred scrapper that people called *The Pirate* for his one pale eye that was likely blind. He had shouted to her, but his warning dissipated, shredded in a flapping shriek of guillemots and gulls. He watched, amazed, as his mother offered the massive beast her hand.

The Pirate swayed and rippled up the beach, stopping just beyond Flora's reach. He stretched forward to sniff at her, in the way that a dog will do. He shuffled a bit closer and, again just like a dog and it wanting to be stroked, he bowed his head and raised it into her open palm. Ciaran could see that his mother was not afraid, that she was talking to the creature as she patted it and scratched its whiskery face. Then, with a grace that belied his bulk, The Pirate rested his enormous head in Flora's lap.

Later, when he asked her, she denied the truth that he had seen with his own eyes.

"Is it The Pirate himself that you have tamed, Mam?"

"The Pirate? Ach, don't be daft."

"But I seen him with you, from the cliffs, and him gentle as a baby he was."

"Gentle as a baby? The Pirate?" She laughed. "Ah son, I'm thinking you best take care when you are up there in the sky, for it seems to me you are become as giddy and as lightheaded as the birds you are after chasing."

"But Mam..."

"You may fetch me some water, if you are wantin' your tea."

Mary McQuaid, that was Tommy Kiernan's sister, said it could have happened as he saw it. "Didn't we used to joke with her and call her *Flora-who-charmed-the-seals* for the way that they would come to hear her singin'...when we was girls together and workin' at the kelp."

"And who was it alive at all, in them days that she didn't charm ?" said Fergus McQuaid.

"Well, thank you very much," Mary laughed. "It is a lucky thing for you I am not an envious woman to hear you goin' on so."

"Ach Mary, don't talk foolish. It were a long time ago. And didn't I marry *you* and all? But it were true all the same. Your Mam was a beauty...and sweet natured with it. She could have had any man." He smiled with the memory of it.

"Was there no one special at all?" Ciaran asked.

"Ach, they was all of them that tried," Mary said. "Doin' chores for your Grand-Da and waitin' for their turn at the dances. Bertie was the worst of them for showin' off on the cliffs."

Mary hung the kettle over the fire and stirred the embers. "We used to say that none of us Rathlin girls would find a man until Flora made her choice," she said. "I mind there was even a traveller from Donegal who made a poem about her and all. But the wonder of it is, she never did...choose, you see. And there were plenty would have had her, even after..."

Fergus cleared his throat and stood. "I'll not be stayin' for tea," he said, "for there's work to be done. You tell your Mam, when she wakes, that I was askin' after her health."

When he was gone, Mary made the tea and a bowl of oaten porridge for Flora. "Could be your Mam will eat something now," she said, and she left him alone to think by the fire.

Winter had followed winter; safe islanded years, protected from the anarchy in Ireland by the certainties of ploughing and sowing and harvesting, lambing and calving, the mending of nets and the tarring of hulls, thatching, shearing, fishing, climbing. They were hard times, after the war, with a man's own work earning him little but more of the same. The landlords had gone, but with them had gone the kelp burning and the money that it brought. Sometimes Ciaran thought about his treasure and the easier life that it might buy. But when he took it from its hiding place and held it in his hands, all such thoughts fled away. There was a rightness and a rhythm to the life he knew and the beautiful golden beads were not yet a part of that story.

His Grand-Da Donal used to say there were all kinds of stories. There were stories heard and stories told, stories that you made and stories that you learned, stories new and stories known. "There is the story that you must share and the story that you must keep all to yourself."

"What is that story, Grand-Da?"

"That is a special one, lad. It is the story that you live...the one that you are."

"Who will tell me that story, Grand-Da? Will it be you?"

"Ach, I cannot. No one can tell you that story, not even a one who loves you like myself or your Mam. You cannot look for it at all; for you see, that is the story must find *you*. And when it does, you will know that it is yours."

So, he had farmed and fished and climbed. He had played his fiddle and kissed the girls who let him. Until, one by one, all the pretty island girls had married island men or had left to find husbands in Ireland and America.

The world did not stand still. It was 1924 and he was thirty-five years old, still fit and strong though years of toil were carved on his fine face. And while he waited for the story still hidden in his treasure, another one, a story that finds everyone, found Ciaran.

Every year, from December to February, Flora suffered from asthma and the coughing fever that afflicted so many on the island. When it was bad, Ciaran moved her into his room, away from the peaty smoke of the kitchen, and Mary came to look after her. Though Flora had taught Ciaran many homely skills, she was too proud to let him help her do her private, womanish things. And Mary knew cures, from herbs and plants, that the Kiernan's had got off a French doctor that had stopped with them after a shipwreck. Now, she stirred docken seed and bog bane into boiling milk.

"She says I'm after poisoning her with the likes of this."

"It is a desperate stink, that brew you are cookin', Mary."

"That is the goodness of it. Muddle it with some sugar and mind she drinks it all before night."

Ciaran listened to the wind and the thunder of the whirlpool *Slough na morra*. From east and west, the tides were fighting to possess the Sound. At this time of the year, when all of nature seemed at strife, it was all a man could do to cling to God. He sighed.

"You mustn't fret. The fever is passed and she will be right as rain by mornin'."

"I have never seen her to be so peaky and frail..."

"You've not been lookin' to see, for she was ever a wee bit of a thing, your Mam."

"...and she is talkin' foolishness."

"Oh aye?"

"She has made me promise that we will take her to the churchyard in the boat. 'I'll not be bouncin' and scramblin' over them rocky roads to my bed,' is what she said."

Mary laughed. "She is thinking on poor Donal, God rest him, and how it was the wheel broke when we was followin' his cart to the graveyard. Do you not remember? It is only natural that she will be thinkin' on such things for she is old now. Ach, so aren't we all, our lot."

Ciaran nodded and shivered.

"Don't you be takin' on so," Mary said. "Your Mam will have a brave few springtimes yet. She'll likely live to see a grandson if you would but stir yourself."

"Ah, Mary. If it were as easy as that."

"Well, myself, I'm thinking that it is not so hard as young men nowadays are makin' it to be." She shook her head. "You are your mother's son and that's the truth."

When Mary had gone, he opened the bedroom door a crack and listened, guilty, to his mother's ragged, breathless sleep. Later, he told her he was thinking to go courting at the Lammas Fair, come August. "It is maybe time I got me a woman to help you, Mam."

"And is that what you think a wife is for, then? You may just as well bring me a hire girl from the fair if *that* is what you are wantin'."

"Could be I'm wantin' some wee'un's and all."

"Ah..."

Mary was only partly right. It was true that Flora was up and about in days. But with the April rains, she took to her bed again, the dampness sitting heavy on her chest. Mary came to stay and Bertie visited every day, bringing news from the village, bunches of purple field orchids, some oranges he had rowed out to a steamer to get.

She asked for Ciaran to sit with her.

"Will you play for me?"

"Aye, Mam. Is it an old tune or a new one that you are wantin'?"

"I am wantin' one that will bring the laughin' back into this room for the both of you are surely miseries to look on."

Ciaran raised his fiddle, the bow poised over the strings. Then he put it down again.

"Play some jigs," Bertie coaxed gently, "...the like we used to have when we was dancing-in the floor of a new-made house."

So he played *The Admiral's Jig* and *Crowley's Reel, Up and About* and *Butter and Calves*. Flora smiled when Bertie shocked Mary with all the rude verses he remembered of *The Foggy, Foggy Dew*.

"You best leave her get some sleep now," Mary said, but Flora snatched at Ciaran's hand and held it tight.

"I will have my son with me," she said.

They left and closed the door behind them.

"Play your Grand-Da's tune...the one he was after sayin' he got off a *sidhe* woman."

"Do you think he did, Mam? Do you think he played for the faery folk?"

"Maybe it was in his dreams they came, for didn't he believe that they did; and they do say that their sort are partial for musicians. Have you not dreamed such dreams yourself?"

Ciaran thought of his waking dreams; of the music that came into his fingers and him walking all alone on the path, of the woman in white who had saved him on the cliffs those many years ago. He had never told Flora these things and he did not want to frighten her with such stories now.

"No Mam, I have not," he said.

A spasm of coughing ripped through her. He held her, sitting up, until it passed. Her frightened eyes, blazing blue as his own against the paper white of her skin, darted about the room.

"Play for me," she said, "for it is quiet and dark and I would have music."

He played, his eyes closed to stop the tears, until she slept easy.

Just before dawn, Mary woke him. "Your Mam is took very poorly," she said. "You must fetch the priest. You best bring Bertie and all."

∞

The sun was cruel hard when they rowed her to the churchyard, turning the sea autumn black though it was nearly May. Bertie and Tommy handled the oars while Ciaran sat astern, his left hand resting on the coffin. When they rounded the point into Cooraghy, two seals came alongside and swam with them all the way across the bay. Just before the mouth of Church Bay, a pod of seals slid into the sea off the sands of *Locknakilly*. They troubled the water around the boat. Bertie and Tommy tried to nudge them away with the oars but Ciaran said, "Leave them be."

"Aye," said Bertie. "Perhaps it is meant to be."

They raised the oars and let the incoming tide carry the shallow-drawn boat over *Clachan Bo* and into the harbour.

Near dusk. The house was crowded with visitors. Most of the islanders had called to pay their respects and, it seemed to Ciaran, most had stayed. Platters of food were consumed and replenished. Quantities of whiskey and poteen disappeared. And as they feasted Death away, a kind of life crept back into the corners, where men talked fishing and fields and scrambling children shrieked with laughter.

Throughout the day, a shield of insensibility had protected Ciaran from the pain of so much consolation. He walked where he was meant to walk because the path came up to meet his feet. He said the prayers and greetings that came automatically to his lips, read the ones that were put before him. Men and women clapped him on the shoulder, embraced him, shook his hand. He was numb and blind to the fear in their eyes.

But now, there was talk of music and games. Someone brought out a tin whistle and Ciaran needed to be in a quieter place.

Bertie had little trouble finding him after a while on the flat rock beside the beach where he went to think. They sat together, in silence, watching the shore emerge from the ebbing tide. A pair of white gulls courted, snowflakes against the darkling sky.

"Do you not feel her still, Bertie?"

"Aye, maybe...for she'll be wantin' to give you comfort, like always. But you must let her go now. She had that hard a life and she has earned her rest."

Ciaran picked up a pebble to throw in the sea. Its barnacled crust reminded him of the treasure. Engulfed by a wave of remorse, he pressed his fist around it.

"It was a hard life and all and I wasna' much of a son to her...Could be I might have made it easy."

"Ach, don't be daft. It is a hard life for all of us, else how at all would we be wantin' heaven? You were a good son. She couldna' wished for better, and so she told me more than once, herself."

Ciaran looked at Bertie. In the half-light his eyes were nearly black.

"Will you tell me something truly?"

"...I will try."

"Why did you never marry?"

Bertie smiled. "She wouldna' have me, son."

"My Mam?"

"Aye. She were a powerful lass in them days. Stubborn as a man, she was."

Ciaran searched the older man's face. Then he turned away and stood, his back to Bertie.

"Bertie," he whispered, "...are you my Da?"

"...Haven't I loved you like a son, all your days?"

"Are you? my Da?"

The heartbeating sea counted them towards the night. Ciaran, his eyes closed, heard Bertie pacing the shingle.

"Did she never say?" Bertie said.

Ciaran shook his head. He wandered into the past, where the men of the *clachan* heave the boat onto the shingle. There is great excitement, for haven't they been to the fair at Ballycastle and sure they will have presents for everyone. Tom Fergus spots them first, rowing in the middle of the Sound. Now the children are gathered on the shore, their mothers watching from the path above. There is Mickey Joe's Bridget and Johnny Mike, Annie McQuaid and the Kiernan twins, Diarmud and Cathal. They throw themselves at their fathers, who are laden with packages, coloured paper sacks and boxes tied with string. And isn't it Bertie who has the most of all? But Ciaran hangs back for his Mam has said he mustn't be greedy of Bertie's kindness.

"Ciaran lad, what is keepin' you? Are you not glad to see your Da Bertie and him come home from the fair itself?" Bertie lifts him and swings him around. "Oof...you are gettin' too big for this, eh lad. Come on then. Lets us find your Mam and see what is hid in these parcels of mine."

There's a red gum ball and a stripey bag of sticky sweet *yellow man* and, best of all, a penny bank with a tinker and a horse. For his Mam, there's chocolate in a pretty tin and a wee china dog with a real red ribbon tied round its neck.

"Ach Bertie...it is too much. You shouldna' done it," Flora says.

Bertie winks at Ciaran. "Do not be frettin' yourself woman. Didn't I win most of this lot at the games and all?"

The chattering procession of families snakes up west along the lane, the children lagging behind, admiring each other's booty. Noisy goodbyes send clusters of adults and children to their own home paths.

"I've a jug for Donal, Flora, will take the miseries off of his bones." They have stopped at the fork by the stone wall that separates their houses.

"He will be pleased to have it, for isn't he roaring since the change in the weather."

"Will you come hear me play, Bertie? Me Grand-Da is after teaching me a faery song."

"Tomorrow, son. I am that tired and in need of my bed."

They go their separate ways.

"Why does not a Da come home with us?" Ciaran asks.

"Your Da cannot live with us. It is not in his nature," Flora says. "But he loves you in his way, child and he is never far away."

"Is me Da in heaven, then?"

He felt Bertie's hand on his back. "Tell me Bertie...is it you?"

"Many's the time I wisht it was," Bertie said. "I loved your Mam. I truly did. But I was never with her in that way."

Ciaran bowed his head. He worked his fists in an effort of control, but when he spoke, emotion choked him.

"You were so good to us, Bertie. Ah, didn't I always hope that you...that she..."

"She didna' want for love, son, nor you neither...not then nor now."

The two men embraced.

A few hundred yards up the shore was Flora's rocky seat. There, by the *frassing hole*, the place where anglers, in olden times, lured the fish with limpets and bits of potato, she used to sit and feed the seals. It was there on St. John's Eve, that was midsummer night, she used to watch the western horizon consume the longest day while, behind her, bonfires blazed the hills.

While they grieved in silence, side by side, a light, seeming to rise from the rocks themselves, gilded the spot. And there was music. The voices of pipes and fiddles shot like shining threads across the fabric of evening. Ciaran held his breath and Bertie stiffened, listening to the music grow louder and nearer. The moving light lit the sky; it tipped the sea chop. The stone-built groyne that held their wee landing place was a dark silhouette against the glow.

Then, the *Barra*, the excursion steamer that plied the Western Isles, hove into view. Her decks were newly lined with electrical bulbs. Strings of them swung between her stacks, casting beads of light, a golden necklace, all around her on the sea. And she was trailing wisps and tendrils of Highland music.

"Well, isn't she a sight," Bertie laughed. They both breathed easier. "Come back to the house now. They're all wantin' to cheer you."

"I know...In a wee while."

"Dinna be long. It will be full night soon and if you catch a chill I'll not be hearin' the end of it from Mary and the rest."

When Bertie was gone, Ciaran settled on his flat rock, pulled his knees against his chest and wrapped his arms around them. For the first time in his life, he felt lonely. Above him, in the house, people who had known him always were wanting to help him. The women were likely already making their plans for how they would do it. And there he sat, staring at the phosphorescent sea, seeing nothing at all. Perhaps he closed his eyes.

He is moaning. A plaintive, animal sound, unbidden and uncontrolled, pours from the darkness inside him, as if his body is a pipe for someone else's music. He holds himself and rocks back and forth, a child's comfort for a man who can never be a child again.

Another voice has joined him. Sweet, unearthly. It lifts his rolling moans into a song. His mother's wordless music that she crooned to charm the seals. The *sidhe* woman dances on Flora's seat. Her dress so fine and white it must be light itself; her arms shape gentle pictures on the air. She sways and sings, her breeze-blown chestnut hair an exhalation of silk.

She has knelt at the edge of the rocks. Her honeyed song knifes through the dark water like a lance of sunlight. A grey spotted bull, with strange pale eyes that glitter in her light, rises to listen. He is old and scarred, massive and ungainly as he beaches on the shingle. But it is a man who comes from the sea. It is a slender, princely man, who sits beside her, dressed only in starlight and water weeds. Seawater glistens his skin and shines his dark, curly hair. He rests his head in her lap and she bends to kiss it.

He has taken her hand to lead her to the shore. He has lifted her up and laid her in the sea. Now, she rides the bull, her fingers twisted in his harness of water weeds, her fine white dress trailing seafoam in their wake. ...*Mam?* But when she turns to look back at the shore, her eyes are full of exultation and release. And then they are gone, the selkie and his bride, beneath the waves.

Ciaran rubbed his eyes. The sea was calm as ever it was on the ebb of a springtime night. He felt refreshed. Sure and it was a powerful healer to give a restless, sorrowing man such consolation and him but sitting beside it a'rowing through his dreams. *What dreams?* he wondered. But all he remembered was the woman in white...and how she had danced away the darkness.

It was night now, moonless and starry; he felt the cold and went to find the warmth of his own hearth.

He heard them playing from the bottom of the path. Candles flickered in every window. They were all still waiting on him. But when he entered the house, the music died away and a hush fell on the room.

"You must not think I'm wantin' you to stop, for didn't my Mam always love a dancin' tune. And she'll not be thinking the more of yous for your long faces, nor myself neither."

"Are you more settled, son?" Bertie said.

"Aye and I am. For aren't we but grieving for ourselves this night, when she is in her happiness with more love than the lot of us could ever hope to have."

He looked around the room. A murmur of *Amens* spread like a ripple of light across the careworn faces of his friends. .

"I'm thinking I will join you," he said. He took his fiddle from the peg by the door and played.

CHAPTER TWENTY

Motherhood

The assistant manager of the shirt factory proffered a blue and white striped rubber ball. "Here, Ruchel, for the boy...It's his birthday soon, no?" Rachel snatched the gift and stuffed it into her satchel. She slipped into her cardigan, gathered up her parcels and pulled on her felt hat. "Next week," she said, calling out her thanks as she streaked down the stairs and out to Orchard Street.

He was a nice man, the assistant manager, always asking about the baby, letting her leave early enough to get to Brooklyn before dark on Fridays. Of course, he docked her pay, but at least she could keep her job. Because of his kindness, though, she would probably miss her connection and arrive too late to see Daniel. Again.

Down in the street, she hitched up her long skirts, put her head down and ran. The pushcart vendors and shopkeepers along the way, accustomed to this weekly sight, waved and shouted greetings.

Heedless, she ran.

To the corner of Essex. Down the station steps, just in time to see the Sea Beach/Coney Island Express pull away. If she had caught it, she could have changed to the local at Brooklyn-59th Street for the ride to 20th Avenue in Bensonhurst. Now, she would have to wait for a Brighton Beach train, change at DeKalb and again at 59th. At least an hour trapped in the tunnels and open culverts of the BMT. By the time she raced the four blocks from the station to Mendel and Helen's, they would have put him to bed.

She bit her lip. Was it so hard for Helen to let Daniel stay up to see her on Friday nights, such a lot to ask? She had begged her more than once. But Helen was stubborn. "He gets cranky," she said. "You'll see him in the morning. It's what he's used to." She never failed to punctuate her refusal. *Babies have routines, you know* or *You don't know what he's like when he's over-tired* or, worst of all, *I don't want you to upset him.*

A low grumble in the tunnel, followed by a sooty gust, announced an approaching train. Scraps of paper and shreds of tobacco spun along the platform. As the train squealed into the station, Rachel reached for her hat and dropped her small satchel, which opened, spilling clothes and presents all over the floor. The train conductor caught the blue and white ball just before it rolled onto the tracks. "Hurry up, Miss," he said, his finger hovering over the button that would close the doors and send another train off to Brooklyn without her. She scrabbled for her things and dashed onto the carriage, trailing nightclothes and lisle stockings from the half-opened case.

Although it was still early, the train was already crowded with working people trying to get home before the Sabbath. Rachel squeezed into a wicker seat and, pressed by men on both sides, struggled with her satchel. They took up so much space, men, with their legs spread and their arms wide. When wriggling in her seat produced no response, she turned and stared at the man on her right until he cleared his throat and pulled himself together. Then she opened the satchel and began to rearrange her belongings.

Except for some night things, a spare shirtwaist and a change of underwear, almost everything in the case was, as usual, for the baby. She was learning to crochet. Her first effort, a blue cotton hat with a chain stitched cord to tie under his chin, was a bit lopsided but it would keep the sun off his head now that it was getting warm. There was a pair of short brown trousers, with a shirt to match, that she'd made during her breaks. Bea sent an alphabet book with big letters and coloured pictures of apples and balls, dogs and cats, printed on shiny cardboard. Rachel thought maybe he was too young for this, but Bea, who taught adult literacy classes, said you couldn't start too soon. She smiled as she traced the stitching on a pair of black leather shoes with her fingers. His first real shoes. Brand new, from a shop. She'd spent half a week's pay on them. They were so tiny. What if they didn't fit? The man in the shop had assured her that they were the right kind of shoes for a child just starting to walk.

These were not birthday presents. Rachel always went to Brooklyn loaded down with packages. "Between you and your father-in-law, he'll be spoiled rotten in no time," Helen said. That was just envy. Rachel guessed that Mendel's pay was more than anyone in the family had ever earned, yet he clung to thrifty, immigrant habits. Most of Emma's clothes were hand-me-downs, passed on by Helen's sister. Helen particularly objected to the macaroons that Rachel brought every week. "What kind of a thing is that to feed a baby? He shouldn't eat so much sugar. It's too hard; he'll choke on it."

But Daniel already had six teeth and Rachel was careful to crumble the biscuits into the smallest possible shreds of coconut and almond paste. He recognised the little brown paper bag and waved his fat little arms greedily when she brought it out. The surprise of sweetness still delighted him.

Helen had a disapproving comment or a piece of smug advice about almost everything Rachel did for her child. If Mendel didn't gently call her away from time to time, Rachel would not have had a moment alone with him. Well, Helen was not his mother. She had a child of her own and this arrangement was only temporary. Everybody said so. Sophie had astonished the whole family by arguing with Jacob about it, the years seeming to add to her boldness as they diminished her stature.

"She's his mother. He belongs with her."

"In a house full of women? Without a father? Some start for a Jewish boy."

"What, you don't live here too? Your whole life you spend teaching little boys. For your grandson, your own flesh and blood, you have no time?"

"I raised my children already. I have no patience for an infant."

In the end, Sophie made him promise, in front of them all, that it was only temporary.

At first it had seemed so simple. Duvi said Bessie always talked about going to Florida. "You shoulda seen the pictures she cut out of magazines. All over the place, pictures."

"You know this woman? You were in this woman's house? Very nice." Jacob was annoyed but nothing Duvi did surprised him anymore.

"Well, she was one of the neighbourhood girls...you know...a good dancer and...that."

Schmuel's father remembered a customer who bought and sold property in Florida. They would find Schmuel, bring him back and make him do the right thing.

But Florida was a big place and Moses Weiss's customer went to jail over a land swindle. And even if they could find Schmuel, what *was* the right thing?

Rachel wanted the *get* so she could look for a decent husband to make a home for her child. A kind man, who made a living was the most she allowed herself to hope for. If, in the night, the rhythm of distant music still sang in her blood, she woke and stifled it. Dreams were fine for foolish, selfish young girls. The child was real, almost more real than she could bear. Someone easy to live with, a man who would take to Daniel, would be enough. Then the Widow Meyer announced that there was no way her son, *the rabbi*, would marry into a family with a divorce.

Rachel tried but could not forget the day she had tied the baby's clothes and belongings in a bundle; everything except the small, linen parcel that the midwife had told her she must keep, no matter what. She wrapped him in blankets and handed him over, barely weaned, to her brother and his wife. The memory choked her with fresh tears at the most unexpected moments. The way she held onto him to the last. His warm, familiar, buttery smell. She had pressed her face against his, stung, by the animal thrill of his tiny heartbeat, his velvet skin.

She did not want these feelings. She had not chosen to love a child conceived in foolishness and violence, born into confusion. Everything would have been so much easier if she had the power to reject him. But she thought she might even tolerate living with Schmuel again if that was the price of having Daniel back.

Now she wiped her eyes with the back of her hand and snapped the satchel shut.

Rain scudded across the roof of the metal subway carriage as it bounced and swayed over the Brooklyn tracks, open to the sky. She closed her eyes, leaned back against the window and nodded to the monotonous motion.

They have called him Daniel, for the book said it means the judgement of God. *And I have heard of thee, that thou canst make interpretations and dissolve doubts...* His mother said, you must not tell him. But he knows the secrets of the heart. "I do not care at all how the child was got. But you must say where they have taken him." *Burden of light, song of fire.* "Have I not come for you, in the way that I promised, yet you will not go wi' me without I bring him." *Dancing, heedless moths, in ever decreasing spirals to the sacramental brilliance of the light, fire, light, fire, light, fire, song, silence, lightfiresongsilencedarkness.*

Rachel sat up and opened her eyes. "Stop! Stop...please st..." The fat man on her right jumped and stared at her. She pretended to cough.

There was no other way. Even if Jacob hadn't insisted, where would they have put him, at Rivington Street, with Ruth and Sarah still at home? People didn't live one on top of each other anymore, the way they did when she was a baby. And who would look after him? Rosa and Abie had moved to the Bronx, to be closer to their married children, and everyone but Jacob went out to work. Sophie insisted Rachel shouldn't have to, but Jacob said she must pay for her upkeep and the child's.

Now that Mendel was the foreman of two warehouses, he and Helen had moved to a brand-new apartment house. It had steam heat, hot and cold running water and every family had a toilet and a bathtub. The babies, Daniel and Helen's Emma, ten months older, shared a room of their own. The parlour, where Rachel spent weekends on a fat, feather stuffed couch, seemed to have no purpose at all, except for sitting. There was even a room just for eating. But for her unease over Helen's growing attachment to the baby, Rachel's visits to Brooklyn might have been as pleasant as a vacation in a fancy hotel.

They reached the busy junction at DeKalb Avenue and Rachel stepped to the middle of the platform to wait for the Sea Beach train. It was just as well that he would be asleep when she arrived. Next Saturday was his first birthday. Rachel wanted to make it a special occasion, so they had a lot to talk about.

"I never heard such a thing...that a child should be deprived because the whole family is afraid of a bad-tempered old man."

Schmuel's sister, Dinah, snapped the tablecloth so hard the opposite corners flew out of Rachel's hands. "It makes me so angry, Rachel. Nobody stands up to him."

"It's not that easy," Rachel said.

"So what's so hard about it? You tell me. A little pot roast, your mother's strudel, maybe a honey cake and some brandy for the men. And presents for the baby...It's only right; he's a year old."

"Helen says he'll be confused with so many people."

"*Helen says Helen says.* Helen knows everything? She's not even a blood relation." Dinah shook her head. "So, did she stop you from bringing him here? *Helen says!*"

Rachel had gone, in a taxi with Schmuel's father, to bring Daniel back to the city for the weekend. Moses Weiss doted on the child, his first, and probably only grandson. If his generosity was also motivated by embarrassment and shame, so be it. Nowadays, she accepted her allies where she found them.

Still, she felt vaguely embarrassed that her champions were Schmuel's family. She scooped a handful of cutlery from the dresser and concentrated on laying Dinah's table.

"We never made a fuss about birthdays," she said. "My father says it's what the *goyem* do."

"Oh please. You know this has nothing to do with that Rachel. Your righteous father can't decide who to punish for his mistake. You tell *me*, it's the child's fault that his father is a *schtick drek*? You should excuse me, Rachel, for being so vulgar. It breaks my heart to say it about my own brother, but we both know it. Your father could have put his foot down. He does it all the time."

Since Daniel's birth, Dinah, had become more a friend than a sister-in-law. Though what she said was true enough, Rachel was painfully aware that it wasn't the whole truth. She wished she could share more with her. Maybe one day she would.

The baby pulled a block from the bottom of a stack he had built, sending blocks skidding off the blanket, out of reach across the linoleum. Recently, he had begun to be frustrated with the crablike progress of crawling. Now he tried to pull himself up on a dining room chair. Rachel caught the teetering chair just in time. He plopped down, squawking angrily.

She knelt beside him, gathered up the blocks and took him into her lap, crooning and tickling him until he jabbered and smiled. Dinah joined them. "So Daniel's going to have a party...Isn't that nice, *bubeleh*?" To Rachel, she added, "If your father comes, he comes. If not..." Dinah looked at Rachel and shrugged.

"He'll come," Rachel said. "God forbid he should be shown up by your father."

Dinah laughed. "You know what? They're both busy grovelling to God, your father and mine. They just go about it in different ways."

She patted the baby's head. His honey-flecked, green eyes glowed. When Dinah had said, "Those he didn't get from *our* side," Rachel realised she had never noticed Schmuel's eyes at all. Now Dinah took his face in her hands. "Such a beautiful boy from such a *tzimmes*, eh little one?"

Rachel stacked the blocks for him. "One...two...three...There, you see? Mommy makes it all better...Now you."

A whistling red top with silver stars wobbled and tipped on its side. The baby, on all fours watching it, sat back on his heels.

"Not bad, eh kid?"

He bobbed his head and smiled. "Geh," he said. Duvi reached across and gave him a wooden horse. Without even looking at it, he dropped it on the floor.

"Not innerested in horses...Okee Doakee...Let's see what else we got here."

"Geh."

"Yeah...right."

The day had gone well. Daniel, despite Helen's predictions, relished the attention of more people than he had ever seen, probably, since his *bris*. He giggled and jabbered and sang along when Abie played the flute. In fact, it was Emma, jealous over the presents, who became fractious and had to be put to bed.

Everyone came, even, as Rachel had predicted, Jacob. There was only one uncomfortable moment, after Moses Weiss unveiled his extravagant present, a car Daniel could sit in. It was styled to look like a little roadster, with pedals his feet could not yet reach. He loved the noisy red and brass horn and grabbed the steering wheel as soon as they put him in the seat. "Looka that...a natural...a real little driver, just like his Daddy," Duvi said. Jacob snorted. "Where will we put it," Helen whined. Dinah took one look at Rachel and decided it was a good time to invite them into the parlour for coffee and cake.

Now, mellow on Dinah's pot roast and homemade brandy, the family crowded around the edges of the front room, over the shop, all the stuffed furnishings pushed back to make room for the baby's blanket full of presents. Balls and stuffed bears, a set of wooden farm animals, a workbench with pegs and a wooden hammer. There was a wind-up duck and a metal pull toy with a seesaw that went up and down and played chimes as it rolled along.

Duvi turned a key and set the duck it motion. It quacked mechanically; its fat orange feet slapped the floor. Daniel scowled and kicked it over with his foot. "Geh," he said and waved to the pile of toys on the other side of the blanket.

"Yeah...pretty stupid, huh? Awright...How 'bout this?" Duvi handed him a teddy bear which he tasted, chewing on an ear. He spat and threw it down.

"It ain't for eatin' Danny boy."

"Geh."

"I know, I know...so you keep tellin' me...Hey...how 'bout this?" Duvi sucked his face in until his lips disappeared in two straight lines along his cheeks. "Bet you didn't know your Uncle Davey had such a funny face, eh kid?"

"*Gehhhh,*" Daniel wailed. He scowled and kicked.

From every corner of the room, female voices spoke at once.

"The top."

"Do the top."

"He wants you to spin the top."

"Okay, okay....Geez...I ain't no mind reader."

"He said *'Again'.*" Rachel and Helen spoke at once. Their eyes met briefly before Helen looked away.

"Your Mama says you want this thing here...Stupid Uncle Davey. Is this here what you want?" Duvi pressed the plunger, making the top whistle and spin. Daniel bounced back on his bottom and clapped.

"Come *tataleh*...Come eat cake with Tanta Rosa."

Rosa lifted Daniel into her lap. "Oy, so big, *kinahora...ein kleyne mensch*, a real little man. Skinny like you, Rucheleh, he won't be...and look at the shoes...real little shoes...*Oy gevalt*, so cute."

"He's almost walking," Rachel said, pleased that the shoes were a perfect fit.

While the adults discussed him, Daniel was content to rest against Rosa's ample bosom breaking honey cake from her plate into crumbs and rolling it into balls that he threw on the floor.

"So much cake, already," Helen said. "He'll be sick."

"Leave him, he's only playing with it," Rosa said. She turned back to Rachel. "Walking? Already?"

The afternoon was fading. Dinah opened the shades and curtains to admit the last of the daylight. Helen began gathering up toys and baby clothes. Soon she and Mendel would take the baby back to Brooklyn. Rachel, aching with this knowledge, snatched at the new topic to delay their departure. "Stand him up and you'll see."

Rosa stood the baby on the floor, holding his hands high against her open palms. His chubby fingers gripped hers. He let go of Rosa and stood for a moment. Then, excited by the adult applause and exclamations, he clapped his hands, lost his balance and sat down. Once again, he reached for Rosa's hands and pulled himself up.

Carefully, he lifted his right foot and took a step. Rosa leaned forward, leading him. Still holding her, he brought his left foot up to meet the right one.

"Look at Daniel walking."

"What a big boy."

Basking in attention, he took another step, a bouncy swing against Rosa's hands. Then he yanked free, swayed, but remained standing. He grinned and gurgled as his accomplishment met enthusiastic approval all round. Rachel noticed that even Jacob's lips were twisted slightly.

Now they were all encouraging him. "Go *bubeleh*," Rosa said. "Go to Mama."

He took one, unassisted step to toward the middle of the room, stopped and looked around. All the grownups were smiling at him, urging him on. He took another step, teetered and stopped to regain his balance. "Go to Mama, Daniel." Rosa repeated.

Now he stood, unsteadily, in the middle of the room, looking first at Rachel, who opened her arms wide to catch him, then Helen, then Rachel again. Neither woman said a word. Puzzled concentration shadowed his face. Rachel held her breath. Matching her concentration to his, she tried to will him forward. Everyone else disappeared; the room, the people melted around her glowing child. He lifted his foot, put it down again and sat back on his cushion of damp diaper.

Helen jumped up, but before she reached Daniel, Rachel had swept him into her arms. She hugged him and stroked his hair. "Who's Mommy's big boy?" she said. "Who's Mommy's big boy? Is it Daniel? Is that who it is?"

"Muh-muh-muh-muh," he laughed.

"Yes, ma-ma-ma-ma-ma." Rachel rubbed her nose against his.

"It's getting late. We should go," Helen said.

"In a minute," Mendel responded.

"The children need to be put to bed," she frowned.

"In a minute!"

Rachel held her baby until all the other guests were gone. He slept against her shoulder, warming her throat with his moist, even breath. Dinah persuaded Mendel to stay for a glass of tea. And another. When Helen finally insisted that they go, Rachel put the child into her brother's arms. He woke briefly to murmur drowsily. "Muh-muh-muh-muh."

"Mommy will come to see you soon," Rachel said. "Now you have to go with Uncle Mendel and Aunt Helen."

CHAPTER TWENTY ONE

A summer full of women

Bertie coiled the climbing ropes while Ciaran arranged the eggs in a pannier. It had been a fine afternoon; the scent of field flowers sweetening under a rain-omened sky and enough eggs for the both of them with extra to spare for the shop.

"She is a fine lookin' woman," Bertie said.

"Aye."

"Peaceful and quiet in herself, they say. The good Father was only just after tellin' me that with all her troubles there is not a harsh word in her."

"Mmm."

The mare tore the long grass at the top of Ruecallan. She took most of the weight now. It was true that a lifetime of hard work had made Bertie fit and hard as most men half his age. But how could he not feel the years when he had seen the back of 65? Though he didn't complain, Ciaran always knew when the older man was plagued by his joints. It was an understanding between them, though they never spoke of it, that Bertie's climbing days were over. He tended the hand rope and saw to it that the mare kept a steady pull on the body line.

Ciaran slung the coiled rope over the pommel. "Do you want to ride her Bertie?" he said.

"Are you after saying that my legs isn't fit to take me home?"

"Ach no," Ciaran laughed. "It just come into my head...and she be saddled and all, that it were a shame to waste it."

"Climb up on her back yourself then."

"I like the walking."

"Myself and all," Bertie grunted.

Ciaran smiled and the two men led the mare along the path, quiet in the comfort of their friendship.

At the top of Kinramher, they paused to admire the island spread out below them, brilliant and stark in the long shadows of late summer. Cooking smoke rose from dozens of cottages. The sun-whitened church steeple punctuated the dark blue bay.

"So, what do you think of her, then?" Bertie said.

"Of who?"

"Of the priest's niece. Who else have we been talkin' of?"

"It is not myself has been talkin' of her, Bertie."

"Aye, but you'd be well to think more on it. A fine lookin' widow with two strong sons; the older one big enough to help you in the fields soon enough. And isn't she young enough still to give you a few of your own before she's done with all that?"

"Maybe."

"So?"

"So, I'm thinking, whatever will Father Rafferty be doin' without his niece to keep his house for him?"

"He'll be doin' what he always done in times past. There's plenty of hire girls that would be glad to be lookin' after a priest and him an old man, with his holy vows besides, to keep them safe."

Ciaran watched the heavy clouds moving in from the west. "It'll cool the leaf tomorrow," he said.

"You'd be well to think more on it," Bertie repeated.

"I have done."

"And?"

"And I'm thinkin' her noggin and spoon is for another."

Bertie sighed and they walked on.

Father Rafferty's niece, that was widowed in the war, was only the latest of the gaggle of women who came nesting to Rathlin that summer. The dances in the hall flashed with courting plumage the likes of which had not been seen since before the Great War.

Ciaran was certain Cathleen was behind it for wasn't it her relation that was the first to arrive.

One rainy spring day, he'd gone to the shop to buy cheese and a bottle of ale. Tom Fergus was helping behind the counter, the poor man. "Will you stay for a bit of talk and a cup of tea," he said, "the while your clothes will be drying by the stove...for it is an unkindly wind is blowin' out there."

"Aye, the rain bites fearsome. It is very cold." He tossed his pullover on the wood stove and settled on a crate of tins, watching steam cloud over the damp wool.

"Cathleen, be a darlin' and put the kettle on."

Cathleen smiled and pushed her sleeves up. "You needn't be wasting your sweet talk," she said, "for isn't it a small thing to be makin' the man a cup of tea."

She pushed Ciaran's pullover aside to make room for the kettle and, as she did so, she noticed the place where he had patched the elbow with a bit of tweed.

"And what do you call that, then?" she said, plucking at the patch.

"It is mending," Ciaran said.

"Ah, so that is what you call it. Myself, I would give it another name all together."

"What's wrong with it?"

"I'm thinkin' there's not a woman on this island could not have done better...even Fogarty's Eileen who is that simple she's scarce fit to boil water."

Ciaran was proud of his sewing. Wounded, he said, "It turns the wet. It is good enough. I canna be runnin' to the women folk every time I have need of a stitch taken."

"Ach, Ciaran. Look at the state of your clothes, man. Sometimes I wonder to God at the way you are become as raggedy as a tinker itself."

"Let the man warm himself in peace," Tom Fergus said.

Cathleen continued clucking and nodding over the patch. "Naeve will see to it. I'm told she is quick with a needle and thread."

It was early in the game and Ciaran had not yet become wary of pursuing the strange, feminine names that everyone soon seemed to be dropping.

"Naeve?" he said.

"My cousin, Naeve, that was my mother's niece from Kenmare down in Kerry. Did Tom Fergus not tell you that she is coming to stop with us...to help me with the children and all?"

Ciaran looked at Tom Fergus, who was, at that moment, deeply engrossed in the pages of a ledger.

"Haven't they had their troubles, my aunt and uncle and all their lot," Cathleen continued, "...with scarce a bit of a roof over their heads since the republicans made a shambles of their house looking for free staters...and my uncle's boat blown to smithereens in the harbour."

"Cathleen, you must not make such a story of it. It were three years ago and more," Tom Fergus said. "And isn't your uncle a porter in Dublin now, at a grand hotel. Would you have our man thinkin' we are that hard hearted to leave our relations sleeping in fields?"

"You may say so, but you know Tom Fergus, that it has never been the same for them since that time of the Civil War. Such a fine fishing boat my uncle had...the likes you would not soon see in this place. And now, with all them children, they have got scarce enough to keep them kind of living."

Cathleen poured the tea and replaced Ciaran's pullover on the edge of the stove. "Naeve will see to this," she said. "They say she likes a bit of dancing and all."

So that was the start of it. And soon there were others.

There was the daughter of Mary McQuaid's sister's husband's brother, that left the convent. "Her father, the holy hypocrite, has no sense in him at all for he canna see that it were a blessing to know she had not the call before she'd her vows taken. So, she will stay with us a while until them Sligo biddies have had their fill of tongue waggling."

Bertie's cousin Fionula that still worked as a laundress took in two sisters, distant relations from Belfast. "Now there is no more work for them at the shipyards, do you know, all the Catholic boys have took to drinkin' and stayin' bachelors. You are not the only man on this island, Ciaran, with a bit of a field and the need of a woman."

Ciaran never did work out the connections of the bleakly plain Donegal girl who came to stay with Mickey Joe's Bridget and her husband. Someone's aunt's husband's sister's child or some such. What did it matter? Sure and she could use a bit of island air; the poor thing looked half starved herself. But wasn't she young enough to be his own child if it came to that?

And there were more. A new barmaid at the pub. A girl to work the wireless at the West Lighthouse. A travelling Gaelic teacher from Derry that had lost her position in the changes and taught in people's houses for her keep. All kinds of women; red haired, blond and raven tressed, large and small, high spirited and hearty, quiet and shy. Every one with a story of loss and troubles. From the Great War, or the war with the English, or the Civil War that set Irishmen one against the other.

Now in the Year of Our Lord 1926, when it looked at last that peace would stay, they came to Rathlin, a place so untouched by the killing that the single men outnumbered the women. The wives of Rathlin, infected with an excess of connubial zeal, seemed determined to stamp out the pagan practice of bachelorhood, once and for all.

So many women. And himself, or so it seemed, the one a brave few had set their caps for. What was a man to do? At first, he warmed to Mary's Caitlin, that was almost a nun. In her silences, he thought he sensed a deepening of dreams. But perhaps they were for another; she would not share them. Could be it were only his own dreams come back to him from her still, dark eyes. For isn't it true that though a man may dream of what he sees, what he sees is often made of what he dreams?

Cathleen's Naeve was eager with presents and offers of mending. She gave him a shirt of white cloth, fit for Easter best, for no reason at all. "You may take it," she insisted. "Isn't it only a bit of practice for Mary Catherine that I am teachin' to sew."

And the priest's niece that was the widow sent her older son to help him guide the plough and lay the nets, protesting when he thanked her for her kindness. "Ah, no, it is a kindness you are doin' me, for he has no man to teach him now but an old priest is all."

Well, wasn't it a grand diversion, for a time. Ciaran could not remember when there were last so many *ceilidhs*, nor when he had last eaten such quantities of currant cakes, so many yeast-risen loaves. He played his fiddle for the dancing and flirted with stories when it was his pleasure to tell them.

But in the end, they were none of them the one. When the stories were told, the dancing finished, he climbed the path alone.

In the two years that had passed since Flora's death, Ciaran had come to enjoy his solitary life. He was not lonely, nor even alone very often. How could he be with his fiddle and his friends, with every part of his work and play close woven to the *clachan*?

Perhaps he had simply learned to allow himself the contentment of it. For in truth, hadn't he always prized those quiet times when his spirit was free to seek its own companions. To gather star music. Or watch cloud islands sail beyond the horizon. To look down from the cliffs as the birds cast shapes upon the sea, himself so high above them that his own shadow darkened on their backs.

For weeks after, the two-room cottage enormous without her, his belief in her happiness as fragile as a dandelion clock, he left her feather bed arranged on the bed frame in his room. He lay, sleepless, in the kitchen alcove, until exhaustion delivered him to a world where nothing had changed and from which he would emerge hungry, the smells of phantom porridge and tea still tickling his nose.

Those were the healing days when grief is jealously held, a possession to be guarded and protected from the intrusive comfort of others.

That summer the sun was more persistent than anyone could remember. Gradually, imperceptibly, time and warmth and light worked as ever they have on the human heart. One day he folded the feather bed, stowed it in the loft where he had slept as a boy, and moved into the bedroom.

Gradually, too, he discovered the satisfactions of self-sufficiency. The years of watching Flora had taught him much that was useful. If he ate more simply, he could fry an egg in bacon fat or boil up potatoes and mackerel or stew a pot of strong black tea. What more did a man need? If the corners held more dust than Flora would have tolerated, the windows more grime, he did not, at first, notice. And when at last he did, he did not much care.

Now, when he chose to, he could mend a tool in the light of a lamp, warmed by whiskey and the fire, listening to the voices that had always been there, waiting, to tell him all the stories that had ever been told.

Flora sings a lullaby. "Her singin' is sweet, is your Mam's," his Grand-Da Donal says, "but lad, if ever you hear the *sidhe* sing, you will know then what sweetness can be...for aren't they fallen angels themselves."

"Are they wicked, then, Grand-Da?"

"Ach no. They are like lost children...waitin' just like us for the Lord to forgive them and take them home to himself."

"But how did they lose their way and them being angels and all?"

"Well now, that is a great mystery. There's them that say it were in the time when the Lord made Adam that some of them were bewitched with love for the mortal man and got left behind. And some say that they are all that is left of broken hearted lovers, that cannot leave this world without they find each other again. There is all kinds of stories of how they come to be and what it is that holds them near us."

"But Grand-Da, is it not wicked for them to love the man more than the Lord itself?"

"Ah lad, that is what the holy fathers would be havin' us to believe. Myself, I'm thinkin' that there is never wickedness in love...only sometimes, powerful sorrow."

If he wondered, as he scoured the leavings of his careless cooking from the heavy cast iron pots, how it was he had come to be doing such womanish work, Flora was there to scold him. *And is that what you think a wife is for then? You may as well fetch me a hire girl from the fair if that is what you are wantin'.*

Could be that I'm wantin' some wee'uns and all.

Ah.

He could watch Tom Fergus gentle his youngest, wee Jenny, to sleep in her cradle and think that was, indeed, what he was wanting. Then, walking home, he would suddenly decide that his childlessness was fit, him being fatherless and all. It was a notion that came and went for it was mingled with another that, although formless, was somehow linked to the golden beads.

They lay at the bottom of the chest for months after she was gone. He would not dare to look at them, but they entered his night world, nevertheless.

They plummeted through milky green water to tangle in fields of bones that waved like eel grass in the currents. Or it was himself, the heavy beads wrapped tightly round his neck, who plummeted through salty ice while skeletal arms reached out to catch him and toothless, fleshless mouths called to him with names that were none of them, yet all of them, his own. He watched in voiceless terror as they melted in a pool of blood that boiled into flame. Once, he sat beside a singing stream, on a hillside where warm grapes ripened and took the chain from soft, wee hands, their skin glossy olive against his golden brown. But mostly he woke, shivering, from horrors threaded through with the mysterious shining chain.

Sleeplessness shadowed his face. "You are looking peaked," Cathleen said. "Are you not feeding yourself, man?"

The useless thing. It was beautiful to no purpose. He had done no good with it. Only bad, in fact; it had made a liar of him. For to keep a secret from the ones who love you seemed as bad as lying itself. Pressed by the dark weight of guilt, he determined to be rid of it. He would take it back to the *Ouig* and bury it where he had found it. Perhaps he would climb a high place and fling it into the sea. But when he lifted the treasure from its hiding place and let it slide, warm, through his fingers, he knew that he could not. If anything, its hold upon him had grown.

The beads were even more wonderful to look at than they had been the night he freed them from their coral shells by the brilliant light of the Talley lamp. He held them close to the candle and they glowed with colours. Almost alive. Almost as if the flame itself had come to dance, mild and harmless, in the palm of his hand. The thing was beauty itself. *It was a gift.* In this harsh world, full of weathers and sorrows, wasn't beauty, the blue of the sky, the flash of a smile, always a gift? The earth had given it to him. And he became convinced that he, in turn, must give it. It was not an object to trade for money, money that could buy food or clothes or shelter or tools. A man could work to earn such things. No, it must be given for itself alone; to share the vision of the one who had made it, to share the pleasure of the first giver, the first receiver. But to whom?

Now Ciaran was a *seánachie*, a storyteller through and through. There was not an event that passed in his life that he wasn't, at once, shaping into the words he would use to tell it. This was not a story he could tell. But he had the knowledge, known to all true storytellers, though few will speak of it, that there is one kind of story better than any other. You may gather a crowd of listeners and make them laugh or weep or quake with terror. You may whisper a tale to one only, that will warm her cheeks and soften her will. Not one of these is as fine as the story that you tell yourself. It will come to you alone, from the stillness of your soul. You need but wait and watch and listen. And so he did.

Once he had taken the treasure from the bottom of the chest, had handled it and succumbed to its charm, his nightmares ceased. Perhaps the thing was living, truly, and had fed him its terrors, locked away in the lonely dark. He dismissed the fanciful thought. More like he had simply forgiven himself his secret, which he had feared was greed but which he now saw as something else; something beyond his understanding but also beyond his power to control. Still, he could not hide it away again. He put it, instead, under the pillow beside him, where he could reach out and touch it whenever it sang to him. He need but feel the smooth, warm beads to relax into waking visions, imagining the one upon whom he might, one day, bestow the gift. In the unravelling fabric of consciousness, he followed threads of almost dreams to other times and places, to stories where it was often she who placed the chain upon him or laid it across his open hands.

Her hair was copper, wheaten, nut brown, smoke; her skin pale as parchment, golden, sallow, chocolate, ebony blue. She wore a robe of linen, a mantel of fur, a coat of hides, a shift of silk, or nothing at all. She lifted his hair to fasten the chain on his neck and he could feel her tender flesh against his bare back, smell the warm spice of her perfume. Sometimes she snatched the beads. At other times she refused them and he had to take her hands in his and force her fingers to close around them. Once even, she was a mermaiden caught in his nets. He cut her free with a curving, bone handled knife and she changed, before his eyes, into a slim young seal, escaping back to the sea, leaving nothing behind but the magic treasure.

When he was wide awake, spinning a handsome girl in a reel or tasting her savoury stew of mutton and barley, he tried to shake free of an obsession he knew to be ridiculous. She was only his imagining. He had never even seen her face or heard her voice, always drifting into dreamless sleep before his mind had formed her whole.

But it was useless. An essential female now abided in his heart. Real or imagined, she crowded out all the others who came seeking husbands in that summer full of women. They were none of them the one.

CHAPTER TWENTY TWO

The Still

At the narrow mouth of Lough Foyle, the Glasgow-Derry steamer waited for the tide in the lee of Magilligan Point. With no boat wind, she rocked in a cloud of her own smoke, sooty ash settling on everything. Ciaran and Tom Fergus had hitched aboard the puffer near midnight, curling up in the shelter of a lifeboat to nap, only to wake at daybreak covered in grit. Tom Fergus had caught a cinder.

"Will you stop troublin' your eye, man," Ciaran said. "How ever will you look standing up for Cathal and your eye a right mess before you've even a drop touched."

"It is a filthy way to cross the water," Tom Fergus said.

"Mmm, but a fast way and all. We'll see Derry in two hours maybe."

"And three hours more before we see the Sperrins," Tom Fergus groaned.

Ciaran nodded. "Could be...could be."

"Myself, I would have rather stood in bed and gone over with the rest of them, tomorrow."

"Ach, man, have you no heart for a bit of adventure? You will forget this hardship soon enough when you are pouring Johnny Craig's drink down your throat. It is that fine, you know."

"Oh aye?"

"Aye. My Grand-Da Donal was after saying it was like angels tears itself."

"Was he then? Well wasn't your Grand-Da Donal after talkin' blether most of the time and all."

Ciaran grinned. "So you are forever tellin' me."

A patrol boat buzzed their bow, laying a stench of petrol fumes on its wake. Constables, off early to spoil the start of some poor bugger's day. Ciaran leaned across the gunwales watching oyster catchers scratch for their breakfast on the clean sands of the bank they called The Tuns, rubbed his grimy fingers and wondered if they would find a wash and a cup of tea in Derry. Tom Fergus was right about one thing. What with the hiring of a cart and the bone jolting ride down to Douglas Bridge and back, it would be a long day's journey to a comfortable bed.

The Kiernan twins, Diarmud and Cathal, had found themselves a pair of lively sisters out of Strabane and made quick work of courting them. They'd danced them round the Feis in July, proposed at the Causeway market, the beginning of August, and set the wedding for the last Saturday of the very same month. The whole island was amazed with the speed of it.

"Well, may Our Lord and all the saints forgive me for saying it," Cathleen remarked, "but you know I will speak my mind. Myself, I'm after thinkin' that with faces on them two the like would give most women nightmares, they'll not be wantin' to chance their fortune for too long and all."

So, tomorrow the Kiernan twins would marry their County Tyrone girls, a big double wedding, with dancing after. Ciaran and Tom Fergus, who would be groom's men, had gone ahead for a supply of what Ciaran assured Tom Fergus was the finest poteen in the North of Ireland.

Even without the journey, buying drink from Johnny Craig was always a bit of a palaver. Ciaran had first gone, as a boy, with Bertie and Donal. Bertie, who had people in Tyrone, had convinced Flora that it was time he saw the world beyond their island home.

"It is a bit of the world with more troubles than a child has need of seein'," Flora had said.

"He'll not be a wee'un forever," said Bertie. "I will show him now the kind of livin' they have there, the way he'll not be pining to chase after it later."

Of course, Bertie was right. He had seen, quick enough, the dreary life those inland people led. Dark and damp and smelling of sod. Not even the whispering forests of trees, the like of which were never seen on Rathlin, would tempt him to stop for long among them.

But Ireland had its pleasures and winkling out Johnny Craig's illegal still, hidden in the foothills of the Sperrins, was one of them. Ciaran watched the patrol boat disappear toward Portstewart. Specials, likely. There was all kinds of lawlessness. He was glad their business was none of his.

They heard the church bells of Douglas Bridge ring three o'clock before they saw the town. It was later than they had planned. They would still be on the road back to Strabane after dark, a thought neither of them relished though it was Tom Fergus who gibbered on about it.

"I know what you are thinking," he said.

"Do you?"

"...that it is because of myself that we will be travelling in the night. And you are wondering who at all might be waitin' for us in these woods with the border no further than a man can shout...is what you are thinking."

"I am thinking nothing at all except maybe of the powerful thirst that come on me when I seen the town."

"You know, man, that those Derry liverymen is thieves and robbers every one," Tom Fergus said.

Ciaran nodded.

"...and they have only to hear the accent of a stranger and straight away they are after doubling the price of a cart and a team of tired horses."

"Mmm."

"So, you must stop at five or six to find the price."

"Or seven or eight, maybe," Ciaran said, "or even ten."

"Aye...or ten..."

"Right."

"...and bargain with every one...You must...else they will steal you blind."

"Mmm...blind."

"Are you listening to what I'm saying?"

"I am that."

Ciaran began to laugh quietly, remembering that, in the end, he had lost patience with Tom Fergus and sent him off to find food for the journey while he, alone, found a fair enough price at the very next stables.

"It is not a laughing matter."

"No, it is not. But I am too parched to be worrying about *your* conscience. And anyhow, you made a right fine bargain for the herrings and the plums... grocer that you are."

The Douglas Bridge pub had not changed at all since the first time he had seen it, more than thirty years before, when his Grand-Da had warned him, "If any of them asks, you must say ought of what we come for."

"But how at all will they know what we are wantin' then, Grand-Da?"

"Look and listen to your Grand-Da and me," Bertie said, "and you will see how it is done."

The ritual exchange of words with the publican, would not have changed either.

"You haven't the sound of these parts about you. Is it far that you have come?"

"Oh aye. Far enough."

"And what is it, then, that brings you?"

"Well, now," he would say as Bertie had said in years past, poking Ciaran's leg under the table when he said it, "could be we are after walking in them dark hills yonder...for haven't we heard that the streams here about run swift and pure."

"Is that what you have heard?"

"Aye...We have."

The publican would nod and wipe the bar with his cloth. Then they would drink and wait. Sometimes the wait was long, sometimes not. When the stiller's boy showed up, that first time, Ciaran had consumed so many lemon barleywaters that he had to run behind the pub before they could go on.

Jack Craig was a man grown now, and like to be the stiller himself soon, but people still called him *the stiller's boy.* He was scarce bigger than Ciaran when first they met and, though they had met many times since, no flicker of recognition would light his face until they were safely away to the clearing.

"If it is streams swift and pure you are wantin', you may come wi' me," he would say. To the end of a winding lane, where the cart would be abandoned, then cross country through dense forest that had terrified Ciaran as a boy. He had clung to Bertie's hand, jumping at the strange scurrying noises, the sudden explosions of bird talk.

"It is the gentle people," Donal had said, "hurrying to hid for they would not have the likes of us to be seein' them at their dancin' games."

"Squirrels," Bertie said.

"Them too."

The woods still made him uneasy for they shrouded him from the signs that set a man straight in the world; the sky, the rip of a current, the curve of a bare hill to show the way. He would not breathe steady until they came to the wee stone cottage in the clearing, the free standing stone shed beside it, with white smoke pouring from the chimney whatever the weather. And, prickling the air all about, a smell that was like no other.

Looking forward to the transaction, Ciaran pushed open the pub door, leaving Tom Fergus to grumble and water the horses. It was usually a quiet place, so he was surprised to find it buzzing full of locals whose talk subsided when he entered. He squeezed between two men at the end of the bar, ordered two pints of ale and looked around. The men closest turned their backs. Ciaran was not offended. Inland people were never over friendly to strangers and dangerous times deadened what natural curiosity they might otherwise have had. The ale was wet and his legs were enjoying their stretch. It was enough.

They *were* dangerous times, those summer days of 1927, for there was trouble again in the South. He and Tom Fergus had left Bertie fretting worse than Flora in her day.

"You do be careful over there...and speak to no man without you have some business with him."

"I will not."

"And if any man insults you or calls you a papist, you turn the other cheek, like the Christian that you were raised."

"Don't I always?" Ciaran had laughed. "Unless I am too sore provoked?"

"You keep your fists in your pockets, do you hear me? Aren't they all saying that the peace has been broken? Now I am an old man, I am full of worries."

"Ah, Bertie, it is only a wedding we are going to. I will see you tomorrow."

"Aye...tomorrow," said Bertie. He shook his head and sighed, "...in this world or the next."

In truth, there had never been much of a peace - only that republicans, seeing there was no winning, had stopped killing other Irishmen for a while. They put away their guns. In attics and cellars, in barns and caves, in sheds and coffin shaped boxes buried at the bottoms of gardens; in places where they could still smell them.

But while most gave up the fighting, some never did. No one who enforced or made the law was safe. Bands of irregulars, intoxicated by the smell of all those hidden guns, calling themselves the Irish Republican Army or the

Brotherhood or other names as old as the history of conflict, still roamed the countryside. They enforced their own laws, gathered levies from smallholders, took vengence on old enemies, settled old grudges.

There are some grudges have only one ending and O'Higgins, who was the justice minister, carried two of that kind around on his back. For wasn't he the one who ordered the killing of so many heroes, back in '23? And didn't he keep thousands more still rotting in Dublin gaols these four years later? Could be he thought he was immortal. But on the 10th of July, someone proved that he was not. All over the twenty six counties, in Mayo and Sligo, Wicklow and Kerry, fires and fighting celebrated the assassination.

Bad times in the Free State could be relied upon to agitate the Ulster Constabulary. Not that they made much difference to folks in the North. Few people cared, one way and another about the goings on down there, for hadn't those Southerners signed away the Ulster Irish, on that paper with the English in '21, leaving them to get on with their neighbours as best they could. It was true enough that most folks had relations on the other side. It was true, also, that bands of republicans were now and then running back and forth to Donegal, though what they got up to was mostly mischief compared with the doings in the South. But the *Specials* didn't see it that way. They say some kinds of hornets will aggravate themselves into a frenzy over a commotion from next door's nest. The *B-Specials*, the ones that were Protestant Volunteers in the old days, didn't need a lot of stirring.

The wait was longer than they expected. The publican was lighting lamps, they were finishing their third pints and still Jack Craig had not appeared. The cold, whispery quiet made Ciaran restless. He soothed his mind with music.

"Hush up," Tom Fergus said.

"What?"

"You are hummin', man...This lot will think you are daft."

"Oh, sorry."

But the music insisted. His fiddle, like that other precious possession, the chain of golden beads hiding under his shirt, always went with him when he crossed the water. Now, resting against his back in the canvas case that Flora had stitched, it wanted to sing.

"Would yous be minding a song or two?" he announced to the assembled strangers. Tom Fergus rolled his eyes but the murmurs of assent were the first words anyone had spoken to them and Ciaran, now bursting with the urge to play, needed no more encouragement than that. He took the fiddle from its case, tucked it under his chin and tuned the strings.

He played *The Waves of Tory* and *McGonagle's Reel, Old Man Tucker* and *Lizzie's Goose*. When he played *Molly Mallone,* a man with a fine baritone began to sing. Soon others joined him. The music warmed the place. He closed his eyes and smiled. He had near forgot his errand altogether when someone snatched the fiddle right out of his hands in the middle of the *Siege of Ennis*.

"Jesus, man! What are you about, playing that one?"

Ciaran recognised the stiller's boy just in time to stop the punch that might have broke the poor fellow's nose.

"It is a grand old tune, is it not?"

"Aye, A grand old *republican* tune...You will bring grief on all of us playing of the likes of that."

"It is an Irish song is all."

"And they will lock you up for the playing of it...after they have broke a few of your bones and all."

"Ach, don't be daft."

"They have done worse, and for less."

Another man spoke up. "It is true enough. Didn't they throw poor Clary in the cells for three whole months, though he was old and as harmless a man can be."

"For playing music?"

"For giving comfort to the enemy, they said, and sheltering them in his shed. But it was lies, when all he done was sing the praises of some boys who stood up for his daughter that was being harassed."

Soon others joined in with stories of their own. Ciaran struggled to imagine how a lively jig could make so much trouble, but he had only to think of Mary Quilley, the island nurse, to realise it must be true. The Specials came to take her away because her brother was a known IRA man, even though the poor woman hadn't seen him in twenty years and never spoke of him except to say he was a bad piece of work. They would have done it and all, but for Father Rafferty, who fetched the English vicar to settle them down. But not before they burned some books she had, that were only Irish faery stories, and half her roof with it.

"I am that sorry if I have caused you worries," he said.

"You must have more care for the way things are, is all," Jack said. Then he grinned. "Well now, enough of this. I suppose it is streams, swift and pure, you are wantin' so you may come wi' me."

Someone put a glass full of money on the bar in front of Ciaran.

"What is this, then?"

"It is for the music," said the publican.

"But it is for myself I play, and for my pleasure only. If you have liked it, it is thanks enough."

"Take it, man. We'll not be emptying the cup, now it is full."

"Ach, no I cannot. Give it over to the priest, the way he can put it to some need or other."

With the ice broken in the pub, Jack Craig talked more than usual. Ciaran was glad of it for there was no other comfort in the leafy gloom, where damp, silky threads broke, invisibly, across his face and whips of bramble tore at his clothes, tangled around his feet. He imagined that the stiller's boy must be sniffing his way through it; there was no path a man could see.

"You may sing if it makes you easy," the stiller's boy said.

"And how may I do that when I must be all the time listening to your feet for sure I can scarce see them?"

"You may breathe, then. There is no one will trouble you, for aren't they all comin' here for their drink."

"Is it the truth? The Protestants and all?" Tom Fergus said.

Jack laughed. "Do you think they are not drinking men themselves?"

Tom Fergus grunted.

"They are and all, you can be certain of that. Constables and soldiers are after drinking from the same jugs as farmers and even the boys from Donegal and Leitrim. There is no fighting differences at Johnny Craig's."

Already, this day, Ciaran had listened to enough talk of politics. And more than enough as well.

"Is it the water makes the drink bite so fine?" he said.

"Could be it is. Though me Da is after saying that the making is in the worm," Jack said. "If the coils is too cold, the stuff tastes of nothing at all. But one degree of temperature too hot and you'll be drinking poison that'll blind you soon enough."

"Well, it is a pleasant drink...better than any other."

"So they say."

"Do you not know it?"

"And how would I know that when I haven't never touched the stuff? Nor me Da neither. You cannot be drinking it if you are going to be stilling it. It is the same for most of the best, you know." He crashed on ahead, leaving Ciaran to stumble dumbly behind, too stunned by this news to express an opinion.

The forest canopy was busy with birds. Ciaran had relaxed and fallen in with Jack's pace when the oddness of it struck him. It was dark now and, like their sea-living cousins, the birds should have been settled for sleep, but they were lively and restless. Jack stopped and held up his hand.

"What is it?" Ciaran whispered.

"I do not know. But we best look sharpish."

"I canna see nothing," Tom Fergus said.

"We best be still and all," the stiller's boy snapped. He bent low and quickened his pace. The crack of rifle shot sent crowds of sparrows into the air. First one, then another, then several together. Jack began to run, the others struggling to keep up with him through the dense brush.

It was a fire fight all right, in the woods some hundred yards beyond the still. They could see the occasional blaze of a gunshot, hear the barks of command. But as they reconnoitred from the edge of the clearing, half a dozen broken jugs gave evidence of fighting there as well. One of the vats was overturned, its contents of fermenting mash a pale, reeking sludge on the ground.

The door of the darkened cottage was barred, from the inside.

"Open up, Da...it is myself," Jack shouted.

After a minute, they heard Johnny sliding the bolts. When he opened the door, the poor old man was shaking like a palsied beggar.

"Are you all right, Da? What the devil is goin' on?"

"The devil take the lot of them," the old man said.

Jack helped him to a chair and lit a candle. The kettle was hot so he made strong tea, stirring in spoon after spoon of sugar. When he dosed the tea with whiskey, Ciaran realised it was only poteen that the Craigs never touched. Jack held the cup and made his father drink. They waited for him to speak as the guns moved back and forth, sometimes closer, sometimes further away.

"Them bloody hooligans..." he said at last. "...for haven't they brought their arguments to my own doorstep...to Johnny Craig's," he said as though he could scarce believe it. In truth, none of them could. Wasn't it a well known fact that Johnny Craig's was a neutral place?

"Who is it at all, that's fighting out there?"

"It was them boys from Gleneely, in Donegal, come over to buy their drink. I'm thinking one of their own lot must have turned informer, for weren't the Specials waiting for them and all. And who at all knows when they will be coming here but their own kind? Or even which way through the woods they will travel."

"They'll not be bothering us again, tonight," Jack said. "We seen them chasing each other to the north."

But as he said it, something harder than a hand banged on the door. Johnny began to shake all over again. Ciaran slid his fiddle from his shoulder and put it on the table.

"Open up in there," a voice shouted. "Unbar the door or we will break it down."

Jack opened the door to a constable who was scarce more than a lad. His uniform, though makeshift, looked new. He had a shiny new rifle slung over his left shoulder and a billy club in his right hand.

"What is your business here, annoying peaceable people in the middle of the night?" Jack said.

"You are running an illegal still," the young constable said. "It will have to be destroyed."

Now, Johnny, who seemed to have recovered at the sound of the young constable's voice, joined them at the door. "Isn't it George Anderson?" he said. "What are you on about, boy? Wasn't you just after buying four jugs with your Da, yesterday a week?"

The young constable twisted the billy club in his hands. "It is none of my doing," he whispered. "The new officers are sayin' you give comfort to the IRA."

"Ach lad, you know I haven't the time for speechifyers and bully boys from either side. And none of that has ever mattered here."

"It is the law must be obeyed," the young constable said aloud.

Johnny peered round the door. Three constables waited beside the shed. One was a stranger, but the other two were regular customers.

"Bloody foolishness," he said. "We shall see about this mischief and all."
The rush of fear that had made him tremble, now fuelled his indignation. He
marched across the yard, Jack, Ciaran, Tom Fergus and the young constable
close behind. "All right," he said, "What nonsense is this?"

"Move aside," the stranger said. The familiarity of his voice startled
Ciaran. He stared at the man, who stared blankly back, but he couldn't place
him.

The old man's courage grew. "What is the matter with you lot? You know
Craigs have been stilling here since before your grandfathers' days."

None of them spoke up.

"Is it money you are wanting? Like them gangsters in Chicago? Is that
what we have come to at last? Well shame on you, then. Shame on you."

Ciaran was confused. Danger charged all his senses. It glowed around all
of them like bog lightening. Yet Johnny Craig hectored the four armed men as
though they were children.

"All right," he said. "Enough is enough. Clear out of here...Go on."

"Will you not move aside?" the stranger said.

"I will not!"

The stranger struck the old man to the ground. Ciaran lunged for his
raised club and grabbed it before he struck again.

And then they were, all of them, fighting, rolling this way and that on the
ground. Someone pushed through into the shed and began emptying the jugs
onto the floor. Johnny Craig tried to stop him and was pushed down again.
Instead of helping his father, Jack ran to fetch a bucket of earth. He shovelled
it onto the peat under the still. What was the man doing when they were all in
the thick of it, hand to hand? Then a finger of blue alcohol flame, beautiful,
smokeless and cold, crawled past Ciaran and he understood. It joined other
rivers of flame, travelling to the edges of the shed, where it lit stored peat and
sacks of potatoes. The sacks went up like paper, lighting the thatch and loosing
potatoes that rolled through the poteen and carried it to every corner of the
place. The alcohol, now warmed, burst, with soft puffing noises, into puddles
of flame.

Ciaran saw Tom Fergus flatten the young constable. He ducked a blow and
shouted, "Get yourself out of here."

"I'll not leave you behind," Tom Fergus shouted back.

"Have you lost your reason, man? Think of your children, for the love of God."

"I'll not leave you behind."

In the confusion of flames and blows, Ciaran was not certain of what happened next. He thought he saw two men, their faces covered with masks of cloth, manhandle Tom Fergus out of the shed. Before he could look again, a timber, one end of it blazing, crashed down from the roof. It knocked his assailant unconscious but it also pinned Ciaran's right foot to the floor. Flames teased his boot and singed the nap of his homespun trousers. He struggled, in vain, to free himself. He was grabbed from behind. A pair of hairy hands gripped his shoulders. He tore them off. They grabbed again. He flailed and struck out but, unable to turn, his blows were wasted. He twisted his head as far as he could and bit a wrist. Something hard crashed into his skull and the world went black.

Now, they were running. Two men supported him under the arms and dragged him through the woods. He wanted to run with them but his right foot didn't seem to be working. When he tried to put it on the ground the searing pain made him gasp.

"Be easy, man...We got you," somebody said.

The floor they threw him onto vibrated and hummed. He felt rubber and metal against his face, saw crowds of shoes around his head. A hoarse voice yelled, "Go...go." He heard the sound of a motor and another thundering noise, the like of which he hadn't heard since the Great War when he'd watched the ships do battle on the Sound. The floor where he lay, seemed to be moving. He rolled sideways, then back again, his mouth tasting mud and leather. Someone's boots. Then he passed out.

CHAPTER TWENTY THREE

In this world or the next

"Are you the fiddler?"

Blinding daylight silhouetted a big man in the doorway. The handkerchief tied over his mouth and nose muffled his voice and his eyes were hid by the flat tweed cap tugged low on his forehead. Otherwise, in his flannel shirt, rough twill trousers and braces, he might have been an ordinary working man.

"Who is askin' ?" Ciaran said.

"That's as no never mind...Are you? Just give us your answer."

The fiddle was gone. It was almost the first thing Ciaran noticed when he opened his eyes - after he realised that he was alone, with no sign of Tom Fergus. He touched the treasure, through his clothes. Then he looked around.

He was beside a motorcar on the floor of a kind of coach house. He tried to stand; pain streaked up from his ankle. His singed trouser leg was slit up to the knee. Someone had wrapped his foot in strips of linen. Using the car for leverage, he pulled himself up, thinking all the while that his bladder was fit to bursting and that it was turning out to be about the kind of morning as it had been a night before. That was when a side door opened and the big man came in.

"So, are you the fiddler?"

"Could be that I am."

"You best come with me, then." He reached for Ciaran who raised his fists, lost his balance and fell forward onto the bonnet of the motorcar.

The big man laughed. "You are a right scrapper you are. I'll grant you that. Look at yourself, man. What are you goin' to do with them grand fists of yours when you have hardly a leg to stand on?"

"I will follow you myself. I havna' the need of helping."

"Come on then." The big man was still laughing.

Ciaran hobbled to the front of the motorcar. He looked around for stick or a bit of a timber to lean on. Finding nothing, he tried again to put his weight on his right foot and grimaced with pain.

"All right now, we have all seen how brave you are. But it is a long way to the bog...if you are crawling."

The big man waited, close enough for Ciaran to smell a gloss of shaving soap over the stink of old sweat and fire. Eventually, he let the man support him and lead him out.

Five men, all of them masked, lounged about a grand room. Ciaran knew he had to keep his wits about him, but it was an effort not to stare. Though he imagined the Manor had such rooms, he had never been inside one. The windows were heavily draped, the curtains drawn even though it was day. The closed doors looked to be made of oak, with big china knobs. Spirit lamps with fine glass covers glittered around the walls and reflected in a gilded mirror above a carved fireplace. The furniture was stuffed and covered with patterned cloth. The chair the big man dumped him into had a silky sort of nap. He felt diminished by the high ceilings. There was no house the likes of this in Douglas Bridge.

Someone knocked and one of the men opened the door a crack. Ciaran heard a woman's voice and watched the man return with a tray of delicate tea things. One of the men offered him tea in the finest bit of china he had ever touched. The man's hairy hand had a loud red bruise and teeth marks above the wrist.

"You..."

Dropping the cup, Ciaran lunged forward and snatched the hand in both of his. Hot, milky tea splashed onto the carpet. In a flash, two other men grabbed him by the shoulders and pushed him back into the stuffed chair.

"Ah, look what you have done now," the hairy handed man said. "The good doctor will be thinking twice before he gives us the hospitality of his house again. I am sorry I had to give you such a crack on the head, my friend

236

but you was bound and determined to go up in flames in that place." He waved at the others and they relaxed their grip on Ciaran's shoulders.

"Where is Tom Fergus?"

"Would that be that fellow you was yelling at in the midst of the inferno?"

Ciaran nodded.

"He is on his way to a wedding in Strabane or thereabouts, if I am not mistaken."

"He wouldna' go without me."

"You are right about that. An awful fight he put up...almost as much as you. We had to tie him and gag him and throw him in a sack before he would see reason. But he will be arriving where he is meant to be, soon enough. You have put us to a lot of trouble, the both of yous."

"We wasna looking for your help."

"Next time we will be sure and get a by-your-leave before we save your skin."

"Why did you save us then?"

"Why? Do you think we are in the business of making widows and orphans out of innocent Catholic families? And as to yourself, weren't you after the same as the rest of us; trying to save poor Johnny Craig, God rest his soul, from them Protestant devils."

"Johnny Craig is dead?"

"He is. And Jack with him, in the explosion of the still. And so would you be and all, if I wasn't after pulling you out and getting the mark of your teeth for my troubles."

Ciaran slumped into the chair.

"Give the man another cup of tea. Or is it something stronger that you are wanting."

He shook his head. What kind of dream was this? Him sitting in a strange man's parlour, while men with handkerchiefs tied round their faces passed cups of tea in pale, flowered cups and talked of destruction with scarce more feelings than if it was the weather. How was he to know what to do or say next? Silently, he asked the Mother of God to pray for them all, alive and dead, and waited for the strength of her comfort.

At last, he spoke. "If you mean me no harm, why are you masked and all?"

"Isn't it to protect yourself that we have covered our faces, for if you haven't the heart to join up with us, best you be ignorant of who we are."

"And why would I be falling in with the likes of you, when I am a peaceable farmer with a home of my own to go to?"

"The likes of us? And what likes would that be, then?"

Ciaran had no idea. What could he know of them except that they were masked? Could be they were killers and bandits for sure they brought the smell of death and the eerie whine of danger to this peculiar tea party. He held his tongue.

"You may not have the choice, my friend, for if it is known you are living, and you be the fiddler himself, you are wanted in Ulster for the murder of the Craigs...and three Specials besides."

"But I haven't never killed no one."

"So you may say, but there is five men dead in the ashes of that place and the officer who got away is after telling them all it was you. Seems you had doings with him before for he is after saying that he should have finished you years ago, when first he gave you a pounding for your boasting in Cushendall. Besides, you left your fiddle behind in Johnny Craig's house."

Ciaran tried to concentrate on the violent events of the night before. So little had been said, he remembered more with his body than with his mind. There was the young constable and an officer, *the new officer* the young constable had called him. When he had commanded Johnny Craig to move aside, his voice had been familiar.

Now, as Ciaran recalled the voice, waiting for a face to coalesce around it, other words came back to him...*I'm thinking you would not be so full of boasts and medals...Jimmy...the finest man for the fiddle...*And he saw a younger man, not in the uniform of a special constable, but in the battle worn dress of a soldier, pulling the arm of a buxom, raven haired girl...*a coward such as himself...heroes all around have need of your comfort...*

Another voice snapped him back to the oppressively elegant parlour. "There was some at the pub in Douglas Bridge, said you was collecting money for the cause and all."

Ciaran shook his head, not knowing what to say...nor even what to ask.

"So, you see," the hairy handed man said, "You will be doing yourself no favours going back among the English, nor your people neither, and you are safe enough with us for now."

"What is this place?"

"You say you are a farmer. What else can you do at all?"

"I can read the tides and follow the fishes."

Some of the others laughed. "Well, that will sure be useful in the middle of Donegal," one of them said.

"Quiet!" snapped the hairy handed man.

"Is it the Free State that we are in, then?"

No one answered.

"You were saying what all you are good at."

Ciaran sighed and closed his eyes. The walls of stone are dark and glassy. The sea birds have gone. There is no hold that is not covered and filled with ice. And below, the sea is black and hungry. "I climb," he said. "...the cliffs."

"Can you read and write?" someone asked.

Did they think he was an ignorant heathen? "Of course I can," he snapped. "Irish and English both."

"You must not take offence where none is meant," said the hairy handed man. "There are many who cannot and isn't it a useful skill and all...There is porridge in the kitchen. Are you hungry?"

For the first time, Ciaran noticed that he was.

"You said before 'if it is known that I am living'. What were you meaning by that?"

"I reckon those bodies will be in a powerful mess when they dig them out of the ruins. Sure they'll be in pieces." Ciaran thought of the Craigs and the fresh faced, sheepish young constable. He felt sick. "...There is no one knows for sure who was killed last night," the hairy handed man continued, "only that they will find the leavings of five and all when they have finished looking. Could be it was Jack who ran with us. We could make it so."

"It is a mistake," Ciaran said. "I will tell them they have made a mistake."

"Will you? And do you think you will live long enough to do it, when they are after believing it is three of their own you have slaughtered?"

Locked in a servant's room beside the kitchen, Ciaran learned the lessons of an accidental exile. On Rathlin, the cliffs still screamed with summer birds, the meadow heathers turned autumn russet and gold. Soon the barley would be heavy and the harvest preparations would begin. Next week he and Tom Fergus were meaning to take the new mare over to Ballycastle for shoeing. After that, the whole *clachan*, men and women together, would see to it that the grain store, the sacks and the implements were fit. And there was Bertie's roof needed mending before the weather changed. It was a cycle he was born to; he had never imagined any other.

"You may stay with the doctor until you are fit for walking. You are no use to us a cripple."

They didn't say what use that was, but he could guess and he wanted no part of it. The hairy handed man had spoken gently enough, but there was powerful menace in the very softness of his tone.

Lost and mute, without the comfort of his fiddle, he wondered how a man could live among strangers. Sure and he must find his way home.

But he could see no way to do it. For it was true enough that if they knew he was living, the Specials would come looking for him, bringing misery and destruction into the lives of his blameless friends.

Perhaps he could get word to them. If there was a priest, maybe it could be done. So at least they would know that he was living and innocent of the things they were saying about him.

But what would be the use of it, except to cause them more grief and worry? Wouldn't they know he could not have done all that killing? Bertie, most of all? *Ah, Bertie.* No, it was best they mourn him and be done with it, for now he could bring them only troubles. Hadn't he already spoiled a wedding in Strabane? Except their prayers, there was nothing they could do to help him.

His head hurt and his ankle throbbed. He could not think anymore, nor weep any more useless tears, so he slept, dreaming of the living, of the dead and of the sea.

Four days later, his ankle healed, he told the hairy handed man, the chief of the little band of irregulars, that their quarrel was none of his. "I am beholden that you have saved me, but I must make my own way from now." They took him, blindfolded, for a long ride in the motorcar. He wondered if now they were going to kill him and, in truth, he was too numbed by grief to care. But when, at last, they stopped, they simply set him on a road in the middle of farm country. He could smell the ripening corn and the earthy tang of beasts.

"Leave the blindfold until you hear us well away. If you walk in the direction you are pointed, you will come to a place called Ballybofey. Could be you will find some harvest work there."

The hairy handed man clapped an arm around Ciaran's shoulders. "Good luck to you, fiddler," he said. And then they were gone.

Part Four

Which of us is not forever a stranger and alone?

Look Homeward, Angel! Thomas Wolfe

CHAPTER TWENTY FOUR

American dreams

A strong looking man stops on the corner of East Broadway and Clinton Street to shift the sack he is carrying from one shoulder to the other. Although he is past the first flush of youth, he is still fit and frequently boasts that he is in his prime. His thick woollen jacket, worn against the grim December cold, does not hide, but rather emphasises the broadness of his shoulders. From the flecks of paint and plaster that cling to his fingernails, the white painted strand in his curly brown hair, it is not difficult to guess his living. And he has, as they say in New York, the map of Ireland printed on his face.

He scans the street for the sign of the three golden balls. What, he wonders, would his grandfather think about the errand he is about? The old man, whose possessions he now carries, never went as far from home as Dublin until he crossed the Atlantic. And then, even in a new world, didn't he keep to his own kind? Yet here he is, in the Jewish neighbourhood, a place he's never been before, sent by a Mohawk Indian and a Sicilian stone mason, come to sell a bag full of things that began their useful lives in Limerick.

John Littlecloud, who lives in Brooklyn and spends his days balanced on girders hundreds of feet above the street, had told him that, unlike some others, the Jewish pawnbrokers in the Lower East Side would give you a price for anything, even old clothes if they were good enough. Tony Manuto, because he played the horses more than was good for him, knew all the best moneylenders. So, he had packed up the little that his grandfather left behind and set out for a pawnshop on East Broadway.

There are two tweed jackets that his grandfather only wore for weddings, funerals and church; a coat and some new linen shirts; a mantel clock and some china ornaments that had been his grandmother's, and a pair of gold cufflinks. The sack also contains the ceremonial sword his grandfather had worn when he marched with the Fenian Social Club and Benevolent Society on St. Patrick's Day. And there's his grandfather's fiddle that he had neither the talent nor the interest to master. Once, he might have kept the sword and given the clothes over to the Church. But he is a practical man. Christmas is coming and so are his wife's republican cousins from Cork. A working man's wages only go so far.

He is surprised to find a young woman behind the counter, expecting matters of money to be dealt with by men; but she seems businesslike and efficient. She is beautiful, in a stern, old fashioned way. Her clothes, he notices, are old fashioned as well, and her heavy chestnut braid. She examines each item he offers and notes it on a piece of lined paper. She runs her fingers across the fiddle strings which exhale a faint dissonance.

That's when, inexplicably, he thinks of the dancehalls he used to visit before the responsibilities of family overtook him. He remembers a girl he hadn't thought about in years; a girl in a spangled dress, with hair like a mermaid, who had shimmied to beat the band.

"Do I know you?" he says.

"No, I don't think so." She looks squarely at him before returning to her work and he realises he must be mistaken. For what had crossed his mind about that girl from long ago was the flashing spirit in her eyes; a spirit that had nearly tempted him, although she was more child than woman at the time. The eyes that have just taken him in, blankly and briefly, are virtually soulless.

∞

Daniel pressed a bouquet of pale green shoots to his face. He closed his eyes and raised his eyebrows, mimicking Uncle Shoe so precisely that Rachel half expected him to declare '*Oy, a machaya*...Such a pleasure...like heaven it smells.'

"Ayuns, Mommy...Smell ayuns," he said and he shoved the bouquet of greens under her nose.

She made a great show of sniffing the present. "Oh, *what* a good smell... Onions...You say it....*Un-yuns.*"

"Ahnyuns."

She hugged him.

Rachel and Helen shelled peas on the porch of Uncle Shoe's white clapboard farmhouse in Connecticut. Memorial Day was a Monday that year and the owner of the shirt factory closed for the day, out of respect for his son who was killed in the war.

Holidays were rare enough, but a long weekend that didn't involve extra hours in the schul or, for the women, in the kitchen preparing a Jewish feast, was like a miracle. Shoe invited Rachel and the boy to come up to the farm to see the apples bloom.

Shoe, who never married, adored Daniel and Daniel loved the farm. A few months before, when Shoe planted the early vegetables, Rachel had spent hours of their precious weekend together travelling with her child, by train, to the little town of Greens Farms. Daniel had followed Shoe from row to row, scattering seed peas and beans, tamping down the soil with a toy hoe. Shoe said Daniel had inherited the family green thumb. Rachel was less convinced. No little boy of three can resist wet dirt.

In April, at the family gathering for Passover, Helen pointedly suggested that, now that she and Mendel had a Ford, they loved taking Emma for rides in the country. Shoe had generously invited Dinah as well. Before Helen had a chance to ask where he would put them all, Dinah declined. Every Memorial Day, she and her father had remembered her brother Nathan, who was buried in France, by putting flags on soldiers' graves in Cypress Hills. Now that Moses was gone, she said, she wanted to keep up the tradition.

So, on a Saturday morning at the end of May, much to Jacob's displeasure as it was Shabbas, they piled into Mendel's car and headed for Uncle Shoe's farm, just over the border on the Connecticut shore.

Rachel put down the bowl of peas and pulled Daniel into her lap. Emma and Shoe had followed him onto the porch, Emma happily chewing on sweet peas, pods and all. Helen tried to prise them from her. "Don't eat those, They're raw. They'll give you a bellyache."

"What are you talking?" Shoe said. "Sweet like candy they are. Better than candy."

"She'll spoil her appetite. It's time for their naps anyway." She took Emma's hand and reached for Daniel who wrapped his arms around Rachel.

"No," he said. "No nap."

"No nap? What then?" Rachel said.

"Go see flower trees."

"Flower trees? You want to see the apple trees?"

Daniel nodded. "Go see appuh trees."

"Well," Rachel smiled at Helen, "I guess that's what we'll do."

Helen shrugged and took Emma inside.

At the bottom of a hollow, hidden from the house by a small stand of maples and pin oaks and sheltered from the salt of the Long Island Sound by a gentle rise, thirty snowy apple trees softened the sky. The rows of younger trees extended to the slope, where Shoe had pushed the limits of the orchard as close to the water as the mixed climate would allow. He had built a low stone wall, from cobbles, to hold back the sand. Rachel perched on it, still and alert to the mingling of blossom scent and sea air. Below her on the beach, Mendel cast a line across the current, hoping to catch one of the bluefish that Uncle Shoe said sometimes lost their way into the Sound. Clover amethysts studded the grassy slope. A Monarch butterfly lit near her. Rachel watched its wings tremble in a breeze that only it could feel, tasted the sweet nectar that it drank. She tilted her face into the sunlight and shared the fugitive pleasure that, even so, must have blessed the first children in the first garden of the world. If she had allowed herself to explore this feeling she would have been surprised, and perhaps frightened, to name it happiness.

In the oldest part of the orchard, Uncle Shoe sacrificed bushels of his embryonic crop for her son's delight. He lifted Daniel into the lower branches of a tree, where squealing and giggling, he stripped the branches bare.

"Uncle Shoe," she called. "Don't let him do that. You won't have any apples to sell."

"What are you worried, Rucheleh? Plenty more trees I got, plenty apples enough. This old tree, it doesn't make such good ones anyway, so let him enjoy."

"You spoil him."

"So *schon*, why shouldn't I? Who else since Weiss, he should rest in peace?"

Rachel nodded. Toward the end of his life, Moses Weiss had lived to indulge his grandson. The old man had stopped hoping that his own son would come home and become a *mensch*. Long before they buried him, his broken heart had set against Schmuel, harder than the January ground they put him in, shovelling away the snow to make the grave. There would be no forgiveness; he left the pawn shop to Daniel with instructions for Dinah to look after it and to teach the boy when he was old enough.

So, Daniel was rich. Rachel wondered whether, when he was old enough to understand, the inheritance would console him for the absence of a father's love. She had no way of knowing whether Mendel's second-hand affection would serve for a kind of love she had never experienced herself. Would it help Daniel to be strong and kind and generous like Uncle Shoe? Would he grow up sure and gentle, brave and loving himself? How could she know, when she had only ever dreamed of such a man, what went into the making of him?

Something in the grass had captured Daniel's attention. A beetle or a worm. She watched him chattering and pointing, Uncle Shoe crouched down beside him, patting his soft brown curls. Perhaps he would grow to blame her. Maybe he would never forgive her for what she had done. Since the annulment, she had heard the whispers. In the neighbourhood, people were saying she had made him a bastard.

Duvi and Councilman Tierney, who was Boss Tierney now, had arranged it after it became clear that, without Schmuel, even a civil divorce was nearly impossible. She had tried to get one as soon as Sarah was safely married and the Widow Meyer's blustering disapproval rendered meaningless. Accompanied by Dinah, for moral support, Rachel had taken all her signed papers to the courthouse. The clerk asked her when her husband would appear in court.

"I don't know. He left me. I don't know where he is."

"Seven years for desertion," the clerk said, stamping the papers and adding "...unless he's a sailor. Then its only two. He in the Navy or anything like that?"

Rachel shook her head.

The clerk shrugged, "Seven years then. Let the court know if you change your address."

"But he could be declared dead in seven years."

"Same thing," the clerk smirked, "Hope your new boyfriend likes long engagements."

"The smug little creep," Dinah spat. "Men, they're all the same." But Rachel, stumbling, stunned and tearful, down the courthouse steps wasn't paying attention. She was thinking about living in the shadow of Schmuel's brutal whims for another four years. Anything could happen. What if he made peace with his father? Who knew what he would want from her. Or from her shining child.

That night, she overheard Jacob telling Sophie, "She made her bed...So now, she can sleep in it."

But Duvi had another idea. "I'll talk to the Boss," he said. "You never know. Maybe he's got a judge in his pocket."

Boss Tierney had a lot of judges in his pocket. One, in particular, had a fondness for pretty girls. And Boss Tierney knew a lot of pretty girls.

"It's easy," Duvi said. "You were only sixteen, and you didn't have no permission. So, it wasn't even legit in the first place."

"We *did* have permission," Rachel protested. "Papa signed a paper at City Hall."

"Yeah? Well, whaddya know, City Hall's a big place. Little pieces of paper in a big place like that? They get lost all 'atime."

"But Duvi, somebody could find out."

"So what? Who's gonna argue with a judge? From the First District Appellate? Besides, who cares about a coupla nobodies from the Lower East Side?"

So, it was done. The annulment made the marriage invalid, as though it had never even happened. It also made Daniel illegitimate.

Where he stood in the eyes of the rabbis was another matter. The *ketubah*, the certificate that proved a Jewish marriage had been consecrated, was locked away in Jacob's chest. To make it the worthless piece of paper that it was, required the worthless man she had married.

Daniel ran circles around Uncle Shoe's legs, a giddy toddler spinning in the sunshine. It was nearly supper time. The questions and the problems could wait.

She strolled towards the house, collecting Uncle Shoe along the way. Daniel dashed back and forth to report on the doings in the kitchen. "Soup and meat and t'patoes and ev'ything..."

"Everything?"

"Hurry up, Mommy, Helen says hurry up. Gotta wash your hands for supper."

The children, animated by fresh air and novel adventures, made supper a lively event. Shoe's new radio, blasting away in the parlour, added saxophones and clarinets to the general din. Once the kitchen was cleared and the children put to bed, Helen complained of a headache and disappeared, with Mendel, upstairs.

Now Rachel sat on the porch swing, riding the dark. Inside, Shoe twisted the dials until softer music emerged from the static. Everyone else was asleep. As a city child, Rachel had, at first, believed that nothing was more black, empty and silent than country darkness. But gradually, over years of summer visits to Uncle Shoe's farm, she had learned to see and hear the night.

Katydids racketed in the bushes while, above them, tree crickets chirped hopeful solos. If she kept motionless, she might hear the soft plop of a toad or the slither of a salamander in the grass. Shreds of moon-limned cirrus stroked the sky. Even the inky woods were animated with whispering, laughing shadows as spirits, too timid to test the daylight, came out to play.

The radio painted ripples of dancing strings. The grass glistens. It bends cool under her bare feet. *Dance for me. Dance only for me.* She spreads her arms and turns slowly to his music, the train of her dress drawing circles in the dew.

"A nice dream, Rucheleh?"

"Hmm?"

"You were smiling in your sleep."

"I wasn't sleeping...I was just..." Rachel blinked and looked around. Uncle Shoe stood over her, proffering a steaming cup. She sighed. "Well...maybe...I guess..."

"I brought you a hot drink. Maybe already you should come inside, it's getting chilly."

"No...not yet." She pulled her shawl up around her shoulders. "It's such a beautiful night."

Shoe agreed. "Always this time of year is here beautiful nights." He sat beside her and set the swing in motion.

"Uncle Shoe, why do you live way up here?"

"What, I should make a farm on the Lower East Side?" Shoe teased. "Maybe plant some apple trees on Orchard Street?"

"No...but...people have farms in Brooklyn and on Staten Island...Mama says when you came to America, there were still farms in The Bronx."

"You don't like it here?"

"Of course, I like it...I love it...but you live so far away. Daniel cried when I told him we were leaving tomorrow."

"So, bring him next week again, on the train. You know, Rucheleh, all this I have by myself. You come stay with Daniel whenever you want, as long as you like."

"You live so far away."

They rocked, the porch swing complaining gently. *Scritch...scratch... scritch... scratch.* The crickets stopped singing to listen. "A *bissel* oil wouldn't hurt," Shoe said.

"You always say that. It wouldn't be the country without the sound of your swing, Uncle Shoe."

"Mmm."

Rachel smiled. "Papa says you live with the goyem."

"Is that what he says? Well..." Shoe laughed and shook his head.

"But why *do* you...live so far away?"

Shoe became thoughtful. "Well, I'll tell you. Some people think that only in the schul God lives," he said, "and that maybe, if you don't live next door, you make too much trouble for him, blessed be his name." He laughed. "So, they think, if the Almighty has to go around the corner, or, God forbid he should have to cross a bridge, *Schon*, already he won't come for the high holidays. Me, I think different.

"You know, Rucheleh, until I took the boat from Hamburg, never in my whole life did I see the ocean. Maybe you wouldn't understand. Because you were born here. But the first time I saw it, I thought...I thought...I must be dead because already straight in God's face I'm looking."

A memory of the feeling rose in Rachel and she nodded.

"A lot of the people were sick as dogs, all the way over. Two weeks vomiting and moaning and praying and cursing the Tsar of Russia for making them leave. And even Franz Joseph they cursed, who was not so bad to us like some others, But me, I was on the deck day and night, like I was made for it."

"So why didn't you go to sea to be a sailor?"

"Me? A sailor? From boats I know? What do I know? I'm a farmer. All those years, pressing suits in Vienna, I dreamed and I saved for my farm in America. So I decided that as soon as I landed, I would find a farm by the water."

"Brooklyn is by the water."

"Don't think I didn't look there first...but, in Brooklyn, by the water is all sand. So I looked at maps and I talked to people and I learned some...you know...geography. Then, one day, I'm in the wholesale market; because I figure maybe there I'll meet a farmer who needs a helper. So, you know, I could go and stay a while, and see if I would like this place or that place before I decided. It wasn't so easy, because in those days, my English is not so good and Jewish farmers, let me tell you, a dime a dozen they're not.

"...So, anyway, this one day I'm talking about, I meet a *Yiddisher* farmer who needs a hired man on his chicken farm in Connecticut. Me, I never even heard of Connecticut. But he tells me it's by the water. So, I went to work for him.

"I didn't know you worked on a chicken farm. You don't even like chicken."

"So, you never asked yourself why? Two years I worked on that chicken farm. Such filth, in my life I never saw. And a stink, Rucheleh, you shouldn't know from it. I'm telling you. A chicken I wouldn't touch if you paid me. But I worked and I saved some more, and, once in a while I got a day off...because, you know, in those days it wasn't every week you got one. So when it was my day off, I went looking for my farm.

"Plenty long I looked. This place was too big, that one cost too much money, another one you couldn't, if you tried, grow even weeds. And then I found this place; twenty five acres, right by the water. With apple trees. Just a few but you could see that they were happy here, and a nice little house. Needed plenty work this house, believe me, otherwise, how could I afford it? But with trees around it, a *shayna* house. So, I went to sit by the water to think and to ask God maybe He could spare me a little advice. 'So *Nu*? What do you think?' I said...and clear as a bell, He says to me, 'Berel' ...that was in the old days before you gave me my name and everybody started calling me Shoe..." He began to laugh. "Your Papa, he should live and be well, would be pleased to know, God still knows my right name...So, anyway, 'Berel,' he says to me, 'This is the place, Berel.' And that, as they say, was that. So, *schon*, a long answer for a little question, *Nu*?"

Rachel laughed. "I wish God would talk to me and tell me what to do."

"God talks to everyone, Rucheleh. You only have to stop thinking so much and listen. And you have to look also, because all kinds of ways God makes conversation. Look at Daniel. You don't think Daniel is God talking to you?"

Rachel had no answer for such a question. Daniel a message from God? For a moment, the beauty of the idea captured her imagination. Since Rabbi Meyer died, years ago, she had not heard God described with such affection and wonder. But then it occurred to her that the message made more problems than it solved. *"Maybe, next time,"* Bubbie Ruchel whispered in her ear, *"You could ask God to be a little more clear."* She changed the subject.

"Dinah wants me to move in with her and work in the store."

"Mmm?"

"There's more room for Daniel there. I wouldn't have to run to Brooklyn every weekend. Mendel could bring him to me in the car."

"So?"

"So, Papa says if I live without my parents, I'll never find a husband. 'Go live on your own, like a shiksa,' he says, 'and see how fast you get a father for your son.' "

"Maybe he's right."

Rachel sighed. "I know."

They left early on Sunday. Helen wanted to take the children to see the Bronx Zoo on the way home. For several hours they wandered among caged animals, Rachel becoming more and more depressed at the sight of them. Lions pining for their lost savannahs, jittery tigers, monkeys screaming in impotent rage, bears chewing their feet. Daniel, like all children, was enchanted by the seals whose trusting faces made Rachel the saddest of all.

"Some life," Mendel said. "Lie around in the bath all day while somebody throws you all the fish you can eat. Pretty good."

Rachel saw ice castles and listened to memories of princes and heroes. She said nothing.

It was dusk by the time they dropped her at Rivington Street. Over Helen's protests, Mendel and Rachel insisted on bringing the children up to see their grandparents. "They're tired. You know your father doesn't have any patience when they're cranky," Helen said.

Helen was probably right; no patience and, as far as Daniel was concerned, little apparent interest either. But Rachel didn't want to disappoint Sophie and Ruth who would be looking forward to seeing them. She and Mendel lifted the children out of the car and headed up, Helen following.

Something was not right. An acrid fog of tension and malice hung on the landing. The doorknob was icy. Rachel shivered, as though someone had walked on her grave.

"What is it," Mendel said.

"Nothing...it's...it's getting cold." She opened the door.

They were sitting, Ruth, Jacob and Sophie, in the afternoon gloom. Jacob still doled out electricity like it was liquid gold.

Sophie jumped up and put on the light. She was distracted. Rachel could see that while she and Ruth fussed over the children, giving them milk and *mandelbrot*, listening to the wonders of the zoo and the farm, her mind was elsewhere. Ruth seemed nervous as well.

Jacob scowled, but since he usually did, Rachel could make nothing of it. "Give Grandpa a kiss," she told Daniel and enjoyed her father's discomfort as he endured the child's enthusiastic affection. After a few minutes of awkward conversation—Sophie didn't even offer them coffee—Helen said, "It's late. The children are tired. We have to go." For the first time in Rachel's memory, nobody argued with her.

As soon as they were gone, Ruth slipped into the bedroom. Sophie picked up a dish rag and set about fiercely scrubbing the table.

"What's going on?" Rachel said. "What's the matter?"

Sophie looked pointedly at Jacob. He cleared his throat. "We had a visitor," he said.

"Who?"

"It was your rich little prince of a son he came to visit."

Rachel sank into a chair. She didn't have to ask but the words came anyway. "What? Who?"

Sophie put her arms around Rachel. "Schmuel is back," she said. "He wants to see the boy."

CHAPTER TWENTY FIVE

Stalemate

His expensive suit was linen. His skin was tanned. Otherwise, Schmuel had not changed at all. He sprawled across his sister Dinah's couch, oozing menace despite his studied nonchalance.

"What do you want from us?"

"What kinda question is that? Do I not have rights? Am I not the kid's father?"

"But why now? After all these years?"

Schmuel shrugged. "News travels slow."

Rachel knew that some news travelled faster than others. No one had to tell her he had heard about his father's will and had come to stake a claim on the child. It was written in the sneer on his face.

"So when you gonna show me this kid? Whaddya call him? Danny?"

"Daniel."

"Yeah. Nice name."

"You can't see him. He doesn't even know you exist."

"Whaddya talkin' *can't*...I tole ya...I got rights."

"No, you don't...The marriage was annulled."

"So I also heard. Pretty slick trick, Pops."

Jacob squirmed. He and Dinah were the only witnesses to the tense encounter now taking place in the rooms above the pawn shop. He had insisted that Rachel must face Schmuel and get it over with. But other than the occasional grunt, he had said nothing since they arrived. Rachel didn't waste time guessing his thoughts; she focused on Schmuel. Her only support came, penetrating and warm, from Dinah.

"So, I talked to this brief, see?" Schmuel said. "...And he tole me I cannot do nothing about this...whaddyacall...annulment, fishy though it may be, because it is, as they say, *connected*. But, this is one very smart brief. And he says that this does not no way change the...uh...situation. 'Cause we was married when the kid was born. And this is a fact which, I don't have to tell you, is written down, permanent, in the Hall of Records."

Rachel bit her lip. "What do you want from him?" she said.

"What I gotta want? This poor kid ain't got no Daddy. How's he gonna grow up without no Daddy to teach him the ropes?"

Rachel swallowed a bitter retort. She could imagine what Schmuel might teach her son.

"Anyway, this kid needs a home. What kinda life is this? He don't even live with his mother? I'm getting married, in a coupla months. Nice and respectable. I got plans."

The news jolted Rachel. Dinah, too, was surprised. She inhaled to regain the self-control she was determined to keep. "You're going to marry *Beh*...the girl you went away with?" A few secrets that Rachel cared to keep, the ones that really mattered, were still her own.

"Nah. Too many chocolates. She got fat. I got me a real classy lady now, educated. Her old man's in the rag trade."

Rachel wondered what an educated woman would see in Schmuel's sleazy charm. But the other woman's preferences didn't engage her interest for long; Schmuel had opened a new line of pursuit. As casually as she could manage, she said, "So, I suppose you'll have to go to a rabbi now...to ask for a divorce."

"Whaddya kidding? I'm gonna go crawling to some old man with a beard? Superstitious crap."

"But how can you get married?" Rachel sputtered. "We don't have a Jewish divorce."

"Oh yeah? Tell that to the State of New York. Listen kiddo, either we are married or we ain't and we never was. You can't have it both ways."

For the first time, Jacob spoke. "This is a Jewish girl you're going to marry? With no *get*?"

"Lemme tell ya something, old man. There are Jews and there are Jews. They are not, all of them, greenhorn *mockeys* like around here, asking the rabbis permission to wipe their asses after they take a shit."

Veins popped out on Jacob's temples. Rachel thought he might have a stroke on the spot. She heard him growl "*Malchamuvis*, devil," but the tight line of his lips never moved.

"Schmuel! That's enough," Dinah blurted.

He shrugged. "Whatever. I ain't tellin' no rabbi my personal troubles so they can make a big *spiel* about me in the schul. They got plenty enough suckers to keep them busy."

"Oh, for God's sake, Schmuel," Rachel snapped. "Why would it be so hard to give it to me? What difference does it make to you?"

Schmuel said nothing. He ran the brim of his cream straw panama through his fingers, sat back and enjoyed Rachel's distress.

His stunning news silenced her. His return had filled her with visions of deliverance. She had never imagined that he would say no. Now she saw herself trapped in a kind of half marriage to a man who could not even be bothered to discard her. She would wither and fade, unable to remarry among her own, unable to find a loving man to father her son, to make a decent home. But she refused to give him the pleasure of her tears. She stared at him until he was forced to speak.

"This *get*," he said, "...this is real important to you?"

Rachel nodded.

"Well, I don't see no problem here...You want the *get*, you let me see my kid."

This was an offer Rachel could not afford to dismiss as once she had dismissed Schmuel for a fool. Even fools can sometimes be clever. And Schmuel was mean.

Jacob leaned forward. She and her child only served to remind him of his failed judgement. He wanted her respectably married and out of his house. He wanted it as much as she did, passionately and selfishly. Dinah, ever practical and sensible would say, "Do it. He'll lose interest, His new wife won't want him bothering with you. Do it and be done with it."

Rachel steadied herself. Coldly, in a silence mocked by sundancing dust, she took the devil's measure. Why had she never seen the bones of real evil that lay beneath his babyfaced grin? His presence so poisons the air that spirits shrink into the corners to avoid it. He holds death in his hand. He stinks of it. His claws drip with blood. There is such a sighing all around. And ragged whispers on the breath of fear. *Do not be deceived by his flowers of reason. His bloody flowers.*

Outside, the melon man turned his cart onto East Broadway, hawking his summer treat as he came. "Watermelon...Cold like ice...Sweet like honey...Spend a nickel...Treat your honey...*Wah-di-muhlown*..." Rachel tried to remember the crisp wet taste, to calm her fancy by anchoring it to the commonplaces of the street. She was a prisoner in her father's house, she reasoned, stifled by pointless rules made by men to please a God who seemed to listen only to them. Schmuel tempted her with a kind of escape. True, it would only be an escape to the sovereignty of another man. Rabinovitz, the matchmaker, had told Jacob there were plenty of decent men just waiting for the *get* to make Rachel a proposal. She would just have to pick more carefully. Now that she was older, she would not be so foolish.

"What have you been doing all these years?"

"Oh, you know...a bit of this...a bit of that."

She imagined it, unpredictable and dangerous. *Do not be deceived. He hunts with the wolves.* She rubbed her eyes with the tips of her fingers but she could not clear away these visions of a soul being consumed by its own corruption. If the price of freedom was exposing Daniel to Schmuel, the price was too high. She would not ransom herself with her son's innocence.

"So what's it gonna be?" Schmuel said. "We gonna make a deal or what?"

"No," Rachel whispered.

"What was that? I do not think I am believing my ears here."

"No...Go away...Leave us alone."

Dinah sighed and Jacob glared at Rachel.

"Looks what we got here is whatcha call a Mexican stand-off," Schmuel sneered. "So Pops...you agree with this?"

"The boy is hers," Jacob said. He was so angry he could barely speak. Rachel knew that she, not Schmuel, was the cause of the anger. She didn't care.

"Yeah, well it ain't that simple. 'Cause the kid is mine too." He gathered up his jacket and hat. "This ain't finished," he said to Rachel. "Like they say in the movies kiddo, 'See ya in court'."

Jacob stormed for days. "A roof over your head forever I am expected to provide? And what would be so terrible he should see the boy?"

"Daniel."

"What would be so terrible he should see Daniel once in a while?"

"He's a *gonif*, a thief."

"You don't know. Aa *schtick dreck*, maybe, with no respect; but the rest you don't know."

"What then? A *luftmensch*, who lives on air? I know."

"He's the boy's father!"

Rachel turned her back on Jacob and left for work.

Dinah said no court would give a young child to its father, especially not a father like Schmuel. But both she and Rachel knew he might get permission to visit Daniel. And then there were Daniel's living arrangements, separated from his mother for most of the week. This was no longer entirely Jacob's doing. Rachel knew she could make her father bend. But what good would that do? Who would look after him while she went out to work? A judge might consider this and let Schmuel and his new wife, whoever she was, keep Daniel for weeks on end.

Oddly, these considerations did not demoralise her. If anything, seeing Schmuel again had galvanised her latent will. Once it had silenced pompous little bar mitzvah boys, set old men to gibbering and praying, brought her any partner she wanted at the dancehalls. Once, she had been able to get her own way when it mattered enough. Perhaps this power had been lulled to sleep by motherhood, or shocked apathetic by her terribly miscalculated marriage. Now, awakened, it listened to voices; it made plans. If her father wouldn't support her, she would find someone who would. Outside the family, nobody knew that Schmuel was still refusing her the *get*. What people did know was that he was back and that he was courting some uptown girl. She had only to wait until they put two and two together. Schmuel, too, had underestimated his opponent.

One Saturday night a month, Jacob's *landsmanschaft*, The Pilsener Mutual Aid Society, hired a hall and held a social. A band of the members played polkas and horas, schottisches and oom-pah-pah waltzes while the young people clustered around the refreshments, drinking lemonade and watching their parents dance. Later, somebody would set up a Victrola and the younger couples would dance chaste fox trots and two-steps to the scratchy music of well-worn records. Old men circulated on the dance floor, using their canes to poke and prod anybody who got too friendly.

These dances were among the few mating rituals approved by the whole community. Sarah had met her rabbi, Yossel, at just such a dance. Now Ruth was keeping company with a barber she met in the same way. Rachel had not attended a *landsmanschaft* dance since she was thirteen. On a Saturday night in June, she loosed her hair, stuffed an *Evening in Paris*-scented cotton ball into her bodice, pushed Bubbie Ruchel's little gold rings through her ears and went hunting for a man.

He was a schoolteacher, a childless widower who lost his wife, Miriam, to rheumatic fever. His name was Aaron and he was delighted to dance with Rachel. He had soft manners, perfect English and appealing green eyes, almost as green as Daniel's. He told Rachel that though the rabbis said a wife should be ruled by her husband, he believed a fair and forgiving partnership was always the best way. He said that he had seen her in the park with her little boy; your *kleyne menscheleh* he said, your little man. To be a father, he said, was his greatest wish. He didn't say that he had made enquiries to Rabinovitz about Rachel. She already knew.

There was no magic. The harsh light of the social hall was not conducive to glamour and romance. And Aaron was hardly the stuff of dreams. But he was reliable, earnest and extravagantly respectable. He would do.

With Rachel's marriage still sanctified by God, Jacob had never before encouraged a courtship. Sophie was amazed that he gave Aaron permission to call on their daughter. Jacob, if he had reflected upon his actions, might have been amazed as well. The neighbourhood read his behaviour as a clear signal that the long awaited *get* was in the works. Rachel was happy that they should. That was probably why Jacob suddenly found himself far too busy with new bar mitzvah pupils to reflect.

Aaron's courtship was as respectable as he was. Weeknights, he called at Rivington Street to eat Sophie's cooking, bringing cakes for the family and sometimes little boxes of *Hopjes*, coffee flavoured sweets, for Rachel. He talked old country Jewish politics with Jacob and impressed Bea with his Socialist views.

Saturday nights, leaving Daniel with Dinah or Ruth, they went to the movies or to the vaudeville theatre. Once, Aaron took Rachel to Carnegie Hall to hear Beethoven's Third Symphony. The music was dense and impenetrable. Immense. At first, Rachel, who had never heard a live concert orchestra before, recoiled at the assault of so many voices. She forced herself to listen and discovered the music had a conscious heart, one soul so old and so powerful that it could raise hosts of spirits to its triumphant service. Levitated by this revelation, she would have risen right out of her seat, sailing on a flourish of horns to play with the phantom listeners who crowded the shadows of the ornate ceiling, but that she grabbed Aaron's hand as an anchor.

He kept her hand for the rest of the concert, holding it, still, as they walked to the subway station after. She wondered if the old wives were right when they said that familiarity bred a kind of affection that, if not better, was more important than love.

He seemed to be fond of Daniel. Daniel, in his turn, indulged Aaron with sunny smiles and laughter, the selfish and impersonal charm that children bestow on those who buy them tickets for the Ferris wheel or wands of cotton candy at the beach.

In July, he took her to meet his mother and at the beginning of August, he proposed marriage. Rachel, who already knew what her answer would be, asked him to wait before speaking to Jacob so that she could think.

"When will you tell him?" Dinah said.

"Not yet. Soon."

"You know this is all for nothing without the *get*."

"It won't matter, you'll see."

Dinah raised an eyebrow.

"Have you heard from Schmuel?" Rachel said.

The city had swallowed him up after Dinah refused him his old room over the shop. But the devil was not far away. His laughter squealed along the trolley tracks. His rasping breath emerged from steaming manhole covers. He winked from stuttering, sulphurous streetlights. Rachel knew he would not be that hard to find. A few questions asked in the right places. Duvi could do it. Or one of his "business associates." She had no desire to find him. He would emerge soon enough, bearing poison and mortal pollution disguised as court documents and birth certificates and visitation rights. Now, she needed time, time to use her hesitation to press Aaron toward a hasty marriage. When Schmuel reappeared, she would be ready for him. She would be well on her way to a respectable marriage, a normal home for her child. No judge would give him the time of day.

Meanwhile, as Aaron sold her his proposal, he sold himself. He made a good living, he assured her, good enough for a comfortable life. They could move out of the city to a steam heated apartment in Brooklyn with private plumbing and extra bedrooms, for Daniel and the other children they would surely have. Maybe a little house in East New York with a backyard for Daniel to play in. He had schoolteachers' vacations. With half pay. There would be summers in the mountains or bungalows on Far Rockaway Beach. Music lessons for the children. Perhaps they would travel, in Pullman splendour, to discover the western wonders of America together.

She raised minor obstacles just to enjoy the spectacle of the ease with which he demolished them.

"You're so much smarter than me. You know so many things. You'll be ashamed of me." He knew, he said, that she was unschooled but clever. He would teach her about the great books, take her to lectures, refine her musical tastes, make her his equal in every way.

Rachel rinsed her hair in camomile and lowered the necklines of her modest dresses.

"I can't cook."

"My mother will teach you."

Gently, subtly, she rouged her lips and cheeks.

When, at last, she presented him with the biggest obstacle of all, he waved it aside.

"He left you for another woman. The rabbis can force him."

"But I don't know where he is."

"His sister..."

"She doesn't know either."

"We'll find him."

Surprisingly, they found him even faster than Rachel had imagined, managing delivery vans for his future father-in-law. Less surprisingly, the exchange of letters and the meeting that followed came to nothing. "She knows what I want," Schmuel said.

Rachel believed that none of this mattered, for by now Aaron was so ensnared in the mesh of his own persuasions that when he suggested a civil ceremony, he was convinced it was his own idea.

"We can go to a rabbi later. He'll come around. You'll see."

And how could Jacob object when he had allowed the courtship in the first place? Besides, she was old enough now to marry without his permission. His dubious blessing, she could live without. The date was set, the justice of the peace arranged.

Then Rachel cooked a meal and Aaron slept badly. That night, a strange woman began to wail.

"It was only indigestion. I told you I can't cook." Rachel touched her forehead. The woman's incessant wailing made her head hurt.

"It wasn't indigestion. The chicken was good. It was fine."

"So, what then?" How could she concentrate with all this noise?

"We have to wait. It wouldn't be right. We have to wait for the *get*."

"But why? Nobody cares."

"Miriam cares."

"What? Miriam is dead."

"May she rest in peace," Aaron said.

Rachel nodded. "Miriam, believe me, is not worrying about you. She has other things to care about now." The wailing became a shriek.

"I don't want to talk about it. What would be so terrible we wait a little while? We need to be in such a big hurry?"

Yes, Rachel wanted to say. Yes. The sooner the better. "Daniel needs a father," she said.

"He'll have a father. A little patience isn't such a bad thing Rachel. Your own way you don't always have to get."

Yes, I do, she wanted to shout. This time, I do. "*A* father?" she said. "He'll have *a* father? You don't want to marry me anymore."

"Of course, I do...only..." Aaron spread his hands in despair. Rachel turned away and looked at cloud faces from his mother's window. Bubbie Ruchel spread her helpless hands, mirroring Aaron's gesture.

"Marry me now, like we planned...or don't marry me at all."

Aaron reached his arm around Rachel's shoulders. She shrugged it off. "Now...or not at all."

"I can't Rachel...I..."

The room went cold, but silent at last.

On an airless Friday night at the end of August, Rachel dreamed of fire. Burning timbers fell, showering her with sparks. Cold blue flames sniffed at the hem of her dress. Men shouted and fists flashed in the suffocating smoke. But no one saw her. No man came to her rescue. She awoke certain that no man would.

In the morning she searched for the paper with the names and addresses that Duvi had found. That evening she dressed carefully, choosing a high-necked shirtwaist that had an old fashioned severity about it. She wanted to look modest and sober. It was longer than the current fashion, but so were all the clothes that Jacob permitted. She braided her hair and twisted it high, anchoring it to her crown with pins. She stood tall and studied the effect in the mirror, pleased at how powerful she looked. She rummaged in the depths of the wardrobe for the dark, fringed shawl that had belonged to Bubbie Ruchel. Although the weather was muggy, she wrapped it around her shoulders.

Jacob was still at schul. Sophie looked up from her cooking when Rachel emerged from the bedroom. "I need some air," she said. She crossed the kitchen and left the flat without waiting for Sophie's reply.

At the corner, she turned left and headed north on Essex Street. It was dusk. The growing babble of radios pouring from open windows signalled the end of Sabbath, pushed forward by people too bored and too hot to wait for a proper sunset. One more home run as the Babe romps toward a season record that may never be broken. More banquets, more parades and more mayors' medals for Lucky Lindy. Ruth Snyder's appeal drags on. Will she go to the chair with her lover, Judd Gray or simply vanish into Sing Sing forever? Another scorcher for the record books as New Yorkers sizzled today folks.

It was an ordinary night, in an ordinary August of 1927, for most New Yorkers a particularly ordinary year. Rachel, angry, determined but more than a little scared, strode onward, wrapped in her grandmother's courage. In her hand, she clutched a piece of paper bearing the address of a house on East Fourteenth Street.

CHAPTER TWENTY SIX

Shelter

Thankful, for once, that inland people were so reticent with strangers, Ciaran walked South. The island music of his speech protected him from too many questions. One pound and some coins, that would have bought the wedding drink, protected him, for now, from hunger.

He had missed the fair and there was no one, now, could pay a man for harvest labour in Balleybofey but, for 6d, the publican gave him meat and bread and let him sleep on fresh straw in his stables. In the morning he told him of a hiring day in Donegal Town.

"If there is work to be had, that is where you will find it. Keep the sunset over your right shoulder, favouring that way a wee bit more each day and you will come to the place in three days walking, two if you are walking hard."

He bought a bottle of stout and two apples for the journey. Then he set off across the vacant, haunted landscape of West Donegal. Fallow fields and roofless cottages, rotting stiles and tumbledown walls. He ate some Victorias from a tree beside an abandoned house, the plums now ripening to feed the birds and the flies. The place was drenched with departure and sorrows to which his own were little more than fresh laid dew. He walked looking straight ahead, grateful for the protests of his still weakened ankle, hoping the pain would crowd away the whispering in his head.

You would not hear me that times have changed...She didna want for love son...nor you neither...not then nor now... Ah, let the man warm himself in peace, Cathleen...You keep your fists in your pockets, do ya hear me...And wasn't your Grand-Da after talking blether most of the time and all?... Give us another...give us another...please Ciaran.

At night he slept in forgotten ditches, overgrown with soft new grass, where no passing stranger might see him weep.

Donegal Town was a poor excuse for a fair. Compared to the great Lammas hiring fair in Ballymena, with its games and races, its music and food and drink, sure it looked to be a grim business altogether. A small gathering of farmers milled about an open patch of ground at the edge of the town. In the centre, a man with bowler hat and a bright yellow waistcoat hawked the labour of men and women, sometimes even children. Ciaran joined the others and watched for a while.

"And what am I bid then for this pair of boys? Fit for all sorts they are, but they are brothers and wanting to go together. Six months or a full year... makes no nevermind."

"I'll have the big lad for three pound."

"I will take on the both of them for five."

"Ah now I know you lot can do better than that. Look at the strength in these shoulders." He poked the older one with his cane and Ciaran cringed as the hungry-eyed boy lifted his shirt to show off his muscles. "I'll warrant they are worth no less than three pound each...for six months is all," the hawker said. Ciaran stared at the ground. It was like the selling of beasts. At Ballymena folks put themselves for hire by carrying a bundle for a sign. He had never seen a middleman in action before. He thought of moving on, of looking for what else this blasted land might offer a willing man. But he knew the hiring fair was his best chance of food and shelter, with maybe a few pounds at the end of six months. He skirted the back of the crowd and joined the queue at the middleman's stall.

"You'll not get the best wages, for you are not a young man," the middleman said.

"I am as fit for work as any."

"Well, you are that. I am only after saying that there is them is younger will be took first. What can you do at all?"

"What there is need of doing. I can work the land or tend the beasts. And I am good with my hands for the mending of things."

"All right then. What are you called?"

"McMurrough."

266

"It is an old name."

"Aye."

"Right then, McMurrough. Pay your *tanner* to our man Tommy, there, and I will call you."

Ciaran felt the treasure against his collarbone. "I'll not be making myself half naked to show that I am fit," he said.

"Well now, I cannot force you. But if you've a fine strong back, it is worth a bit on your wages."

"I will take whatever is offered."

"Suit yourself."

Ciaran gave sixpence to the man called Tommy and sat down in the grass to wait.

The ordeal was less humiliating than he had imagined. When he took off his woollen jacket, his strong shoulders and powerful arms were clear enough through his pullover. No one demanded that he undress further and, looking for comfort wherever he could find it, he took a certain pride in the lively bidding his appearance generated. In the end, he went with an old man called Keegan who was willing to pay six pounds, plus board and lodging, for six months labour. He was to look after a dozen milch cows and their calves on a farm near Killyclegg, Keegan said, and do general labour about the place.

"I don't hold with drunkenness," Keegan said, "but you may take two pints a week at the public house as part of your keep." Ciaran nodded. "Well then, fetch your kit and we'll be goin' ."

"I haven't any."

"Are you meaning to tell me, man, that you have nothin' but what you are standin' up in?"

"Aye."

Keegan studied Ciaran as though reconsidering his decision. "I'll not ask you how you came to be in such a straitened circumstance for sure it is no business of mine, but you are too well fed for a man of the road. And I'll have no troubles or politics under my roof."

"I will bring you none."

"All right...all right...but we best stop first and get you fitted out. You may take some credit against your wages."

At a shop near the diamond, that was a place where three roads met in the centre of Donegal Town, Ciaran bought socks, a change of clothes and, feeling the first discomforts of a few days' growth, a cheap cut throat razor and a piece of soap. He bought a seaman's duffel bag to stow them in. By the time he was finished, he had spent nearly two of the promised six pounds. When he slipped the duffel bag over his shoulder, the light touch of the strap across his chest reminded him of his canvas fiddle case, now lost, with the fiddle, forever. He was quiet for the first hour of the journey.

They left the town along the way that Ciaran had entered it; already earning his keep, he was at the reins. Then they turned west beneath a range of mountains Keegan called the Blue Stacks. Mid-afternoon, Keegan brought out a basket covered with a tea towel and they ate cold mutton, soda bread and a cake spotted with raisins, the lot washed down with milk.

"Your missus makes a fine cake," Ciaran said.

"Ach, that she did in her time, but it were not my missus made the cake for hasn't she been gone now these ten years and more. It is Molly, the hired girl, done it."

"Ah."

"She is a good girl, Molly. You'll not be bothering her or interfering with her at all."

For the first time in days, Ciaran laughed. "Ah Mr. Keegan," he said, "if it were only that simple. For isn't it the women and the girls who are, most of the time, after interfering with myself?"

Keegan softened and shook his head. "Aye...you do have that look about you." He too laughed. "And wasn't my Tim always saying the same and all. You are a bit like him, now I look at you."

"You have a son then?"

"Four...and grandsons besides...though you'd scarce know it with three of them in America and the one in Australia."

"Was it the troubles that sent them away?" Ciaran could not imagine abandoning a father without there was good reason. Warming to the man, he thought of Bertie and swallowed hard.

"Ach, no. It were adventuring that lured them off; and the making of their fortunes."

"They left you behind?"

"Ah well, wasn't they wanting that we should all of us go together? But my Colleen was ever a frail bit of a thing. Sure and she would not have lasted the fortnight's crossing on one of them stinking steamships. Coffin ships they used to call them, you know. My Tim is all the time after me to sell up and join him, now he is a sheep farmer in a place called Nebraska. But I am too old and settled for all of that."

Ciaran absorbed this information as they rode on in silence. The afternoon was fading and the past few days had taken their toll. He was profoundly tired. He hoped he would get a night's sleep in something resembling a bed before his work began in earnest. "Is it much further we are going?" he said.

"Not far. Just beyond them hills."

"So, it is just you and the hired girl live there?"

"And Johnny Boyle who tends the sheep. You best take care in your dealings with him, for isn't he a scoundrel and a layabout as well."

"Why do you keep him, then?"

"Well you may ask, for haven't I wondered to God the same thing myself? But he is good with the beasts and you will not find his like for shearing in all of Donegal."

It was a grand place Keegan had. The low built farmhouse was whitewashed and slate roofed, set on a hill, apart from the working buildings. There was a shed for lambing, a grain store and a large walled enclosure for the stables and the milking byre.

After Ciaran helped him stable the horses, the old man led him to a lean-to attached to the end of the byre. A big old rain barrel, its sides soaked through and covered with moss, stood beside the door. Inside, it was bare but for two iron beds covered with rough woollen blankets, a crucifix on the wall between them. "You may stop in there, with Johnny, while you are here. It is plain but comfortable enough. When you have settled yourself, come up to the house. The girl will be putting out the supper."

"I think I will not. I am that tired and not hungry at all."

"That's as may be," Keegan smiled, "but you must eat with us and all for it is an early start you will be making tomorrow, and how will you do it without you have food in your belly?"

Not since the Great War, when he manned the rocket with the others, had any man given Ciaran an order. This one was clothed in smiles and friendly tones, but he understood it, nevertheless. He stuffed his duffel bag under one of the beds, not daring, even, to sit on it for fear that he would be overcome by sleep. Outside, he plunged his head into the rain barrel, letting cool water course down his neck before he shook it out of his hair. Then he climbed the hill to the house.

The kitchen was dark, lit by the last of the summer daylight and a single oil lamp. It was near as plain as the room in the lean-to. Keegan introduced Ciaran to the others and showed him where to sit at the bare wooden table. Ciaran bowed his head when the old man said Grace. Looking up, he saw Johnny Boyle wink at him. Molly, the wee hire girl, that was not more than thirteen or fourteen, was staring at him. He fixed his eyes on his plate and kept them there throughout the meal.

It was cold mutton again, and a dish of potatoes and buttermilk. They ate silently until Keegan wiped his plate with a chunk of bread and pushed back his chair.

"Molly and I will see to the beasts tonight," he said. "I will show you what is to be done tomorrow. We rise with the sun and you must do the milking before breakfast but you may have a cup of tea first. You may rest for one hour middle of the morning and again in the afternoon. Molly will summon you for your meals."

Ciaran nodded.

"I will expect 12 hours of work from you every day, for aren't we all doing the same. But you may have Sunday after Mass to yourself - except for the milking, morning and night. The beasts are no respecters of the sabbath. You may take one shilling a fortnight out of your wages, for your pocket. Molly will see to the bedclothes and the washing and mending, but you must look after the hearth yourself. I think that is the lot of it. Sure and if I have left anything out, we will know soon enough."

Ciaran continued to nod, afraid now that if he stopped, he would commence to snore right there at the table.

"You do look destroyed with tiredness, man," Keegan said. "Best you be getting to your bed."

"I will that, Mr. Keegan, sir." He rose from the table. "I thank you Molly, for wasn't it a fine supper you were after giving us." Both Johnny Boyle and the old man looked up in surprise. As he made for the door, the girl touched his arm. "I will bring you your meals to where you are workin', if you are hard on it," she smiled. Johnny Boyle winked again. Instinctively, Ciaran disliked the man.

CHAPTER TWENTY SEVEN

On Keegan's farm

Johnny Boyle lounged in the doorway of their shared quarters, watching Ciaran unload clean milk churns from the cart.

"Hard on it then?"
"Aye."
"Keeps you jumping, does old man Keegan?"
"It is the beasts make the work. I do not mind it."

In truth, he did not. In the three weeks on Keegan's farm, the rhythm of new toil, working all the hours of daylight, and a few more besides, was a kind of solace.

And it was true, also, that the beasts set the pace, for there is nothing concentrates the mind so much as the screaming of cows, their udders bloated with night milk. Four of the ladies had dried off and had to be watched as they would be calving soon. And there was a heifer had to be got ready for her first encounter with the bull, hired out by the local dairy.

After milking he drove the animals to pasture, stopping for porridge or a bit of soda bread before beginning the arduous daily mucking out of the cowsheds, the washing of the buckets, the spreading of clean straw. Sometimes Keegan worked beside him, cleaning tools, mending a well head, reseating a gate, making ready the winter feed. The man spoke little but seemed fair enough. Boyle never joined them, having Ciaran assumed, his own work keeping after the dogs and the large flock.

Afternoons, he took the churns to the dairy, just past Killyclegg, exchanging them there for clean ones. Usually, the old man set him an errand or two in the town. "McMurrough, will you fetch us a ha'penn'orth of iron nails and a tin of paraffin." Or "The girl is needing a spool of white thread and a paper of needles. Ask after it at the shop." He wondered, sometimes, why Keegan didn't make a list, for sure there was something wanting almost every day. Could be the farmer didn't trust him with more than a few pennies. It didn't matter. There was little enough time to be wasting in Killyclegg with the churns to be stacked and the horses to be stabled and fed before the beasts became restless for the byre. He let them settle themselves while he ate with the others. Then there was milking again before his work was done.

"Do you not fancy my cookin' Mr. McMurrough? You have scarce touched your meat."

Ciaran pushed tough, stringy bits around the edge of his plate. Mutton again. Sometimes Keegan would wring the neck of an old hen, past her laying, or there would be boiled bacon for a change. But it was almost always mutton. Never a man to worry about his belly, so long as there was sufficient, Ciaran was surprised at how much he missed the salty tang of cured mackerel, the bland comfort of a bit of boiled cod.

"It was grand Molly...but..."

"I'm thinking the man hasn't the room for honest food, what with the sampling of all them sweeties from the ladies of the town," Johnny Boyle laughed.

"Whatever are you on about, Boyle?"

"Isn't it the blacksmith's daughter Peg, I hear is feeding you tea and cakes?"

"Ach, man, it was the once only, to pass the time the while her father was shoeing the horse. I am that sorry that ever I told you."

"Well, I'll warrant there is more, and sweeter still, whensoever you are wantin' it. For isn't she all the time asking me when at all you will be comin' to the dancing."

Ciaran had no heart for the Sunday night dances in the town. "I am not a dancing man," he said.

"More straight to the business, eh? I'm guessing that would be your way. Why waste time with dancing, when the ladies are warm enough just for the looking at you?"

"You know Boyle, you are a fool, man."

"Am I? Do you think I haven't eyes to see the fluttering and the preening goes on every Sunday morning at the Mass? If there is a fool at this table, sure it isn't myself, for there is softer rides than cart horses can be had all around you."

Molly blushed and looked down at the table. Ciaran frowned. "That is enough of that kind of talk, Boyle," Keegan said.

But Boyle had plenty more of that kind of talk. When he wasn't spouting rubbish of some other sort. The man breathed blether, endless and, apparently, endlessly amusing to himself. He could remember and relate every hand of poker he had ever played, every horse upon which he had ever chanced his money or anyone else's. It was, Ciaran soon discovered, a horse race and not his skill with the flock, that kept him tied to Keegan. For hadn't he lost a packet of the old man's money, got for the selling of some sheep at a fair, on a filly that went lame a furlong from the finish. Keegan, Boyle said, had given him the choice of being brought before a magistrate for thieving or working off the debt at pauper's wages. "And wasn't I a fool to myself then, for it would have been better to take the magistrate and gaol and be a free man by now. Ah but she was a beauty, that one, a runner born and bred. You could see it in her eye. You can you know...see the way they are wantin' to win. So how was I to know that her fetlocks was made of glass?"

Most of the time though, he managed to bring the talk around to women. He had only to pull off his boots for bed and he was off, expounding for twenty minutes on his bunions and of a girl he used to know who had the softest hands for soothing them. *And by the way, do you know, she had the softest thighs and all.*

"Do you never tire of listening to yourself talk, Boyle?"

"Am I keeping you from your sleep, then?"

"Aye, you are. And the beasts will be keeping you from yours in the morning if I am late for milking."

"Right then. Off you go to dreamland. Me Mam used to be saying that to me when I was wee and she was after tucking me up for sleep."

"Mmm."

"Ah, those were they days, eh? What I wouldn't give for a woman to look after me the likes of that. With a bit of the other, of course. Are you asleep man?"

"Mmmph."

"There was a girl I used to know in Dublin, who...Did you know I was in Dublin once? Are you listening, man? Well anyhow, this girl, she was..."

One day in late in September, when he returned from the dairy, Ciaran found Boyle, as usual, idling in the yard, waiting to flap his tongue in the breeze.

"Have you no work of your own to do?"

"I will have work enough tomorrow, my share and more, when I have fetched the ram from Grogan up the road. So now I am after conservatering my strength."

"You will be seeing to the ewes yourself then?" Ciaran allowed himself a smile.

"Touché my man, touché. I'm pleased to see the spirit of lewdness come alive in you at last. For sure I was beginning to have a serious concern about the state of your health. Ah, but wait...wait...If it isn't the very Flower of Sligo herself is about to grace us with her presence. And just when I was warming to this interesting talk."

Molly crossed the yard, carrying a basket of folded bedlinen.

"My goodness, don't you look a picture of loveliness today, Miss Molly," Boyle said.

"Good day to you, Mr. McMurrough," Molly said.

"Good day, Molly."

"What's this...Haven't you none of your sweetness for me today, darlin'?"

Ciaran frowned as he stacked the churns.

The girl put the basket on the ground near the lean-to, brushed a loose hank of hair off her face and sighed. "Do yous have need of washing today?" she said.

"Well, that would depend upon what you was meaning by your question now, wouldn't it?" Boyle said.

"I'm sure I do not know what you are talking about, Mr. Boyle, except that I know I must be gettin' on with my work."

This was not the first time Ciaran had witnessed Boyle's bantering harassment of the hire girl. It was wearing his patience.

"I was only meaning that there is all kinds of washing a tired, sweating, hardworking man, such as myself, has need of."

Ciaran looked up in time to see the girl blush. "Leave off of such talk, man," he said. "for she is scarce more than a child. Let the girl get on with it."

Molly lifted the basket and made for the lean-to. Boyle blocked the doorway. "It is only a bit of blether to lighten the day. Isn't that the truth of it, sweetheart?"

"Mr. Boyle...please...Will you leave me pass? I've the beds to change."

"Ah...what is that lovely smell you have about you today, Miss Molly? Sure and it is heaven itself."

"It is only the washing soap on the sheets is all."

"Is that what it is? And here I was thinking that maybe the old bastard was after plying you with eau de cologne. For aren't you alone all the day with him in that big house, not to mention all the night, and never a smile for me."

Ciaran slammed a milk churn on the ground. "Let her be or I will see to it that you do," he said. He was steady and quiet but Boyle had no wish to test him. "Keep your hair on, man. I was only havin' a bit of a laugh." He stepped aside and let Molly pass.

"Boyle!" Keegan's voice rang out from the gate at the end of the yard. "I don't keep you to wag your chin. Be you about your business."

"Yessir, Mr. Keegan, sir."

Supper that night was grimmer than usual. No one spoke until addressed by Keegan, and after Grace he said nothing until he had finished his food.

"A fine meal, Molly." Keegan, unlike Boyle, had adopted Ciaran's habit of thanking the girl for her efforts.

"Thank you, Mr. Keegan, sir."

"McMurrough."

"Sir?"

"Have you not been sleeping, man?"

"I sleep well enough."

"You look to me like maybe you are not...and a man that is wasted from the lack of rest is little use to me with the calving scarce a week away."

Ciaran had no idea what response was expected of him so he said nothing.

"I have been thinking, McMurrough. Here am I alone with the girl in this big house. And maybe there are those who think it is unseemly."

"They are fools that think it."

"That's as may be, but it is a small place, Killyclegg, with some in it that have little enough to do but mind the business of others."

Ciaran wondered where this talk was leading. Boyle scraped his chair back and started to rise. "I'm thinking I will stretch my legs a bit and maybe stroll down to the pub."

"And I'm thinking you will stay put until I have done, Boyle."

Boyle scowled and sat back.

"You know," Keegan said. "There was a time when this house was full of the noise of men. And I am thinking, what is the use of all these empty rooms and you not fit for work because you are tossing and turning the nights away in that damp, cold shed?"

"I am not complaining."

"I know you are not. But I see what I see. Not like some others who see what they are idle enough to imagine." He glared at Boyle.

Ciaran picked at his fingernails. He wanted no bother with Boyle, or anyone else.

"So, McMurrough," Keegan said, "...there is a box room beside the kitchen will suit you better. You may move your things into it tonight."

"And is there a room to save myself from the chilblains and all?" Boyle said.

"You, Boyle, may stay where you are."

Alone in a room that was almost his own, Ciaran sat on the edge of the bed and savoured its homely comforts. The room had a chair and a washstand with a basin and jug. There was even a wee peer glass for a proper shave and a rough linen towel beside it. On the sill of the window overlooking the kitchen garden, the girl, Molly, had arranged a vase of field flowers.

He was grateful, of course, to be relieved of the clatter of Boyle's tongue. But if, that night, he drifted closer to peace than he had in weeks, the cause lay elsewhere. For the first time since his arrival at Keegan's farm, he took the treasure from the bottom of his duffel bag and held it close against him while he slept.

CHAPTER TWENTY EIGHT

The Petitioner

She wanted to run, but she walked. Proud, measured steps along the sidewalk. She would show them that she had left because she chose to, not because they had driven her away. Because they had not.

They stood in the open doorway behind her, the women calling names at her stiff, straight back, shouting *madwoman* and *witch*. She could hardly hear their voices for the maelstrom of buzzing and wailing that issued from the house on East Fourteenth Street. Her chin trembled but her eyes were dry.

She wanted to run but she did not. She would not offer them the easy comfort of believing that they had frightened her with their power, with their smug assumptions, with their threats and their mockery.

Because they had not.

If they imagined that they had humiliated her, she would not prove them right by running away in shame. Perhaps, at first, it *was* the sting of humiliation that had set the thing loose, sent it pouring, stinking and bilious, out of her mouth. Now it would not be contained and soon it would consume them. *Someone will be sorry.* She shivered and clutched at her shawl. She was more afraid than even they could imagine. But it had nothing to do with them.

The heavy door slammed, shutting them in with the mindless, churning moans and screams, returning silence to the darkened street. They didn't hear it. They didn't know. But they would. Soon, they would look into the face of the woman who would be the bride and see what Rachel had seen when she watched it, fascinated by the awkward beauty of the rage on its plain, coarse features. They would look into her eyes and see, as Rachel had seen, that they were the colour of ice.

The sound of the slamming door still echoed in the deserted street when Rachel lifted her skirts and ran.

Rachel had found the house on East Fourteenth Street ablaze in an aura of its own light. From every window, blue-white incandescence cut across the yellow haze of the streetlights. Above the door, a bright bulb glittered under a bubbly glass cover. More light poured through the etched glass panels of the door.

It was a narrow brownstone; four storeys above the ground and one half-hidden behind the stairs. This was no friendly stoop, made for summer socialising, but a grand, railed flight of a dozen steps at least so that, from the ground floor rooms, the occupants of the house could safely look down upon the rest of the drab street.

Seeing it for the first time from across the road, Rachel was dazzled. Her uptown march had been single minded and determined. But now, confronted by the house itself, contemplating the people who dwelt there, bathed in such brilliance, she faltered. She had only a vague idea of what she would say, hoping the words would come to her when she needed them. The house bustled with people and activity. She could see a great deal of coming and going between the ground floor rooms. Who would greet her at the door? How many people would listen to her? Would they even let her in?

For a long time she lingered in the shadows, waiting for the impulse to cross the street. From time to time, she closed her eyes and steadied her breath. No one passed between her and the house on the silent street. Finally, she pulled Bubbie Ruchel's shawl tight around her shoulders and crossed over.

The elaborate railing was twined with wrought iron flowers, roses and daisies, ribbons and leaves; frozen and black but not dead, for when she grabbed it, they vibrated, humming with frantic, unvoiced music. The door knocker, in the shape of an animal's head, a lion or, perhaps a wolf, grinned at her from between the two glass panels of the door. Its brass teeth glittered and when she lifted it to knock, they bit her. Startled, she pulled her hand away and saw blood on her fingers.

A black woman, wearing a dark blue dress and a white apron, opened the door. It was a moment before Rachel, struck dumb by the elegance of the hallway behind her, realised that she was the maid. A crystal chandelier bristled with electric lights that reflected in mirrors and on the surfaces of dark, polished wood. A patterned carpet covered the floor. The hallway exhaled the terminal sigh of roses and gardenias.

"Can I help you?" the maid said.

Rachel craned her neck to see around her. Vases of white flowers squatted on tables. More flowers, tied with ribbons, poured out of white cardboard boxes casually left on chairs and on the floor.

"Miss?"

Rachel remembered her purpose. "Does Mr. Franks live here?" she said.

"Which Mr. Franks do you want, Miss? Mister Arthur or Mister Joseph?"

Rachel had no idea. Before she could respond, an elderly man came into the hallway. "Who is it, Lucy?" he said.

"This lady is asking for Mr. Franks."

"Yes?" the man said.

Rachel, dizzy with nerves, took a deep breath and was sickened by the burning scent of flowers. "Can I see Mr. Franks?" she said. "My name is Rachel Weiss."

"Weiss? Are you a relative of Samuel's? We haven't met any of his family yet. I'm so glad you could come. Come in, come in." He took both her hands in his and drew her into the house. "Oh, you've cut yourself. You're bleeding."

The man spoke like a gentile. Puzzled by his accent, Rachel gestured vaguely. "It's just a scratch...the door" she said.

"Yes, I know. I'm so sorry. It's the new door knocker, it has a spur. We have to get it fixed but there's so much to do before a wedding...even, nowadays, for the father. Lucy, go get the peroxide and some cotton."

Rachel still didn't know whether she was in the presence of Mister Arthur or Mister Joseph but she knew she had found the man she had come to see.

"Come, come," he said, leading her into a large, decorated room reeking still more of expiring flowers. "Sit. We'll clean up your hand. Then you can join the others. Rebecca's in the upstairs parlour with the other girls. So how are you related to Samuel?"

Rachel, absorbing the fact that Schmuel's intended was called Rebecca, didn't answer. While the man fussed over her cut hand, she took in the room. Most of the furniture seemed to have been removed and what remained, some long tables and a number of small, straight backed chairs, was pushed against the walls. The tables were covered with white damask cloths and edged with swags of white crepe paper, caught with white satin ribbon bows and small bunches of white roses and ivy. Lengths of white crepe paper and ribbons criss-crossed the ceiling and curled from the chandelier.

"There," the man said, patting her cut finger with cotton. "That's better. It doesn't look too bad. I really am terribly sorry. So, you were saying how you are related to Samuel...a cousin...or?" He smiled.

Rachel was not accustomed to gentility in the behaviour of men. There was an innocence in his good manners that was almost seductive. Disarmed, she might have doubted her purpose had not a burst of female laughter from an upstairs room reminded her that she had not come here to be charmed, that there was no other way.

"I'm his wife," she said.

The man continued to smile. In fact, he was so slow to respond that Rachel wondered if she had actually spoken or, in her heightened state, had only imagined herself speaking. It would not have been the first time this had happened to her. "...his wife," she repeated.

He sat in the chair beside her, still smiling. Only now she noticed the effort of it in the twitching corners of his mouth.

"I beg your pardon?"

Rachel wondered if he had heard her. He was an old man. Maybe he was hard of hearing. Speaking slowly and clearly, she repeated, "I'm Rachel Weiss. I'm Schmuel's wife."

"Yes, yes. I heard you the first time. I'm just not sure I see what you're trying to tell me."

It seemed obvious to Rachel. "I got married to Schmuel four years ago." she said.

A long, tired sigh escaped the man's lips. "Oh," he relaxed. "You're his *ex*-wife. Samuel told us he was married before."

Rachel sensed an unmistakable chill and the whispering and shuffling of watchers. Determined to stay strong, she gripped her hands in her lap to stop them trembling. "Not exactly," she said. "The rabbis say we're still married."

"What do you mean? Not exactly? Look, I don't understand what you want. Why did you come here? Tonight of all nights?"

Although she had observed them, for the first time Rachel took in the significance of the flowers, the ribbons, the blazing lights.

"I want...I want my divorce."

"But you have one. Or an annulment, anyway. It's the same thing." The man's voice was rising. He stopped to collect himself. "Samuel explained the whole thing to us. I know all about it. He said that you were only children, that your fathers forced you." Rachel smelled his impatience. "He said you got an annulment."

"I did."

"So that's that," he exploded. "You're not his wife anymore."

The man's agitation was oddly soothing. "In God's eyes, I am," she said quietly.

The man crossed the room, then turned and studied Rachel from the far corner. When he spoke again, it was with the slow, modulated tones one uses to calm a fractious child, to address an imbecile, a halfwit.

"My dear young woman," he said. "In my day, I know, divorce was unheard of. Sadly, it happens in this modern world. You have to accept these things and get on with your life. Do you understand what an annulment is? That it's just like a divorce?"

"Of course I do," Rachel snapped. "But how can I get on with my life without a *get*?"

"Without a what?"

"A *get*...a *get!*"

"I'm afraid I have no idea what you're talking about."

Rachel was stunned. She had never considered that the father of the bride would not understand what she wanted. The whispering rose to a hum.

"Young woman," he said, "I don't know why you're here, but my daughter is getting married tomorrow and I'm a busy man. I have guests in my house. Now, if it's money you want, I..."

"I don't want money."

"Then *what!?*"

"Make him give me my *get*."

"Your what?"

Now it was Rachel's turn to lecture a child. "A *get* ... a Jewish divorce from the rabbis. I can't get married again without it...and neither can Schmuel."

"What nonsense is this? You mean where the rabbis make him walk around you three times, saying *I divorce you, I divorce you, I divorce you?*" Astonishingly, the man began to laugh.

Unprepared for his derision, Rachel hesitated. She was uncertain of the formalities and put that way, it did sound ridiculous. "It's the Law," she said. "I'm still married to him until..."

"How dare you come into my home, the night before my daughter's wedding like some kind of raging fanatic? How dare you!? You speak like an American woman, like you were born here...so what is all this ridiculous, ...this...this ghetto superstition? I don't believe this is why you came. You're after something else. Out with it. What do you really want?"

It had seemed such a reasonable plan. She would go to the father of the bride-to-be. She would put the facts to him and the thing would be arranged. She had not expected to arrive on the eve of the wedding, but why should that make any difference? Even in normal circumstances a *get* could be obtained in a matter of days. These people had money and influence. Surely, they could summon a rabbi out of his bed, someone from their fancy congregation, to do it at once.

Rachel had no experience of people like this; Jews who spoke like Christians and ridiculed the Law that she had been raised to believe was written on stone, once and for all, on Mount Sinai. In the Lower East Side, even atheists respected Tradition.

A coil that she, herself, had begun to wind one spring afternoon long ago in Mishkin's storeroom, tightened in her belly. Her frustration, in the face of this stubborn, uncomprehending disregard, became anger. She clenched her fists to contain her tension, unaware that her body betrayed her. She was rocking in her seat.

"Do you think I want you to pay me to go away?" she seethed. "Is that all you know about? Is that how you solve everything?... *Pay me!?*...For what? Do you think I want him *back*? Is that what you think? What for?...That worthless, conniving...You're welcome to him...If he's the best your money can buy."

The man winced and seeing that she had touched a nerve, Rachel relaxed enough to feel the burning of her eyes. She was not going to cry. She stopped to catch her breath.

"My God, I only want to be free of him," she said. "...I only want to be free of him."

"Daddy, who was at the door?"

"Rebecca, go back upstairs to your friends."

Rachel turned to look at the woman who spoke. At once, a puzzle was solved. It had never been difficult to understand why Schmuel wanted a rich, uptown wife. Now she knew why an educated woman would marry Schmuel. The woman's fashionable dress of crepe de chine did not conceal her short, dumpy figure. Her skin was mottled. Rose coloured blemishes clustered around her nose and chin. To describe her face as plain would have been a kindness. And she was old. Well past thirty, at least. Although Schmuel's appearance was wasted on her, Rachel understood that by objective standards he could be called handsome. The answer to a homely maiden's prayers, in fact. She almost smiled.

She understood, as well, why the man had winced. She could imagine his distaste for Schmuel, for his coarse speech and sly manners, for his flash clothes and ghetto roots and, because the man was no fool, for his motives. He must have held his nose when he consented, aware that his bank account was his daughter's most attractive feature but unwilling to deny her what was probably her last chance.

"Who is *she*?" Rebecca said.

She had no manners either.

"Rebecca, go back to your party. I'll take care of this."

Her father's refusal to identify the shabby stranger intrigued Rebecca. She lingered in the entrance arch.

"Was there someone at the door, Arthur?" An older woman, also short and dumpy, joined them. Clearly, she was Rebecca's mother though her face, in its day, must have been a better one. Poor, homely Rebecca. Such a disappointment to her parents. The woman's nostrils flared when she looked at Rachel. The humming rose to a buzz. "Hello...you are...?"

Rachel didn't respond. The woman raised an eyebrow and turned to her husband, who, outnumbered by curious females, had no choice but to answer.

"This is Rachel Weiss...she's..."

"Weiss?" both women said.

"She's Samuel's ex-wife."

"What?" Rebecca snapped. "What do you want?"

"Go upstairs, Rebecca. Your mother and I will deal with this."

"No...I want to know what she wants."

Rebecca's father sighed. "It seems," he said, "that your fiancé neglected some sort of Orthodox formality. She's says they're not divorced."

"Of course they are. Annulled. He had to get the annulment papers at City Hall before we could get the marriage licence...I saw them...*You* saw them."

"I know."

"So...what..."

"I want a Jewish divorce," Rachel said. "He can't marry you because he didn't give me one. He's still married to me." Her voice caught in her throat and she realised she was losing control. "I don't want to be married to him any more...Make him give me the *get...Please*."

"Are you *crazy*?" Rebecca shouted. "You mean where he dances in circles around you and says..."

"Rebecca!"

"No Daddy. I can handle her. She's just an ignorant little tramp. You think I don't know about you? You think Sammy didn't tell me how you tricked him? How you were fooling around the whole time you were married? I know about you."

What was she talking about? A subway rumbled under them and the floor began to shake.

"You're pathetic, you know that? Pathetic. And you have some nerve coming here tonight. Sammy said you were nuts...that you would..."

"Rebecca! This isn't helping."

"Who does she think she is, coming here?"

"Arthur, make this woman leave."

"If you would both just let me handle this..."

Now they were all yelling at each other. Rachel trembled and watched the exquisite rage in Rebecca's twisted face. This trembling had a life of its own. It pushed outward, stretching her arms and fingers, rising up from her gut to press against the bottom of her throat, forming there words that tasted of ash. She began to expand.

"Make him do it," Rachel said.

They all stopped talking at once.

She rose from the chair and continued to rise. "Make him do it, or you'll be sorry."

They were staring at her, all three of them. She towered above them.

The man recovered first. "Are you threatening us?"

"You'll be sorry." The words were carried on whisps of soot and ash.

"Get out of my house," the woman said. "Get out of my house or we'll call the police."

The floor continued to shake. Rachel reached out for balance, grabbing up a swash of ribbons and roses from the edge of the table. Her cut finger throbbed.

"If you don't make him divorce me," she said, "You'll be sorry." So many voices poured through her throat, she thought her neck would burst. Black soot swirled around the room, turning liquid when it settled on the furniture, the decorations, the three people impaled upon the fury of her huge brown eyes. It dripped and stank.

She held the crushed handful of ribbons and flowers in front of her face. "If you don't make him divorce me..." the escaping voices howled, "...in less than a year, this will be black."

Rachel sank, exhausted, into the chair. All over the room, spirits gibbered and shrieked. There were many she had never seen before, but the ones she knew were weeping. She threw the crushed wedding decorations on the floor. Where she had touched the roses, they were stained with her bloody fingerprints. Bubbie Ruchel covered her face with her hands and fled.

Panting, she surveyed the chaos that seemed to frighten her more than the others. Her own dreams and visions, now twisted and ugly, whipped around the room. She saw peddlers, fiddlers, birds dripping with bile; heard songs and whispers and laughter now transformed into dissonant wails. Something important, something essential, had poured out of her with the shuddering curse. She had never felt so empty. She looked into Rebecca's eyes and knew that the bride-to-be was already dead.

"Witch!" the bride's mother screamed. "Madwoman!"

The bride's father yanked her from the chair. "Get out of here now or I'll have you arrested."

She pulled her arm free and walked out of the house. They stood in the doorway, yelling after her, their voices joined with the screaming frenzy of her own soul that she had left behind. She waited until they slammed the door. And then she ran.

CHAPTER TWENTY NINE

Letters home

Lowell, Massachusetts
November 17, 1927
Dear Michael,

Your letter filled us with joy to hear that your Mary has had a fine girl at last and that her lying-in was mercifully short. I trust to God that you are all in good health, as are we, thank the Lord. My most fervent prayer is that this year we will once again be spared the influenza. The weather is now wet and bitter cold and, as you know, it will be worse soon enough, though pretty with it when the snow comes and the children out in it all the day like eskimos. We had thought our Billy would join the other four in the mill this year, but the nuns say he is that clever that it would be a sin to take him from school. Could be he will even go to the Jesuit college in Boston. So I will be taking in laundry for a brave few winters more. It is a great sadness to me that, you are so far away and, with Christmas coming, I think of you and home often.

With all my love and blessings, dearest brother,
Your loving sister May

Ciaran had too much time on his hands. He milked by candlelight now, both morning and night. And though the beasts needed more looking after, crowded for warmth as they were in the cow-byre, there was little else to do.

"Is there no mending needs doing, Mr. Keegan?"

"The thatch was lookin' thin over the turf pile. Could be the wind will lift the scraws and then we will have a job of work to do this time of the year."

Ciaran had noticed the bare patch days before. He had already cut lengths of sharp red grass from the bog, bound it into locks with rushes and woven it into the thatch.

"I done it yesterday," he said.

"Well then, you may look to see if the wall is sound along the upper meadow."

He didn't bother to say he had done that as well. The walk to the high fields and upward into the foothills of the Blue Stacks passed the day. Then he would climb to the highest land around, if you could call it climbing, to look out for the sea. Keegan said it was some five miles to the west but, even in clear weather, he only saw it when he closed his eyes. Sometimes he might forget himself that way, listening for lost music in the gathering wind.

"You missed your tea, Mr. McMurrough. Did you not hear me call you?"

"I did not, but it is no matter."

"Sure and I would have brought it to you, but I could not find you at all."

"You must not worry. I wasna hungry."

Brooklyn, New York
November 12, 1927
Dear Gran,

Thank you for the medal of the Virgin you sent me for my First Holy Communion. I will wear it always and think of you. Mommy says it looks just like the one her Gran gave her when she was little. That's my class in the picture. I had to stand in the back because I am the tallest girl. Can you see me in the middle of the back row? Mommy made me curls with rags. I always remember to pray for you in my prayers and I ask Grand-Da who is with Our Lord to pray for you too.

Love, love, love
Sally

Sunday nights, he drove the cart into Killyclegg and waited for Molly outside the church hall. She didn't like the lonely walk home after the dances and Keegan didn't trust Johnny Boyle, "and him full of drink", to walk with her.

Sitting in the dark, the cart pulled up beyond the spill of light, he heard fragments of escaping music that scarce touched him at all. The town had

288

no fiddlers. The wheezing of concertinas and the occasional whine of a gramophone record bore little relation to the songs he knew or the ones that still hummed across his fingers.

"Why do you never come to the dancing, Mr. McMurrough?" Molly said.

"I have no dancin' in me, Molly girl," he said, and it was an honest reply.

Once she asked, "Have you lost your sweetheart?"

"What at all has given you that notion?"

"Sure and you have lost something for why else do you not come to the dancing, when it is plain that there is music in you."

"Well now," he said, wondering all the while at the powerful intuition of women, even those that were scarce women yet, "the truth of it is, that I haven't never found her."

"I don't believe it, a pretty man like yourself."

Ciaran laughed. "It is the truth and all. Gracious, Molly, you are bold for a wee girl."

"I am *not* a wee girl," she said.

"No, you are not. And there will be young lads aplenty after courting you soon enough. So you best be thinking on the ones you fancy."

"It is not a young lad that I will fancy."

"Will you not?"

"No. It is a man of experience that I am wanting...such as yourself...to teach me the ways of the world."

They had reached the house. Laughing, Ciaran handed Molly down from the cart. "I'm thinking there is little enough I can teach you except that the ways of the world will get you in a powerful lot of trouble, so you best take care." He turned the horses toward the stables.

"Mr. McMurrough," she called. "Would you like for me to bring you your tea in the morning?"

"No thank you. Good night, Molly."

He found Keegan in the kitchen, smoking his pipe in the near dark.

"Will you take a whiskey with me, McMurrough?"

"Thank you, sir, I will." Not having been invited to sit, he remained on his feet.

"You must stop *sirring* me, man. I am no more gentry than yourself."

"Yessir," Ciaran said and Keegan sighed. "I'm thinking the girl has took a shine to you," he said.

"Maybe, but it is no matter. Haven't I godchildren older than she?"

"You are a family man, then?"

It was not the first time Keegan had tried to draw information from him. Once again, he failed.

Ciaran knocked back the whiskey and put the glass on the table. "I will be off to bed, then, for it is few enough hours before the beasts will be needing me."

"Aye. Good night, God Bless."

"And you and all."

"Oh, McMurrough...I near forgot. When you are up to Killyclegg tomorrow, will you leave word at the church for the priest to stop here when next he is passing."

"I will. Are you all right?"

"Of course I am. I have got me a letter from my Kevin, that is a fisherman, and I am wanting the priest to read it to me."

"Can you not read?"

"What use did I ever have to do it until my sons went off? And by then I was too old a dog to be learning such stuff."

"If you are willin', I can read it for you."

"It is the truth?... Well what are you waiting for, then. You must read it to me now. I will get the lamp."

And so, that night in the beginning of December, Ciaran unfolded three sheets of onion skin paper, and, by the light of a paraffin lamp, discovered a whole new way of living.

Machiasport, Maine
28 October, 1927
My Dearest Father,

I have not wrote for so long because I did not want for you to be burdened with our troubles these months past. You must not worry for we are all of us fine and healthy now and I am working. Betty was poorly with a summer fever. Thank the merciful Lord she is now recovered and fierce as ever. There was a Nor'easter in September and we lost the boat. She broke free of her moorings in the night and smashed to splinters on the rocks. Sure and it broke my heart to see it, but Betty says we must count our blessings that it happened in the night and not when my boys and me were out pulling in the pots. Now Father, I will tell you that I was sore tried to think of blessings and me owing so much money. There was $9 owing to the *doctor for Betty's sickness and $16.15 to the grocer and $22 for the rent and $3 to the nuns for wee Gabriel's schoolbooks. And I was all the time thinking of my pots, that will be busy catching lobsters whether I can get to them or no. For, you know Father, that those creatures are such cannibals, it is near sinful to leave the traps loose in the sea...*

Ciaran smiled, remembering the time that storms had kept Mickey Joe from pulling in his pots for a whole week. When, at last, they hauled them up, they were full of half eaten creatures that had been after destroying each other for days.

... I sold the pots to another fellow, that gave me $25 for all 50...

Fifty lobster pots! Ciaran was amazed.

and now I am working in the sardine factory with my oldest, Donal. The wages is $14.60 a week for each and with the money from Betty's eggs and chickens we are able to put something aside every week. Me and two others, that lost their boats and all, are saving together for a new one that we will buy in a year or two. Betty says she can't hardly wait because of how I smell of sardines. Now Father, I hope that you continue well and contented. I am often heartsore with thinking of you and my brothers and my most fondest wish is that you will relent and join us here for it is a place where children don't go hungry, even after troubles the like that we have had.
> *Affectionately,*
> *Your faithful son,*
> *Kevin*

Keegan's eyes were shiny when Ciaran finished. He folded the letter and gave it back to the old man. Then he left him and, without further talk, went to his bed and to a sleep rocked with tides.

Trenton, New Jersey
November 28, 1927
Dear Cousin Dougal,
> *Have you seen the talking pictures? Donny and me went yesterday and it was swell...*

When the travelling picture show man came to Killyclegg the week before Christmas, more than one local was ready to stand Ciaran the penny price of admission and a pint after. He brought a spidery looking contraption, with arms and metal reels, a noisy paraffin generator to run it with and five moving pictures. By then, Ciaran had read so many letters from America he was eager to see the lot.

Two days after he had read Keegan's letter, Mary Halloran, that was a widow hired to cook and clean for some bachelor brothers up the road, arrived at the farm.

"Mr. Keegan is after telling me that you can read, Mr. McMurrough. Is it the truth?"

"It is."

She pressed a small, square envelope, spangled with strange looking stamps, into his hand. "I'm thinking it is from my granddaughter in America but I cannot be sure. If it is not a trouble for you, Sir, would you read it to me. It will be a week or more before the good father has the time to spare for me."

"It is no trouble at all, Mrs. Halloran. Come sit yourself down in the kitchen and I will do it."

"I cannot pay you nothing, Sir, but there is some shirts was my late husband's, may the angels comfort him, could maybe fit you."

"I am needing no payment...and you must not call me Sir."

He took her into the kitchen and read a thank you letter, written in a childish scrawl, from a wee girl in a place called Brooklyn.

That was the first. Word spread quickly. That week, two other fellows from farms so far away they had to come on horseback, showed up with letters for him to read.

Sunday, after Mass, he was collared by the priest.

"Might I have a word with you, Mr. McMurrough?"

He nodded warily, wondering what business the priest wanted with him.

"I hear you have been reading letters for some of the country people."

"I have...and what of it?"

"You needn't worry, man, for isn't it a great service you are doing them?"

"It is no trouble."

"Do you write as well?"

"I do."

The priest touched his chin and nodded. "Do you know that I have the care of three parishes with near four hundred folk in them together?"

Ciaran knew that the priest sped off in a motor car after Mass to serve it again at another church, but the number surprised him.

"So many? It is a wonder for one man to have the care of that many souls."

"Aye, and haven't I often said the same to the Bishop. But it cannot be helped, for there is only a living for one priest is all, between them."

Ciaran waited, unsure where the priest was leading.

"I would be most beholden if you were to help me."

"Myself? But what do I know more than the next man about the Church?"

"Ach, not with the Church, Mr. McMurrough. With the reading and the writing. Sometimes I am so pressed, it is a fortnight these poor folk have to wait before I can read a simple letter."

"Is there no one else can read in the town?"

"Oh aye, a few...the shopkeeper and the publican, and the man who runs the dairy. But farm people can be wary of townsfolk. You are like themselves, one of their own. It would be a grand blessing, Mr. McMurrough. May I say, from the altar next Sunday, that you will do it?"

"Aye. You may."

So two afternoons a week, after the priest made his announcement, Ciaran read and wrote letters for anyone who came to Keegan's farm. Sometimes they asked him to supper, gathering all their relations and friends from neighbouring farms, to listen to the news from far away.

He tried to refuse payment. Weren't the letters themselves payment enough? They came from all over, America and Canada and Australia, even once from Mexico. So many lives, so many stories. But folks would insist, bringing him a warm pullover or a cake, forcing a penny into his hand.

Scranton, Pennsylvania
December 2, 1927
Dear John,

I am hoping that it is time someone at home wrote to me. I have not had one single letter since I left home and I am sore afraid that something bad has happened there...Well John, I am working now in the mines. The pay is $3 a day, that is better than the land, though the work is hard and full of dangers. I hope you will be happy and surprised to know that I am saving to be married. The girl I mean to marry is in service so I must repay her passage before *we can be wed. With luck and God's blessings, we will go to the priest in April or in May. Well John, tell Mother not to be worried about the £6 I borrowed as I mean to send some money soon. Please tell Father that I am sorry for the hard words I spoke before I went. Dear Brother, will you tell me whether or not you have the reading of my letters in private as, if you do, I will send you all about myself and my life here.*

> *Your faithful brother,*
> *Thomas*

November 17, 1927
Dear Friend Henry,

My sister Louise and me were so glad to receive your letter and learn your happy news. We are well and all. I have got a good position with a good Catholic family. I have the care of three children, two boys and one girl. The lady has not the slightest airs about her at all. Sometimes she works, herself, right beside me! My sister is not far away on the subway trains. Sundays, after church, we go to the pictures together. She is keeping company with a nice young man that works as a waiter in a grand place. Now Henry I want to thank you for all you have done for Frank. He is all alone in the world with nobody to care for him but me and Louise that are so far away. You know Henry that it is the most terriblest thing of all to be lonesome with nobody to talk to, so we will never forget all your kindness to poor Frank. Now Henry, will you please see to it that he has potatoes sufficient for what he is wanting and also some onions and carrots if you have to spare and send me the bill. God will reward you, Henry, for your goodness to our Frank. Here is 1 pound and 10 shillings for the rent. I am sending you, also, 1 pound for you to have a treat.

> *In fondest friendship,*
> *Mary Callahan*
> *c/o Mrs. Malone*
> *155 West End Avenue*
> *New York*
> *America*

Gary, Indiana
December 15, 1927
Dear Tom,

Once again I am in expectation that we will have a letter from you soon for it has been long enough since you have wrote us with news of home. Minnie is that fretful that you have not got the Christmas things that she was at pains to send you more than one month past. I

294

am still working in the steel works and with Joseph and Francis now old enough to join me we have enough for Minnie to give up the cleaning of peoples' houses. Sure and it is a blessing for us all, for wasn't she all the time suffering with the pains from her joints and never stopping from complaining of it. My oldest son, Connie, was in an accident in the steel yard. He got his leg crushed so bad it was cut off. He has got him a new leg that cost 125 dollars. He cannot do no more hard work so he is learning the telephone trade. Will you write soon and tell me how are my cousins and friends and all the people that I knew? There are many Irish here but it is mostly folk from Cork and Wicklow and I have never yet heard the sound of a home voice since I left. We keep you ever in our hearts and prayers. Minnie says to say she hopes the Christmas things is useful for the way that you are living.

Your loving brother,
Cornelius

Since boyhood, Ciaran had taken little interest in the picture shows. When he was eleven or twelve, he and Tom Fergus had watched images of scantily clad hootchy-cootch girls in a tent at the fair. They did things that made him blush while the lap of his trousers bulged. In the boat home, they were both so quiet that Bertie and Fergus McQuaid thought they were sick.

"Do you see now what comes of spending all them pennies I give you on sweeties, boy?" Bertie said. "Ah well, your Mam will soon sort you with a dose of something."

The anticipation of cod liver oil prompted a confession. Bertie had studied him gravely then. "Whatever will your Mam say?"

Ciaran's eyes widened. "Bertie, you will not tell me Mam," he wailed.

"Will I not, then? And why wouldn't I tell herself that you've been lookin' at naughty pictures at the fair?"

"Ah Bertie...*please.*"

Bertie smiled. "Well, all right then, maybe. For won't it be myself that will have the tongue lashing and all. It will be our secret. Man to man."

Bertie shook with silent laughter.

"Must I be telling the priest at confession?"

Now Bertie laughed out loud. "No need to give Father Rafferty such a shock as that...and him an old man and all. I'm thinkin' maybe, just this once, you can take it up, private like, with Our Lord...When your Mam's not listening, mind."

Later, when errands took him to Ballycastle, he'd stopped a few times at the picture palace. They were mostly comedies he saw and there seemed little point to them. To be with a crowd of laughing strangers was lonely and unsatisfying when a man could be making music or sharing stories, raising a pint with friends or flirting with a pretty girl.

But in the week before Christmas, his curiosity about America, a place where everybody seemed to be getting on in one way and another, drew Ciaran to the shows in the Killyclegg hall. Surrounded in the clattering, whirring dark by people who, if not his friends, had learned, at least, to call him by name, he was mesmerised. The stories were daft as ever. But the pictures! Now, at last, he could see what he had only imagined, see the places that had been little more than scrawled words or smeared postal marks on the dozens of letters he had read.

While the others gasped and bellowed at a fellow in round black spectacles who clung to the hands of a clock high over a city, Ciaran was impressed by the view from the cliffbuilding hanging over a flowing sea of motor cars.

In the weak, flickering light thrown by the travelling impresario's projector, he saw neat, white painted houses made of wood surrounded by gardens of grass and flowers; oceans of waving corn; shiny trains of railroad cars that stretched forever; bridges spanning wide, chaotic rivers, giant chimneys spewing smoke and fire. Cowboys galloped through strange, dusty landscapes and commanded vast currents of beasts. Ciaran had never seen so many beasts. Ordinary people, even poor people and travellers wore clothes that looked like Sunday best. And sunlight. Everywhere, so much light.

Sure and this was stuff for dreaming. And so it would have remained, but for the letter Keegan received, the week after Christmas.

Sweetwater, Nebraska
December 3, 1927

Dearest Father,

I was glad to receive your letter and to learn that you are well and fit. But Father, it troubles me to know that you have got another hired man to help you. Sure and it must be a sin for you to be all alone with strangers in that bleak place when you have sons and grandsons and myself that is doing so well. Mary and me had a talk about it, and my brother Ned, who is on the telephone now, is agreed that it is time you came to us for a visit. It is all decided and I will not hear of you denying us. I have wrote to my Uncle George in Six Mile Cross. Now Father, you know that he has a fine place, but four sons and their families also, that are near grown, so there is scarce enough for all of their lot. My cousin Jimmy, who is the youngest, is agreed to help me here, for I have more than myself and my hired men can do with the flock near 500 head. He will come to fetch you in the week after the new year and you must go with him on the boat, for I will not hear other. I have sent him your passage and all that is needed. His brother Eamon will come and all, with his wife and two boys, to look after the farm and the beasts while you are with us. My brother Ned will meet you in New York and after you have had a good visit with his lot, he will put you on a train west to me. Now Father, I know you will be proud and stubborn, but you must let me do my duty by you. You will be that astonished by your grandsons. The oldest is near as big as I was when I first left home. And my Eileen, that is now twelve years old, is so like my mother that is in Heaven you will weep to see her. I am sending you 10 dollars for you to treat yourself in New York. Mary and me will pray for you to have a safe and easy crossing.

Your faithful and loving son,
Tim

Two notes of inky green money rested on the table where they had fallen when Ciaran unfolded the letter. For a long while Keegan said nothing. He slid the money about the table with his fingertips. At last he spoke.

"I'm thinkin' I must have become a doddery old fool without I was even lookin'." he said.

"Ach, you are not. You are as fit as hard work can make a man."

"Oh aye? Sure and it must be that I am walking the last road for why else at all would my own children be after making plans for me and telling me what to do."

"He is only missing you, in the way that a son should and wanting you to share in his good fortune."

"Maybe...maybe."

Ciaran wondered if there would be a place for him once the old fellow had gone and his nephew moved into the farm. From what Boyle had told him of other hire farms, he did not care to take his chances again, and him not getting any younger. But he kept his worries to himself.

"It is ever a good thing to be with the folk who know you," he said quietly, "whether you be an old man or a young one."

Keegan nodded.

"And what a grand flock of sheep the man has. Could be he is needin' the help of more than his cousin and all."

Keegan looked up and, in his eyes, Ciaran saw fear and anticipation and joy, all mingled together. He knew that once the old man crossed the Atlantic, he would not return.

CHAPTER THIRTY

Another Crossing

The fo'c'sle wash-house was freezing. When the chief trimmer poured the last bucket of fresh hot water into the tin trough, Ciaran joined the scrum to get at it first. In seconds the cold air would have turned it tepid and it would be muddied with ash and soot. Using his sweat rag for a flannel, he scrubbed at his arms and legs, watching the skin turn from black to blue to silvery grey.

All around him, other men were doing the same. There were eight on his watch, four trimmers and four firemen. The other crewmen called them the black gang and it was easy enough to see why. They worked naked in the stokehold and bunkers. Except where their feet had been encased in heavy leather boots, every inch of their bodies was blackened with greasy soot.

Sometimes Ciaran imagined he would never feel clean again. Ten days out and already he had forgotten what his mouth had tasted of before it tasted of coal, what the air he took for granted had smelled of before it smelled rancid with other men's sweat. An intractable channel of black outlined his fingernails. Although he had given up shaving for the voyage and never looked at his own face, he knew from other men's faces that his eyelids were rimmed and shaded, black as a gypsy woman's. He squeezed dirty water out of the rag and dried himself as best he could. He could scarce believe that in ten days more he would be in New York. Whatever fancy had propelled him on this journey, his American dream was now little more than a hot steaming tub to soak in all by himself, a big chunk of clean white soap and a brush with which to scrub his skin pink and raw.

When Keegan had told him he would have to go before the time agreed, he was only surprised at the speed of it. The year was three days old when the old man's nephews, Eamon and Jimmy, along with Eamon's wife and sons, arrived at the farm. Ciaran moved back into the lean-to with Johnny Boyle.

"Ah, man," Boyle said, "when it comes to doling out the cosy comforts, isn't it the truth that blood is always thicker than water?"

"Not near so true, Boyle, as that you will always be wasting breath on what is too plain to need saying."

"You need not take so hard a line with me...seeing as we are both sure to be men of the road together soon enough."

"You may speak for yourself."

"Do you fool yourself, then, to think there will be a place for you when that new lot settles themselves?"

Ciaran grunted. He had no illusions on that score, but he had no intention of taking to the road with Boyle. The one blessing he could count was that he would see the back of the man at last.

A few days later, Keegan asked him to stay behind for a whiskey after supper. He knew well enough what was coming.

The old man filled two small glasses and set them on the table. He emptied his, staring at Ciaran all the while, then poured himself another. The others had gone to the pub, the women to their rooms. The house was quiet.

"My nephew and his sons look to be hard workers. Do you not think so, McMurrough?"

"Aye. They are willing enough."

"Mmm. I'm thinking they will keep the place good and proper while I am away."

"Aye, while you are away."

"Drink up, man, and I will pour you another."

Ciaran emptied his glass and watched Keegan, who was clearly uncomfortable, fill it again. If there were a way to do it, he would have spared him the trouble of speaking, but he believed it was not his place.

"And Thomas, Eamon's oldest, looked after the beasts for his Grand-Da, that was brother to my Colleen, may she rest in peace."

Ciaran nodded.

"...So...I'm thinking...He is fit for the work and all."

"He is that."

"You know, McMurrough, it is a good farm that I have...that makes a kind of living..."

"Mmm."

"...for them that cares for it...but...well..."

The old man's embarrassment mystified Ciaran. Wasn't he only a hired man after all, with no ties of blood or even friendship? But a kind of respect had grown between them that now prompted his tongue.

"You may be easy," he said. "I know it is a burden to be feeding a man when there isn't work enough for him to earn it. When would you have me be going?"

"I will pay you your wages for the full term."

Ciaran expected nothing less. Hadn't they shook hands on six months at the fair? And it was none of his doing that it was to be less.

"There is a hiring day in Donegal Town, day after tomorrow. There will be a few that needs a man this time of the year for there is always some that goes home to their own for Christmas and never comes back. I have spoke to the priest...He will take you there in his motor car."

Ciaran could scarce imagine the powerful hardship that would lead a man to run off before the end of his term and his wages still owing. He would not put himself out for hire again. But Donegal Town was a big place, with a harbour and all. Once there, he would make his own way. Could be he might join up with a fishing crew or some such. He downed his second whiskey and relaxed into its warmth.

"I will go with the good Father, then," he said.

Keegan filled the glasses a third time. Now the deed was done, he seemed to want company. Ciaran was willing to indulge him. It cost him little enough and besides, wasn't it a fine bottle he was pouring?

"You are a puzzle to me, McMurrough," he said.

"Myself? I am a simple working man, no more nor less."

"You are a good worker, I do not doubt it. But there is more to you than you are willing to let folks see. Sure and it is plain enough that you have fallen on hard times."

"So have many and all. A man's troubles is his own business."

"You are right. I am not meaning to pry. But I'm thinking that you have not the heart of a man who lives by the hire of his back to another."

"A man must live any way that he can."

"Mmm."

While they drank and talked, firelight played shadow games on the walls and danced in the bottle of spirit. Ciaran put a fresh turf on the sputtering hearth. When he returned, he saw that Keegan had poured him yet another. He had not drunk so much whiskey in a long time. It muddled his head and oiled his tongue. He was not the hired help no longer. He and Keegan were just two drinking men.

"So you are goin' out west to be a cowboy, then," he said.

Keegan laughed. "Seems to me, I will be more of a *sheep* boy."

"A sheep herder."

"Aye, that and all. Grogan that keeps the ram was saying that first I must be sowin' a few wild oats in the city. At my age! It is such notions that comes of keeping a ram. I'm thinkin' that I've first to find some oats to sow."

"You will find them or sure they will find yourself and all." Ciaran listened to the sound of his own words, not finding much sense in them, but enjoying the *craic* nevertheless. "What does he do," he said.

"Who? Grogan?"

"Ach no. Your son that is livin' in New York."

"Ah, that would be Ned."

Keegan sat back in his chair, smiling.

"Aye? Ned?"

"Oh aye. Well isn't he a clerk in a bank; a real city gentlemen he is. Do you know, he wears a proper church goin' suit to work?"

"Is that a fact? And does he have a family and all?"

"That he does. Two girls and a son that's near grown, imagine that."

The whiskey was singing and somewhere, along the way, Ciaran had lost the thread. "Aye," he said. "What? Imagine what?"

"That I am to be gallivantin' around America. A man of my years and all."

"Well won't it be a grand adventure for you?"

"It will...it will...Ah, if only I done it when I was a younger man."

"Aye, younger..."

"Like yourself and all. For sure it seems to me that you are prime for adventure."

"Ah, Mr. Keegan..."

"You may call me Joseph."

"Joseph...Joseph. Well Joseph, If I were to say the adventures I have had; more than enough I can tell you."

"What nonsense is this? You are young and fit."

"Not so young as all of that."

"Younger than myself by half at least. And no ties to keep you that I can see. Have you never thought, yourself, to cross the water and make your fortune, man?"

"I have not."

"Well, sure enough you should."

The next morning, sober, but with a head that wished God had never made whiskey, Ciaran thought about his talk with Keegan. He remembered only fragments but those stayed with him over the next few days. On Friday, when he climbed into the priest's motor car, his pockets were heavier with his wages and a bit extra that he had earned from the letters. His duffel bag was heavier too, crammed with the bits and bobs he had been given; a thick warm pullover, two shirts of linen, a pair of hand knitted socks. But heaviest of all was the choice before him. Fate and memory pushed him, inexorably, to the edge of the cliffs.

The ground is safe and solid beneath his feet, hard but sure. Beyond, the wind screams fierce over the roaring sea. Yet the wild birds sing so free. And isn't it the truth that he is skyborn himself.

"Sure, can't I lie on my belly to look over, first?"

"You will never do it that way, son," Bertie says. "Push off lad...Jump...Go on now. It is just like flying, I promise you. You must trust to me and to the ropes."

It was God who held the ropes now. If he would not grow old and bitter, at the beck and call of sullen strangers, Ciaran knew that he must jump.

He had no plan. He had no idea, even, how it was done. It could not be a matter of money for folks much worse off than himself had done it, folks near to starving had crossed the ocean to start afresh. On the journey to Donegal Town, he waited for an opportunity to broach the subject with the priest. It came soon enough.

"Folks will miss you, Mr. McMurrough, now they have to wait again for me to read their letters."

"There are so many have relations over there. Do you not sometimes think it is powerful sad?"

"Sometimes, sometimes. But it can be a hope to the ones left behind...to see that a man can better his lot. And there is little enough to keep them here. I wonder, myself, why more don't up and leave, even now. There was a time they were going in their hundreds and thousands. But it is not so easy as once it was."

"Is it not?"

"No. Years ago anyone could go down to Rosses Point, beyond Sligo, and get on a boat. Now they have made a new law and you must have a sponsor. A friend or relation that is already an American. Or else you must post a bond of money. Hundreds of dollars."

Ciaran had nearly seven pounds in his pocket. He could not imagine where he might find hundreds of dollars.

"Oh," he said.

"Are you thinking of going, yourself, Mr. McMurrough?"

"And what way would I do that? When I have no one there nor no money neither?"

"Mmm...Sure and you will not hire yourself out again, a man of your abilities?"

"I do not know at all what I will do."

"Would you not think of going back to your own people?"

Briefly, Ciaran considered saying that he had no people. But he would not tell falsehoods to a priest. "I cannot," he said.

"Oh."

They had come down from the hills of the Blue Stacks to the coastal plain. Ciaran closed his eyes. As he inhaled the salty air, he could not help but smile. When he opened his eyes, the priest was studying him.

"I have heard...," the priest said, slowly, "...that some have worked their way across...on the merchant ships."

"Have they?"

"Aye. I have heard of young men of my parishes, who have taken the Sligo steamer to find work in Glasgow. Next thing, the family is receiving a letter from Brooklyn or Ontario or some such place."

"And how do they stay, once they have got across? With the laws and regulations that you were telling of, to keep them out?"

"Well...I suppose that there are ways to do it...and maybe people to help them...maybe Irish people ...once they have got there. I do not really know, mind, only it is something I have heard."

"Ah."

The priest said nothing more about it until they came into Donegal Town. When he left Ciaran at the diamond, he shook his hand. "Good luck to you, Mr. McMurrough. God Bless." he said. Then, casually, as an afterthought, he added, "If you are wanting the station, it is that way."

Ciaran watched the priest drive off. Then, following the way he had pointed, he walked to the train station and bought a three shilling ticket to Sligo.

The daily boat from Sligo stopped at Derry en route to Glasgow.

"Must I get off in Derry?" Ciaran asked the ticket agent.

"Ah no, the customs men come aboard."

"Is there a boat for Glasgow only?"

"Aye, Once a week. You must wait till day after tomorrow."

"I will have a ticket for that one."

"One pound then...One pound six shillings if you are wantin' a sleeping berth."

He bought a one pound ticket. As he counted out the money, the ticket agent leaned across the counter and whispered to him.

"Are you runnin', man?"

Ciaran was startled. Did he look like a desperado? "From what?" he said.

"It is all right, man. You needn't say." the ticket agent said. "But, you have the Northern way of speakin' and...well...let's just say that with you wanting to give Derry a miss and ...let's just say, I am with you lads."

Ciaran wondered which *lads* the ticket agent thought he was with. In the papers he had read about so many of them, all with different names, all fighting with each other.

"I am just wantin' to go to Glasgow for the work they say is there."

"Mmm. There is the British law that meets the Glasgow boat and all, you know."

"Oh aye?"

"They do. But once you have passed them, the place is lawless enough."

Ciaran sensed that, the like priest, the man was after helping him. He said nothing.

The ticket agent scribbled something on a piece of paper and passed it across the counter with the ticket. "My cousin Morris is a harbour constable there, himself, for the immigration," he said. "When you are landed, you ask for Morris Riley. You give him this and tell him Florrie sent you. He will sort you out all right. Remember now, Morris Riley. You do your business with him and no one else."

Ciaran took the paper. "I am much obliged to you," he said.

"It is little enough a family man such as myself can do...Up Ireland, eh?"

Ciaran soon discovered a secret world of people who made things happen. They did it for reasons of their own. Sometimes politics, sometimes money, sometimes, it seemed to him, just for the thrill of the risk. It was a world of nods and winks, of half-finished sentences, false names and meaningful looks. For a man whose biggest knowing crime had been the purchase of a few jugs of poteen, it was a revelation. He found that the less he said, the more these folk would assume, the more they would offer. So he said almost nothing and within a few days he was bound for New York on the *Prinzessin Louisa*, a German freighter loaded with Scottish tweeds and glassware, and crewed by a veritable league of nations.

He'd spent the last of his money on a licence and a seaman's book in the name of John Murphy. The dockside publican who was a *crimp*, a man who hired for the shipping agents and did a bit of business on the side, had grinned when he sold Ciaran the documents. "What a very popular name, nowadays," he had said. "And I'll wager your mother was a Smith...Mary Smith if I am not mistaken. So Smith, ah, Murphy...that will cost you sixteen pounds."

"I have no more than three pound left."

"I will take it from the advance on your wages. You are signed on for a year, so they'll not be bothered over giving you two weeks money for a start."

"Two weeks money? How much is my wages?"

"Trimmer's pay is eight pound a week."

"Eight pound?" Ciaran was astonished. It was a fortune.

The *crimp* laughed. "Don't you worry, mate, you will earn it."

The *crimp* had not been wrong. Sure and it was mule's work he was doing. After ten days of breaking and shovelling coal in the dust laden gloom of the bunker, the muscles of his back no longer ached but his chest hurt when he breathed, his eyes dripped and burned. Four hours on the move. The metal deck of the bunker, hot from the fires of the stokehold below, would burn a man's feet, right through his boots, if he stopped to rest. Four hours off. Barely time for a wash, a feed and a kip. Often, he was too tired to eat. He forced himself, to keep up his strength. He had seen tired men collapse and leave the skin of their hands and faces behind on the scorching deck.

Ten days more and he would be in America, swallowed by the anonymous crowds to be spat out again, he hoped, in a new story. But for this knowledge, he might have convinced himself that he had fallen into Hell. This, he told himself, was merely a hellish way station. Purgatory only feels endless to the souls that are in it. Though he wanted to dream of after, to imagine and plan how it would be when this ordeal was over, for now his spirit was exhausted. When he wrapped his arms around the duffel bag that he used for a pillow and rested his face against it, his sleep was dark, and as silent as the dead.

CHAPTER THIRTY ONE

The Golem

"Only three dollars? But they're solid brass. My grandmother brought them from Poland."

The woman across the counter had seen better times. Bald spots shone in the brown velvet collar of her Chesterfield. Coarse white stitches peeked from seams she had tried, with little skill, to patch. But her hair was elaborately arranged, a habit suggesting she had once been accustomed to leisure. The pearls in her ears were large and creamy.

"I could give you another two dollars for the earrings," Rachel said.

The woman touched her earlobes and her eyes filled up with tears. "They were a wedding present...from my husband," she said. "...I can't."

Rachel examined the brass candlesticks again. They were heavy, but they were not solid brass. The bases were filled with lead. Hollowware.

"These are dented," Rachel said. "Three dollars is fair. They're not worth more."

Dinah, who had been in the back room sorting saleable clothes from the rubbish for the rag man, came into the shop. "Mrs. Peretz, good morning."

The woman nodded, but now tears were coursing down her cheeks and she couldn't speak.

"What's the matter?" Dinah said.

The woman held out the candlesticks. "...three dollars," was all she could manage to say.

Dinah took the candlesticks and turned them in her hands. She looked at Rachel. "Well," she said. "they're very nice. From the old country?"

The woman nodded.

"Maybe a little more." She gave the woman another dollar from the cash box.

"A mensch you are. Like your father before you, may he rest in peace."

"Why did you do that?" Rachel asked when the woman had gone. "She'll never come back for them. And they're dented."

"It's almost Christmas. Somebody will buy them."

Rachel frowned.

"Rachel, that's the woman from the trolley accident. Her husband lost his leg."

"Oh."

"My father always said once and a while, a little extra...it's good for business."

"Oh."

After that, Dinah kept a sharp eye for neighbourhood customers whose troubles she knew.

People said Rachel had a heart like a stone. Sometimes you could see them, the ones from the neighbourhood who knew what was what, lingering on the sidewalk, waiting outside until they were sure to be served by Dinah. From the morning after that August night, when she arrived at Dinah's, wild and terrified, she had been that way. No one knew why. Not even Rachel.

"Maybe she's upset about Aaron," Sophie said. "Maybe she took it harder than we thought."

"Maybe," Dinah agreed, but she didn't really believe it.

"You were raving like a lunatic," she told Rachel. " ...English ...Yiddish ...God knows what else. You didn't make a lot of sense. What happened?"

But all Rachel could remember was that she had been to the house of the bride. She had become angry. They had thrown her out.

"I'll never have the *get*," Rachel had said, "...or a Jewish husband." And as she spoke, she felt oddly free of the chains that had bound her to her father. Free of the The Law. What did it matter? His impatience, his rules, his scorn? Why, with no hope of a respectable escape, should she stay under his roof another day?

She looked around the room. It had been Nathan's; a good size with space enough for an extra bed for Daniel. "Can I stay here?" she said.

"Of course you can."

"No...I mean *stay* here...and work in the store."

"Rachel, your son *owns* the store. Do you even have to ask?"

Dinah showed her the basics; the balancing of value, cost and price that produced a profit. But Dinah could not teach her how to defend herself against the demons that swirled into the shop with every hard luck story.

If she seemed stony, it was precisely because her heart was not. Her soul, that once danced and sang with spirits, now prowled in silent desolation. Hungry for companionship of any kind, it soaked up other people's darkness like a sponge.

The regulars, drunkards and luckless card players, supported their vices with a never ending cycle of pledge and claim. Their possessions made a weekly circuit through the shop. They were easy to satisfy and easy to bear. But others, the ones with stunned expressions of defeat, who needed money for food or rent or schoolbooks or grandma's funeral, gripped their belongings, their knuckles turning white, as they held out for a better price. Until she learned to build a wall around herself, these customers assaulted Rachel with their inner turmoil.

So she numbed herself with numbers. She made a joyless game of it, became expert. Most people cannot see another's emptiness. So they imagined she was cruel while unnamed days consumed the seasons. They thought she was heartless as time accumulated to be discarded, like numbers in a ledger column once the total has been proved. Soft September came and went unnoticed. October pranced its party turn, all sun and colours. Wasted. She spoke as little as possible and only when she had to. She ate what Dinah cooked, when Dinah made her. Enough to keep the hunger pangs at bay; no more. Nothing tasted of anything anymore. Nothing smelled of anything. She didn't dream for fear of nightmares. And only Daniel, her child of light, could make her smile.

She wanted him with her. Certainly there was room enough and she and Dinah could have taken turns in the shop. There was nothing to keep her from marching off to Brooklyn and reclaiming her child at last. Nothing but Schmuel.

His court threats had, so far, produced no summons. Maybe he was too busy being a newlywed. Still, nobody knew what he might do next. Legal papers or not, he could show up at the pawn shop at any moment, demanding to see Daniel. Both she and Dinah agreed that, until Schmuel showed his hand, Daniel was safer far away from East Broadway, safer in a home that had a man. At least for now.

So she compromised. Weekdays, Daniel stayed with Mendel and Helen. On Friday mornings, Mendel delivered him to Rachel. Together, they fled to Uncle Shoe's farm for the weekend.

"Mommy, tell me a story."

"It's so late...Mommy's tired. Aren't you too tired for a story?"

"Nope."

"Well, maybe...First show me how you can take your clothes off. Can you do that? All by yourself?"

"I can."

"Okay. Show me."

"...but the hands parts gets stuck."

"I'll help you. Come on."

"Tell me a story."

"What kind of a story? How about the Three Little Pigs?"

"Nope."

"Goldilocks?"

"She's naughty. The wolf gonna get her."

"There are no wolves in Goldilocks. Bears. Button your pyjamas."

"The wolf eats bad children, Tanta Rosa says."

"I remember. That's what Tanta Rosa says."

"Yup. The wolf gonna eat Emma."

"Daniel! What kind of a thing is that to say? The wolf will eat *you* if you don't watch out. Saying naughty things like that."

"I gonna punch him right in the face."

"Oh you will, will you? That sounds pretty dangerous. The wolf has big teeth you know."

"I got big teeth."

"Mmm hmm. Well, I wouldn't worry about it. There are no wolves in Connecticut. And anyway, even if there were, Uncle Shoe wouldn't let them in. Come on you; under the covers."

"Tell me a story."

"Oh Daniel, I don't know any stories."

"Yes you do. You know lots."

"Not now. I can't remember any."

"Yes you *do*!"

"You know what? Why don't you tell *me* a story?"

"Okee dokey, I gonna tell you 'bout the wolf that's gonna eat Emma."

"That's enough of that."

"Emma punchéd me right in the face."

"Well, that wasn't very nice of her. Did you tell Aunt Helen?"

"Nope...Emma says that's tattle tale. You know what, Mommy?"

"What?"

"When I get bigger than Emma, I gonna punch her right back."

"Now Daniel, what did I tell you about hitting girls?"

"I am. I gonna punch her. I don't like Emma...Mommy? Can I come stay at your house?"

"Oh, Daniel," Rachel sighed. "Soon, baby...soon."

He was the bracing breeze that clears the air. The sweet, sharp pain of life lived. When the weekends ended and Mendel came to take him, the deadening fog rolled back. The cycle of the days; rise, dress, work, sleep, rise, dress, work, sleep, wait for Friday. The parade of pathetic transactions were always the same; sad stories, shabby treasures, exchanges of money.

One customer, however, stood apart from the others. He came with different motives—*For old time's sake*, he liked to say. And the treasures he brought were never shabby. Mr. Stein, *The Man*, still brought gems of value and style, if dubious provenance, to the shop on East Broadway. Once or twice a month, a man from the Jeweller's Exchange made the rounds, visiting the local pawn shops and small, second-hand dealers. He was always pleased to buy what Mr. Stein's "friend" or his "wife" had grown tired of.

"Happy New Year, Mrs. Weiss."

Rachel knew he called her that out of respect, because she was a mother, but she bridled, nevertheless.

"Happy New Year to you. Please, Mr. Stein, just call me Rachel."

"You don't mind I should be so familiar?"

"No, I don't mind. I'll get Dinah. She's in the back."

313

Rachel had no talent for stones. A diamond, a spinel, a piece of glass were all one to her. Usually, she busied herself in the storeroom when Dinah dealt with Mr. Stein. But today the blue velvet roll he unwound contained a dozen lengths of knotted pearls. Despite herself, Rachel lingered. Busying herself with a ledger at the other end of the counter, she watched furtively as Dinah passed the unfinished strings of silvery white, pink, cream and yellow through her fingers or tested the grain against the front of her teeth. She wondered how he would explain possession of what appeared to be a dealer's job lot of pearls. There was always a story and Dinah always indulged it.

It was Dinah's opinion that, although the goods were probably stolen, it was not Mr. Stein, or even his minions, who did the stealing.

"Does he look like a cat burglar to you? Can you picture him sticking up a jewellery store?"

Once Rachel might have laughed. Now she just shook her head.

"No," Dinah said, "I think people pay him this way. People who owe him."

"Owe him for what?"

"I don't ask because I don't want to know...And you shouldn't ask either."

"For my anniversary," Mr. Stein said.

Dinah nodded.

"My wife...you know...she doesn't like to try on in the store because, in case...you know, somebody should see, they'll know, God forbid, how much I spent. Oy, women, such ideas. Like the world isn't full of worries enough."

He smiled and shook his head. Dinah smiled too, but Rachel could tell she was smiling at Mr. Stein's boundless gift for lame stories.

"But, you know pearls; it's like they're alive. The colours, it's very personal. You can't just buy a string of pearls. Especially once a woman is, you know, a certain age. So, I figure, I'll bring her a few different kinds...like a selection... and then she'll choose."

"What a good idea," Dinah said. "They're very lovely."

"Of course. What else? Only the best. But these uptown jewellers, they don't like to take back. Maybe they think it doesn't look good. Like their fancy schmantzy customers will think they're in the pawnbroker business. So the money they give you, you shouldn't know from it."

Dinah clucked her tongue.

"So I say to myself, why should I take peanuts from some snob, can't even trouble himself to be polite, when I know two nice girls downtown, could use the business, could give me the same price, maybe better?"

Rachel buried her nose in the ledger while Dinah and Mr. Stein negotiated a price and engaged in small talk about the lowering skies and the likelihood of more snow. He had folded the money into his pocket and was turning to leave when Rachel heard familiar laughter. Low and nasty. She went rigid, afraid to look up from the books, afraid to see him sauntering into the shop. But no one had come in. Mr. Stein, his hand already on the door had stopped and turned.

"Oy, I almost forgot," he said. "So guess who walked into my office the other day, looking for a job? Your brother still has plenty of chutzpah."

"My brother? He works for his father-in-law."

"You didn't hear already? They threw him out a coupla weeks ago."

"Why?"

"What? You don't know? Oy, I thought..."

"Know what?"

He was not alone. Others were laughing too. Cackling and snorting and squealing. A chorus of scorn. *Play with us if you dare.* Rachel would have reached up to cover her ears but her hands weren't empty. A small bloody mass squirmed in her joined palms. She blinked hard and shoved her hands under the counter.

"She died, right after Christmas."

Clearly, Mr. Stein had not expected to be the bearer of what must have seemed to him to be intimate, family news. For a long, awkward moment, the three stared at each other.

"What did she die of?" Dinah said.

"Do I know? Some women's thing. First, she was expecting, then she wasn't expecting. Something about the baby wasn't where it was supposed to be. Something like that. I thought you knew."

"We don't talk anymore," Dinah said.

"Oh."

Now that he had brought the subject up, Mr. Stein seemed unsure about how to drop it and leave. His lips moved like a drowning fish. Thoughts seemed to bubble up only to be swallowed before they broke the surface.

"So, anyway, you know, people like that...I guess...I suppose...they got no use for people from this end of town, except if they have to, if you know what I mean. So, her father fired him and threw him out of the house. Next thing you know, he comes to me for a job. I'm telling you, a minute he didn't waste."

"Did you give him one?" Dinah said.

"I'm thinking about it. Some good connections he maybe has now in Florida, if he was fixed up, you know, with the right kind of outfit. And then, this place is still a good business."

Rachel had gone so still she was barely breathing.

"This place?" Dinah said. "He has nothing to do with this place."

"Yeah, I know...But it belongs to his kid, no?"

Mr. Stein had been edging back to the door. Now, his hand rested on the handle once again. "Look, I'm sorry you had to hear from me, but news like that...Who knew? So I'll see you next time," he said, and he made his escape.

Rachel watched Dinah lock the shop and pull the shades. Dinah was saying something but Rachel couldn't hear her for the shrieking and growling. Dinah bent her face close to Rachel's. Rachel could feel her warm breath, see her lips moving, but the sounds that came out made no sense. Then Dinah put her hands on Rachel's shoulders and shook her.

"Rachel!"

One day you will go too far.

"Rachel!"

"I'm bad," Rachel said, "...evil." She was shivering now, so violently that Dinah was not sure what she had said.

"Rachel, what are you talking about? This has nothing to do with you... Nothing!"

"I cursed him," Rachel said. "I cursed them both."

"So what? So you wished him *tsuris*. Who wouldn't? If anybody up there paid attention to curses, the streets of New York would be knee deep in corpses. Now stop this nonsense. Stop it right now."

"He'll come here. He'll make trouble for us. He'll take away my son."

"Stop it, Rachel! Stop it! This doesn't change anything. He has no rights here, you know that."

Rachel didn't stop shaking until Dinah put her to bed and rubbed her back until she slept.

He didn't come, though she watched for him in the flat grey shadows of January. He didn't come, lunging through the door on gusts of snow hissing wind. If she had been quiet before, she grew quieter still. And watchful. But he didn't come.

Terror so intense cannot endure. The spartan fuel of menace and threat will not sustain it. The spikiest peaks of fear, unfed, soon level to a tolerable background dread. Jingling bells on the door announced every new customer. Eventually Rachel stopped jumping when she heard them. The dull routine of work reasserted itself, punctuated by radiant weekends with Daniel.

In February, winter made a last, brutal stand against spring. The storms brought heavy, waterlogged snow that set in frozen gargoyles along the streets. When the temperature rose, their vaporous steam mingled with thick fog from the Gulf warmed sea. Then the freeze fell again. Everybody had colds. On a Thursday night, early in the month, Helen telephoned the shop.

"Look, he has a temperature," she said. "I don't think you should take him outside in this weather. Why don't you come here? Mendel can bring you after work tomorrow."

So Friday, Rachel dressed in the warmest clothes she owned, pulled galoshes over her shoes, wrapped a muffler around her face and neck and plunged into the frigid night. As usual, she had misplaced her gloves. She stuffed her hands into her coat pockets.

The fog was cold but bright with trapped city light. It obscured all but a few yards of icy pavement ahead of her. She found her way by instinct, slowly, impatiently, but forced to concentrate on the effort of making way. At some intersections, she could not see the woolly glow of the traffic lights and had to search the dense blankness for the telltale slices of headlights, had to listen for the labouring engines of crawling motor cars, the bell spangled whine of trolleys.

The fog played capricious games with sound. It was difficult to say whether footsteps were across the street or coming up right beside her. Was the saxophone she heard coming from a jazz cellar right under her feet or from blocks away? It was impossible to tell. The strains of a violin haunted salt scented air that rolled up the crosstown streets. Bell buoys rang in the rocking waves and sea gulls bickered. She even heard the dark sigh of a foghorn that must have been miles away.

By the time the spotlights of the West Side docks rose before her, a brightening aura in the murk, her teeth were chattering and the muffler, sodden with her breath, was chaffing her face. She hoped Mendel had thought to keep some coffee hot.

317

CHAPTER THIRTY TWO

Shipmates

"Keep her blowin', Mister." The seaman at the end of the long wooden table voiced the common sentiment as he muttered into his coffee. There were grunts of agreement all round. For three days they had been stalled in the Ambrose Channel, just outside the port. No tugboat crew would risk such heavy fog to steer in a load of fancy glassware and expensive cloth. So, blind, they hove to the wind, the ship's powerful engines groaning impotent against nature's sleight of hand.

Other ships surrounded them, doing the same. They could hear the whistles and bells, the ringing slap of rigging and the bovine shudder of foghorns.

They'd had their share of weather and more, this voyage. The men were tired and even the old hands were nervy, knowing the dangers of New York's Lower Bay, the crowd of ships hemmed in by land so close a man could hear the rumble of trains, the shouts of brawls in dockside bars.

The blast of their own siren was a comfort. But as the watch wore on and the lookout tired of staring into the void, the regulation two minute intervals grew to five, then ten, then longer.

"Keep her blowin', Mister."

A storm, two days before, had flooded the compartment, leaving two inches of sea water and coal dust to slosh back and forth across the deck. Ciaran, stretched out in a lower bunk, trailed his hand in the cold, murky water to stay awake. At any moment, the fog might lift and he would see the place that fate, and his own awakening will, had sent him to make a life. While other men snored, Izzy Katz, in the bunk above, was talking about a miracle rabbi from a place called Chelm. Izzy told good stories, full of strange, foreign words, but right now Ciaran was having trouble staying with him. More than anything, he wanted to be standing on deck, watching the ship slip past the massed towers of Lower Manhattan that Izzy had described.

"What kind of a name is Katz?"

"It's a name...It's your business?"

"Ach, no," Ciaran said. "It is never no business of mine. I am only after wondering where you come from. For sure I haven't heard no man's talk the like of yours." He wondered, as well, what he had done to make the man so touchy. Could be it were the shock of the accident had put him in a temper.

They had been working side by side when a hidden fire in the coal released a burst of hot clinker and ash that sprayed them both. It singed the hair on Ciaran's leg, but Katz, whose right hand had taken the worst of it, had gone off to fetch the first aid kit, fixed to the forward bulkhead by the companionway. No one else seemed to have noticed. Ciaran could not watch the man struggle, one handed, to open the jar of tartaric without offering to help.

He smeared the sour black ointment on Katz's hand. When he wrapped it in gauze, Katz winced. "Your fingers are near cooked," he said. "Do they pain you much?"

"Not so much...Coulda been worse...Right over my favourite part my hand was. *Danks Gott*, coulda been much worse."

They both laughed. "You know what?" Katz said. "I think a mensch maybe you are."

"A what?"

"A *mensch*...A person, you know, like a human being."

"Oh." Ciaran raised an eyebrow. He sensed a complement was intended though what it could be, when to be a person was no more than any man was, escaped him.

"So I give you a *bissel* advice... Some things you don't ask. You, of all people, should have the *seychel*, the sense, to know this."

"Myself? Why?"

Katz scowled and studied Ciaran. "Me you're asking? Some memory *you* got. *Schon*, already you forgot my face?"

Ciaran's brow creased. He had no idea what the man was talking about.

"Well, you *I* remember. First time I see you, whisky you are drinking . Maybe you wouldn't drink so much whisky, more you would notice."

"What?"

"At McGonagle's, the crimp in Glasgow. Right before me you went in. You think I don't see you come out with papers?"

"Did you?"

"What? I'm gonna make it up?"

"Oh...I..."

"I think, John Murphy, a little more careful about what you ask ...because, I think, already, we got the same kind name. *Vershtay?*"

Katz never did say where he came from. "I'm a Jew. It makes a difference? One place from another you would know?" And he was prickly. Until he finally understood that Ciaran's questions arose from simple curiosity, were not traps suffused with hidden meanings, he was argumentative and wary. Ciaran had never met a Jew. He knew no more about them than what the priests taught from the Bible, which seemed to him, in truth, a pretty confusing story. Sometimes they were the villains. But other times they were heroes. There was Daniel and Moses and David, who was a musician and a lover of women, just like himself. And weren't the priests all the time saying that the Lord himself was a relation of King David's, so he must have been a Jew and all. It was a puzzle. Maybe it was the sort that Father Rafferty was after calling a mystery. But Ciaran didn't trouble himself over puzzles the like of that. And wasn't Katz a fine fellow after all, with a gift for stories old and new.

"You have a spirit that shines, lad," his Grand-Da Donal used to say. "Wherever you go in this world, it will find you friends...or folk will see it, and they will find you." Halfway to America, in the middle of the Atlantic Ocean, Ciaran had found a friend.

"So she says to him, 'Get me a chicken'."

"A chicken?"

"Sure...What else? 'A chicken and bread and while you're at it, you shouldn't forget, some carrots and an onion, maybe a parsnip...and candles... because otherwise, everybody is already talking that the rebbe's wife don't have...even to make Shabbas'."

"What is that? shabbas?"

"What is Shabbas? Shabbas is Shabbas...You know, like *you* have Sunday... so *we* have Shabbas...Same thing."

"Oh, aye, shabbas...With chickens?"

"Oy, it's a long story. So anyway, this woman, a tongue she's got, you shouldn't know from it...'All the time,' she says, 'you float around...your feet don't even touch the ground. Everybody else's troubles you got time for...Your own children you don't got time even to feed'."

"Was he magic, this rebbe fellow?"

"Magic? What are you talking?"

"To float around... and his feet not even touchin' the ground and all."

"Of course not. This is a Jewish story. It was...like...holiness...from God."

"Oh."

"...So he says..."

"Izzy? Do you think there will be work when we get there?"

It was a good story, but after the storm had lifted, and before the fog, Ciaran had seen the glow of New York on the western horizon. Ever since, he had thought of little else. He could scarce imagine it, a place that, two days out, could set the sky ablaze the likes of that.

"Plenty snow in New York, I betcha." Katz said. "A good strong back like yours...Work you don't gotta worry."

Ciaran sighed. America had called to him, powerfully, irresistibly. Hadn't she astonished him with his own notions, ideas that were in his head all along, ideas he didn't even know he had? He could not believe that all she wanted from him was the shovelling of her streets.

"I have had my fill of diggin'," he said. "I did not cross the ocean for to be doing more of the same."

"So what kind work you want?"

"I do not know, myself, what kind of city work that I am fit for."

"Like I said, you shovel some snow, maybe sweep a street. You get some money in your pocket and you look around. Plenty kinds work in America...So, where was I...Oh yeah...So the rebbe says..."

"Izzy, tell me about New York. Tell me why they made you leave."

"Like I said before, politics."

Ciaran's heart sank. He had thought that, in America, politics was just another word for talking.

"It was union trouble. I'm telling you, on the docks, with the unions, there was plenty trouble, years ago. So, we had a strike, and they said I was socialist agitator. Me! A communist, they said."

Ciaran didn't really know what a communist was except that, in the papers, they always seemed to be in the middle of strife. "And were you?" he said.

"Who knows? Such names they put on things. Decent pay I was for. Rights. You know what I'm saying? In America, they tell you, everybody got rights. So the working man? He shouldn't have rights also? I'm asking you. If that makes me a communist...so maybe I was."

"They made you go because of what you were after believin'?"

"Well, there was a fight. The papers said a riot, but believe me, I seen plenty riots when I was a kid. They don't know from riots. But anyhow, some people got killed. Not by me, I swear to God. But who knew, in such a *meshuggah* mess, who did what."

"Why did they not just put you in gaol?"

"Because, I got no American papers yet...whatcha call citizenship. You don't got citizenship, a real American you're not. Any time they want, out you go. And my English was not so good then either. So that was that. Next thing you know, I'm on boat to Hamburg...and my papers got big stamp, 'Undesirable alien'...You get that stamp, *is nicht*...finished."

"But now you are goin' back?"

"What else I'm gonna do? Ten years already I was in America. Twelve years old I was when I came. A whole village...together we came. You think I got someplace to go back? You think I got anybody left in old country even knows my name? So in America, nobody knows my *new* name either. This time, I got smart. No more unions. I get off this boat, I ain't coming back."

Ciaran nodded. "What are the folk like, in New York? I have heard they are a fast and grumpy lot."

"Some are, some not, like anyplace. Smart they are, sharp. You be smart too. You keep your eyes open and your mouth shut till you know who you are talking to. You listen good; you use your brains. You be okay."

In the end, he heard the city before he saw it. When the weather lifted enough for an escort of tugs to tease the *Prinzessin Louisa* into the Port of New York, Ciaran's watch was breaking up the remains of the coal in the Number 1 bunker, making room for the lading of more. By the time he went above, the crew was tying her up in a slip beside a warehouse and the fog had settled again.

On the dock below, dark eddies of men swept aside the landlost clouds. Try as he might, he could see little beyond them. Perhaps that was a stack of windows, a suggestion of brick and stone, a bit of cobbled street. Perhaps not. Now and then, a motorcar crawled past at walking speed. He might have been anywhere. But for the sound.

Every kind of noise at once, every sound he could imagine. Voices, motors, machines. Sea birds and horses and hissing steam. Bouncy modern music, its source unseen, approached, passed and faded away. People argued and laughed. They walked and ran. These sounds merged with strange, unidentified rumbles, gratings and whines.

The wonder of it was, this cacophony made a kind of music, a clamorous pulse that quickened Ciaran's own.

"Does it not drive folk mad, all this noise?"

"What noise? Today everybody stays inside, it's so cold. This is quiet. Wait till summer...Everybody's got their windows open. *Then* is noise."

"Is it the truth?"

Izzy laughed. "Tell you what, tomorrow, we got money, I show you New York. I got friend is janitor for two buildings. We get a room, then we get *lukshen* soup. I know a place...so good, like you never tasted in your life."

Ciaran could not argue with that. He supposed he would discover what kind of beast this *lukshen* was soon enough. He smiled and rubbed his bristly chin. "Well," he said, "I'm thinking, if I am goin' to be a city fellow, I best not be lookin' such a ruffian." And he went to find the ship's barber.

He had more than a hundred dollars in his pocket, three weeks wages, less three pounds towards repayment of his advance. He had worried, knowing that he would not return to work off the sixteen pounds, that this might be stealing and had considered paying the two week's money all at once. But he did not want to arouse suspicion. And besides he had no idea what a dollar was worth or what it was good for in New York. The negotiations over his debt delayed him at the purser's office and now Izzy was well ahead of him in the queue for the immigration stamp.

Two fat men in blue serge uniforms with red, white and blue patches on their sleeves had set up a wee table at the top of the gangway. One of them wore a thick scarf and a hat with fur. Sure and it was cold enough, but Ciaran, energised as he had not been since his days on the cliffs or lifting his fiddle before the crowds at the Feis, scarce felt it. He pulled his woolly cap down over his ears, adjusted the strap of his duffel bag across his back and shoulders and waited.

The queue snaked slowly forward. The bareheaded man examined each seaman's book, wrote in a kind of a ledger and said something to his companion. Then the man in the furry hat selected a rubber stamp, from a selection lined up in front of him, and stamped the book. The formalities seemed quickly done. Ciaran inhaled, testing New York with another of his senses. His nostrils, still clogged with coal dust, refused him any information. He noticed that the coal even seemed to colour the steam of his breath.

Izzy came abreast of the table. He winked at Ciaran as he handed over his book. The bareheaded man looked at it. Then he took a pair of wire rimmed spectacles from his pocket and looked at it again. Because of the distance, Ciaran could not be sure, but he thought maybe the man was smiling.

The bare headed man leaned across and said something to his colleague. Now there was no mistaking the turn of his spirit. Both men laughed. Maybe they were the sorts who were after giving Jews a hard time. Izzy had told him that even America had such people.

"So Katz," the bareheaded man said. "That *is* your name? Katz?"

"What else? That's what it says."

"I see what it says...You're a Scotsman, are you?"

"I been living there."

"Mmm hmmm...And you got this here licence in Glasgow?"

"Like I said, it's where I live."

"I'm sure you do."

Ciaran's palms began to sweat. He shoved his hands deep into his pockets to keep them from freezing. His blood sang in his ears.

"Well, nice try Katz...But you see, we're on to this guy...this whatshisname..." he ran his pen down a page in the ledger, "McGonagle...Jeez, you know, he's getting sloppier all the time."

Ciaran was rooted to the spot. The urge to run, to hide, would have been irresistible but that his concern for Izzy riveted him to the scene unfolding less than twenty feet away. *You keep your eyes open and your mouth shut...You listen good... You use your brains.*

"This is how it is, Katz...or whatever your name is...So long as you stay aboard, you ain't committed no crime...But we can't take the chance that you might be a sleepwalker...or maybe you got a taste for the Polar Bear Club, if you know what I mean." He turned to the officer-in-charge. "You got a brig on this tub, or you want we should lock him up?"

The officer bristled at the word tub. "We can't afford to lose a trimmer," he said. "We'll take care of him."

Ciaran wished that Katz would look up, to understand and take comfort from the silent prayer he was making for him. But Katz stared at his feet as two crewmen led him away without a struggle.

Softly, slowly, as calmly as his screaming nerves would allow, Ciaran faded back into the queue and returned to the sleeping compartment, where two firemen were still packing up their gear.

"Back so soon, Murphy?" one of them said. "Can't even kick you off, eh?"

Ciaran muttered something about needing the head. Once on deck, he made his way aft, to the Number 1 coal bunker. It was empty but warm from the fires below. He was supposed to return, to help fill it, in three days' time. No one would bother with it before then.

He settled into a dark corner and tried to compose his thoughts. He must make a plan, for there was no way he would shovel coal for three weeks back across the Atlantic to an uncertain fate. If Katz's book was suspect, then so must his own be and all. And if the books were suspect here, whatever would the British constables, who lined the Glasgow docks, make of them? Sure and they would find out who he truly was. So much had changed since that fiery night in Douglas Bridge, he had near forgot that he was a fugitive. Now he saw the stark consequences of this voyage.

In the Free State, his life was rootless and lonely, but safe enough. For the first time since the daft impulse to sail away had overtaken him, he realised that life in America could be as rootless and as lonely as any place that was not his home. And for this flimsy chance, he had put himself in mortal danger. For if the bleak future he had left behind seemed endless, the one to which they might return him stretched no longer than a hangman's rope.

After dark, he would look around and decide what to do. He had no idea what that might be; only that he would not go back, that he must escape.

CHAPTER THIRTY THREE

Into the dark

He was warm in the bunker but hungry and thirsty. Prowling the decks when the way was clear, he'd found sufficient ice and rusty condensation to slake his thirst for a while. But he had not eaten since yesterday breakfast time and it was near dark of the second day. He dare not go near the food stores for fear of alerting one of the skeleton crew still aboard. If he were to have strength enough to carry out his plan, it must be done tonight.

Last night, after dark, he had crept out to look around. Almost at once, he saw that a port side escape was out of the question. Although the top of the gangway was open and unprotected, smoked poured from the chimney pipe of a wee timber hut at the bottom. It was a guardhouse sure. And shimmying down a portside line was nothing but a fool's end with the ship rocking against the fenders in the weather blown chop.

Starboard was another matter. The ship was a good thirty feet narrower in the beam than the slip in which she was tied. Four lines of sturdy rope, fixed to bollards on the pier, held her steady. Because of the big winter tides, the crew had set plenty of slack in the lines.

Each line was strung with a rat stop, a shallow metal cone, maybe a yard across at its widest, that was meant to keep the nasty creatures from visiting with their relations. They would cause him little bother, except for that he would have to swing out round them, one handed. Well, he had done much the same on the cliffs, though Bertie wouldn't like to know it.

The likeliest line ran to the dockside off the starboard bow. It was shorter than the rest and there the pier was thickly fendered with sisal and big chunks of cork. This fender, which was above low water, was near two feet across the top. A man could stand on it easy. If he were careful, he might scarce even touch sea water.

The pier itself was made of old wood pilings. There were plenty of places a climber such as himself could grab a hold of. And further along, maybe ten feet to the right, was the wooden ladder that would welcome him to America.

There was even a kind of stone built depot where he could warm himself before he went on his way. Before his troubles began, he and Izzy had watched the dock labourers manhandle rope-tied bundles of tweed into this warehouse. Later, he'd seen the crew of warehousemen leave, all together. And after, a big man, who looked to be not much younger than himself, came out and locked the door. Ciaran reckoned the stone work was knobbly enough for him to reach the windows, high off the ground. He could get inside, no trouble at all. He fancied he might even have a soft kip on one of them bundles of tweed.

But after the excitement of his reconnoitre, he realised that his muscles, still tight with the tensions of the day, needed sleep. So he had spent last night and all of today in the Number 1 bunker. The bell that summoned the few men on board to their evening meal reminded him of his empty belly. It also told him he could safely slip out into the early night of winter.

Brute cold. The temperature had dropped and, at first, he gasped at the shock of it. He waited to steady himself. Now was no time to be shivering. He had been lucky to have scouted through the fog yesterday. Tonight it was blinding thick. Big lights, from the corners of the warehouse he supposed, turned it to a wall of white. Where it had settled on the lines, it had turned to ice. No matter. Though the end of the starboard bow line disappeared in the murk, he remembered that the rat stop, positioned close to the pier, pulled the line downward almost within reach of the fenders. His hands could bear the cold long enough to slide down the length of it. And once he'd passed the rat stop, he'd only to swing over to the thick sisal platform, with no climbing of the ice slicked rope at all.

He looked around once more to make sure the way was clear. The fog was so heavy it scarce mattered. A man twenty feet away would never know what he was about. He heaved his duffle onto his back, tightening the strap across his chest. Then, he climbed up onto the gunwales, hooked first his feet and then his hands around the line, quickly asked the Mother of God to keep mind of him, and pushed off.

Pausing for breath at the rat stop, he thought that though he ached all over, it was no worse than a bit of rough climbing. It minded him of Rathlin, the way the gulls were talking all around him. But melancholy can be a comfort. And wasn't it a fine adventure? Could be he would live to make a story of it for his grandsons one day. The notion made him smile. He hoisted his legs around the line to shift the weight from his hands and arms. It had not been such an easy glide as he had hoped. The rope was rough and uneven, bare in places, covered with sharp ice in others. If not for the calluses of three weeks shovelling coal, his hands would be shredded and bleeding by now. Ah well, at least the job of it warmed him up.

Or was it the water that was doing that? For now he was close enough to see it, three or four feet below him, and to see the feathers of steam rising off of it. Sure and it was warmer than the air, maybe warm as a bath itself. He almost wanted to reach down and dip his hand in. But he was not fool enough to do it. Wouldn't the air ice it on his hands in no time at all? Already he could feel his forehead crisping over with his own frozen sweat.

His arms rested, he examined the rat stop, its pointed end facing him, and planned his way around. Then he took a deep breath and set about the risky business. Slowly, he lowered his legs from the rope, being careful to keep his knees bent and his feet clear of the sea. He slid his hands to the rat stop, one after the other, until his right hand was touching the metal point. Then he set his body in motion, building up the sweep of his swing until he could reach out to hook his right leg around the line on the other side. Now, shifting as much weight to his right leg as he could, he grabbed for the bottom of the cone with his right arm.

There he rested for a moment, his right elbow cradling the sharp edge of the base. The awkwardness of his jacket and the weight of his duffel bag made the work heavy going. He almost leaned his face against the cone, stopping himself just in time. Sure wouldn't his cheek freeze right to the metal? Aye, it was a near escape.

It was quick work to slide his right arm down and catch up the line with his hand, just past the bottom of the thing. Then he eased his left arm up the slope of it until he could grab for the line with his left hand.

Panting like a horse and it after finishing a race, he was past it at last. Only his left leg swung free. He didn't bother to bring it up. With his goal in sight and less than two feet to travel to be within reach of it, he made the distance in one swift hand-over-hand. Then he let down his right leg, and swinging both legs together, landed his feet on the fender.

The Mother of God herself must have been after hearing Ciaran's prayers and sending guardian angels to look after him this night. For just as he was about to let go the line, his feet slid off the side of the fender and almost into the water itself. The ice on the sisal had crunched and given way under his feet, sure enough, but greasy oil and algae lurked beneath it. Well, he could not hang from his hands this way for long. They didn't ache any more but he could not feel much of the tips of his fingers neither. He would have to aim his feet closer to the wood pilings. He hoped he could grab onto something before the weight of his duffel toppled him backwards. He thanked the Lord for taking him this far and threw himself at the pilings.

He landed safe, his feet sinking into the soft fibres atop the fender, his arms hugging a loose piling. It was only then that he realised how lucky he was. For the pilings were oil soaked and slick as well. Only one or two had shrunken away from their neighbours enough to offer any purchase at all. In his blind flight, he had found one of these.

Where they were not frozen over, the pilings were, all of them, fouled with engine oil. And the surface of the fender was not near so level as it had looked from above. Though only six or seven good paces would put him in reach of the ladder, it would be a slow and steady work of balancing with nothing sure to hold. He felt the cold penetrating his clothes to his clammy skin. His feet, though dry and wrapped in all the socks he owned, were going wooden. How much longer would they be any use at all?

"You didna' come this far to be lost for a bit of the shakes," he whispered to himself. But there was no going on without that the trembles must pass. He clung to the piling, counting his breaths, inhaling the sharp and wakening smells of tar and salt.

The ladder shone like a stairway to heaven itself. He could almost see an angel hovering about at the top of it. He shook his head and the angel took the shape of a sea bird. She was a gull, sure enough. Pure white, the like he'd never seen before. She watching there and her all aglow in a halo of fog. Just why this bird should give him heart he could not say. For wasn't she only being curious in the way of sea birds ever? But heart he found now; enough that moments later he arrived at the end of the fender, the ladder no more than an arm's stretch away.

Perhaps confidence had made him too easy. Maybe it was his hands, painful now and weak with the cold. But as he reached his right arm and leg for the ladder, he felt his left foot sliding down. He had one rung of the ladder within his grasp when he found his fingers clenched in an empty fist. He was falling, the duffel bag pulling him backwards into the sea.

There are those will tell you how a man can see his life pass all before him in such a moment as this. Though it be a good story, they are fools that tell it. For the colour of panic is brighter than the heart of a noontime sun that will blind a man sooner than show him the truth. And the rushing roar of fear will deafen him.

But the fatal sea seduces and consoles that part of man born of it. In each of us the same. In restless blood, the tidal ebb and flow. And the sea is ever ready to welcome home its own. *If I let you, you can ride me like a lover. If I want you, I will keep you...*

In a whole sea girt lifetime, Ciaran had never felt salt water close around him with no ground beneath his feet. Now, before breathless panic overtook him, he marvelled at the soft, buoyant warmth of the black, dark silence. He turned slowly downward. How long can a man fight his fate? He was so tired and the water thick and warm as mother's milk. Above him, someone was shrieking, screaming raucous into the night. Why? And then his lungs echoed the noise with screaming pain.

Almost against his will, certainly without his conscious effort, his legs and arms began to flail. The motion pushed him upward through the surface to gasp lungs full of painfully frigid air. And with the shock of cold, his senses returned. The sea gull was hopping back and forth at the top of the ladder. It was her fierce cries had summoned him and pierced the sea itself. His arms slapped useless at the water. Soon his heavy jacket and the duffel, soaked through, would drag him down once more. But the sea had brought a stinging life back to the exposed skin of his hands and face. With one last desperate reach he felt his fingers close around the ladder. He pulled upward, part of him still reluctant to leave the bath warm sea, and dragged himself, still burdened with the sodden duffel, to the top of the ladder.

Now, as he lay gasping on the dock, collecting his strength for one last dash to the warmth of the warehouse, he heard voices. A woman and a man talking in the doorway. They went inside and closed the door behind them. He would have to wait until they were gone.

Half walking, half crawling, for he had lost all feeling below his knees, he struggled to a pile of pallets against a wall of the building. There, he could settle himself for a while, unseen by both his shipmates and the folk inside; sheltered, if only slightly, from the cut of onshore winds.

Soon he would be safe. Soon enough. Safe and warm. Maybe he would find a kettle in there and he could make himself a cup of tea. He would wrap himself in soft Scottish tweeds while his clothes dried against a stove. And he would fetch the golden beads from the bottom of his duffel, that he had not dared touch all the while across the sea. Ah, they were warm and lively against his skin. And weren't they gentle, them Scottish tweeds, thick and warm. He pulled some close, feeling the nap under his chin. His hands didn't hurt no more, now his fingers were hugging a thick mug, hot through from the tea. And a bit of whiskey in the tea and all. But where was this lot of feathers coming from? Sure it wasn't that bird that was watching him and her all alone. And whatever was she doing flapping right up to his face when all he wanted was to drink his tea and sleep in peace. To sleep in peace. A gentle snow fell. He was smiling when he closed his eyes.

Part Five

Where lies the final harbour, whence we unmoor no more?

Moby Dick, Herman Melville

La mer, la mer, toujours recommencée

Le Cimetière marin, Paul Valéry

CHAPTER THIRTY FOUR

A man with the sky in his eyes

Strange weather. Even for February when anything was possible. In a cold snap that should have cleared the fog and locked the skies solid, a soft snow had begun to fall. Delicate caps of Queen Anne's lace, tatted from the mist itself, powdered over the treacherous patches of ice.

Unbalanced by her weekend satchel, full of presents for Daniel, Rachel slithered across the warehouse yard. Reaching for the bell cord, she fell forward, and smacked the flat of her hand hard against the door. She was rubbing it when Mendel answered.

"Why didn't you put down some sand? I almost broke my neck."

"Well hello," Mendel said. "Good Shabbas to you too."

"Oh...yeah...Good Shabbas. Mendel, it's really slippery in the yard."

"Mmm." He studied the snow and sighed. "Some drive it's gonna be to Brooklyn. Come inside, get warm."

They were brother and sister. The intimacy of blood coloured their conversations but had not yet bridged the distance of almost a generation of years between them. A young man's observations, unseen and unknown by the child; a child's hunger, hungrier and more intense than an adult will ever remember. Much goes unsaid, is forgotten by both; it chills a gulf that only maturity can warm and dissipate. And so, as they snaked through alleys of stacked crates marked *Fragile* and *This End Up*, bundles wrapped in brown paper, tied with thick twine, they were, at once, formal and familiar, careful and heedless. Staccato puffs of condensation echoed the blunt rhythm of their talk.

"Daniel? Did you see him this morning?"

"He's fine. Helen makes too big a deal. He's got a runny nose. So who doesn't."

"Did you send for the doctor?"

"She called…on the telephone."

"So? Did he come?"

"He didn't have to come."

"Are you sure? How can you be sure?"

"He's all right, Rachel. I'm telling you. Nothing with nothing. Chicken soup and some Vicks on his chest and that's that."

Rachel knew she would not be satisfied until she saw for herself.

In a corner of the warehouse floor, by the pot-bellied stove, Mendel poured her a cup of bitter, boiled coffee. Then they climbed a wooden staircase to the row of heated offices.

"I have to finish this," he said as he sat behind his desk. "…Insurance papers. A coupla bundles broke open. Then we'll go."

"Anything good?" Rachel said.

"I dunno, maybe…Some kinda material. Wool. You'll look when we go down. You could maybe make a coat."

Two sides of Mendel's office were half walled with glass. While he wrote, Rachel stared out, imagining of scenes of Daniel's suffering against the darkened warehouse. She saw him feverish and flushed, tossing on a sweat soaked pillow. He awoke, overheated and terrified, calling out her name. He held his head and cried. *Hurts Mommy. It hurts.*

"Are you almost finished?" she said.

"Mmm hmm…In a minute."

"You're sure he's really okay?"

"I told you."

He blotted his papers, stood up and stretched. Then he opened the window a crack and peered out.

"You know, Rachel," he said. "…I think we should go by subway. The bridge it's gonna be like glass already."

"You mean I came all the way over here for nothing?"

"What can I do? Look at it. I only got a Ford, not a snow plough."

At the window now herself, she saw that Mendel was right. The snow was falling fast. Its cold, enlivening smell freshened on her face. Well, it was not a long walk to Cortlandt for the train. And the subway would be quicker anyway. As she closed the window, a low, animal groan rose up from beneath it.

"Mendel, I think there's a dog out there. Maybe we should let it in, out of the cold."

"What? So it can crap and pish all over my warehouse all weekend long? Forget it. Strays know how to look after themselves. I better telephone Helen or she'll worry."

Thick magic falling through a windless night alive with mystery, every streetlight a bride in shifting lace. Every footfall swallowed in creamy silence. How tenderly it surprises the skin with kisses, melting cool. How innocently it confuses the eye. Soft and inviting the bed it lays. Cruel nature at her most beguiling, promising the sweetest, gentlest death.

How could anyone name such pleasure *storm*? If not for Daniel, Rachel thought, she could happily sit for a while, in this stillness like no other, listening, trying to catch the impossible sound of gathering snow. She was entranced. As Mendel turned to lock the door, she virtually danced into it. At once, both feet flew out from under her. Reaching blindly for any support to stop her fall, she snatched at the loose pile of pallets, bringing one down with her, sending several more, further along, to the ground.

That was when she heard the long, deadfall whisper of a sigh.

"Did you hear that?"

"What?" Mendel offered his hand to help her up.

"Over there. Someone's over there."

"I told you already. Stray dogs, I got no time for."

But she had already scrambled to her feet and was stumbling to the end of the row of pallets.

A beautiful old man lay back against the wall, his stiff white hair and his features lightly masked in snow, his arms tightly wrapped around some kind of sack. She brushed snow from his oil blackened face and as her finger touched his cheek she shuddered and snatched her hand away as if seared. His skin was cold. Dead cold. She began to tremble, unable to tear her eyes away. The dead man was smiling. Not the fearful grinning death rictus she had seen actors simulate at the pictures. His face was lovely, serene. As though he had fallen, dreaming, into paradise.

"Oh," she moaned. She hugged herself and rocked. "Oh...oh...oh." But whether this was sadness or terror or awe in the face of such a peaceful death, she could not have said.

"Oy, *nisht du gedacht*." Mendel was right behind her.

He knelt and felt the man's wrist for a pulse. Then he pressed his fingers into the side of his neck. In the still falling snow, neither of them noticed the weak exhalation that escaped the man's lips.

"I'm not sure," Mendel said. "I think, maybe, he's alive."

He tossed his keys to Rachel and pushed aside a pallet that had fallen over the man's leg. "Come on. Help me get him inside." Struggling together, they dragged the man, his arms still clutching his belongings, into the warehouse.

Once inside, Rachel was amazed at the ease with which her brother, strong from years of warehouse work, lifted the man over his shoulder and carried him up to the office. He rested him against the radiator, warm with residual heat, and gently pried open one eye. They were both startled by the flash of summer blue.

"He *is* alive," Mendel said. "The poor man." He examined the man's face while Rachel watched white flakes of salt ice soften and fall from his dark, curly hair. Mendel wiped oil from his cheeks with a handkerchief. He was not old at all.

"The poor man," she agreed, but it was not pity or compassion that rose in her throat and stopped her breath.

"Take off his clothes," Mendel said. "...while I go find something dry to put around him."

"You want me to undress him?" Rachel was shocked.

"Rachel, this is no time to be *Miss Priss*. The man is freezing to death. Take off his wet clothes."

Timidly at first and then with an avid interest that shocked her all over again, she began to peel off his clothes. When she pulled him forward to take off his jacket and shirt, he fell against her, his dead weight almost toppling her, his chin pressing against her shoulder. She held his head, as she settled him back against the radiator; his damp curls licking her fingers, his rasping breath moist on her face. She took off his boots. Then, quickly, she unbuttoned his trousers and yanked them off.

He was pale, in his half frozen state almost as white as marble. And like a marble statue, she could see the muscles defined in his arms, his chest, his legs. Rachel who had been bride, mother and dream lover, had never seen a naked man. Did all men look like this? Men who could use their voices like hammer blows to stop time itself? So vulnerable? So breakable? She felt the warmth of her reddening cheeks. Embarrassed for his helplessness, she turned away, took off her coat and laid it over him.

Last of all, she pulled off his sodden socks. What strange feet. Fine, almost iridescent skin connected his toes, one to the other. Although it was years since she had unwrapped the small linen parcel, given to her by the midwife, now, looking at the man's toes, she was reminded of Daniel's caul. Gently, she spread them to touch the web. She was shocked when he pulled away.

"I...I'm sorry," she said.

He was staring at her, his eyes so sky full she could almost see birds soaring in their cloudless depth. Higher and higher. They play courtship games with the sun. She pulled her eyes away and when she looked again, his were closed, the arcs of his lashes dark against his cheeks. Where Mendel had cleaned his face, now lines of coal dust scored it, traces of black tears. Perhaps she had imagined it all. But she could not shake the feeling that something had entered with him. *Only remember.* Something powerful and familiar. Something she had felt before that had brought her nothing but grief. *No! Never again.* By the time Mendel came back, carrying a bolt of soft brown tweed, Rachel had rebuilt her wall of protection.

Mendel sliced off a length of cloth and bent to wrap the man. "In the bottom drawer of my desk, there's some slivovitz. Get it." Rachel obeyed. "You know the pot-bellied stove downstairs? Where the men make coffee?"

"Uh huh."

"Go mix up the embers with some fresh coal...We'll heat some water."

She waited in the office doorway watching Mendel rub the man's hands and blow on them.

"Well?" he said.

"Mendel, maybe we should call the police."

"What?"

"So they can send an ambulance or something."

"Don't be stupid."

"But..."

"You think business this man wants with the police? Somebody this desperate to get into New York that he jumps off a boat?"

"Maybe he just fell off...by accident."

"Use your brains, Rachel. From boats in harbours, sailors don't fall. This man is an illegal."

"We don't know that. We don't know anything about him."

"Believe me, I know."

"How? I mean...he...we..."

"Look Rachel, I know what I know. You didn't go through Ellis Island, you weren't born then. You didn't see what people would do, the ones they wouldn't let in, what they would do to stay. I was only seven but believe me, I understood plenty; how bad they wanted to be in America. And I saw plenty. I saw and I remember."

"We got him out of the cold. I don't see why he's our business now."

"Oy Rachel," Mendel sighed. "Someday you'll grow up. Maybe then you'll know that to be a human being is everybody's business...Go put coal in the stove."

Mendel stirred slivovitz into warm water and offered it, but the man remained too profoundly unconscious to drink. Although he groaned and shifted from time to time, the mixture only wet his lips and dribbled down his chin.

"We have to get him out of here," Mendel said. "...somewhere where we can warm him good." His brow creased in thought. "That bed in the room behind the shop...where the old man used to sleep...It's still there?"

Though Rachel could think of dozens of objections, she knew Mendel would counter them all. She recognised the adamantine set of his mouth, having seen it on her father's face often enough. And somewhere deep within herself, a hungry whisper dared her to acquiesce. *Why not? See, play, remember... Company.*

They settled him, with his clothes and possessions, in the back seat of Mendel's Ford, garaged behind big, swinging doors at the end of the warehouse. By the time the car crawled out into the storm, she thought she had silenced it.

"This is crazy Mendel...He could be a criminal or something."

"Tomorrow, already, he'll be on his feet, to go. So in the meantime, I'll stay."

"Helen..."

"There's a snowstorm so I couldn't get home. It's so strange I should sleep at my sister's, whose got plenty of room? I'll call her."

"What will Dinah say?"

"She'll make soup and fill hot water bottles. About Dinah I'm not worried."

The headlights threw a hypnotic tunnel of light ahead of them. Rachel stared at the pattern of illuminated flakes, trying to stop her unruly mind from making patterns of its own. Suddenly, she felt her lap, looked at the floor, and twisted to see the floor behind her.

"My bag, I left my bag in the yard."

"The gates are locked. Nobody's gonna climb over them in this weather."

"It's full of presents for Daniel."

"It'll be there, it'll be there...I'll get it tomorrow."

"I should have gone by subway myself. Daniel needs me."

"Daniel is sleeping."

"He'll miss me. He'll wonder why I'm not there."

"Three years old he is, Rachel. You think he has any idea, one day from another?"

"I should have gone myself."

Mendel sighed. "Do you ever think about anything besides what *you* want?" he said.

Rachel was too surprised at the distaste in his voice to defend herself. Mendel had never spoken to her like that before. And she could hear, in the silence that followed, that there would be more.

"You know, Rachel...ever since you were little, you were special. Smart. When you were just a baby, you used to come out with such things would make everybody...I dunno...amazed. Mama said you used to talk about Bubbie Ruchel like you already knew her. From her pictures, maybe, you guessed... Who knows. Things you couldn't even know, Mama said, you knew. So tell me something, Rachel, how come you're so smart, you know so many things, so how come you never know what really matters?"

Mortified, Rachel turned away to hide her stinging eyes. Bessie swam into the dark. *Raaachel! What's wrong with you? Don't you know nothing?* And Aaron. *Your own way you don't always have to get.* Was it true?

Neither of them spoke for the rest of the journey.

Mendel was right about Dinah. When they arrived, Mendel carrying the unconscious man like a sleeping child, she barely asked a question.

"What happened?" she said.

"We found him in the snow. He needs to be warm," Mendel said, and she was off fetching an eiderdown, blankets and one of her father's flannel nightshirts, from the upstairs bedrooms. "Fill these," she said to Rachel, giving her two hot water bottles and sending her to the kitchen.

Rachel found them talking about the man when she returned. They'd been through the pockets of his coat and had found a seaman's book with the seal of the International Seamen's Union on the cover. Salt water had washed away all the writing inside it. They found a sodden roll of money, but it was American so they were none the wiser. Dinah agreed with Mendel that he must be an illegal immigrant.

" It makes you think," Dinah said, wrapping his arms around a hot water bottle, "...to do such a thing on a night like this. Such troubles people have." She clucked her tongue sympathetically.

He looked no better, almost as white as the pillowcase, now soiled with grease and coal dust from his face. Dinah and Mendel said they should take turns sitting with him. "So he shouldn't be afraid...to wake up in a strange place, full of junk," Dinah said. Rachel didn't want to. She wouldn't say why.

Mendel sent her to empty his duffel bag and spread his things to dry. "They shouldn't rot...if it's all he has. Maybe you'll find something so we'll know if he has people, family, somebody we can send a letter...Go...Make yourself useful at least."

In the bathroom, upstairs, Rachel pulled clothes from the bag and spread them on the radiator and the sides of the cast iron tub. Two linen shirts, old fashioned and, she noticed, sewn by hand. A soggy sweater, hand knitted in a plain stitch. A pair of homespun trousers like the ones she had pulled off him. A rag that might once have been a towel and a little piece of soap. A lethal looking razor.

Something heavy and lumpy was wrapped inside the last shirt. As she lifted it from the bottom of the bag, a string of beads slipped from the folded linen and clattered against the tub. Kneeling on the bathroom floor, she stared at them, astounded.

342

They couldn't be gold. They were far too thick and heavy. Surely the stranger was poor; she could see that from his clothes. Where would such a man get a string of gold beads? Were they stolen? Was that what he was running from, why he had been trying to hide? Maybe if he knew she had found them, he would rise up and murder her in her bed, murder them all. No, she remembered the sweetness of his sleeping face. They could not be gold. They were probably just lead, coated with some coloured metal to look like gold. She lifted them out of the tub.

They were not beads, precisely; more like a chain, each thick link intricately graven with a knot pattern. On some of them, the knot design was inlaid with flecked blue stone. Lapis. They *were* gold. They were made by hand. And they were blood warm; growing warmer as she held them. She was so startled, she almost dropped them.

Now she lifted the chain and held it against her face. It hummed and smelled of the sea. *I found it by the shore and you must have it now.* But she is frightened. "When he comes to take it back, he will take you also." He only laughs. "He may try," he says. She hears her own cries in the whirlwind. The beads are melting in the pool of his boiling blood. In the place by the stream, at the bottom of the vineyard, she kisses the back of his neck as she adorns him with the collar of gold. She can smell the olives in his long braided hair and together they watch the fair-haired strangers climb the hill from their long boats. *It is the bond between us and I am the promise unbroken that will not rest until I find you.*

"Rachel!" Dinah called from the bottom of the stairs. "Bring down a bowl of hot water and some soap." Rachel came to her senses rocking on the bathroom floor, the mysterious golden chain, still pressed against her face. It fell from her fingers. She had no idea what she was doing there, or why her face was drenched with tears.

"Okay," she tried to shout, but her voice was choked.

"What?"

"Okay."

She filled the pitcher with warm water and put it, together with a towel, soap and a washcloth, into the basin. Hastily, she splashed cold water into her burning eyes.

Now she did something inexplicable, even to herself. If she could have remembered why she did it, still she could not have explained it. But she never had to. No one ever asked. She bent to pick up the golden chain and slipped it into the deep pocket of her dress. Then she made her way down to the room behind the shop.

"I'll do it," she said. "You go eat something."

When Dinah and Mendel had gone, she lifted the stranger's head and arranged the towel over the pillow behind it. Slowly, with such care she might have been anointing a prince, she washed his face.

∞

Ciaran opened his eyes. A young woman bent over him, washing his face with a soft cloth lathered with scented soap. I am dreaming, or else I am dead, he thought. Her hands were fine and delicate, her skin fair. Her light brown faery hair was a halo around her small face. But when she turned her gaze upon him, her huge round eyes as dark as night itself, he shrank in terror.

"Don't be afraid," she said. "You're safe."

But though her voice sang to him as pure and clean as the finest fiddle, he did not believe her. For in her sad eyes he had seen such hunger as he had never in his life looked upon, a hunger that seemed to pull the very soul out of his body. He turned his face into the pillow.

"What is your name?" she said, her voice like the siren's song itself, so that despite his fears he had to answer.

"I am Ciaran," he whispered.

"Ciaran," she repeated, and she smiled.

Then she reached into her pocket and, before his dazzled eyes, she brought out his own treasure that he had just been dreaming of. Dizzy, he gripped the bed to keep from floating into her strange, compelling eyes. *Sure and I must be dead.*

Slowly, she bent closer to him. Gently, so gently that he barely felt the cool touch of her fingers, she placed the golden collar around his neck. She took his hand, that was limp and willing, and folded it around the beads.

"I am Rachel," she said. And he felt safe.

CHAPTER THIRTY FIVE

Interludes

Sleeping and waking, stitched together in a seamless state of dreams. He did not know how long he stretched his bones or where at all he was. Or with whom. So he watched and dozed and listened from the safety of a feather bed. There were three of them, who came and went; the one he thought of as the *sidhe* woman and two others besides. There was a man and a short, plump woman, with olive skin and cropped black hair, who fed him clear soup, bits of toasted bread and sweet black tea. "Feeling better?" she smiled. He nodded before drifting off again.

The wind picked up. Outside a Nor'easter whooped and bayed. In the kitchen, Dinah ladled soup for the family, while below them, the stranger slept.

"Would you listen to that," she said. "We should only thank God we have a roof over our heads, *Nu?*"

Mendel nodded. "Think, if we didn't find him. If he was out in this. On my own worst enemy I wouldn't wish it."

"I wonder where he comes from...What kind of troubles he has, you know... because why else...?" Dinah said.

"If he wants, when he can, he'll tell us. If not, *schon*, maybe it's not our business."

"Mmm."

"He's an Irishman," Rachel said. "His name is Ciaran." Mendel and Dinah both stopped their spoons mid sip and stared at her.

"What? *What?!*...He told me."

Ciaran watched the man, a strong looking fellow, with muscular arms and hands as big as a bare knuckle fighter, peel dollars from a thick, wet wad and drop them into a crockery bowl on the table beside the bed. "I don't want it should get rotten, all stuck together," the man said, "so God forbid, when you need it, it wouldn't be worth beans." The man smiled too, in a bashful, friendly sort of way. He had a gentle face.

"Oh, aye," Ciaran said. He wanted to say more but he was too tired to think of what it might be.

The *sidhe* woman, tall and young, with clouds of chestnut hair, stepped out of his singing dreams to sit beside him, still and solemn. Unlike the others, she rarely smiled. In fact, only once, when she had whispered his name soft as music, and dressed him in his gold, could he recall her smiling. Maybe it was a dream. She did not tend to him, like the others but only sat beside him sometimes, her eyes mirroring the wonder in his own. Could be she was a dream altogether. He remembered listening to her croon and watching her dance circles onto the starlit dew only to wake and find her singing still as she worked at some job or other, filling boxes, tying bundles of clothes with twine, singing softly to pass the time. But no, she must be real for the beads were real enough. She had lifted the neck of the flannel nightshirt to hide them under it; his secret now hers and all. How strange it was, for the first time, to share his secret with another. How easy he felt to do it. Why? And then he remembered that she had told him her name.

"Now you're doing this?"

Dinah watched Rachel heave another bundle of old clothes onto the growing pile by the front door of the shop.

"Why not now? What else have I got to do in this weather? Anyway, when they shovel the street, the rag man will come around. It's time we got rid of all this stuff."

"You'll wake him. The poor man needs to sleep."

"I'm not making any noise. You can't even breathe in there. A perfectly good room, full of junk nobody wants. We could have a fire or something. Mice could make nests...rats even, who knows."

Dinah shook her head. "All of a sudden you decided this?"

"Daniel could play in there while we work, if we cleaned it out."

"Oh, I see."

Clearly, Dinah did not see at all, but that suited Rachel who was, herself, not sure why now, of all times, the state of the store room seemed so important.

She was the last to look in on him at night, tiptoeing down the stairs after Dinah and Mendel had gone to bed, and the first to assure herself that he was still there in the morning. So, it was Rachel who found Ciaran wandering in the shop early Sunday. He had wrapped himself in a blanket and was leaning on the counter, his legs wobbly from so much sleep.

"Oh. You're up...uh...You must be feeling a little better."

He had colour in his cheeks and a pressing question on his mind.

"Good morning Miss Rachel. Would you tell me please, where is the bog?"

"The what?"

"I am sorry to trouble you but I am near desperate for it." While one hand clutched the blanket, his other, unconsciously hovered near his groin.

Rachel saw he would need help to stand. She blushed. "Oh...I...uh... My brother will..." She shouted up the stairs. "Mendel! Mendel come down!"

She listened to him interrogating Mendel on the way up—*What is this place? How did I come to be here? Who are you all that have been so kind to let me stop with you?*—relieved to let Mendel explain, still vaguely ashamed of her initial impulse to abandon him to the forces of law and order.

In the kitchen, Dinah was starting the coffee. "Is he on his feet?" she said.

"Just about."

"So...?"

"So what?"

"So, did he say anything to you? What is he like?"

"Oh...you know...He's..."

What could Rachel say? He was a man and a stranger; what, besides trouble and sorrow, could ever come from him? And yet...and yet... She remembered the flush of colour on his cheeks; the gentle, shy music she heard when he spoke; the way her fingers, of their own accord, wanted to play in his hair, to stroke his throat. What could Rachel say, who had awakened to no other love but that of instinct, a mother for her child? How slow the mind can be to understand what the blood has always known. She changed the subject. "I'll make breakfast."

"You?"

"You don't have to be so surprised. I know how to cook an egg."

"Fine. Go ahead. Make breakfast." Dinah grinned and shrugged.

They gathered around the kitchen table, the three of them awkwardly watching Ciaran, the air thick with unasked questions. He seemed a bit steadier now, still wrapped in the blanket, eating Rachel's streaky scrambled eggs and drinking, he said, the first cup of coffee he had ever tasted.

"Sure and isn't this the finest eggs a man could wish for," he said as he tactfully pushed some uncooked egg white and a bit of shell to the edge of his plate. Rachel beamed. "Ah," he said, "so there is a smile in you after all, lass... But would yous look at the rest of you, staring at me like I was Lazarus himself, arisen from the dead."

"You almost were, I'm telling you." Mendel said. "If my sister didn't find you..." He shook his head. "Well, Thank God, it didn't happen. *Kinahora*, you're a lucky fella'."

"Was it *you* found me then?"

"Well...I..." Rachel could hardly bear the innocent blaze of Ciaran's eyes. She looked down at her plate.

"Ach, you have saved my life and all. Lord knows how I will thank you for it."

"It was...oh...just...it was nothing."

"It was never nothing," Ciaran said. "Though I will tell you, myself, I was thinking the Lord himself was after deciding my life was worth nothing at all, with my fortunes that I would not wish on no man. But isn't my faith restored, now I have met three fine folk such as yourselves?"

He stirred another spoon of sugar into his coffee and, once again, an awkward silence descended that, once again, Ciaran broke.

"You must not mind me askin', for I mean you no ill with it, but are you Jewish people?"

Mendel cleared his throat. "We are," he said coolly.

"It is only that I heard you say some words Izzy Katz was after using, that was my shipma...that was my friend, is all. He was a grand fellow that I am missing already."

"What happened to him?" Rachel said. Both Dinah and Mendel frowned at her.

"Ah well, I do not know for certain. Only that maybe he was not so lucky as myself." Ciaran fell silent. He looked thoughtful.

"Are you Catholic?" Dinah said.

"I am that I suppose."

"Would you like us to get you a priest?"

"A priest? Ach no, for I do not think I am dyin' anymore at the moment."
They joined his laughter, the discomfort of strangeness dissipated for now.

Rachel and Dinah cleared the table, while Ciaran stretched and patted his
stomach. "Isn't it a powerful thing, what a wee bit of food will do for a man.
I am thinking, now, that I have put you to trouble enough and it is time I was
goin' on my way."

Rachel had not dared to think about his leaving. "Oh no, not yet," she
blurted. "You can't...you...you...You're not well enough yet. It's miserable and
cold outside...and...and...besides," she enjoyed a small triumphant surge, "your
coat is still wet."

"My sister is right," Mendel said. "A couple days, it wouldn't hurt, you
should rest some more. Is there somebody you want we should call? You have
maybe some relatives or friends could be worried about you?"

"There is none but you lot knows me here," Ciaran said. "But I must find
myself some work to do and a room to stop in."

Rachel held her breath.

"It's Sunday. It can wait a little while," Mendel said. "You have some ideas
already, what you'll do?"

"I will find me a pub, I suppose. For I'm thinking that a publican can
always say where there is work to be had."

Rachel had no idea what a pub was or what Ciaran was talking about. But
Mendel laughed gently. "We don't have pubs here," he said. "We don't even
have barrooms anymore, since Prohibition."

"Oh aye, I mind I heard about it and all. But I scarce believed it. Is it the
truth then, that a man canna buy himself a wee drink and him parched with
thirst?"

"It's true all right. It's not gonna last much longer, if you ask me, because
you can still...you know...in private, have a little something. And believe me,
everybody does. But pubs, like I read about in books, never. The saloons,
maybe, in the old days, you know, with cowboys...maybe that was like a pub.
I dunno."

349

"Ah well, I must have a me look around, then. Where there is people living, there is always work, one kind and another."

"Look, don't worry about it now...You'll stay a little, get strong with Dinah's cooking. I'll ask around. Who knows? A man wants to work, something there's gotta be for him to do."

Ciaran nodded.

"Meanwhile, why don't you take a bath, have a shave...So you'll feel like a mensch again."

Two women left alone with a stranger in the uncommon pleasure of a lazy Sunday. When the skies cleared, Mendel hiked out into the luminous snow to get a snow shovel from the warehouse and to find Rachel's bag. Rachel telephoned Helen to talk to Daniel.

"No more fever," she reported to Dinah. "He wanted to know if I was coming tomorrow."

"He's only little, Rachel. He'll play in the snow. He'll manage till next weekend."

"I know."

The sound of running water emerged from the bathroom.

"Did you tell Helen about...him?"

"No...I told her Mendel was digging out the car, that he'll be home later."

"You're probably right. She'd only make a fuss."

Lost in their own thoughts, they drank coffee in a house at peace with itself. Dinah said she might bake. "It's that kind of a day," she said.

"Can I watch. Will you show me?"

"Sure...All of a sudden you want to know how to bake?"

"For Daniel..."

"Oh."

"Listen." Rachel looked toward the bathroom. "Can you hear that?"

Dinah nodded and smiled. On the other side of the door, Ciaran was singing. "I don't know," she said, "is it just me, or does the house seem different today...you know, good...like a home should feel?"

Rachel was stunned. All morning, she had sensed this good feeling, a river of light, growing in intensity until it flooded her to bursting. But she had nurtured it in secret, never guessing that it could be shared. ...*like coming home.*

"Sometimes," Dinah said, "I think, maybe...I don't know, you'll think I'm being silly."

"No I won't. Tell me, please."

"Well, sometimes I think that maybe when you do a *mitzvah*, you know, a good deed, maybe then, you can feel God smiling."

Rachel sighed. "I found him," she said. "I *found* him, Dinah."

"I know you did, Rachel."

The women had ironed his clothes and set them in a pile in the corner, his socks neatly arranged on top. Even his shoes felt soft and supple. Could be they'd rubbed the salt away with grease. He eased himself into the hot bath, sinking back to wet his hair, then resting against the cool, white enamelled tub. As he reached for the cake of white soap, he could not help but smile to think that one of his American dreams had come true at last.

The real America was still little more than his memories from the picture shows. He had seen nothing but the fog bound dock and the inside of this house. Well, he had met some real Americans anyhow. And grand folk they seemed, though he knew little enough about them. The brother and the sister, Rachel. And the other one, who was likely a sister and all. Or maybe she was the brother's wife. He would find out, he supposed, for his heart had told him they would be his friends.

Although he was curious about them all, it was Rachel, now that filled his mind. Sure and she was a beauty. But something else about her, something strange and uncommon, had captured his imagination. No man could deny he'd had his share of pretty girls, and more maybe, but none had touched him the like of this. Almost a girl she was, yet so serious and solemn when she had watched beside him, as though the spirit that looked out of her round, dark eyes had been to forever and back, as though a part of it watched and pulled at his own from that faraway place. And where her fingers had brushed his neck, when she gave him the treasure, couldn't he feel the tingle still? He was not sure how he knew it, but he was certain she had not told the others about the golden beads. Why?

Ah, it was idle to think such wild notions. Didn't she show him a smile, over breakfast, that was like daybreak itself. His heart swelled just to remember it. He closed his eyes to see it again. He would make her smile that way again.

351

Could be he might ask her to show him the sights. There was that boat that Izzy spoke of, went back and forth right under the nose of the Statue of Liberty, and all them skyscrapers he had yet to look upon.

It would be grand to go about the place with a woman on his arm, and a sweet one and all. Hadn't it been long enough since he had done it? Not since Rathlin. *Ah.* Quite unexpectedly his eyes filled with tears. He wiped them away. It was a sorrowful thing to think of home and wouldn't he always be heart sore to do it? But those ones he left behind had the comfort of each other. Could be that imagining he was with the Lord had made them easy and all. A living man must find what contentment he can. And he must know it when it looks him in the eye.

His muscles had gathered strength from the warmth of the water, but it was cooling now. Testing the tap, he was astonished to discover there was more hot water still. He caught the square soap as it floated past his fingers. He had never seen a cake of soap to float before and it smelling clean as a pretty woman's curls. Singing softly, he soaped his arms and chest. Then he lathered his hair and slipped back into the water to rinse it. Oh God, sure and there must be baths the like of this in Heaven.

They'd rinsed the salt out of his pullover, that Flora had made him. Though it was fragrant and soft as new, he decided not to wear it, for wasn't it near summer warm. Through the wee, curtained window, now steamed over from his bath, he could see the sky was summer blue and all. Sure and the weather did not change so fast as that?

Determined to get a better look, he wiped condensation from the glass, pulling away in surprise at the shock of cold glass. This nice, warm feeling was inside only. But he had seen no hearth at all. He pressed his nose to the window. Below he could see a yard, all full of snow, surrounded by houses made of brick. A tree, its bare branches encased in glassy ice, sparkled where it reached into the sunlight and quivered with quick, wee birds, brown mostly, but one of them astonishing paintbox red against the snow.

A heavy knock on the downstairs door jolted Ciaran from his admiration of this postage stamp of a scene. Ah, this was getting better and better. They were having Sunday visitors likely. And there was he, feeling so bath soft and clean and sociable all together. He even grinned into the mirror as he wiped a bit of shaving soap from his ear and ran his fingers through his damp curls.

A hubbub of voices rose from below, the two women and someone else, a harsh new rhythm he had not heard before. Then he heard Rachel shout. "Get out of here. Go away...Just leave me alone." And he was out of the bathroom, dashing to the stairs.

From the top, he saw the two women in the open door. Dinah was in front, almost blocking the entrance with her body. Outside, a fellow in a topcoat and a fancy brimmed hat, the like that gangsters wore in the picture shows, was leaning against the door that Dinah was trying to close.

"What is the matter here?" Ciaran said.

The man ignored him. "I have not got no interest in you," he said to Rachel. "I just figure on coming home for a while. Things didn't work out like I planned. I suppose you heard."

"This isn't your home," Dinah said.

"Oh yeah...that is not no way how I see it. Don't you know that home is where when you gotta go there, they gotta let you in the door."

"I don't *gotta* let you in anyplace."

By now Ciaran had reached the bottom of the stairs, where Rachel trembled so violently he could feel the air vibrate around her. Instinctively, he reached out his arm to calm her.

"What are you after, Mister?" he said.

"This ain't no business of yours," the stranger said. "This here is whatcha call a family matter." He leered at Rachel. "Hey, doll, where'dja get the Paddy?"

"You stopped being family when you broke my father's heart," Dinah said. "Go find some tramp to take you in."

"Whaddya talkin' about?"

"The women do not want you here. Now, why don't you be a peaceable fellow and be on your way?"

"Cute," the stranger said. "Now butt out." He put his hands on Dinah's shoulders and tried to shove his way in.

Ciaran let go of Rachel and snatched the fellow's hands off Dinah, putting himself between them.

"Take your hands off the woman," he growled.

"Big man," the fellow sneered.

"Aye, I am. Big enough for the likes of you." He saw that the man's eyes were craven. "Are you after chancing your fortunes with me?"

The stranger glared at him but did not make a move.

353

"Right then. I didna' think you were. Now go on, get away from here. Leave these folk in peace."

As the man turned away, Ciaran saw Mendel come up behind him, a big, flat shovel over his shoulder, a satchel in one hand. He could not say, for sure, how much Mendel had seen, but his distaste for the fellow was clear enough.

"What are you doing here?" Mendel said.

"Keep your shirt on. I ain't hangin' around. The company you keep stinks," the man said, and he shambled off.

"Are you all right?" Ciaran asked Dinah. She nodded. He took Rachel's hand and brushed a vagrant curl from her forehead. Her eyes were full of tears. "Ah now, do not fret, lass, for hasn't he run off with his tail between his legs and all. You must not be frightened of such a worthless fellow as that. Who is he at all?"

Rachel did not answer. "He's my brother," Dinah said. This news surprised Ciaran, but not more than the hatred in her voice. By now Mendel had come inside and was easing the women up the stairs. "It's all right. It's over," he said. "What did he want?"

"To stay here," Dinah said.

"Here?"

Mendel whispered to Rachel, but Ciaran, following them up, couldn't make out the words. He was puzzled by the entire encounter. Could be he had stepped into some family quarrel that truly was no business of his.

In the kitchen, Mendel opened a bottle and poured dark, syrupy liquid into four wee glasses. He gave one to Rachel and patted her shoulder. Then he offered a glass to Ciaran, who sniffed at it cautiously.

"Drink," Mendel said. "Homemade. It's good."

It was a sort of brandy, sweet and thick. He could not remember drinking the like before, yet the taste was familiar.

"I'm sorry you got dragged into that," Mendel said. "It was...you know... family..." he waved his hand.

"It is myself that is sorry," Ciaran said, "...if I have put my fists where they did not belong. But the fellow was harassing the women and I will not stand by for none of that, nor bullies altogether."

Mendel nodded. Ciaran watched a look pass between the three of them, full of meanings he saw but could not understand. No one spoke.

Mendel sat back and stared at the ceiling for a long while. Then he leaned forward and studied Ciaran's face. "You're all right," he said. "I think, maybe, you got a good heart. Look, maybe, already, you got some plans of your own so, you know, I wouldn't want to stop you. But, well...if you need a job, I could use you in the warehouse."

CHAPTER THIRTY SIX

So close to rest

Five-thirty a.m. of a weekday morning and the garbagemen's reveille was in full blast. Their slope-backed khaki coloured truck wheezed down Chambers Street, pushing along a solid racket of shouts, curses, laughter, the grinding of gears and the crash of galvanised iron ash cans against pavement.

Ciaran barely noticed. One month in New York and already he had acquired the selective sensitivities of the city dweller. Well, wasn't it that or go mad altogether? For the place was never quiet. Nor dark neither. Even now, hours before sunrise, it was bright enough for a man to read the papers, no trouble at all. And when, at last, the day broke, the sun came timid as a shy lass to the dancing, so that you never even noticed until there she was, watching from the side of the hall.

He trudged on to work, head down and blinking against the cindery March gusts like others all around him. Like them, his thoughts were far from the noise and the filth. And like them, too, he carried his lunch in a newspaper parcel tied with string.

There would be, he knew, a piece of Dinah's chicken and, he smiled to think of it, a raggedy slice of bread that would be Rachel's handiwork. She was not, as herself was quick to say, much use in the kitchen. It was no matter. For the filling of his belly was a small thing, though you would not think it to see how eager she and Dinah watched him try their strange new food. Mostly it was tasty enough; some he would have to get used to, he supposed. His lunch parcel likely would include a kosher dill pickle, wrapped in waxed paper. He had not heart enough to tell Rachel that he could not bear the smell of the thing, so proud was she to have chosen him a fine one, nor that every day he traded it away to another fellow for an apple or an extra hunk of bread. Some kinds of secrets were harmless enough.

Sure and she had secrets of her own. Didn't they all?

He was a proper lodger now, in the room behind the pawnshop on East Broadway. In less than five weeks' time, he had settled into their household and they had warmed to him almost like family. Yet much remained unspoken, between himself and his new friends.

"We were going to rent it anyway," Rachel had said. "...so you might as well have it, since you need a place to stay and we need a boarder." Ciaran watched Dinah's eyebrows climb skyward. "and you helped me clean it out and everything. And anyway, you're already here. If you want to stay, I mean."

Of course he did. Was there ever any doubt? From the moment she had pinned him with those eyes that held the past and future all mingled together. From the moment she took hold of his secret in her cool, wee fingers. How, then, could he move on careless as a traveller? But life, like stories, wants for means and reasons. So he said it was a fine thing to stay safe among friends for now and him knowing no one else at all in New York. And he agreed to give them three dollars a week from his wages, to pay for the room and his meals.

None of them had troubled to ask how he came to be freezing to death in the place that they found him, though Ciaran was certain Mendel knew it well enough.

"This week, already, I'm gonna be too busy to start a new man. We got a German ship, the *Prinzessin Louisa*, still unloading. And then it's got cargo still to take on. So five, maybe six more days it's gonna be."

Ciaran nodded. "As long as that?" he said.

"Yeah. The snow, you know. It slowed everything down. So in the meantime, you'll take it easy, look around. And then later, I got more time, I'll show you the ropes. You ever worked a forklift?"

At the end of Chambers Street, Ciaran turned and navigated north toward Pier 25, through staggering sailors and their ladies who drifted in and out of cheap boarding houses and brothels, illegal boozers and gambling joints masquerading as all night cafes.

On the wharves, longshoremen and stevedores scrambled, agile as monkeys, over and around the freighters, lined up two deep in the slips. In good weather, swinging daredevil from the ends of steam driven cranes, wielding baling hooks like lances, they could strip a ship down to an echoing shell in hours, the pyramids of goods dumped at warehouse gates. They seemed a burly and aggressive lot. Ciaran had read of their rough union politics in the papers, thinking sadly of poor wandering Izzy Katz all the while. But, he supposed, it was only their jobs made them seem so, for sure they went home to wives and children, mothers and sisters and sweethearts, like all the other men who worked the waterfront.

Ah well, didn't he have a sweetheart himself now, at last. Sweetheart. The sound of it fluttered about his brain. So frivolous and airy a word. It seemed scarce fitting for the speechless tenderness that lately overtook him when she turned quickly, her long plaited hair slipping over her shoulder to reveal the curve of her neck. She would hug the wee lad, Daniel, running her fingers carelessly through his hair and Ciaran wished he were a wee'un himself that could command caresses, simple and open, the like of that.

Aye, she had a child. It was not a secret, nor was it secret that the bully who had come to the door that Sunday after the storm was Daniel's father. She never said why the fellow, that was called Schmuel, aroused in her such potent dread. It puzzled Ciaran, as well, that the child lived with Mendel and his wife when there was room and time enough for him at East Broadway. Could be she would be after telling him soon enough if she was meaning for him to know. And if she were not, it were no matter. He did not grow up Flora McMurrough's son without learning a thing or two about the deep and private ways of women.

When Mendel delivered Daniel to the shop, that first Friday morning, Ciaran was more surprised by Rachel's quicksilver laughter than by her motherhood, both newly revealed.

Daniel was a fine looking lad, his skin darker than hers, his eyes green and flashed with gold; only the warm brown of his hair was like her own. And his laughter.

She played clapping games with the child and singing rhymes, fed him sweet things and milk, listened patient to his tales and told him stories of her own.

"We go see flower trees?"

"Not yet Daniel. The flower trees are sleeping under their blankets."

"And snow?"

"And snow."

"Let's wake'em up!"

"We can try but I don't think it'll work. We'll build a snow man instead. Come on, head up so I can put on your hat."

"Nope."

"Daniel, it's cold outside. Now be a good boy and let Mommy put on your hat."

"Why they sleeping?"

"Hmm...Well, after they made the apples...you remember?"

"Umm hmm."

"...so after that, they were so tired, they decided to take a little nap for a while. And then the Northwind came, so now they're hiding from him."

"The Northwind blowed and blowed so everybody has to go inside."

"That's right. That's just what happened. But he'll get tired soon and go away."

"I don't like naps." He spun around, his arms wide. "Wake up! Wake up, flower trees! Come see Daniel make a snow man. I gonna give the snowman my hat."

"Oh you think so? Hold still, I have to button your coat."

"Mommy, where do the flowers go inside?"

"Oh my, I'll have to think about that one. On the train."

"Well, don't you know lad, they are not really sleepin' at all, for like yourself they are not much for naps. You see, just about right now, I reckon they are after dancin' with the wee folk," Ciaran said.

"We folks?"

"Aye, them that are in their faery caves, that be deep under the ground, where it is always warm as summer."

"Will they come out?"

"Myself, I'm thinking that they will when they are ready to do it and not before. Your Mam is right. For they do not fancy the cold."

"Oh. Mommy? Why does that man talk funny?"

She chided the boy for his manners but everyone laughed all the same. Within the joyful noise, woven through it and around it, Ciaran experienced a sensation that was, for himself, entirely new. It was true enough he had been drawn to Rachel from the first. But this attraction was hedged about with caution, darkened by the memory of a secret, otherworldly moment they had shared.

Now, in the sun bright kitchen, his fears were cast in sharp relief and he saw them for foolishness. Ach, wasn't it the truth that he was scarce himself then? A man ought not to credit dreams over much and them coming out of his fevers and delirium itself.

Absently, he fingered the treasure through his shirt. Well, could be she was only after giving him what was his, no mystery to it at all. He might have wondered why she kept the beads a secret from the others, for he was sure that she had. But, just then, she smiled at him. So, he wondered, instead, if this new sensation might be love.

He'd scarce time to explore the feeling or enjoy it at all, when she was gone; she and the boy, all bundled against the cold, out the door with a satchel.

"Are you goin' then?" he said.

"We'll see you Monday. Say bye bye to Mr. McMurrough, Daniel." The door closed behind them.

From the kitchen window, he watched them disappear down the street and round a corner. If he knew where they were going, he could go there with them, in his mind like, to imagine her laughing with the child in some different place. But however could he ask and him no more than the lodger? Then Dinah answered his unspoken question. Sure and she must have sensed it, in that way that women have.

"Her uncle has a farm in the country," she said.

"A farm?"

"Yes…Right by the water. Daniel loves it."

"Ah."

Tompkins Brothers Dry Goods Storage had two warehouses at the end of Pier 25, one each for import and export. Mendel managed both for the bankers that owned them. There had not been any Tomkins Brothers for years, he said, but the name remained emblazoned on the buildings, peeling white paint against the dark red bricks.

"Why do not these banker fellows put their own name on it then?"

Mendel shrugged. "Too cheap, I figure. Paint costs money."

He had put Ciaran to work in the export warehouse, unloading the trucks that, already this morning were lined up in a queue outside the gates. It would be a long twelve hours heaving goods around. Mendel said he would maybe show him the receiver's job one of these days. Ciaran didn't fancy it, standing on the loading dock with a log book, making tick marks on truckers' manifests. He didn't say, of course, for he was that grateful to Mendel.

Instead he got on with the work at hand. If it were dull, it was hard and physical, which suited him well enough. He passed the time imagining the places that sent the cardboard boxes and wooden crates he loaded onto pallets. From all over America they came. Armchairs from Grand Rapids, shoes from Maine, printed cottons from the mills of Lowell that he had read about in letters, engine parts from Michigan. Sure and it was a regular geography lesson. And besides, weren't the fellows grand.

At first, mindful of Izzy's advice, he kept himself to himself, watching and listening. But how can you know folks without a bit of talk? And a bit of drink and all? Ah sure, he was not going to perish without it but now he had some money, and it coming regular, it were a shame not to spend it in a friendly way.

"Do you not miss a pint, now and again?"

Together with Weegie Gianelli and Frank LaPlant, mates from work, he had gone to see a fearsome game called ice hockey, played with sticks in a big arena. Later, over long, red hotdog sausages and bottles of cream soda, the two others had argued the merits of the teams. "You believe it, dere ain't nobody can play dis game like de Canadians, I betcha," LaPlant said. "Aah, whaddya talkin'?" Gianelli countered. "The Rangers gonna wipe the floor with them Canucks. They're gonna be champeens this year. Ain't no other team can beat New York."

Ciaran, who didn't understand the finer points of the game nor the partisan loyalties, as heated as politics, had begun to feel a powerful thirst.

"What kinda pint you got in mind, Mac?" Gianelli said.

"I'm thinking, right now, how I would fancy a beer or a bottle of ale maybe. And I was only after wondering how a man is meant to do without it."

Both of the others laughed. "Tell you what," Gianelli said. "You come with me, payday...We eat *ah beetz* and maybe drink something, you won't be thirsty no more."

"What is a beets?"

"You'll see...Best you ever tasted."

Ciaran didn't argue. People were always after saying the same to him. Was there nothing these New York folk wouldn't boast over? If it were not the biggest or the best, than sure it was the worst; either way, it were never less than the most a thing could be. "Well you know that Capone? Meanest guy in Chicago? He came from here first, didn't he. You think he could learn to be so tough in Chicago? *Pah!*" Gianelli once said. It seemed that even their villains were more villainous than anywhere else.

The next Friday, after work, Ciaran and Gianelli ate flat bread, spread with a spicy red sauce and stringy melted cheese, in a café called Lombardi's in Little Italy.

"*Ah beetz*," Gianelli said. "Good, hah?"

Ciaran, his mouth full of cheese, could only grunt.

"Good, Mama...Always you make the best," Gianelli told the fat old woman who served them.

"You good boy, Weegie," she said. "You come anytime. I cook for you special."

"So...Mama, you maybe got something to drink. Me and my friend here is thirsty."

The woman scrutinised Ciaran. "Is okay, you friend?"

"Is okay, Mama," Gianelli laughed.

"She is your Mam?" Ciaran asked, when she was gone.

"Aah no,"Gianelli laughed. "'Iis just, you know, like respect."

"Ah."

After a few minutes, she brought them two bottles labelled near beer.

Ciaran had heard of the stuff that had none of the spirit of proper drink.

"Yeah, yeah," Gianelli said. "You taste. You see."

So he did and didn't he learn that in New York, even a little old lady could be a criminal.

He drank four bottles and he was feeling fine enough when, for no reason at all, he thought of Rachel in the kitchen at East Broadway.

"I best be gettin' on home," he said.

"Whatsa matter? It's early yet. Plenty more where this came from. You doan like?"

"I like it fine. But it is a long way since morning and I am wantin' my bed and all."

"Eh, Mac," Gianelli winked. "You got some girlie waitin' up for you?"

"Ach no, it is only my tired bones I am thinkin' of," he said, but he hoped that maybe he did.

∞

Ciaran looked at his new wristwatch as he came abreast of the warehouse gates. Ten minutes to six. Time enough for a cup of tea with the others before punching in. The watch strap nipped against his wrist. Now that his work day bore little relation to the rising and setting of the sun, he had need of wearing the thing, but he had not yet become accustomed to the feeling of it. It was all right. It minded him of Rachel and her fixing it on him in the pawnshop when he bought it for two dollars and fifty cents.

She'd helped him pick it out from a box they kept under the counter. Hadn't they, all of them, looked alike to him? But she showed him how some of them had words of love cut into their metal backs and she said as how it were bad luck to be wearing somebody else's fond wishes. *To M with love forever, J; Always remember today, M&D; For Tom, Love Ann; Kisses and Hugs from your Honey.* Bad luck or no, it were sad enough to see all of them bits of love scattered in a cardboard box for strangers to pick over. So she'd helped him to find a plain one and worked the metal buckle for him with her soft fingers. Crossing the yard, he grinned. Most mornings, now, he pretended to struggle with it still.

"Hey Mac," Greenbaum, the head receiver, who was partial to kosher dills, caught up with him. "You got something for me today?"

It was one thing to fancy that she was his sweetheart, but another all together to make it so. For though he wanted to court her, open and agreed between them both, by the end of March little more than shy smiles and hesitant gestures had passed between them. Ciaran was sure she liked him well enough. For didn't she show him little signs of fondness all the time; like when she troubled herself to cut his hair, though there was a striped barber's pole on nearly every corner that could do the same for two bits only. Or that time she showed him the box of real Irish tea she had found, so he could have his morning cup the way he liked it and all.

He wondered what it was that was stopping him from asking her to walk of an evening, or maybe to go to the dancehalls that he had heard talk of. Sure and he was never a shy one with the women. But every time he thought he might, she seemed to know it. Then something darkened in her already dark eyes and the words dried in his throat.

Once, when she had gone off with the boy, as she did every weekend, he braved a lunch time talk with Dinah that was always plain spoken, with no sides to her at all.

She'd given him a bowl of soup all floating with wriggly, white wormy bits. He poked at them with his spoon.

"What is those in the soup?"

"*Luckshen*," Dinah said.

"Oh...What is that?"

"You know, noodles."

Dubiously, he poked the *luckshen* things again. *Use your noodle* folk sometimes said, when a fellow was acting thick as two planks. Sure enough they didn't look like brains at all. He tried another tack. "How do you catch them then?" he said.

"Catch them? You make them...From flour and water and eggs." She near exploded with laughing. "I'll have to remember that one...catch them...oy, I'll have to tell Rachel, when she comes home." Suddenly, she caught herself. "Oh, I'm sorry. I didn't mean to hurt your feelings...but..." And she was off laughing again.

She seemed in such good spirits, Ciaran judged the moment fit for what was on his mind.

"It is all right," he said. "For isn't it the truth that I am a country fellow still and that stupid sometimes. Could be that is why Rachel has no time for me at all."

"Oh, no...Don't say that." She was still chuckling. "It's a pleasure to rent you the room, believe me. It's just that, well, Rachel she has, you know, things on her mind."

"Things about that fellow? Your brother, that is the lad's father?"

"Yes."

"Is she...are they wed?"

"They were. Not anymore."

"So they are divorced then?" The word sat uneasily on his tongue.

"No, annulled."

"Ah." He hoped she didn't hear his relief.

"So, then," he said, "such a pretty lass must have a fellow or two, I'll warrant." Sipping his soup, he had pretended no more than casual interest, but Dinah was wiser than he was clever.

"No, nobody," she said. "You like her, don't you?"

"And why wouldn't I? She is a fine, sweet woman...but..."

"But what?"

"I'm thinking maybe she would not care to keep company with a plain working man, the likes of me."

"Did you ask her?"

Could be it was Dinah's good nature, so kind and sensible, that made him open his heart to her. Or maybe it were only that he had kept that part of himself locked away for so long, it was bursting to be let out. "Ah Dinah," he said, "Haven't I tried. More than once and all. But she will not let me. Isn't she like a wee bird that will watch you from safety for the whole of the day, singing to you all the while. But when you reach out a friendly hand to give it a bit of bread, it's off and away."

Dinah sighed. Ciaran thought she was going to tell him something, but instead she commenced to clear the lunch things from the table. He worried that he had taken liberties. Wasn't she family and him only the stranger in the rented room. "I am sorry if I have spoke too plain," he said.

"It's all right. It's just that...well... Men, good to Rachel they haven't been. So, I guess maybe she's afraid, that's all."

"Ach, I would never cause her sorrow. Sure I would not."

Dinah studied him. "No, I think maybe you wouldn't. Why don't you try again. You never know. She could change her mind."

She smiled. She was a good woman, Dinah, with strength to her soul that minded him of Flora, though she were near the same age as himself.

"I will, Dinah," he said. "I will try again."

However could he not, when he had waited that long to find her, a quiet woman with a song about her? If she could look into his eyes and know what it was that was in his heart, and he believed that she could, whatever did she see there, among his soft feelings, to fear? He had dreamed of her; now he could wait for her.

"They are good, these *luckshen* things," was all he said.

CHAPTER THIRTY SEVEN

Riffraff riff

"You have? Oh Sammy, ain't that sweet. Who woulda thought you was a Daddy?"

Schmuel Weiss may have left New York a two-bit sprat; he came back a gold-plated shark. He still had a weakness for yellow haired women with big appetites and the blowzy blond who wallowed beside him on the damp, tangled sheets was as hungry as the best. She was one helluva looker too. Too bad he wasn't planning to stick around.

From his own point of view, life had handed Schmuel a raw deal. But, along the way, he'd picked up a couple of important lessons. Number One: if you got looks, yellow haired women are a dime a dozen. Number Two: there isn't a dame alive won't give you a headache if you stick around too long.

This one was beginning to give him a real three banger; always complaining, *gimme this, gimme that,* starting to get the idea that all she had to do to open his wallet was close her legs.

He was wise to that routine. *Plenty more where you came from, Doll.* While all over town, good men and bad struggled with eternal riddles, Schmuel figured he had it all worked out. Love'em and leave'em. Get what you came for and take a powder.

"Is he a cutie? Does he look just like you, Sammy? I bet he's a real cutie."

"Yeah, yeah. A real cutie."

He ran the flat of his hand along her inner thigh and pushed open her meaty legs. Then he pressed his face into her salty crotch. Yellow haired all over. Holy shit.

"I wanna meet your kid."

Schmuel looked up from the business at hand, so to speak.

"You what?"

"Yeah, I wanna meet your kid. We could take him on the Ferris wheel at Coney Island. It'd be fun Sammy. Come on."

"Can we talk about this later, Babe?"

She snapped her thighs shut. "Nah, I wanna talk about it now."

Christ! He slid up against the headboard and lit a cigarette. Dames. Nothing but trouble, every one of them.

The Man said as much after he cruised back into New York. "You had it made in the shade," he said. "Nice little business. Good location. I coulda put plenty of customers your way besides. All you hadda do was wait. So instead you take off with some cheap blonde. You know what your trouble is, Buster? You think with your dick."

Yeah, well not anymore. Bessie fixed that, the fat slut. Dragging him all the way to Florida, land of opportunity. Like she thought they could live on coconuts or something. More like land of mosquitoes and three inch cockroaches. So he finally gets himself connected, gets a cushy job working security on one of them off-shore gambling joints. Jeez, he was this close to being a made guy. And whaddya know? The bitch is two-timing him with some pansy college boy.

Man oh man, those casino ships was something else. First class cabin, first class booze, room service round the clock. Women, gambling, a snort of snow now and then. You take enough money twelve miles off the Florida Coast and you can get away with murder. He sniggered, remembering that he had, a couple of times.

"What's so funny Sammy?"

"Nothin'. If you ain't in the mood, whyncha' have a snooze or something. I got stuff to think about."

He coulda been happy as a pig in shit. And all he had to do was walk around flashing a piece and looking tough in case some spoiled rich kid didn't feel like paying up. So Bessie, she gets pissed off. She's bored. There's no place to go. Same old faces every day. Nag, nag, nag. You'd think he was married to her or something. So what if he started spending a little time with the working girls? A guy's gotta get some peace and quiet.

Next thing you know, he catches her fucking some skinny-assed kid. In flagrante. The works. So he busted the kid's jaw. How the hell was he supposed to know he was related to the boss?

The big blonde on the bed beside him turned onto her stomach. *Marone*, what an ass.

"Tell me about your kid. Does he take after his Daddy? How old is he?"

"Not now, Babe." He pinched her fat behind.

"Ow! Jeez, you didn't have to do that."

"Yeah, I know. The Devil made me do it."

"Ha, ha. I need a drink." She flounced out of bed.

"Get me one, while you're up."

"Get it yourself."

This broad was definitely on her way out. Maybe if had listened to the alarm bells in the old days he wouldn't have ended up with some heavy in a row boat pointed at the Florida Keys. Well, at least they didn't make him swim. Or mess up his face too much. A guy's gotta get lucky sometime.

Florida was old broad heaven. Rich old broads. Once Bessie was history, it didn't take him long to work out that a man with his looks and his talents could get by pretty good. Oh yeah, it was a helluva hustle, a real pain in the ass most of the time. Until he met Rebecca. Boy oh boy, there ain't nothing like a grateful dame to make a guy feel like a million bucks. Especially when her old man *has* a million bucks, give or take a couple of million. At first, he figured she was good for a few weeks pocket money, the usual. Then one night, they're walking along Palm Beach, full moon and everything, real hearts and flowers, and he's got her talking about her dreams and wishes. Dames love to talk about that kind of shit. So she tells him she always wanted a kid, but she can't have one. Too dangerous, something like that. She's crying and everything, the poor old cow.

That was when Schmuel had the first real brainstorm of this life. All of a sudden, he sees himself drinking champagne, the real McCoy, on a honeymoon cruise to the islands. Giving some fancy manicurist an extra big tip and a pat on the tush. Buying Cuban cigars in Dunhill's. By the box. Having his suits custom made. Sure, he'd probably have to push papers around a desk in an office now and then. But what the hell? He'd get himself a blonde secretary, a real goer. Office doors got locks. So maybe he'd have to give Rebecca one once in a while, just to keep her sweet. It wasn't like she could complain, or, with a face like hers, go find it someplace else. And besides, she'd be busy with other things, wouldn't she?

"I got a kid," he said.

"Do you?"

"Yeah, a little boy. Cute as a button." Schmuel had no idea what his son looked like, or even that his name was Daniel, but he figured his kid had to have looks. Anyway, women thought all little kids were cute as a button.

"His mother ran away with a shoe salesman," he improvised. "Naturally, he dumped her when he found out she had a kid. The poor little shaver. Who knows what kind of life he has now, with no father and a tramp like her for a mother."

"No!"

"Yeah...A real American tragedy."

"Why don't you get him away from her."

"Aah, you think I didn't try? But she's the mother. You know how it is. Now she won't even let me see him anymore."

"Oh that's terrible."

They walked along the beach in silence. Schmuel let his sad story sink in. He knew he was onto a winner.

Finally Rebecca spoke. "My father knows some very good lawyers," she said. "Maybe he could help."

"That's real considerate of you to offer. But why would your father help me?"

Rebecca turned to him, beaming her pathetic, crooked smile. "If I wanted him to Sammy. Daddy would do anything for me."

I bet he would, Schmuel thought. God, he coulda been in like Flynn if it wasn't for Rachel and her dumb family.

"I'm afraid you failed to share some very important facts with us, Mr. Weiss," his fancy Park Avenue lawyer said.

"Like which?"

"Like which? Yes, well, for example, the fact that City Councilman Tierney has taken a special interest in the young woman's situation."

"Whaddya talking about?"

"Well, we understand that her brother is Councilman Tierney's ...um ... accountant, and a very trusted employee."

"Oh yeah?"

"Yes, I'm afraid so. So, under the circumstances, it would not be in our firm's...interest...to become involved. You understand, I'm sure. Perhaps someone else."

Yeah, he understood. The stupid bitch was connected and she didn't even know it. Otherwise, why was she so afraid of him? Unless he was packing, people weren't often afraid of Schmuel Weiss, so it was not an emotional state he failed to notice. He could smell it a mile away. She put up a good front, he would give her that. But she was scared. What the hell did she think he was gonna do to the kid anyway? Turn him into chopped liver?

The blonde beside him was pouting and drinking straight gin.

"Hey Babe, you got anything to eat in this place?"

"No," she sniffed. "You said you'd take me for *chinks*."

"Right. So go put some clothes on and fix your face."

"What's wrong with my face?"

"Oh, man, there ain't nothin' wrong with your face if you want the whole world should know you been screwin'. Maybe you better chew a coupla *SenSen*, while you're at it."

"You're a real prince Sammy."

"So I been told."

What would it hurt if he spent a little time with the kid? He sure as hell wasn't gonna learn which way was up from her, or those fanatics she called a family. Maybe if he gave the kid a few smarts, he could make something outta the business when he grew up. Not that he was that interested anymore anyway. What was he gonna do with a kid? Now that Rebecca was dead and he was out on his ass all over again, he didn't need no excess baggage. Sometimes he wondered whether Rachel didn't have something to do with that too. Old man Franks sure got funny if anybody mentioned her name.

Schmuel sat up, pulled on his trousers and counted the money in his wallet. Forty bucks. Rebecca's father used to say, if you gotta count it, you ain't got enough. Maybe he put it more refined like, but that was the general idea. He thought about asking for a raise, but decided not to press his luck with The Man.

"I should have my head examined," The Man had said. "But your father did me a lot of favours. He was a righteous man, you know what I mean? I figure I owe him, may he rest in peace. I suppose you got a mean streak could be useful."

So he put him to work collecting nickel and dime debts for peanuts commission. It cheesed him off, those two women running a penny ante junk business on East Broadway, when he could turn that place into a gold mine.

Sure there would be the usual business through the front door, plus a coupla' new customers The Man would put his way. But that was only the beginning. While the big blonde slammed around in the john, Schmuel entertained himself imagining a regular empire of vice. High stakes poker in the back room, high class hookers upstairs. Word would get around. He'd be raking it in in no time at all. By the time the kid was old enough to notice, they'd both be loaded.

Sure, his old man said Dinah had to run the joint, but he didn't say what kind of joint she had to run. He'd have to work on Dinah of course, but hell, she was family and blood had to be thicker than water sooner or later. He pictured his older sister decked out like a madam and laughed out loud.

The only fly in the ointment was that weird witch Rachel. It was like she had some kinda spell over Dinah. As long as she was in the picture, he was getting nowhere fast.

Useful ideas were not frequent visitors to Schmuel Weiss's grey matter. So on those rare occasions when they did drop in, they lit him up like bolts of lightning, incandescent genius. If it wasn't an oxymoron, you might even say the idea that came to him now struck him dumb.

The stupid bitch was scared he wanted her kid. That's why little Danny boy lived with his uncle in Brooklyn. Like he couldn't go around to Bensonhurst whenever he felt like it? You'd think by now she'd have it figured out that he couldn't touch the kid or, anyway, that he had no interest whatsoever.

But, if she thought he did, maybe he could scare her right outta town. If she thought she had to take the little brat away herself, so God forbid he shouldn't be corrupted by his bad old dad, who knows how far away she'd run? He just had to lean on her. Aand keep leaning.

"Hey Babe," he called. "Take it easy with the paint. I'm takin' you to see my kid."

CHAPTER THIRTY EIGHT

The Fiddle

Musical instruments frequently crossed the counter of the shop on East Broadway. It is a fact of life that for every child with musical talent, there are fifty ambitious mothers. On the Lower East Side, there were a hundred. Perhaps they were more ambitious than most. When they looked out of their windows at their little Jacobs and Leahs, Abrahams and Esthers—or by 1928, their Stanleys and Shirleys, Harolds and Elizabeths—dashing about the April warm playground of the streets, they did not see what others might observe; snot-nosed boys fighting over games of stickball, knock-kneed girls dragging dollies in painted wagons. No, indeed, they saw doctors, lawyers and dentists, rabbis and rebbitzens, school teachers and nurses and prosperous housewives with hired help in the kitchen.

Now naturally, such nascent professionals and their wives had to be crowned with culture and accomplishment. Families who shivered in cold water flats, with bath tubs in the kitchen, somehow managed to spare a few pennies a week for the music master, who was also the man who sold dish towels, clothespins and candles off a pushcart all day long, or the singing teacher, who worked as a Cantor but was really an opera star manqué.

But just because Great Uncle Schlomo was the finest violinist in Lvuv didn't mean the talent was a family gift. Buying second hand was prudent. What is ambition without prudence but simple foolishness? Later, when it turned out that little Harold had a tin ear, or more frequently that he would rather play baseball than practice, you could always sell it back.

So the shop did a brisk trade in fiddles and flutes, clarinets and silver plated cornets; usually the same ones, travelling through the shop again and again. That was why, on the same April morning that Schmuel and his lady friend were planning an outing, Dinah was so surprised to find a fiddle that had been collecting dust since December.

"Rachel, why is this still here? You bought it before Christmas."

"I don't know. Maybe it's too expensive."

Dinah examined Rachel's handwriting on the tag.

"Thirty-five dollars!? What kind of a price is that?"

"I thought it was worth it."

"Maybe on 57th Street. Rachel, a lot of people around here don't earn that much money in a month."

"I know. But it's not just a fiddle. It's a violin."

"What?"

"It's a nice one. It's full of music."

It was true the fiddle was a beautiful instrument. The belly was formed of a straight-grained, golden wood, the back and sides of handsomely figured maple, the pegs of rosewood.

"Full of music? I swear to God Rachel, the things you say."

"Here. Look."

Rachel took the fiddle and gently tapped the strings with the bow. It was so finely made, that even in her awkward, ignorant hands, it sang. The whole instrument seemed to sigh.

"Well that's very nice," Dinah said. "But if nobody can afford to buy it, who's ever going to know?"

"Well, I thought..."

Dinah stared at Rachel and shook her head. "You don't *want* to sell it, do you."

"I just thought, maybe Daniel could learn, you know, when he's older."

"Oh, I see. Rachel, if you don't want to sell it just take it upstairs and put it away. If people think we're asking that kind of money, they'll go someplace else. If you want to keep it, keep it."

"No, I...I'll think about it."

She put the fiddle on a shelf in the back with the goods that might still be claimed.

"Good day to you ladies. Are you still hard on it?"

Ciaran was early. A wildcat strike among the longshoremen had shut down the West Side docks. There were no goods to move, so Mendel had sent the men home.

"Some fellow had words with a foreman, likely." Ciaran told the women. "It will be over in a day or two and we will have a powerful lot of work to do after."

Ciaran did not see the sense of it, that men with steady wages should be so troublesome to keep others from their work and all. But he kept such opinions to himself. Wasn't it a warm afternoon, the sun shining and no work to do. Could be he might persuade Rachel to go walking at last.

He headed upstairs for a wash and a cup of tea. "Would yous like a cup yourselves?" he asked.

"I'll make it." Rachel said.

"No, you are busy with your work. I will bring it down, no trouble at all. You are lookin' right lovely today, Rachel," he smiled at her. "Must be this fine spring weather has given you a spark."

He made the tea milky and sweet, the way his Mam had showed him. They all drank it that way, now he had weaned them off their bits of lemon. Dinah said it was self-defence. "You make it so strong, there's no other way to drink it," she said.

After, though he worried he might be in their way, he was reluctant to go. She *was* looking fine. And quiet and sweet. And he was after asking her today.

He poked about the shop. "I am thinking of getting me a gramophone the likes of this," he said, handling an old fashioned one in the corner. "Or maybe I will get me one of them radio sets, so I will know what is what, the way the other fellows won't be always thinking that I am ignorant."

"I don't believe they think that," Dinah said. "Anyway, you can always come upstairs and listen with us."

"I do not want to be a bother, that is always under foot." But he remained under foot.

Customers came and went. A woman paid three dollars and fifty cents to reclaim a humidor, a silver locket and a pair of combs. A fellow pawned his grandfather's gold watch. "It is a sad thing, that," Ciaran said.

"Don't worry about Maxie," Dinah said. "He plays poker tonight. He'll be back for it on pay day."

"Is there nothing at all I can do to help you, the way the work will go quicker?"

Rachel, who had said very little, passed him a deep cardboard box filled with odds and ends. "A bunch of stuff got mixed up when we were cleaning out the back." she said. "See if you can find anything that's been here more than sixty days."

Earnestly, he set to work, digging through a jumble of wind up alarm clocks, cut glass candy dishes, china ornaments and silver plated ladles, examining the tags.

"Gracious. Whatever is this for?" He held up a muskrat boa, its feet, tail and glassy-eyed stuffed head flopping about.

"It's to wear. You know, women wear them around their necks," Rachel said.

"With grinning teeth the likes of that?" He shook his head, frowned and dipped into the carton again. Sure, there must be a story in with all these bits and pieces. It came to him soon enough.

"Well now, would you look at this?" A rose gold ring with a pearl and a tiny diamond chip gleamed from a little blue box. "Do you know, I once found such a ring, near the same, in the belly of a fish?"

"In the belly of a fish?"

"Aye, I was after cleaning it for my tea, the fish you see, when I saw the thing. I woulda fed it to the seals, with the guts and all, but that it was twinklin' at me the like of this one."

"What happened to it?"

Well, isn't that the best question a seánachie can hear and it whispering from the soft lips of a pretty girl?

"Ach, wasn't I sure amazed? So I showed it to me Grand Da. Now, he says to me, Ciaran, he says, if it is by a thorn bush you have found it, straight away you must put it back, for you know that is where the wee folk are after dancing and sure it belongs to one of them. They will be wantin' it back. And if you have found it in the gizzard of a bird, you must take it to the cliffs and throw it to the wind, for it will be magicked, like as not, and bad cess to any that finds it."

He snapped the box closed and dropped it back into the carton. "Just like that one it was," he said.

Rachel nodded. She waited for more. Ciaran reached into the cartoon, pulled out a candlestick and read the tag.

"Is there another of these?" he said.

"What?"

"The tag says they are a pair. Where is the other?"

"Oh, somewhere. What about the ring?"

"What about it? It is a fine one."

"Yes, but the one you found. What if you found it in a fish?"

"Ah, right, sorry. I was after losing the thread of it with lookin' at all these treasures here. So anyway, it was all right, you see, for my Grand Da says, Ciaran, lad, if you have found it in the belly of a fish and you catching him fair and square, well then, it is a gift from the sea and yours to give to the one you love."

"And did you?"

"Aye, I did sure enough."

"Oh." Rachel turned away to dust the trinkets under the counter. Ciaran stifled the urge to grin. He waited a few seconds before he spoke again.

"Didn't I give it to my Mam?" he said. "For I was only a wee lad at the time and she didna' have a such a fine, pretty thing of her own."

Looking up, he surprised her in a smile, but, as always, some sorrow caught her heart and wiped it away. She looked away quickly.

"There's some more things back there," she said.

They worked together in silence. Dinah at the ledger, Rachel dusting and seeing to the odd customer and Ciaran examining the goods in the back of the shop. Then Dinah snapped the ledger book shut. "Well, that's that." She pushed her stool away from the counter and rubbed her eyes. "Look at the time. I better start supper. Are you okay to finish and close up?"

Rachel nodded.

"I'll see you upstairs later," Dinah said. As she passed Ciaran, she raised her eyebrows and seemed to tilt her head in Rachel's direction. It was only a slight movement and maybe it was only his wishful thinking that made him see it. No matter. He was going to ask her. Today he was going to do it.

But with Dinah gone, the chill of Rachel's reserve settled over them both. Though he longed to break through it, he could scarce even catch her eye. What was it in her that stopped him speaking a few simple words? She liked him, clear enough. It was there in all the wee signs. And yet, just when he felt it most, something froze between them. Was it that bully made her so afraid of men? He wondered if the cowardly fellow had beat her.

While outside the Lower East Side went about its never ending, noisy business, the shop was quiet as a Monday morning church. Ciaran never liked the quiet. He began to hum.

At once, Rachel looked up.

"What is that, that song you're singing?"

"It is just a tune, came into my head. Are you bothered by it?"

"No, I...I just thought I heard it... somewhere."

"Ah, maybe. I do not know where I have got it myself. It just come to me, is all."

"Oh."

They both turned back to their tasks. That was when he saw the fiddle. Hidden away it was, in the corner of a shelf, golden and glowing. It was a fine one, truly, made with a loving hand. He fingers ached to hold it, but as he reached out to touch the fiddle, he heard Rachel singing and, instead, he turned to watch her.

She swayed slightly to the music, looking just like a girl full of dancing and her waiting to be asked. And it was his own song she sang, but different. Embellished with silvery ornaments, slides and delicate trills, it was magic to hear. She would be a fine dancer. He imagined his fingers holding her waist, her lightness as he spun her and the damp warmth of her flesh that his hands would sense moving under her thin cotton dress. Her curls would fly and brush across his face so that he would smell them, taste them.

She sang the tune through twice, apparently unaware of him, and then she stopped.

"My goodness, Rachel you have took my heart indeed with your lovely, sweet voice."

"My voice?"

"I havna heard such singing ever."

"Singing? Was I singing?"

"Aye. Do you not even know it?"

She shook her head and Ciaran saw she looked near fainting. He was at her side in an instant.

"What is it?"

"I...I don't know."

"Sit yourself down...Here." He pulled up the stool and sat her on it. "I will get you some water. Do you want me to fetch Dinah?"

"No...it was nothing. It's warm in here. Maybe I'm just hungry."

"You are certain?"

"Yes."

Ciaran was not convinced. "I think I will fetch Dinah anyway."

"No don't, please. I'm okay now...really."

"All right. If you are sure."

Ciaran remembered what Dinah had told him, that men had not been good to Rachel. Had he done this, caused her to go pale and weak with fear when all he had wanted was to be close to her?

"Is it myself has frightened you? I know you have had troubles enough with men folk."

She looked surprised.

" Dinah said," he continued. "Are you afraid to be alone with me? Is it that?"

"Afraid of you. No...it's just..." She shook her head and would not say more.

He waited, concerned, to see the fair bloom return to her cheeks. When at last it did, before his very eyes, it was almost as though she had willed it back.

"You see. I'm fine. Don't worry about me."

"It is a wonder, after your turn, but you are looking better now. Have you been standing up all through the day?"

She nodded.

"Ah. Could be it was only a bit of a rest you were needing. Sit yourself a while, for I have found something, sure enough, will give you heart. Would you look at this fine thing was hidin' here in the shadows?"

"The fiddle?"

"Aye, a right beauty it is too. I'll wager it is full of music, just waitin' to be set free."

She smiled.

"You see?" he said. "I knew it would cheer you, and I have scarce even touched it."

"Do you know how to play it?"

"Aye, I do. Might I try it?"

"Yes, if you like."

He raised the fiddle to tune it, listening with concentration for the instrument's own voice. He smiled at Rachel before he raised the bow.

He played a lively reel and then another. He played soft lilting ballads. Eyes closed, he let the music take him where it would. The whispering glens of Rathlin sang through the fiddle and with them restful feelings of home. Now and then, he stopped to talk about his playing. "It is a faery song. My Grand Da, that learned it from the wee folk, taught it me." And, "Ah, Rachel, the way folk loved to dance to that one. It was a fine sight to see, I can tell you." But it was this home feeling that he wanted to share, peaceful and safe, if only she would let him.

Some say the fiddle speaks with a lover's voice that only the stoniest heart can resist. Ciaran wooed Rachel in the way that he knew, telling stories with his fingers that he hoped she could hear. When he could, he stole a glance at her. She was not watching him, but watching the music itself, seeing, as he did, the pictures it made. Now he sensed that he must ask her, now with their spirits singing shared music, before the shutters closed again.

"One day, maybe, I will have a fiddle of my own as fine as this one," he said.

"Maybe one day," she nodded and replaced it on the shelf. As she turned, he caught both her hands in his. Full of hope, he spoke her name, but before he could say more, the telephone on the landing rang. Then Dinah called.

"Rachel, It's Helen for you. I told her you were busy but she wants to talk to you now."

"It must be Daniel," she said. She dashed up the stairs, leaving the touch of her fingers still warm in his.

Helen was hysterical. Her fury buzzed down the line.

"I never agreed to get in the middle of this, Rachel. I never agreed to that. I never said I would deal with him. You know that. You know..."

"Tell me what happened? Did you let him see Daniel?"

"First you said he'd never come back. Then you said he'd never come here and make trouble with Mendel. Now what, Rachel? Now what? I won't have him here with his cheap women. My Emma shouldn't have to see such women, like that."

"Stop! Tell me what happened. You didn't let him in, did you?"

"Of course I didn't let him in. I talked to him downstairs, through the hall door. You should have seen the tramp he brought with him."

"Did Daniel see him?"

"I told you, I didn't let him upstairs. I didn't even let him into the building. Look Rachel, for Mendel to be like a father to the boy, that's one thing. I'm not getting into fights with my in-laws over that. He's a pleasure, Daniel, God bless him. But nobody ever said that *schtick dreck* would come here. Everybody said *never...not a chance.* 'You think he wants to start something with Mendel? Mendel is twice his size. Mendel's friends are dock workers.' That's what your brother Duvi said. You think I don't remember?"

"What did he say?"

"What did he say? What did he say? He was drunk. What did he say. A garbage mouth on him you shouldn't know from it. I wouldn't even repeat. Oy, if my neighbours heard. This is a respectable building Rachel. There are CPAs, dentists living in this building. Respectable people. That they should think we keep company with gangsters and whores. *Vey iss mir.*"

"But what did he want?"

"Oh...wait till you hear. This is the best part...He and his *shiksa* floozy, and I'm telling you, through the door I could smell the whiskey...they wanted to take Daniel on the Ferris wheel...to Coney Island! Rachel are you there? Rachel?"

"Yes, I'm here...I..."

"Rachel, you have to do something about him. He can't come here. In a state like that. Not like that. You have to deal with him, do you hear me?"

"I hear you."

"I mean, I love Daniel like my own..."

"I bet you do," Rachel muttered.

"What!?...I didn't hear you."

"Nothing...forget it."

"This I can't forget. Like my own, Daniel is. But scenes like that, in front of my neighbours. You have to do something Rachel. This is your mess. You made it. Otherwise, otherwise..."

"Otherwise what?"

"I don't know...Well, what would be so bad he should have a look at the child? Supervised. If he came here decent."

"Helen! Don't even think such a thing."

"Well, all this carrying on. I have my own child to think about. You do something Rachel. And fast."

A murmur of voices from the kitchen. Crouched on Daniel's bed by the window in her room, Rachel wondered, briefly, whether they were talking about her. *He must think I'm mad.* But now, the fog, the aching sense of doom were gone. Helen's call had blown them away.

This was something new. Schmuel had never tried to see Daniel in Brooklyn, though it was no secret he was there. Nobody thought he wanted to take on Mendel, Rachel's big brother in every sense. Physical confrontation was not Schmuel's weasel style. That's why he showed up when Mendel wasn't home.

Helen and her precious respectability. Did he know that if he showed up, drunk and noisy, a painted whore in tow, he could make her cave? Rachel didn't believe Schmuel was that smart. And what did he want anyway? He didn't give a damn about Daniel. She didn't waste time thinking about what he wanted or what he planned. All that mattered was that she couldn't trust Helen anymore.

Otherwise. Rachel could just imagine what *otherwise* Helen had in mind. Sooner or later, she would decide that it wasn't worth upsetting the neighbours over a little family squabble that was her in-laws' problem anyway, and she would let him in. A supervised visit, she would call it. She'd tell him to wear a decent suit, to come sober and without his lady friends. Then she would ship Emma off to her parents for the day and invite Schmuel for coffee and cake. She might do it more than once. She might not even tell anybody.

Daniel had to come to East Broadway. She and Dinah could handle a little intimidation. Her stupid sister-in-law. Didn't she realise that's all it was. Schmuel would never force his way into Mendel's house. He would never challenge Mendel by pushing Helen around.

But he had beaten Rachel in the past. He might do it again. Even before he forced himself on her that August night, he used to knock her around. The whole family suspected; nobody ever raised a hand.

So the old problem remained. In her wilful ignorance, she had stepped into the whirlwind and now she must ride it. The solution that offered itself, so naturally, so easily, filled her with fateful sadness.

She pulled her knees up and rested her chin on her folded arms. A pair of white gulls twitched the greening branches of the backyard tree. How simple and uncomplicated to ride the wind and never worry about guilt and sorrow and death, to dream of nothing more than slow, fat silvery fish and garbage dumps heaped with rotting fruit. She wished she could be so blissfully unaware. Why was she cursed with eyes that saw but never understood? Now, for Daniel's sake, she would feign blindness.

They had finished supper. Dinah was pouring coffee.

"You're all right?" Dinah said.

"Mmm."

"So?"

"So, I don't trust Helen. It's time Daniel came to live with us."

"Schon, Good. It should have happened, already, a long time ago."

"Maybe."

"Rachel, you know you don't have to worry about my brother. He's just a little shit. We can handle him. Together we can do it. And you don't have to run away to Connecticut every weekend either."

"I like going to Shoe's farm."

"All right. But just so you know, you don't have to. Here." She put a plate of blintzes with applesauce on the table in front of her. "You should eat something. Ciaran said you nearly fainted."

"I'm not hungry. I'm all right."

"Eat."

Rachel pushed bits of food around the plate. Feeling Ciaran's eyes on her, she sensed he wanted to speak but, caught in the middle of a family crisis, was too polite to start.

"Did you hear Ciaran playing the fiddle? Wasn't it wonderful?" Rachel said.

"I heard, I heard. Such talent, right in our house. Who would have guessed?"

"Ach. It was nothin'." he said, and they both watched him blush. He was so easy to look at.

"Will you play for us again?" Rachel said.

"I will, if that is what you are wantin'."

He put his cup down and leaned his elbows on the table. His shirt stretched taut over the muscles of his back and shoulders.

"Rachel," he said. "If I am speaking out of turn, you must say, for I know this is never no business of mine...but we are friends, are we not?"

"Yes...We're friends."

"Well, I will tell you, then, I would not let no one harass a friend of mine."

"Thank you," she said. "But you don't need to worry about my troubles."

"And what kind of a friend would I be if I did not?"

She nodded.

"I wanted you to know, is all...Won't it be grand to have the wee lad with his Mam, the way it should be."

Rachel nodded and another awkward silence descended. Ciaran finished his coffee and rose to go. "Well, I will leave you to it. Sure and you must have family things ..."

"Don't go," Rachel said. "I...I want to talk to you."

"What is on your mind, lass?"

"I've been thinking. Would you like to have the fiddle?"

"The fiddle? Aye. Who would not? But it is far too dear a thing for the likes of me, with my wages and all."

"No...I mean, you can have it."

Dinah put down her cup and stared at Rachel.

"I could not. However could I take such a gift, when you have already been that kind to me and all?"

"It's a shame that no one plays it. You could play it while you're here. Maybe you could teach Daniel and buy it that way...with lessons."

"Ah now, if I was to earn it in that way...Well, that would be different."

"Then it's settled. You can have it."

"Ach, I scarce know how to thank you. I will teach the lad like my Grand Da taught me. He will take to it easy, I promise." Now he looked for permission in her face. She let him find it.

"Rachel," he said, "I was thinkin' too. It is a fair mild evening, do you not think so?"

"Yes."

"And isn't the twilight grand and golden? So I was thinkin' Rachel...will you come walkin' with me tonight?"

"Yes," she said. "Yes, I will."

CHAPTER THIRTY NINE

Undertow

Dangerous water. The Long Island Sound, now tranquil as a lake, was exposed and unpredictable too. From the shore, Rachel watched Ciaran at the oars of her uncle's boat. She strained to see Daniel, but he and Uncle Shoe, who held him, merged into a brown blur. The little boat slipped into the morning shadows of Pine Rock, the uninhabited island half a mile off Uncle Shoe's beach and disappeared. They were after the big bluefish that ran where it was deep and cold this time of year.

Rachel was not happy about the outing. Every summer a swimmer or two succumbed to the forceful tides that swept between The Race and the entrance to the East River. And pleasure boats often came to grief among the giant freighters waiting, in the centre of the Sound, for a berth on the East Side docks. "It is a short pull only," Ciaran had said, "and I'll not take her into the shipping lane, so you need not worry yourself."

But was she gripped by unease and had been ever since Ciaran and Shoe first mentioned putting the twelve foot dinghy back into the water.

It had rested, keel up, on the beach for years. "Strength for rowing I haven't got no more," Uncle Shoe had explained. "Maybe, years ago, when everything on a farm you did by hand. But now I got a tractor, I'm not in such good shape. And so young, anymore, I'm not besides...So, she sits on the beach and reminds me about the good old days. Who knows, even, if she'll float."

"It is a fine, wee boat, she is," Ciaran had said. "I can make her seaworthy, no trouble at all."

And so, every weekend since the middle of May, after he finished helping Uncle Shoe in the fields, Ciaran sanded and tarred and painted the dinghy while pale wet phantoms haunted Rachel's sleeping and waking dreams.

Twice she had taken the little linen sachet from the box it shared with Bubbie Ruchel's golden *chai*. Twice she had held it to her face and listened to the midwife's remembered words. *It will protect a loved one from drowning and accidents at sea.* The third time, she put it in her handbag.

"It is only because you do not know the ways of boatmen that you worry so," Ciaran said. "But isn't it only dreams and all?" He didn't understand about Rachel's dreams. And what could she say, when she didn't understand them either?

Then three weeks ago, at the beginning of June, the boat was ready and they announced their intention of fishing off Pine Rock. Actually, it was Daniel who brought her the news.

She had been watching them eat the lunch she cooked, understanding, at last, the mild pleasure Dinah and her mother enjoyed in the giving of food. Dinah was teaching her. She could make soup now and she knew how to tell when a chicken was cooked enough but not too much. None of them hid bloody bones and raw flesh under the potatoes anymore. Or choked down woody, dry mouths full just to be kind.

At Ciaran's whispered prompting, Daniel thanked her for the meal.

"Maybe tomorrow I'll make a surprise and we can have a picnic on the beach for lunch."

"No, no picnic tomorrow. We going fishing in the boat... Keern an' me an' Unca Shoe."

Rachel raised her eyebrows. "Oh?" she said.

"Now lad...Did I not tell you, you must first ask your mam?"

"Can I Mommy? Can I?"

"I'll think about it."

"Please, Mommy!"

"I said I'll think about it."

The weather had spared her the need of such thoughts. In an unseasonably hot and humid June, Sunday morning dawned, crashing with thunder and sheets of driven rain. The following weekend had been much the same.

But today, a Saturday morning in the middle of the month, the sky was overcast but high and bright. She knew there would be no keeping them from the boat. So instead she pressed the linen sachet into Ciaran's hand.

"What is this?" he said. He began to untie its thin blue satin ribbon.

"No...don't open it. Don't look at it. Just put it in your pocket and keep it there."

"All right...all right. But what is it at all?"

"It's...it's a charm...you know, a kind of a lucky charm."

"Ah, like a four leaf clover, or maybe a rabbit's foot. It is some such thing as that?"

"Yes. Some such thing as that."

"Well, all right. My Mam was after putting store in tokens the like of that."

"Promise me. You must wear it in your pocket when you go on the water... always."

"All right...I will."

"Always...Promise me. Say that you promise."

"Gracious, Rachel. Such a palaver. We are only after goin' out to that wee pile of rocks that is that close you can hear a man shout. But if it makes you easy, I will promise."

She had waved them off and watched, admiring Ciaran's power at the oars despite her fears, until they disappeared behind the island.

She squinted up at the heavy sky, hoping it would hold and glad of the distraction she had planned. After she cleaned upstairs, she was going to make a honey cake. To be more precise, while they were away, she was going to *try* to make one. If she failed, again, they none of them would be the wiser. Somehow Dinah could not communicate the mysteries of baking.

"So then you mix in the flour..."

"How much flour?"

"You know...enough...so it feels right."

Enough, the magic Jewish ingredient. So far, Rachel had not mastered *enough*. Ciaran had a sweet tooth and Rachel's pride suffered every time he brought back boxes tied with string from the town's German baker. He stopped there most Sundays after Mass.

He went to church regularly now. "All the while, in my troubles, I was thinking God had no time for me at all. But, do you know, it was myself had not the faith to trust that he was lookin' out for me. So now, you see, I must make amends."

"Do you mind that I don't go with you?"

"Ach no. Haven't I seen enough foolish wickedness. More than enough and all. Sure, Our Lord never asked for all of that in His name. Besides, I do not think that the Lord would be after making so many different kinds of folk if it were not his pleasure to do it."

Uncle Shoe said much the same the one and only time they spoke of Ciaran's religion.

"Oy, Rachel," he had laughed. "I bet your father has plenty to say. His own daughter keeping company with a goy."

They sat on the porch, chatting and swatting at mosquitoes while Ciaran and a high school boy from the town cleared irrigation ditches, making the farm ready for the hot, dry months.

"I don't know what my father thinks. He doesn't talk to me. Not since I moved out."

Uncle Shoe shook his head. "And my sister?" he said. "You took him to meet her already?"

"Yes...Sometimes we go to Kandel's deli. I think Mama's worried he's too old for me."

"There isn't enough *tsuris* in the world? My sister has to make up things to worry about? When you were little, she used to worry that you were born old...I'm telling you, that's what she used to say. So now you're too young? If that's all that's bothering her, I wouldn't worry."

"Well, she says she wants me to be happy. And he asked for seconds of her chopped herring so I guess she liked him."

"So are you? Happy?"

"Yes," she said. "But sometimes I'm afraid."

"Why? What's to be afraid? He's a mensch Rachel. He loves you, he loves the boy. So?...Something else you are not telling me?"

"No...it's just that...What if he goes away? What if something happens to him?" Because of me, she thought, but didn't say. "Maybe I don't deserve to be happy."

"What are you talking? Here, to be happy everybody deserves. It's even in the Constitution. I remember, from when I went to be a citizen." He had laughed and Rachel had laughed with him.

"Well maybe," she said. "But I can't help it. Sometimes I get scared and I don't even know why."

"You know what I think, Rucheleh? I think that's what love is. The minute you love somebody, you get scared. That maybe they don't love you. That maybe they'll go away. That, God forbid, they'll die before you do. You think, I don't know, all kinds things. I was in love once. You didn't know that."

"You were?"

"Sure I was. Such a beautiful girl. If you would only see her..."

"Why didn't you marry her?"

"She died Rucheleh. She had tuberculosis and she died. It happens."

"Oh. I'm sorry."

"It was a long time ago...In Vienna yet. But you know what? Good memories, I still got. Here," he put his hand over his heart, "she never gets old. So all that being afraid, where did it get me? God does what he has to do... Come on, too much sad talk. I think maybe I would like a glass tea."

Rachel put the kettle on. "Does it bother *you*, Uncle Shoe? That Ciaran is Catholic?"

"Me? Me it should bother? They all think I'm an atheist already anyway. What's to be bothered? You know, all the time the rabbis say that love comes from God. Where else? So if this is what God wants, who am I, I should argue?"

Now Rachel fed logs to the stove to heat up the oven. She cleared the kitchen table and set out honey and flour, eggs and salt. *What God wants.* Was it as simple as that? Was that why it had been such an easy slide? In Ciaran she had seen a man who could make her feel safe, protected. For his sake, she had tried to resist looking for more but her heart had found it anyway. *Heaven's choice?* She smiled and shook her head. Maybe Rabbi Meyer was right, with his sweet story long ago.

They had courted the way that New York couples did in those days. She liked romances so he took her to the pictures, holding her hand while she wept along with Janet Gaynor and Norma Shearer. They tried the dancehalls a few times but, in the end, preferred to sway to radio music in the parlour while Dinah busied herself elsewhere. They looked for surprises in each other, the way that lovers do. And found them. He liked the hot dogs at the Polo Grounds, though Rachel thought they smelled like the Javelle water she used to whiten his shirts. And he had an astonishing capacity for black and white ice cream sodas. She was wild for baseball and swore like a sailor when she thought the umpire was unfair to the Giants. "You are ferocious," he told her. "Myself, I woulda been in terror if not that I was laughin' so hard."

At night he fiddled and they talked. He told her stories, of changeling children and devil cats and magic islands. He could weave a story from almost anything. In fact, he often did. Once, he brought home enough mackerel from Fulton Street to feed the whole family, including relations, twice over.

"What are we going to do with all of these?" Rachel had said. "Why did you buy so many?"

"Well, you see…" he drawled, and Rachel knew she was in for a story. "… there I was, just walkin' along, minding my own business like, when this fellow comes up to me. I suppose he could see that I was an Irishman and all, for they do say it shows upon my face…So, anyway, this fellow tells me that he has got some mackerel have swum all the way across the oceans, from the Irish Sea itself. Ach, what kind of blether is this, says I, for aren't they only wee fishes that canna' swim so far as that? 'Well, wasn't it cod I was after?' says he. 'Them big, stupid ones that will swallow anything and most of the time do not even know where they are at all.' And it was a fine catch he got, himself. Some of them near a hundred pound in weight and more. So it was all right, but sure it seemed to him that there was a powerful lot of flapping and wriggling going on amongst these cod, for you know, they are the sort of fish that have no fight in them at all. So he cuts one open, right across its shining white belly…and do you know, it is full of mackerel that it has swallowed whole, and them still lively and all. So then he cuts another, and sure enough he finds the same. Well, this fellow, takes one look at these mackerel and knows for sure and certain they are Irish, for what other sort would be that feisty and pugnacious all the way across the sea? So, myself, I have a sniff of them and sure enough this fellow is right, for they have that bit of Irish about them. And so I bought the lot."

Rachel shook her head and smiled. "Maybe the cod fish wasn't the only one who swallowed something whole."

"Do you think so? Could be, could be." Then, completely deadpan, he said, "Well anyway, I was thinkin' to show you how to salt them, the way they will keep for months and months. We can put them in a box in the yard. Fine eating they are. Lovely. You will see," and a slow grin spread across his face.

He told her about Rathlin, his life there and how he came to leave it. "If only you could stand atop Kinramher to watch the floating islands of the sea. And the cliffs of birds that are such a wonder. Do you know that the seals cry just like babes in arms to warn folk when the fog is rolling? My Mam used to sing to them and feed them and all. Folk called her Flora that charmed the seals....Ah Rachel," he would sigh," If only my Mam had known you...and Bertie and the rest."

Sometimes, when he talked of home, he grew melancholy. Then music, and later kissing, could lift his spirits.

She told him about her childhood, about her time at Mishkin's and, as much as she dared, about her marriage.

"He had a mistress," she said. "He used to hit me."

"Did you love him ever?" he asked.

"He was handsome. I was too young...and I was stupid."

"Why does he upset you so, now that you are done with him?" he asked.

"He's evil," she said. She would not say more and he did not press her.

She told him about when, as a child, she walked to the sea and of the punishment that followed.

"Ah, but it was only out of love, he did it, Rachel. He was lookin' after you in his way, is all. For sure it was powerful strange for you to do it and you only a wee bit of a thing."

He did not understand, who had never been despised. Rachel, a wanderer for too long in unremembered darkness, warmed to his innocent tolerance and was humbled by it.

It was a gentle and ordinary courtship, for love, even magic and eternal— and what true love is not?—requires permission to be called by name.

By the middle of May she had invited him to join her and Daniel on their weekend jaunts to Uncle Shoe's farm.

Daniel took to him at once, following him like a puppy and mimicking his expressions.

"Will you be a good boy and eat your peas and carrots?"

"That I will, Mommy, sure nuff."

For his fourth birthday, at the end of May, her son demonstrated his fiddling for the family assembled at East Broadway. Duvi came, and Ruth with her barber beau. Mendel brought Emma and Helen, grouchy as always but curious about *Rachel's goy*. Sophie was there, but Jacob, Sarah and her rabbi stayed away.

Ciaran and the child had prepared the recital as a surprise, with secret lessons and practice in the room behind the shop. Daniel could just about hold the instrument and bow properly. He could play a C as sweetly as Ciaran and scrape out the rest of a painful octave.

"Keern says I doing right fine for a wee man. Do you not think so, Mommy?" he said, and everyone but Helen had burst out laughing.

That morning's mail had included a package for Daniel. At first Rachel thought it was a present from Bea, in Washington now, working for a congressman. But it was postmarked New York. The handwriting was unfamiliar. Perhaps because of this, she had opened it at once. It was a stuffed rabbit, powdery blue, the sort of toy Daniel had long ago outgrown. She tore open the card.

Dear sonny,

 Your Daddy's real sorry he can't come round to see you and Mommy on your birthday. You must be a big boy now. Happy Birthday kiddo. I'll be seeing you real soon.
 Love, Daddy

Rachel stuffed the toy and its wrappings into the ash can. She crumpled the card and was about to throw it away when she was struck by the odd realisation that while it annoyed her, she was not frightened. Not long ago, just the mention of Schmuel's name raised goose bumps on her arms. But, as she stared at the wadded paper in her hand, she felt almost nothing. Smoothing the card, she read it again. *I'll be seeing you real soon?* Was that some kind of challenge? A warning? In fact, other than the faint distaste of handing something Schmuel had touched, the card had little impact. She threw it away.

Daniel's birthday card was the first of several notes from Schmuel. During the next two weeks, a new one had arrived in the mail every few days. They were always the same, a couple of words. *I hear you're going away. Bon voyage, sweetie. See you around. I got my eyes on you.* They were ridiculous, pathetic.

Was this the most he could get up to? After all this time in New York, all the bluster, the threats of court, the dark hints of unspecified persecutions, was this it? Why on earth had she imagined he had changed, had somehow become more dangerous? He was a small, weak man and he always would be.

She showed some of the letters to Ciaran.

"I will find him and put a stop to this," he said.

"No, you don't have to. They're only letters. Sticks and stones, you know what they say. I'm not afraid of him anymore."

It was true. After a while, she recognised the handwriting and dropped the letters, unopened in the bin beside the sink.

Uncle Shoe's kitchen seemed dark for so early in the day. Reaching for the light cord, Rachel realised her fingers were gluey with flour and honey. The table was splattered with flour coated puddles of honey and egg. How did Dinah manage to do this without making such a mess? Still, the mixture in the bowl looked about right. She wiped her hands on her apron and poured it into the pan. Then she put her hand into the oven and counted seconds. One... two...three...four...five...six...ouch! That was about right too.

One o'clock. Surely, they had caught a fish by now. Had the sky turned a slatier grey? Maybe not. Trying hard not to think about the little boat bobbing about in all that water, she busied herself with cleaning up the kitchen. Then she straightened the parlour, letting her hand linger on the bedlinens before she folded them off the couch where Ciaran slept.

When the cake was done, at two, Rachel hardly noticed her success for now the sky had visibly darkened and a light rain fell. Where were they? How long could it take to catch a stupid fish? She wrapped herself in a shawl and ran down to the beach.

The island pines shredded shifting mist. On the spit of land that marked the edge of Uncle Shoe's property, pin oaks and sycamores marched into clouds that, here and there, touched the steely surface of the water. Rachel listened for the slap of oars. All was silent. No birds called, no voices carried across the Sound. And in the awful stillness, the turning tide whispered to the sand. *In veils of spindrift, I reclaim my own. If I want you...* The blood rhythm made her giddy. How easy, almost comforting, to surrender to familiar dooms of love.

But no pale, sea garlanded phantoms rose before her now. She saw Daniel, lips blue and teeth chattering, the time Uncle Shoe had let him stay in the water too long. By now he must be soaked to the skin, maybe even showing the first signs of a summer cold. My God, he'd never had whooping cough. What was she thinking, to let them go in such weather?

And she saw Ciaran, deathly white among the pallets, slipping into heaven with a smile. What if he drowned? He should be so lucky. He wouldn't have much to smile about when she gave him a piece of her mind. How could he? How dare he take her child out in a boat when the sun wasn't even shining? They might be lost in the fog and drifting into the shipping lane. Maybe they'd already been rammed and capsized, or worse. And to stay out so long. Daniel must be starving. All they took with them was a thermos of coffee and a few bottles of pop. How had she let Ciaran and Shoe charm her into such a hare-brained, stupid, dangerous... Two grown men who should have known better... worse than children themselves.

She stormed up to the house and spent the next two hours pacing herself into a rage. She didn't even notice the blue of the clearing sky. When, at last, they returned, she greeted them like a fury.

"And what time do you think it is?"

"Mommy, I catched a fish."

"Not now, Daniel."

"I catched it all by myself. Keern ony helped a little..."

"I said, not now Daniel. Go upstairs and take off your wet clothes and get under the covers."

"I not wet. We went in a cave. Keern cooked a bird in the dirt, Mommy. Look at the fishes, Mommy!"

"Oh Daniel!"

"Come on *tataleh*," Uncle Shoe said. "Come, we'll get washed." He took Daniel's hand and led him upstairs.

Rachel glared at Ciaran. "Well?" she spat.

"Well what? What are you on about, woman?"

"Where have you been...Look at the time."

"We have been fishing. You know that."

"All day? Hours and hours?"

"Well, lass, these bluefish are not a clever lot but they are not so dim to be jumpin' into the boat just because you wave a bit of herring under their noses."

"It's not a joke."

"I am not jokin'...Whatever is the matter with you at all? It is a fine welcome you have given us. And the boy...to remember, on the very day is he after catching himself his first fish."

"I was so worried. Then it started to rain. And there was fog. I thought you...I thought that..." Rachel's words tumbled one after the other. She felt foolish now they were safely home, but embarrassment only fuelled her outburst. "It's so dangerous on the Sound. You could have drowned. When I think of you and Daniel out in a storm. How could you?"

"Ach, Rachel, do you trust me so little as that, to think I would put the lad in harm's way? Do you think I have so little sense as that? I scarce had to smell the weather and we made for the island, straightaway, until it cleared.

"But you were gone so long...and I didn't know..."

"Well, I am that sorry the place has got no telegraph office. Next time, I will be sure and send you some smoke signals, the like red Indians use to warn the woman folk they will be late for supper."

"If there is a next time."

"If? Ah...I see you are not fit to be talking with until you have calmed yourself." He turned and reached for the door.

"Where are you going?"

"I am goin' to clean a fish."

CHAPTER FORTY

Episodes in counterpoint

A squall of seagulls harried the Staten Island Ferry as it steamed between Governors Island and the Statue of Liberty. On deck, Schmuel Weiss raised his collar against the brisk morning and frowned at the birds. They were giving him a headache. From a chased silver pocket flask, a souvenir of better days, he poured a jolt into his coffee. A guy's gotta do the business, but what a way to spend a Sunday morning, eh?

Some business. He'd left a nice cosy bed and a strawberry blonde to do it. She was easy, this one. A good time, a few laughs and no aggravation. You get what you pay for, he supposed. If not for this penny ante job, he would have paid for the rest of the day. Instead, there he was at the crack of dawn, drinking coffee from a chipped cup, breathing in the low tide garbage stink, on his way to collect a measly few bucks from some dope in the boondocks.

By now he shoulda been raking it in at East Broadway; by now that dippy broad Rachel shoulda took the hint and hit the road. But she had surprised him. She didn't scare so easy. She was gonna make him work for it. She was gonna make him get heavy and getting heavy was a lotta trouble. Getting away with it was even more trouble than that. The last thing he needed was a broken nose from one of her brothers, or from that muscle bound mick he heard was still hanging around. Not to mention Tierney's mob.

Schmuel sighed. Whatever he did, it would have to be smart. He'd figure it out. Meanwhile, a blast of the ship's whistle reminded him that he had to see a man about a debt. In the middle of nowhere. Christ. Who the hell lived on Staten Island anyway? In his breast pocket he carried a paper with the address of one *J. Johnson* and the notation $175.00. He'd known a few Johnsons in his day. Maybe this loser was one of them. Nah. Nobody he knew would live with the cows in Podunksville. Still, you never know. Deep in Schmuel's subconscious, the smallest germ of an idea began the long, laboured process of sprouting to the surface.

He caught a taxi outside the ferry terminal in St. George. "Nice day," the cabbie said. "Takin' a Sunday to smell the grass?"

"Yeah, to smell the grass." Busy, Schmuel wasn't really listening. He took a neat automatic from his pocket, popped out the magazine and removed all the bullets but one.

At about the same time that Schmuel was playing with his Luger in the back seat of a cab, Joey Johnson rolled over, stretched and yawned. The morning sun threw a leafy pattern on the bedroom ceiling. He listened to the birds and thought about his garden. He smiled. Who woulda thought that Joey Johnson would end up a family man, heaving pig carcasses for a living and growing roses for pleasure. In a place with a hick name like Tompkinsville, no less? Go figure.

Angie was still asleep but he could hear the girls playing in the next room. Determined to snatch a bit more rest before they burst in demanding breakfast, he snuggled up against his wife's warm shoulder. *His ball and chain.* He teased her with that. "Well wasn't you the one what put me behind bars, Angie doll?"

"A good thing too."

"Dontcha' never miss the high life though?"

"You can keep it. I like the life we got."

He couldn't disagree. Anyway, she didn't really put him inside, except, you might say, in a manner of speaking. She was on his mind so much in those days, her and her big belly that was getting bigger all the time. So first he got twitchy and then he got sloppy, which in his line of work at the time was not so smart. Next thing you know, he had earned himself eighteen months in the joint.

Well, it was an occupational hazard, he philosophised. He'd just been unlucky. "It'll be a breeze," he told Angie. "I'll watch my *Ps* and *Qs* ... Ten months, tops." But he spent the whole time remembering the way she looked when they took him away, thinking about his kid being born while her old man was doing time upstate. What kinda start in life was that? It was a tough ten months. Spider Johnson, *as was* in those days, read the writing on the wall and knew that his career as the slickest second story man in New York was over. He left his prison clothes at the gatehouse. He left his old moniker there as well. He was Joey Johnson now. And he was straight.

Once, he and Angie had lived like a couple of swells. The money his father-in-law, the pork butcher, paid him now didn't stretch to flash clothes and taxis to the racetrack. Hell, he barely made ends meet. Last month he even missed a payment on the nickel and dime debt he was still clearing up from the old days. Ah, but this was better. He thought about his daughters, each of them, in her own way, a reflection of his wife. This was better.

As Joey Johnson breathed the sigh of a contented man and waited for his Sunday morning peace to be broken by peals of girlish laughter, Schmuel Weiss climbed out of a cab and took in the layout of a single family house on Staten Island. It was small and neat, wood-framed and painted yellow. Jeez, it even had a white picket fence with roses. Just like in the pictures. Any minute now, Mary Pickford would come skipping round the corner and wave, *too-de-loo*. Cute. He stretched and squinted into the sun. The day was turning out to be a scorcher. If he got this business over with fast, maybe he and the strawberry blond could make it to the beach.

He stopped at the gate to pick a rose for his lapel and, what the hell, another for the lady of the house. Then he marched down the path and up the porch steps. As he always did, Schmuel tried the door before reaching for the bell. Christ, it wasn't even locked. This really was hicksville.

In the kitchen garden of Uncle Shoe's farm, Rachel dug radishes and scallions for lunch. Somewhere out of sight, Ciaran helped Shoe turn up market onions to dry. An occasional burst of male laughter, breaking the summer stillness, told her they were near. It was a reassuring sound after the careful, quiet supper of the night before.

She had put Daniel to bed, still murmuring drowsily about his adventure and his fish. When Ciaran disappeared out of doors with his fiddle, Uncle Shoe joined him. She had listened to their voices, below her on the porch, until she fell into troubled sleep.

This morning, she woke to find the parlour empty, Ciaran's blankets and sheets neatly folded off the couch. A twist of panic gripped, then loosened when she remembered it was Sunday and he was at church.

Growing up in Jacob's household, Rachel had never learned how to apologise. Harsh words were common but once spoken were never spoken of again. The whole family colluded in the pretence that bad temper, casual unkindness and petty cruelty were somehow neutralised by ties of blood. Maybe the soul is immortal, but the human spirit is not indestructible. Rachel knew that corrosive secrets, hurts, resentments and fears, had etched them all. She was determined to apologize for her outburst as soon as Ciaran returned.

But when he did, she found that she could not, afraid that to remind him of her anger would be to discover something had changed between them. For he was subdued, different. Not distant, precisely, but distracted. His kiss seemed almost absent minded, quick and dry. Looking not at her, but through her, he held her face, then slid the fingers of one hand down her neck to the base of her throat. Her eyes reflected in his, a corridor of mirrors, infinite and dark, and her morning panic quickened. She pulled him, hard, against her.

"Gracious, Rachel...What is this?"

Her arms tightened across his back.

"What? What is this?" he said. His voice was warm; his lips grazed her face. Perhaps she was mistaken.

Burying her face against his shoulder, she mumbled, "I...I'm just glad to see you, that's all."

"Glad as that, are you?" he laughed. "Ah, Rachel...Myself and all...myself and all...But I must go now and help your Uncle, for I have promised."

He hugged her quickly. As she watched him go, Rachel's hand strayed to her chest, where she could still feel the imprint of his golden beads.

"Could it be? I do not believe my eyes here. Spider Johnson as I live and breathe! Ain't it a small world? I heard you was in the joint."

"What the...?"

A dapper, slightly familiar little man lounged in the doorway. He held a white rose in his left hand. The other was in his jacket pocket. Alert at once, Joey Johnson slid up against the headboard and threw a protective arm around his still sleeping wife.

"Cushy set up you got here," the little man said. With his right hand, he gestured vaguely, indicating the room. He was holding a dark and compact little pistol. "Nice...very nice."

Joey Johnson didn't want to frighten his girls or wake Angie. His mind racing, trying to guess who he had offended, who would send a hit to catch him in bed on a peaceful Sunday morning, he hissed at the little man.

"What the hell do you want? What are you doing in here?"

"The door was open so I just figured you wouldn't mind a little company... Folks droppin' in, so to speak...Seeing as how you live in such a folksy part of town and all."

Angie stirred. "Joey, what is it...Joey?" Seeing the stranger, a gun in his hand, she clutched at her husband, trembling. "Oh my God, Joey," she whimpered.

"Ssh baby," he whispered. "...the girls..."

"Mommy wake up. Come on, Mommy. We're hungry." His children shouted from the hall.

"Go back to your room," He called, but it was too late. The two little girls, clamouring for breakfast, froze behind the man with the gun.

Joey Johnson fought to control his voice. Whatever this was about, the man with the gun had not yet pointed it at anything in particular.

"Who the hell are you anyway? What do you want?"

"Hey, Spider...whatsa matter with you? It's me, Sammy Weiss. I just come round for a little chat. Whatsa matter? You don't got no time for your old pals no more?"

He settled on the end of the bed. Angie scrambled out of his way. "So how you been? Imagine that, Spider Johnson holed up way out here in the boonies. Now, who woulda guessed?"

"What do you want?"

"I told you. We got things to talk about...business."

"I ain't got no business with the likes of you no more."

"Now what kinda thing is that to say? That ain't very friendly." The little man examined the gun in his hand. "That ain't very friendly at all. Oh, hey, Missus. I brought you a flower." He shoved the rose at her. "You see what kinda nice guy I am? Now why don't you be a good girl and make a cuppa coffee for your old man and me."

Angie gripped her husband's arm. He peeled her fingers free. "Go on," he said. "It'll be all right...go on. Take the girls downstairs with you."

Reluctantly, Angie rose and backed out of the bedroom.

"Black, three sugars. You got that? You won't do nothing silly now, willya?"

Angie shook her head. Joey Johnson listened to his wife comforting his daughters as they descended to the kitchen. "It's all right," she said. "It's just one of Daddy's old friends playing a joke. Don't be scared."

Weiss lounged on the end of Joey Johnson's bed, polishing his gun with a corner of his jacket. "So, now, Spider...So how you doin'? You must be doin' okay."

"I get by."

"Oh yeah? Looks to me like you get by pretty good. This here's a pretty nice place."

"It belongs to my father-in-law."

"No kiddin'? And I bet he don't ask you hardly nothing for rent. That right, Spider?"

Joey Johnson nodded.

"So, here you are, livin' the life of Riley; good lookin' wife, coupla kids, nice rose garden, practically rent free. So tell me something Spider. How come you don't remember you still got obligations to your friends."

"What the hell are you talking about?"

"Hey Spider, don't you know what I am talkin' about? You trying to tell me you don't know I work for The Man?"

Joey Johnson relaxed. "Is that what this is about? One missed payment? You telling me you break into my house and scare my wife and kids over a lousy twenty-five dollars? Get outta my house." He swung his legs over the edge of the bed, but before he could stand, Weiss had pointed the gun at him.

"You do not wanna do nothing too sudden like, okay? I just wanna talk with you. You know, Spider, business is business; I do not gotta tell you that. So what kinda business would The Man be runnin' if he does not notice when his books doesn't add up at the end of the month? You see what I'm sayin'?"

"I'm good for it. My kid needed to go to the dentist."

"That right? Well that's a real touching excuse. But hey, every moocher's got a story. The world is full of deadbeats. Sometimes you gotta make an example outta one a them...so's the other deadbeats know what's what." Weiss aimed the gun at Joey Johnson's head and cocked the trigger. He pinned him to the bed with his fish cold stare.

The kettle whistled in the kitchen. Joey Johnson listened to the mingled voices of his wife and children and weighed up what might happen next. He could hardly believe the little punk would shoot him over small change. But Weiss's motionless face was full of menace. He thought about trying to disarm the gunman. Though he had been agile enough in his heyday, he had never been a man of violence and he had no desire to test his reflexes against a cocked pistol. Not with his innocent family downstairs. His ears rang and his heart thudded. Joey Johnson held his breath.

Outside the window, crows bickered. Weiss's finger tightened on the trigger. There was an empty click and nothing happened.

Weiss burst out laughing. "I gotcha didn't I? I really had you goin' there. Man oh man, you shoulda seen your face, " he snorted. "I bet you was sayin' your prayers."

Joey Johnson went limp with relief. "You stupid sonofabitch," he panted. "You stupid sonofabitch...You wouldn't kill me over peanuts."

Weiss smiled. "Nah, you're right. Too much aggravation."

"Get out of here. Get the hell outta my house. I'll pay when I'm good and ready." Once again Joey Johnson tried to get up. Then Weiss was on top of him, shoving him against the bed and holding him there with surprising strength.

"Like you said, I wouldn't kill you. But, after all, even peanuts add up. Maybe I'll just give you something to remember me by." Held down by Weiss's left knee and the flat of his left hand, Joey couldn't see the gun. But he heard the unmistakable pop of a Luger. A bullet whizzed into the mattress and he felt its hot wind next to his knee.

"So? Now I got your attention? We can talk man to man, peaceful like?"

Joey Johnson nodded and Weiss relaxed his grip.

"This is the thing, Spider. You gotta pay The Man. You gotta pay The Man today."

"I ain't got no money in the house. Next week, when I get paid. You got my word."

"Yeah, well, you have not been so good at keeping your promises lately, know what I mean? And I ain't that interested in making a career outta ridin' on the Staten Island Ferry."

"Next week, I swear to God."

"Nah, I don't think so."

"Man, I ain't lyin' to you. There ain't no money here."

"Maybe I got an idea...A business proposition. It just come to me that maybe I could help you out."

"Yeah? What kind of proposition?"

"Well you see, Spider, just like you, I got a problem. I need a favour...to solve my problem, if you see what I mean... and Spider old man...you are just the expert I could use for the job. You do me this favour, you pay your debt, earn a little money for the wife and kiddoes besides and at the same time, you help me out...with this problem we got. Then we're quits and everybody's happy."

Joey waited, staring at the gun.

"So whaddya say? We got a deal?"

"What kind of favour?"

"Just up your alley, my good man. See, I know this joint, on East Fourteenth Street, is just stinking with ice. Fancy *tchatchkis*, I'm telling you. First class. Belongs to this ugly old broad. And I been thinking, what's she need it for? She's blind as a bat anyway. Maybe it could use a new home, with somebody who could appreciate it better."

"I don't do that stuff no more. I'm retired."

"You surprise me Spider. With your debts, you could afford to retire? Hey, I even know a fence would not ask no questions, would not even know you from Adam. Just in case you're worried some joker might get to thinkin' you are back in business, so to speak. Piece of cake."

"I don't do that stuff..."

"So you said already." Weiss released Joey and strolled over to the window. "Nice place you got here...Real nice. You do that garden all by yourself?"

"Yeah."

"A regular country squire," Weiss chuckled. He brought a Zippo lighter out of his left pocket and flicked it to life. Through the flame, he stared at Joey, the cold menace returning to his eyes. "Like I said...a real nice place."

"Oh, Jesus Christ..."

"It's up to you Spider. We got something to talk about, or what?"

Joey Johnson looked around his bedroom for inspiration. Wherever his eyes rested, he was reminded of all he had to lose. His wife's shoes casually tossed beside the wardrobe, her hairbrush and toilet water on the dresser. There were framed baby pictures of his daughters on the walls and a green sweater Angie was knitting for the little one folded on a chair.

"Yeah," he sighed. "Yeah...We got something to talk about."

Ciaran and Shoe leaned on pitch forks and surveyed their work. Onions, scattered across three quarters of the field, ripened in the sun. In the midday heat, the rising scent of onions distracted Ciaran with thoughts of food. Shoe sent Daniel to check on the progress of lunch.

"Very quiet you are, all of a sudden," he remarked.

"I am?"

"Maybe you got something on your mind?"

Ciaran had spent most of the morning thinking about Rachel. Her powerful fear and anger was ever a sure sign of love. Wasn't his Mam the same those times he gave her cause to fret. He had hoped and dreamed she would love him, almost from the start. But now he was sure of it, he did not know what fit and respectable thing he must do.

Sure and he had enjoyed the comforts of women in the past. But Rachel was different. She was not some girl in a pub. She was the mother of a child. His love for her was a fine and decent thing. Yet, he was a man for all of that. At night, especially if they had been kissing, he ached all over so that he scarce had a minute's rest. Sometimes he had only to look at her to feel the urgent pain of wanting to lie with her. Lately, the dreams of her that woke him, damp and shameful, near drove him to confession. He knew it was time for a wedding. But how? He was bursting to talk of it with Shoe yet lost for how to begin.

"No," he lied. "Only the work, for haven't we both been hard on it."

When Weegie Gianelli's brother got married to a Protestant girl, they went to a justice of the peace, that was a kind of a judge, Gianelli said. "My Nonna Maria, she nearly had a stroke, they didn't go to a priest."

"Where do you find such a fellow...a justice of the peace?"

"Why? You thinkin' about getting hitched?"

"I was only after asking...to be sociable like...for a bit of talk is all."

"Oh, Just for a bit of talk?"

"Mmm."

"Yeah, well it's easy. They give you a list at City Hall when you bring your papers."

"Papers?"

"You know, your birth certificate or maybe your immigration papers; so's you can get a licence, so it's official. And then, at City Hall, they give you a list. Nothing to it."

"Aye...Nothing to it."

Now Shoe shrugged. "It's your business, I guess, if you don't wanna talk. But not even a song? Most of the time, if you ask me, you're better than the radio. You sure everything is...you know, okay?"

"There is nothin' It is only that...that. Shoe, did you ever...were you ever?..." The words refused to come. "Well, isn't powerful heavy work, digging onions, to be talking all the while?" he said.

"Mmm." Shoe stared at him and shook his head. "You're a hard worker that's for sure. If the boys I hire from the town put in work like you, so worried about my old bones I wouldn't be."

Ciaran leapt at the change of subject. "What are you on about?" he said. "You are fit enough and strong."

"Yeah, sure, now. But how much longer? So young I'm not, for a long time already. How long before I have to sell up?"

"You are thinkin' of selling? To strangers?"

"So what else? How else I'm gonna retire?"

"Have you not thought for Rachel's brothers to help you?"

"My nephews," Shoe laughed. "They come to see the apple trees, for a picnic. You think they wanna dig onions for a living?"

"They would learn to do it soon enough. Any man would...to keep a bit of land. And such land as this, by the sea and all."

"I dunno, I'll see. Maybe, if God's got a good idea, it shouldn't be too much trouble for him, he could tell me about it already, before my back breaks from old age."

As they laughed together, Daniel appeared, out of breath from running. "Mommy digged begetables from the garden. She says, 'Lunch in a minute. Wash your hands.' I gotta go help now." He dashed off.

Walking down to the house, Shoe set such a leisurely pace that, at first, Ciaran worried the older man's bones really were troubling him. Something was, for he was frowning. At last, he spoke. "You and my niece," he said, "...you are...you know...all right?"

"Aye."

"You're not mad at her...for yesterday I mean."

"Ach no. Wasn't she only fearful for us all?"

406

"Mmm. So, the two of you, what, five, six months you've been keeping company? So, you must be already, you know, making some plans?"

Ciaran sighed. Now the subject had been broached he could no longer restrain himself. "Ah, how can I?" he said. "How can I promise her, with myself no better than a fugitive?"

"A fugitive? From the law? I don't believe it. What did you do?"

"Why nothing at all, except that I come here without a by your leave."

"What?"

"We haven't never spoke of it, but I know that you know the way that I come to America and all..."

"So?"

"So I am after doin' it in a proper way. And even if she will have me, I haven't any papers for the licence."

Shoe began to laugh. "Two sentences you haven't put together since this morning. This is why?"

"Aye, maybe. And it is no laughing matter I will tell you."

"I'm sorry, but here I was all the time worried that you were gonna go away or something...because, you know, a mouth she's got, God bless her...that you would break my Rucheleh's heart."

"Ach, I would never...but..."

"What's the matter with you? Ask Duvi to talk to Tierney."

"Why?"

"Yesterday you were born? An Irishman, just like you he is."

"So?"

"So he *fixes* things. You think for one of his own, for a *landsmann*, a little thing like a wedding licence he wouldn't fix? Come on, let's go eat."

CHAPTER FORTY ONE

Light

The smell of green apples. In little more than a month they would harvest the early trees. The sun baked scent of ripening fruit sank into the dusk like soft fog. Rachel dropped her needlework into her lap, leaned back against a tree and watched the sun dip behind Uncle Shoe's house.

She was restless. Though the urge to apologise had lessened, a taste of words unsaid remained. He must have sensed it too, for at supper he ate very little and when he asked would she go walking with him on the beach, he was almost shy.

"Isn't it fine, Rachel, the night so mild and ourselves not having to leave until tomorrow?" he had said.

Because the docks were crowded with summer shipping, Mendel rearranged the work schedule into round-the-clock shifts. She and Ciaran had both been pleased that it gave them an extra night at the farm this weekend. Now she worried she had spoiled it with her tongue.

"Rachel," he had said. "Would you be after walking with me by the shore?"

She was so startled by his awkward tone, as formal as when they had been strangers to each other, that she did not, at once, respond.

"Later...when you have done here and....Ah...Well, will you?"

"Yes." she ventured. "Of course I will. Is something the matter?"

"And what would be the matter for ourselves to go walking on a grand summer evening?" He had grinned, then, and seemed to be himself again so she let the strange moment pass.

But, when she finished in the house and went out to the porch, she found him drinking tea with Uncle Shoe, deep in a conversation that stuttered to a halt as soon as the screen door slapped shut behind her.

"No moon tonight," Uncle Shoe said.

"Aye...no moon."

"But nice, clear."

"Mmm...clear..."

Disturbed by the feeling that her presence was unwanted, Rachel took a crochet hook and a ball of worsted yarn out to a favourite spot in the orchard.

She could see them now in the orange glow of the porch light. What were they talking about so intently, their heads bowed together? Surely it was not her outburst, for she heard them laughing. And once, she caught the particular lilt of Ciaran's storytelling voice. But, being excluded from men's talk, though not unusual, was always irritating. She attempted distraction in the needlework, chained a few stitches then realised she had no idea what she was making and set it aside on the grass. The old tree was warm. Through apple-heavy branches, she looked for Polaris in the purpling sky.

It is the lonely star, the star for wishing. *Let go. Do this for me.* If she could lay upon the wind, she would rise to where warm currents fold the clouds. *Let go.* She would cast moving shadows on the backs of sea birds; follow the wakes of dreaming fleets, dive to scan the faces of the sailors. So she might find him then. Under the lonely star, the star for wishing. *Do only this for me. Let go.* But she holds fast. The northern sky pales starless; cold carrion wind rakes the blood coloured sea.

"Rachel?"

Ciaran was holding her hand.

"Rachel? Lass?"

"What? Oh...I..." She rubbed her eyes, sat forward and touched his face. "Oh, it's you," she said.

"Sure and it is." He looked puzzled. "Rachel, you didn't half give me a turn with your eyes wide open and staring at me like you was blind itself. Were you sleepin'?"

"Yes, I guess so. I must have been sleeping." She noticed he was carrying the beach blanket. "Are we finally going for a walk?"

Crossing the orchard, Rachel, now fully awake, remembered her earlier curiosity.

"What were you talking about for so long? You and my Uncle."

"Oh, you know. A bit of this and a bit of that. The price of onions mostly."

"Really? Onions?"

"Mmm," he grinned, lifting her over the stone wall. "...as you might say."

Almost wordless, side-by-side, they scoured the sand for treasures. Once she bent to collect a pink striped scallop shell. He found her rose quartz and a nacreous clam no bigger than the nail of her smallest finger. "A fine wee miracle," he called it.

They walked as far as the piney wood at the end of Shoe's beach. Beyond, a granite outcrop, sparked with mica, formed a natural boundary wall. He spread the blanket high up under the trees, cushioned by fans of evergreen needles that exhaled resin when they crushed them sitting.

"Why are you so quiet?" she said.

"Am I?"

She nodded.

"I suppose it is the smells of the evening that I am enjoying, the ones the sun has squeezed out of the day. Do you know, there was none the like of this on my island, that I can remember, nor trees the like of these, neither."

He put his arm around her waist and held her against his warmth.

"Look you," he said pointing to the western sky, where the sun had disappeared below the horizon. "There is the evening star...The first. You must make a wish. Quickly now."

"You too."

"I have done."

Night saturated the deep pine shadows, the only sound the tolling of a bell buoy and the slow slap of the sea that rocked it. Ciaran's silence, that had at first filled her with an easy comfort, worried her now. Leaning against him, she could feel his tension. He held his breath, at the point of speech, only to release it in a ragged sigh. In the reflected light of a far off anchored ship she saw a fullness in his eyes. Had he taken her here, to this dark corner of the beach, because something between them was about to change? She sensed he was trying to steady himself to tell her. Rachel, who was newly and only tentatively acquainted with happiness, was afraid.

"What is it?" she said.

But he shook his head, so full of feelings he could scarce speak. He let go her waist and took both her hands in his, turning them and stroking them with his fingers. When at last, he spoke it was in such a breathless rush that she understood his words more in the remembering than in the hearing of them.

"Such tiny wee fingers," he said. "Do you know that I am near twice the age that you are now? Ach, Rachel, am I daft to think that you might care for me, old fellow that I am? That you might... in the same way that I...that...Ah, will you marry me, lass? Do say that you will. For I am lost to myself with love for you."

Did she hesitate while she listened to his words spin, rushing with the blood in her ears? Was that why worry creased his face now? She would kiss it away, tasting the heat of his flush, his salt soft eyes, the damp tender nap of his mouth. How was it possible to feel the timeless power of his soul yet know she held it, fragile, in her hands; to feel such joy and such terror, all at once? The night was full of voices, swarms of spirits. Even the leaf-dancing trees urged her inevitable answer. *Let go. Do only this for me.* And all the while his words, "Say that you will" echoed across the nightfall sky.

She sensed choruses of declarations and promises made as she said, "I will. Yes. I will."

She shivered and it crossed his face like a breeze passing. So he held her. For a long time they remained together, rocking to the rhythm of mingled heartbeats, their silence eloquent against the agitated night.

Then with almost ritual solemnity, he unfastened his golden beads and offered them to her across his open palms.

They had never spoken of them. Nor, since the first time, had Rachel looked on them fully, though she had often felt them when he pressed against her. Even in the moonless dark, the beads expressed a fiery glow. Now she was timid to touch them.

"What are they?" she whispered.

"I do not know for certain," he said. "Only that they are yours."

"Mine?"

"Aye. Before ever I found them, long ago, they were yours. Only I....Ach, sure you think I am daft...telling stories..."

She held her fingers to his lips and shook her head. Why would she think him daft, who had sensed his coming, always, in the surge of her own tides?

"They're beautiful," she said. "Magic,"

"Aye, magic."

He placed the beads upon her, lifting her curls to fix the catch and brushing her neck with his lips. She turned her face into his hair. The simple gesture, made to stay the moment, bloomed with ardour. She took his head in both her hands and pulled his mouth to hers, arching her back the better to slide beneath him. A terrible emptiness had reawakened, limitless and lonely. It was a hunger that had no object but its own satisfaction, no instrument but her entire self.

He was needful too. She could feel his pulse, racing with hers. And though he whispered, "Easy, easy," and tried to gentle her with love words newly coined, his body shaped to answer her, blind, as together they searched for home.

Selfish and unselfish, the giving and receiving, all one in a fury born of long restraint. They fell upon one another in a confusion of lips, fingers and tongues, damp skin and rumpled fabrics. Modesty, convention fell away. But canvas, linen and leather did not. They sat back, panting, forced into a conscious act by the inevitable predicament of clothes.

He rested his hands on her shoulders, exploring her face with eyes blown black, their blue light vanished in arousal and darkness. Voiceless, he asked; for answer, she fingered his belt buckle.

Slowly, deliberately, they undressed each other, learning as they went. Currents of feeling that Rachel had only imagined now schooled her body, set free of all awareness save touch and smell and taste. Of nectarines and candle wax and salt. The yielding satin of his chest but for a silky path of hair that quivered in her breath. Even his love sounds had the warmth of touch, vibrating between her breasts, across her belly. Her fingers followed the line of his groin. He shivered when she touched him there. "Ah, such tiny wee hands," he sighed. She wanted, then, to enfold him, to cradle and protect this, his most vulnerable self, cool and warm, hard and fragile all together. In the glancing heat of his palm against her thigh, she shuddered and crooned, spreading wide, opening to let him find her where she waited for him now, to swim with him through blood warm seas and caves of night while shoals of silver flashed her inner eye.

Then, with a cry almost of pain, he flooded her, filling every part of her dark secret soul with waves of spirit light. I am glowing, she thought. And she

imagined, drowsy against his fragrant arm, that they had lit up the shore like a
beacon fire that guides the traveller home.

She woke dizzy, falling upward into the sky. Night, cold stars against the
black, had come on hard while she slept. An arm lay across her belly, wet and
quivering with tiny sea creatures, tangled water weeds. She held her breath,
blinking until she saw that it was only starlight, shimmering in beads of sweat
on Ciaran's arm. She eased herself up to look at him, asleep beside her. He
was drenched. Even his hair dripped shiny with sweat. He stirred and groaned
when she lifted a corner of the blanket to wrap him.

"You'll catch a cold," she said.

"Mmm..." He reached up to pull her close again. "You must warm me
then, love. Will you keep me warm?"

"Always," she said. But on her back, she felt the mocking stars.

CHAPTER FORTY TWO

The set-up

July was easy. Lucent evenings in parks flowering with girls in summer dresses. Italian ices in pleated paper cups; they licked the sticky syrup from each other's fingers and chins. They strolled shimmering sidewalks, their scents mingling in each other's clothes.

At night they were explorers. After that first headlong rush, they now ventured carefully into new worlds of sensation and trust. By the end of the month, Ciaran had moved upstairs, Dinah shifting her belongings to Schmuel's room to make a space for him. If she noticed shadows under their eyes, or heard floorboards complain as Rachel, at first light, crept back to the room she shared with Daniel, she didn't say. Dinah was a realist. Besides, Ciaran was family now.

July was easy; so easy that it might have lightened August's sultry burden of secrets past.

∞

"Stein must be getting senile." Dinah paced back and forth in the room behind the shop. "What could he be thinking? Sending us a man like that, a thief."

"Maybe *he* didn't send him," Rachel said.

Dinah frowned. "You know *I* never liked doing business with him. But, it was my father. Oh, you know." With the back of her hand, she wiped sweat from her forehead.

Rachel didn't know much; only that the shop's relationship with the Man went back a long way, before she was born, in fact, to the days when Moses

Weiss gambled and kept women. After the old man died, Mr. Stein remained a customer; a debt of gratitude, he said. Out of respect for her late father, Dinah would never turn him away. But they had no other customer like him. Until this sweltering morning late in August.

Neither of the women doubted that the goods he brought were stolen. Although the customer was well dressed, his speech was common. He had a charnel house smell about him. Rachel, who had felt queasy all morning, nearly gagged. "He smells like he works in a butcher shop," she told Dinah. Where would a man like that get the sort of gems he had spread before them on the counter? Even the Man never tried to sell them such valuable stones. Or so many.

"My grandmother left me some jewellery," he said. "I got a friend tells me maybe you can give me a good price."

"To pawn?"

"No...I got no use for it."

It had been a slow morning. August mornings were. Who needs to borrow money to pay the coal bill or wants to buy a warm old coat in the summer? Rachel had been stitching a sleeve of the yellow silk dress she would wear in September when she and Ciaran stood up before Judge McLaughlin. They wanted to marry in Uncle Shoe's orchard, but Tierney's reach did not extend into Connecticut. She would not have come up to the counter at all—other people's jewellery always made her sad—if not for the astonished look on Dinah's face.

The customer unrolled a quilted satin case. Its contents tumbled out, a handful of tangled pirate treasure: a diamond choker with a sapphire clasp; a pair of ruby dress clips, in the shape of roses; a gold mounted cameo more elaborately carved than any Rachel had ever seen. There were chains and rings and lockets, bracelets paved with glittering, multi-coloured stones; a gold brooch of two, long tailed birds with emerald eyes, a pink gold watch with a ruby crusted case cover. He opened a pale grey velvet box to show them an amethyst parure and another, of red leather, with a man's wedding ring that looked unworn.

"Wait here," Dinah told him. The two women retreated to the back room where, now, they considered what to do.

"Maybe Stein thought he was doing us a favour," Dinah said. "I don't want we should offend him."

Rachel, at the window, watched Daniel race around in the pedal car he had nearly outgrown. Two other little boys, from the tenement that shared the courtyard, clamoured for a turn at the wheel. "Daniel, be a good boy and share," she shouted. "I don't like this," she told Dinah. "It's dangerous. We should send him away."

Dinah nodded. She had, apparently, come to the same conclusion. She went back into the shop. Rachel remained in the doorway.

"I'm afraid we can't help you," she said. "We don't handle this kind of thing."

"My friend said you ladies knew the score."

"What friend?" Rachel said.

"Aah, come on," the man smiled. He spread his hands, palms up. "My friend said you wouldn't ask no questions."

Rachel crossed to the counter and pushed the gold and ice cold stones at the customer. "Your friend was wrong," she said.

"We couldn't possibly give you what they're worth. We don't keep that kind of money around," Dinah, ever the diplomat, added.

"I could leave it with you. Hock it. You know, until you find a buyer."

"No. I'm sorry. This is really just a second-hand shop. We don't get much call for..."

The customer shrugged. Without another word, he gathered up the jewellery and left.

Rachel felt dizzy. A fresh wave of nausea swept over her. She sat down, leaning forward on the stool to settle her stomach.

"What is it? You look terrible," Dinah said.

"It's the heat. I never like it when it gets so hot."

"You want to go upstairs to rest?"

"I'll be all right in a minute...maybe a glass of water."

"Tea is better when it's hot," Dinah said. She went upstairs to make it.

Violin music, from someone's radio across the courtyard, filtered in through the open back windows. Rachel thought of Ciaran; the way his face softened when he played. She had seen the same look wash over him when they made love. Her spirits lifted, she took up her sewing once again. She was still alone in the shop when the three policemen came in.

Two of them wore uniforms. The third, a plainclothes detective, flashed a badge. None of them were local. They were following up some robberies, the plainclothesman explained, asking questions at the second hand places around town, that sort of thing. Had she seen any unusual customers lately?

Rachel shook her head. She and Dinah had not committed any crimes. It was better not to get involved.

"We're looking for some items. Jewellery. Maybe you've seen some of these, Miss?" He gave her a typewritten list. All the customer's pieces were there, carefully described. She could see them, feel their cold weight. But she shook her head.

Dinah arrived with the tea. "These policemen want to know if we've seen any of this jewellery?" Rachel said, her brow creasing as she handed Dinah the list. "I told them no."

Dinah examined it. "No, sorry," she said.

Outside, someone fiddled with the radio, tuning it through static to an overheated, warbling soprano.

"We'll look around for ourselves," the detective said.

Now Dinah became impatient. "Look, the store is full of junk. There are boxes of things all over the place. You can't just start looking around."

"Yeah, we can. We got a warrant. Suspicion of receiving stolen property." The detective slapped a document on the counter. Rachel leaned over to read her name and Dinah's, and the address of the shop on East Broadway.

The two policemen and the plainclothes detective went about their business. Practised, efficient, they would have seemed careless if they were not so thorough. They emptied cartons, cleared shelves, moved cabinets away from walls. They made Dinah open the safe, then seemed unimpressed with the contents of the strongbox. They shifted objects. When they returned them, it was only to an approximation of their original position, intensifying the shop's normal, chaotic disarray. Watching them, Rachel wondered if, perhaps, she should have told them the truth in the first place. It was too late now.

The radio voice of the warbling soprano fractured, adding multi-layered static to the laughter and screams of children at play. "What's out there?" the detective said.

"Just a courtyard...Please...you'll scare my little boy."

The detective glanced out the window. "Okay. There's nothing special out there anyway. Where's the door to the cellar?"

In less than an hour, they were finished. "Looks like we got a bum tip," the detective said. "Sorry we troubled you."

"A tip?" Dinah said. "What do you mean *a tip?*"

"I ain't at liberty to talk about it, lady. Who knows. Maybe you got an enemy? Somebody wants to make trouble for you? It happens."

Rachel impaled the detective with a glance of her huge brown eyes. "Who would want to do that to us?" she said. Her voice dripped with more innocence than the hapless detective could resist. Against his training and his better judgement, he had to continue.

"To tell you the truth, Miss, I don't know who called the station. But we got a tip-off that we'd find...uh...certain items from a heist on East Fourteenth Street. Maybe you saw it in the papers?"

"And you can get a search warrant any time some anonymous crackpot calls you up with a story?" Rachel, who had gone cold at the mention of the address, saw that Dinah barely controlled her temper.

"Well he knew what we were looking for, the items. Exactly. So we figured he was kosher. Somebody on the inside, with a grudge. Anyway, like I said, sorry for the trouble."

When they were gone, Dinah locked the shop. Then she and Rachel surveyed the confusion. Only a habit-trained eye would have noticed anything out of place in the shop itself. Upstairs was different. Every kitchen cupboard hung open. All the mattresses were crooked on their frames. The parlour furniture had been moved about and one of the upholstered chairs was sporting a sofa cushion. But the disturbance was less extensive than they had imagined.

Dinah put the kettle on. They sat silent at the kitchen table until its whistle prompted Dinah to cut the atmosphere with words. "East Fourteenth Street," she said. She shook her head. "The bastard. He thinks he's so damn clever."

July had been so easy that August had almost slipped by without unhappy memories, without a single thought of Schmuel. Now, to Rachel's surprise, she found she was more angry than frightened. He was like an evil tempered child breaking toys he couldn't play with. Besides the disruption of a slow day's business, what real harm had he done? "Do you think he's trying to put us out of business?" she said.

Dinah's laughter was mirthless. "Put us out of business? Rachel, he was trying to put us both into the Women's House of Correction. You know this has to stop."

Rachel's uneasy stomach floated up to her throat. She went to forage for dry bread. "We should straighten up," she said.

"Are you listening to me?"

"Mmm. I'll do the bedrooms. You do the kitchen."

"What's the matter with you? We have to talk about this, Rachel. Who knows what stupid scheme he'll come up with next?"

What was there to talk about? He was like a canker sore that erupts every now and then. So it hurts a little. Leave it alone and it goes away until the next time. Pick at it and it can poison your blood.

"There's nothing to talk about. It's over. I'll make lunch for Daniel and then we'll straighten up."

"What are you going to tell Ciaran?"

"Nothing. I'm not going to tell him anything. What? So he can go looking for Schmuel and make more trouble...No...It's not important...Not now...*Please* Dinah, not now." She found some saltine crackers and washed them down with water.

Dinah raised an eyebrow, watching Rachel stuff crackers into her mouth. "It seems to me *now* more than ever," she said, but Rachel knew she would keep her own counsel.

∞

In the bathroom of a two room apartment on the Bowery, Schmuel Weiss slapped eau de cologne on his face, straightened his tie and winked at himself in the mirror. Not bad. Tonight, he and the strawberry blond were going out on the town. A little celebration in honour of settled scores. Hey, they might even grab a meal at Ruby Foo's. What the hell, he was gonna be flush, in a few minutes rolling in dough. And that would be just the beginning.

There was a sharp knock at the door. Schmuel came out of the bathroom just in time to see Spider Johnson shove his way into the room past the strawberry blond. He was carrying a brown paper bag.

"Sweetheart, my banker has arrived," Schmuel told the girl. "So how much didja get?" he asked.

"They won't ask no questions. They know the score. Piece of cake. You asshole," Johnson sneered. "Here!" He dumped the bag's contents on the table. Jewellery rolled and skidded across it and onto the floor. "Give this to your boss. Keep it. Do whatcha want with it. We're square." He grabbed a gold bangle bracelet and waved it at Schmuel. "This here's for my trouble. My Angie'll like it."

He turned on his heel, stopping briefly at the door. "You just remember," he said, "I was on the inside. I got friends too. Don't you never come near me or my family again." He was gone before Schmuel had a chance to utter a reply.

The strawberry blond was transfixed by the haul. In the silence that followed the slamming of the door, she wandered over and began to finger the jewels.

"Leave it," Schmuel snapped.

"I was only thinking, Baby," the strawberry blond said, "it's gorgeous, but how we gonna eat with it?"

CHAPTER FORTY THREE

Endgame

"So what's it gonna be? You in or out?"

Schmuel Weiss considered his cards. He felt what was left of the wad of notes in his pocket, looked at the other players and then around the club. Manny Schwartz, who booked speciality acts for after-hours joints, had just come in with a bunch of his girls; too many for him to handle on his own, that was for sure. Schmuel noticed a giddy blond stripper for whom he had once made a play. She was a good sport, he remembered; maybe he'd try again.

"You win some, you lose some. Ain't that right boys?" *Schmuel call me Sammy* Weiss sighed. He threw down his cards and pushed away from the green baize poker table. "I think I'll stretch my legs at the bar."

It had taken him almost a week to get rid of the ice. The strawberry blond didn't hang around. When he finally found a fence willing to take the stuff, it was a real case of beggars and choosers. In the end, after he'd handed Johnson's money over to The Man, he was left with a lousy three C notes for himself.

Well, a stake is a stake. It sure as hell didn't make no sense sitting around like some kinda loser when he had money to burn. Anyway, he had a feeling that his luck was about to change. "Yeah, sure, tonight's the night," he told his reflection as he adjusted his fedora. But, he was in a sour mood when he hiked across town to Stutz Feinstein's speakeasy, in the cellar under a pool room at the end of Delancey by the bridge.

That was how, in less than an hour, he'd managed to drop $150 in a poker game. Now he elbowed in to Schwartz's noisy crowd at the bar. "Buy you a drink doll?" he smiled at the blond.

"Sammy Weiss! Hey cutie. Well ain't you a sight for sore eyes. How you been keepin'?"

"Not bad, not bad. So what'll you have?"

Before Schmuel had a chance to get the bartender's attention, Schwartz had ordered drinks for the house.

"So, this is some kinda special occasion? He pick a runner at the track?"

"Manny's wife just had a kid," the blond said. "We're helpin' him to celebrate."

"Whaddya know."

Schwartz shoved a Cuban cigar at Schmuel and slapped him on the back. "I got me whatcha might call a son and heir now," he said. "Ain't that something? Ain't that something?"

"Yeah," Schmuel knocked back a drink. "That's something all right."

While Schmuel was getting well oiled, for most working people the weeknight was drawing to a close. In cafes all over town, waitresses wiped down tables and set out the breakfast cutlery. Movie palaces and theatres disgorged crowds into the subway stations. In the dancehalls, bands struck up the last waltz.

Ciaran and Rachel dawdled outside the Canal Street Theatre, not yet ready to go home. It had been an evening for celebration. First, Duvi had come up with the goods, a marriage licence valid in New York for the next twenty-one days. As a wedding present, Tierney had surprised them with an almost blank birth certificate for Ciaran. The seal of the City of New York was already stamped through the date and the clerk's signature. That made it official. "Tierney says, you write in whatever you want," Duvi said. "Just don't lose it 'cause there ain't no copy in the Hall of Records, if you see what I mean... and besides, it cost a bundle."

Then, they had gone to Kandel's deli for supper and while Sophie stuffed them to bursting with brisket and potato kugel, they persuaded her to defy Jacob and come to the wedding.

After, they went to the pictures. Now, with a freshening wind livening what had been a steamy day and a bright crescent moon playing tag with the clouds, they talked about nothing in particular. They had been to see *A Girl in Every Port*. Rachel thought Louise Brooks was strange and wicked. Ciaran laughed. "I canna see why you say so. A face like an angel the woman has...though mind, myself I'm thinkin' it is paint makes her look so good as that." He squeezed Rachel's hand.

They walked with no particular destination in mind, but drawn, unconsciously perhaps, to the source of the salty breeze. Before long, they found themselves leaning on the railings of the Battery, at the bottom of Manhattan.

With a great blast of its ship's whistle, the Staten Island Ferry pulled into its slip a few hundred yards away. Ciaran counted the coins in his pocket. "I want to ride the ferry," he said. "Come, let's us go out on the sea for a bit of a while."

"Now? In the middle of the night?"

"Ach, Rachel, it is not so late as all that. It is one of them things that everyone talks of, and I haven't never done it, nor seen the green lady close up, neither. Unless you are too tired."

In fact, she was. Lately she was always tired. But she didn't want to disappoint him. "No," she said. "I'm fine. Let's do it."

He took her hand and, together, they ran to catch the boat.

"You know, it makes you think..."

"What does?"

"Aah...life...you know what I mean?"

"Yeah, sure." Drunkenness had turned Manny Schwartz into a philosopher. After a few hours of enjoying Schwartz's largesse at the bar, Schmuel had no idea what the man was talking about. But it was always a good idea to humour the guy who was buying.

"Whatsa matter, Baby? You feelin' down?" the giddy blond said.

"I'm awright," Schmuel said, but the buzz in his head was turning nasty.

"Come on, cheer up. It's a party." The blond took a small, mother of pearl box out of her handbag and gave it to Schmuel. "This'll put some gasoline in your tank, Toots," she said.

Schmuel snorted a generous pinch of coke and gave the box back to the blond. "Go on, enjoy yourself," she said, so he gave his other nostril a treat. He licked the back of his hand. In no time at all, the world was a better place. Even the buzz was kinda like music.

"So you was sayin'?" he said to Schwartz.

"Well, what I mean is, this kid I got. Nowadays the world's his oyster. He don't gotta turn out like his old man, hustling the strip joints. He could be anything he wantsa be. Christ, he could even be President of these United States. Now ain't that somethin'? Even his old man couldn't do that."

"Oh yeah? Why not?" Just about then Schmuel was feeling like he could be the Tsar of Russia, at least. If they still had one that is.

" 'Cause I wasn't born here. You some kinda dope? You gotta be born here."

"Oh, right. I forgot. Jeez, my kid could be President too."

"Whaddya talkin' about? You ain't got no kid."

"The hell I don't."

The poker players started to laugh. "Yeah, ain't you heard?" one of them said. "He's got a kid with that weird dame who runs the pawn shop on East Broadway. She won't let him near it. The way I heard it, he never even seen this kid."

"That right?" Schwartz said. "You got a kid you ain't never even seen? That ain't right, you know...That ain't right at all."

"Whaddya talkin'? I can see my kid any time I want...take him out to Coney Island, fishin' in Sheepshead Bay. You name it, we done it."

"Bullshit," the poker player said.

"You don't know shit from Shinola," Schmuel snapped. "His mother and me, we got an arrangement. I wanna bring him out to teach him to play poker, all I gotta do is show up and the kid's mine."

The poker players laughed. "Booze talkin'," Schmuel heard somebody say.

"Right now, I wanna show my kid a party, teach him a little poker? I could even bring him down here and his old lady wouldn't lose any sleep over it."

"Oh yeah?" the poker player said. "I got ten bucks says you can't."

"Count me in for a fin," somebody else said.

In minutes, more than a hundred dollars was riding on Schmuel's boast. "So, wise guy," the poker player said, "You gonna put your money where your mouth is?"

"You're damn right I am." He pulled the giddy blond off her bar stool. "Come on, sweetheart, we're goin' to get my kid."

"Jeez...You're nuts."

"Right...Where you hidin' that snow, Doll?"

Changing weather. While the ferry churned back and forth across the harbour, the wind kicked up and clouds darkened over the moon. They had been on the water for hours. At first, Ciaran's pleasure had been almost childlike. "Look you there," he said, pointing at lower Manhattan. "Isn't it a wonder? Like the night sky itself. Ah love, isn't it a grand thing that I have come to settle in such a place as this? Sometimes, I canna believe it. And with such a one as yourself and all."

Later he became quiet, a light smile playing over his face. The sea seemed to content him in ways Rachel did not understand nor share. Now, although she was cold and tired, she was loath to intrude. She snuggled up against him for warmth but shivered nevertheless.

"You are cold, Lass. Come, I will buy you a cuppa tea. Or could be there is chocolate for drinking below."

A clock over the counter in the salon showed it was two in the morning. "Ach, Dinah will be beside herself," he said. "And yourself that is destroyed with tiredness. Why did you not say?"

Rachel found herself too exhausted to answer. They settled on a bench against the bulkhead. Her head felt so heavy, she dropped it against his chest. All the while he was talking, words that made little sense but soothing as they merged with the humming of engines. "I do not know what come over me, Lass...It is a thing that happens, sometimes...by the sea." His voice trailed away...*by the sea...by the sea...*

Barren rocks, under the wailing stars. And on the flaming hills the beacons burn for no one. *Wake up.* Cold in the darkness of alone, tormented by the screaming sea birds. You chose, you chose. You kept your secrets. *Wake up.* And Bubbie Ruchel is weeping for her bloody roses all scattered on the ground... Bubbie Ruchel is... What? *Wake up.*

"Wake up, Rachel. The boat is docked. Come...we must go ashore now. We canna ride across again when you have need of your bed."

"Something is wrong," she gasped. The hard yellow light of the salon hurt her eyes.

"You drifted away, Lass. Come on now."

"Something is *wrong!*" She grabbed his arm and pulled him toward the companionway.

By the time Schmuel and the giddy blond turned the corner onto East Broadway, they were shrieking with laughter. Her mother of pearl box was now in his pocket and he had helped himself, liberally, to its contents along the

427

way. He was feeling prime.

Midway up the block, someone opened a window, looked out and then slammed the window shut. "Ssh, ssh," he gasped. "We don't wanna wake up the whole neighbourhood now, do we, Doll? This here's a respectable street, know what I mean?"

The girl giggled.

At the door, he fumbled in his pockets. "Well, whaddya know. Guess I musta' lost my keys," he snickered. "But look what I got here. Want some?" He snorted some coke but the girl was laughing too hard and she blew hers away. "Hey, hey, hey. Watch it. That stuff costs money, you know."

"Yeah, I know. It's my junk, remember?"

"Oh, yeah, right. So, now whadda we gonna do about this door?"

He turned and slammed his shoulder against it. "Ow! Jeez. Guess I ain't no Victor McLaglen, eh Doll?"

"George Raft."

"What?"

"George Raft, that's who you remind me of. George Raft."

"George Raft? That right?" Schmuel smirked and straightened his tie. "So, okay, so what would George Raft do in this here situation?" He kicked the door. It remained closed, but he felt it give a little. He backed away and kicked it again. It gave a bit more. Third time lucky. The lock splintered off the frame and the door fell in.

Dinah, in her nightgown, was already halfway down the stairs.

"Hey Sis. How you doin'?"

"Why are you here?"

"That any kinda way to talk to your brother? To welcome him home and all. And in front of his lady?" He turned to the blond. "You're my lady, ain't that right?"

"Sure Sammy," she giggled.

Dinah glared and held her ground in the middle of the stairs.

"So, anyway, Sis. We're in the middle of this big celebration over at Stutz Feinstein's place. 'Cause Manny Schwartz...Remember him? His old lady had a kid. And I get to thinkin', this here is one helluva good time, know what I mean? So I come to take my kid to the party."

"Are you out of your mind? For God's sake, it's the middle of the night."

He started up the stairs but she blocked his way.

"So where's the witch and her boyfriend? You all on your own here, or what?"

When Dinah didn't answer, he tried to push her aside.

"Get out of here now or I'll call the police."

"Sammy, maybe this ain't such a good idea," the blond whined.

"Whaddya talkin'?" There was no way the bitch was gonna make him feel small in front of a woman. Once this week was enough. He grabbed Dinah by the arms, twisted his body and threw her past the blond down the stairs.

She lay, for a moment in a motionless heap.

"Jesus Baby, I think maybe you killed her. I don't wanna do this no more."

Dinah groaned and raised her hand to her head.

"Nah, she's all right. Come on." He grabbed the blond's wrist. "Let's go find my kid."

Rain had started to fall. Rachel and Ciaran raced along East Broadway heads down against the weather. That was why they didn't notice the open, splintered door until they were upon it. They found Dinah coming to her senses at the bottom of the stairs.

"What has happened?" Ciaran said. "Can you stand at all?...Have you broken any bones?"

She waved away his attentions. "Schmuel...He..." She burst into tears.

Rachel raced upstairs, Ciaran close behind her, her every breath a prayer. The child's bed was empty; Daniel was gone. Screaming his name, Rachel sank to her knees among his bedclothes, now strewn on the floor. Ciaran knelt beside her and gathered her into his arms, as if he could take her grief and terror into his own body. If she were not half insensible, she would have felt him stiffening with rage.

CHAPTER FORTY FOUR

If the sea demands it

He ran, oblivious to the sheeting rain. The lad was screaming. Did no one else hear him crying, pitiful, for his Mam? Did no one wonder at the sight of them—for Dinah had said—the foxy fellow and his painted whore, staggering, drunken through the city with a frightened child? What kind of place was this where they would take the boy in the middle of the night? What kind of men were they that were there?

But Delancey Street was empty, the shop fronts shuttered and dark. And was it the child he heard wailing or was it fury itself? Piercing, chaotic, driven. For sure he would kill the man with his own bare hands if Daniel came to harm. He would wring his coward's neck, slaughter him like a hen for the pot. Or tear him to pieces and leave him to rot, carrion for the seabirds to feed upon. He had never thought to do such a thing. He was not thinking of it now. It was a fact and all this body knew it.

His thudding heart and the pounding of his feet against the pavement matched each other, beat for beat, as he ran the roaring streets.

When the fear came, in waves of panic, Rachel couldn't catch her breath. She would settle for a moment listening to Dinah, so steady and reasonable even with a lump the size of a robin's egg coming up on her forehead. "Ciaran will find him, Rachel. It will be all right. He won't come to any harm." And

"He had a woman with him. No woman would let him hurt the boy. It isn't natural. Not even a woman like that."

But then she would remember those first few minutes; the way, even as he held her, the two of them listening to Dinah's account of the night, she could feel him growing insubstantial beside her. Soon, he would be far away; no more real than a dream, the dream that he had been and would be again.

"If you hurry, you can catch him," Dinah had told Ciaran. "He was falling down drunk."

She tried to go with him then, to hold onto him as long as she could, but he spoke to her like a stranger.

"Where do you think you are going? Stay with Dinah. She has need of you."

"I'm going with you."

"No. Stay here."

"Please, I have to go with you."

"You will not!" he bellowed. Both women jumped at the power of his voice. She could only obey. And then he was gone.

Now, she and Dinah sat on the top step, holding hands.

"How long?" Rachel said, "...how long has he been gone?"

"Five minutes...less than five minutes. He'll find him. He'll bring him back."

Rachel began to rock and sigh, remembering a gentle face and eyes the colour of the sky. "Oh God. I'll never see him again. He won't come back."

"Don't be silly," Dinah said. "Of course he will. Ciaran will bring him back. He'll be upset, but he's only a child...he'll get over it. Children forget."

A grief soaked sob escaped her lips. "It isn't Daniel."

"What?"

"Don't you see? It isn't Daniel."

"What then... Ciaran?" Dinah pretended amazement. "You don't have to worry about Ciaran. You know my brother is afraid of him. He's twice the man Schmuel is...ten times."

But Rachel was not reassured. She knew Dinah was worried too.

"I have to go after him."

"What can *you* do? Wait here with me. It's better this way."

"No...I have to be there with him...I have to stop...to change...to...to...I have to go after him...*Please* Dinah, don't try to stop me."

432

Dinah cupped Rachel's face in her hands and stared hard into her eyes. "I'll go with you, then," she sighed. Together, they followed Ciaran into the night.

The little mother of pearl box was empty and Schmuel had come down hard. He was beginning to regret the whole thing. What did he need this aggravation for? The kid bawled and wriggled for blocks. Leaving, Schmuel noted with disgust, kid snot all over his lapels. Any minute, he expected somebody to hear all the carrying on and call the cops. But nobody butted in. Some town, New York.

When he couldn't take the screaming anymore, he slapped his hand over the kid's mouth. "Sammy, you're gonna hurt him. He's only a little kid," the blond said.

"Okay...You're so smart. You shut the brat up then." He shoved the kid into her arms.

After a while, the kid stuck his thumb in his mouth and quieted down. "Whaddya wanna do that for?" Schmuel said. "Only babies suck their thumbs." The kid stared at him, his eyes wide open, but it was like he didn't even see him. Weird.

Now, on the sidewalk outside Stutz Feinstein's, it was the blond who was giving him a hard time.

"Maybe this ain't such a good idea, Sammy, takin' a kid in there."

"Whaddya talkin' about. It's a party. What kid don't like a party? Besides, I got money riding on this."

"He's scared Sammy. And some of the fellas...maybe they won't think it's such a gas, you know. Anyway, Stutz'll be bullshit if you bring the kid down there."

"What's this? What's this? I thought you was a good sport."

"I was high. I ain't flying no more and I ain't bringing no kid into a speakeasy. It ain't right. Here, he's your kid, you take him." She pushed Daniel at Schmuel.

"He stinks like a toilet. Christ, he shit in his pants."

"The woman is right. You are frightening the child. Now put him down."

It was the mick, panting and gasping like he'd run all the way from East Broadway.

"Where the hell did you come from?"

"Leave the boy be and you and I will settle this like men, eh?"

"What is it with you? Always butting in. It's my kid. I'll do what I want."

"Put the boy down." The Irishman advanced.

"Back off," Schmuel growled. He squeezed Daniel so hard that he squealed. "Keern!"

"What's that? Some kinda name? That your name?"

The Irishman kept advancing, pressing Schmuel backwards up Delancey Street.

"Put him down I said. If you hurt the boy, you are a dead man."

Schmuel fumbled in his pocket. "Big talk. I guess you don't hear so good. I said back off." He pointed his Luger at the Irishman and cocked the trigger.

"Oh man, I don't want no part of this," the blond said. She sidled over to the door of the speakeasy and disappeared inside.

With his druggy bravado fading fast, Schmuel realised there was no way he could take the Irishman in a fair fight. He wasn't that big but the guy looked strong. And if he used his piece right in front of Stutz Feinstein's, there would be hell to pay. One more place in New York where his face would not be welcome. The cops on Stutz's payroll only turned their heads so far when they looked the other way. So it was kind of a standoff.

Well, at least he could use the gun to hold the guy at bay while he tried to figure out what to do next. But the Irishman kept crowding him and Schmuel kept backing away.

"I told you, keep your distance."

"Give me the boy."

"Jeez...Don't you know no other song?"

Schmuel was beginning to wish he'd never bothered to get out of bed. It wasn't like he really wanted the kid anymore. What the hell was he gonna do with him? But he was not about to hand him over to the witch's heavy, just like that. After all, a guy's got pride. "Tonight's the night," he muttered to himself.

"What?"

"Nothin'...So what we gonna do about this here Mexican standoff?"

"You are goin' to put the boy on the ground and stand away from him."

"Nah...I don't think so."

Just about then, it occurred to Schmuel that if he made a dash for Clinton Street, he could maybe make it to the corner of Broome before the Irishman caught up with him. Then he could ditch the kid in some alley and disappear into the night. The more he thought about it, the more he liked the idea.

He glanced over his shoulder to gauge the distance and was astonished to discover that while he was keeping his eye on the Irishman, the stupid mick had forced him backwards onto the westbound ramp of the Williamsburg Bridge. Shit. Now what? They hadn't gone that far, but it was maybe eight, ten feet to the ground. He was fast on his feet but he wasn't no athlete. He'd have to put the kid down to jump clear. Back to square one.

Except for the rain, it was too goddamned quiet. And he was getting fucking soaked. That was why he hadn't even noticed he was standing in the middle of the gutter. Not a car in sight. Well, who goes to Brooklyn in the middle of a weeknight? Nobody. They roll up the sidewalks there at ten o'clock.

Yeah. Nobody.

Schmuel had an inspiration. If he could draw the sucker way up onto the bridge, right out to the middle, he could do what the hell he wanted, even fire a pistol, and who'd know.

"You want the kid, you come and get him," he shouted. He turned toward Brooklyn and ran.

∞

Daniel was too quiet. Mute with terror, he was. If not for the boy, Ciaran would have tried to grab the gun. The fellow was staggering with drink. And anyhow, if he was meaning to use it, sure he would have done it already. Ciaran had more experience with fists and billy clubs than with guns. He could not be sure what Schmuel would do. Until the child was safe away, he had only his voice, the steadiness of his nerve and a few quickly uttered words to the Mother of God to defend them both. He was murderously angry. But he was also helpless.

And then, to his amazement, the fellow began to run towards the middle of the bridge.

Ciaran gave chase, keeping what he guessed to be a safe distance from the gun but never losing sight of Daniel. So close was he focused on Daniel's head, just visible, bobbing limply on Schmuel's left shoulder, that when, about halfway to the first tower, the gunman reached out his right arm and fired, he never even saw it. In fact, he scarce heard the noise of it, no more than a hand clap it was.

Schmuel's aim was wild. Ciaran kept running, dodging the yellow pools of the streetlights. Schmuel fired twice more. Ciaran heard a bullet zing off the railings.

They were nearing the first of the two towers that supported the bridge; an ugly, cross-braced structure of steel girders from which the many levels, the promenade, the subway and trolley tracks, the east and westbound roadways, were suspended. The girders were like ladders climbing into the sky. And the corners of the tower, made of beams joined together, were a size a man could hide himself in. A platform jutted out over the water, carrying a sort of footpath around the tower where it crossed the level of the roadway. It was from this footpath that the tower could be gained.

Sure the thing would be easy enough to climb. Even carrying Daniel, he could do it, no trouble at all. If he could but get the child clear of Schmuel, they could scramble up into the tower and, shielded by the confusion of metal, wait for the fool to use up all his bullets. Then he would carry Daniel through the tower to the promenade and safety.

His chance came soon. Quite unexpectedly, just after he had passed the tower, Schmuel stopped and put the boy down. Ciaran realised that, drunk or no, the man's aim would be much improved without the burden of the child, who stood motionless, seemingly unaware that he had been set free.

As Schmuel squinted into the rainy dark, looking for a target, Ciaran slipped sideways onto the platform. He navigated the footpath with stealth, working his way around the tower until he was almost within reach of Daniel. He filled his lungs and lunged for the child.

Almost at once, he saw Schmuel raise the gun. His sober instincts faster than the gunman's, Ciaran dove for the footpath, shielding Daniel with his body. A bullet whizzed over their heads.

At the same moment, Rachel shouted. "There they are. I can see them Dinah...Over there!"

The sound of her roused Daniel from his trance. "Run boy, run fast to your Mam," Ciaran whispered. "Do it." As the child ran off, Ciaran leapt onto the steel tower and began to climb.

Daniel trundled toward her. He was stumbling blind, his arms spread wide, his eyes tight shut. Rachel broke into a run. When she caught him up, he shrieked in terror.

"It's all right, Daniel. It's Mommy....Sha, sha...it's all right."

Dinah was right behind her. The three of them, crouched in the rain, held onto each other, weeping and shaking. Between hiccoughing sobs, Daniel was trying to tell them something, but all Rachel could make out were the repeated words *bad man, bad man,* and *gun.*

"It's okay now, Daniel. Mommy's here and Aunty Dinah. Don't be afraid."

"Bad man, bad man."

"I know...I know. It's all over now...We'll go home." While she said the words, made the noises to comfort the child, her relief was tempered with dread. Some prowling thing was there. It danced hungry in the shadows. And it was not yet sated. "Where is Ciaran?" she said.

"Keern!" the boy wailed.

Then she heard him, his commanding voice coming to her from so high above that, had she not heard him use that same tone earlier, she would have thought the voice supernal.

"Go home, woman. Take the child and go from here."

Her eyes darted to the tower. At the same time she heard a clattering in the steelwork, as though someone had thrown a rock with great force, a rock that ricocheted among the girders. Daniel's incoherence suddenly made sense.

"Oh my God, Dinah...He's got a gun."

Horrified, she watched Schmuel climb onto the platform railing. Would he climb into the tower himself, chasing Ciaran from level to level? But no, he seemed to lack the courage. Instead he leaned on the tower for balance, looking for Ciaran amid the tangle of metal. She saw him raise his arm again. She did not hear the gunshot, but she saw the flash of flame and heard the clatter of the ricochet.

She had let this happen. She had let him near her. Knowing all the while that she had loosed devils, she had let him love her. She had welcomed him, creature of light, into a darkness she alone had made. Once, when Uncle Shoe's generator failed, they had fumbled for candles in the dark. Ciaran lit a match and, by the light of it, they found the hurricane lamp. "Do you know," he said, "there is a saying of the priests, that the dark is never stronger than the light. For you need but strike a match and a whole universe of darkness will be brought low. It is a fine saying. Do you not think so?"

It was a fine saying and for a time she had let it soothe and beguile her. But it wasn't true. Darkness had followed her soul through generations, finding her again and again, accusing her in voices strange but familiar. *You. You. You.*

437

Yet she sensed he had always been there, waiting to return, to light her emptiness for a little while. Why, if she could never make it right?

But what if she could? If she had set the thing in motion, couldn't she stop it as well? Hadn't he tried to tell her so himself. *Strike a match. Bring the darkness low.* If she could only let go her fear.

She hugged Daniel and pushed him against Dinah. "Take care of him," she said. And she ran to the tower.

"Well, whaddya know. It's a family reunion." Schmuel pointed the gun at her. "Don't come any closer if you know what's good for you."

He squinted into the structure of the tower. "You picked yourself a regular monkey...But I figure he can't stay up there in the trees, so to speak, all night now can he?"

"Please, let us be. He never did anything to you. Why can't you just go away and leave us alone? He was only worried about Daniel."

"Yeah, well I don't take too kindly to stupid micks stickin' their noses in where they ain't wanted. Anyway, what did he think I was gonna do to the kid? It's my kid ain't it? Did he think I was gonna throw it off the bridge into the fucking East River?"

Schmuel tried to twist himself around a girder, without losing his hold, to get a better look. Rachel couldn't see Ciaran but she knew he was above them, maybe as high as the promenade deck. If she could distract Schmuel, keep him talking long enough, Ciaran might run down the promenade to get help, the police or something. As soon as the hope occurred to her, she knew it was a false one. Ciaran would never leave her alone with Schmuel. Already, she could feel him working his way back down through the scaffolding. She would have to try something else.

Schmuel seemed to have spotted his quarry. He raised the pistol.

"No...wait. Talk to me. I can give you what you want."

"Oh yeah? Like what? My father's store maybe? You finally got in mind to hand it over?"

"You know I can't. It isn't mine to give."

"That supposed to mean somethin' to me?"

"Something else is...mine to give. It's worth more than the store. Lots more. You can have it."

At last she had captured his interest. He dropped his gun arm to his side.

"So talk."

Rachel didn't talk. Instead she reached inside the neckline of her blouse and felt the golden beads. They were cold. How odd. Cold as a dead woman's jewels. She undid the clasp and raised the beads up so that Schmuel could see them in the light. "Take them. They're old, very old. They must be worth a fortune. Just take them and go away."

Schmuel put the gun in the hand he was using for support. He snatched the beads and held them up to his face. He tasted one.

"What d'ya take me for? Some kinda schmuck? Piece of shit" he said and he flung the beads over the railing into the salty East River, far below.

Rachel watched the golden beads arc through the light that illuminated the platform, then disappear into the darkness. Her eyes filled with tears.

"Oh God," she said. "What *do* you want? What will it take for you to leave us alone?"

"Don't you get it? Can you give me back my reputation? I'm *askin'* you ...my name? You think I don't hear them laughing behind my back, calling me a loser because I let a coupla broads push me around? Doll, you have not got nothin' that I want no more." He put the gun back in his shooting hand.

That was when Rachel realised that he would kill them both. He would do it without a thought for the consequences and he would do it for no better reason than that it would make him feel good for a little while. At the same time, she and Schmuel both saw Ciaran slipping down through the girders. Now, with nothing to lose, she snatched at Schmuel's gun arm.

Ciaran watched appalled. He had scarce believed his eyes when Rachel appeared below him on the lighted platform. What was wrong with the woman? Had she no sense at all, to try to reason with a man who was half mad with drink and who likely had no scruples at all when he was sober? He could not hear them at first; he could barely see them through the downpour, lit up like a wall by the light of the platform. He did see the treasure disappear over the railings, surprised at how little it touched him with his thoughts all for Rachel. For a few minutes he had been working his way back down toward them, looking for an opportunity to knock the man from his perch. When Rachel struggled for the gun, he was scarce ten feet above them.

"No!" he shouted, but they didn't seem to hear.

"Get off," Schmuel said. He whipped his arm back, catching Rachel full in the face with the barrel. She fell against the railing, blood on her mouth.

When Schmuel turned and pointed the gun at Rachel, there was no mistaking his intention.

With a roar of pain and disbelief that set the whole tower singing, Ciaran flung himself, head first at Schmuel, catching him mid-section. He felt Schmuel's arms fly upward as the man flailed backwards over dark water. He heard the peculiar snapping noise of the gun going off over his head. And then they were both flying.

∞

So much noise. Laughing and screaming and talk, all kinds of talk, in languages she didn't understand. People rushing back and forth, all kinds of people, every which way. Rachel was afraid. Then she heard the splash. Duvi was wrong. You *could* hear a rock hit the water. It made a big echoing noise under the bridge. That was the sign. She would have to cross the bridge to Brooklyn another time.

A lady was touching her. Rachel recoiled. It was not a good thing to talk to strangers, or to let them touch you. Papa said. The lady was crying and talking fast. Rachel didn't understand most of what she said. She had a little boy with her, a pretty little boy. He was crying too.

Rachel realised that her clothes were all wet from the rain. Somehow, she had cut her lip. Her belly hurt too. The lady looked kind. "Will you take me home now?" Rachel said.

The lady helped her to stand up. Then they walked, the lady, the little boy and Rachel, through the crowds of strangers on the Williamsburg Bridge.

"Papa will be angry," Rachel said. "I'm not allowed to go on the bridge."

∞

In day that followed, sometimes she seemed to remember. She would sit in the parlour, clutching pieces of the dress that would not be completed, her silent tears staining the yellow silk. When she was in that state, she said nothing.

At other times, she was back on Rivington Street, worrying about punishments, asking Dinah, whom she took for Tanta Rosa, to tell her stories.

There were days, and these frightened Dinah the most, when she seemed to be somewhere else entirely; terrified, agitated, saying things that made no sense at all. She uttered guttural sounds and words that Dinah was almost sure were foreign.

She took little interest in Daniel, bestowing upon him, when she became aware of his presence, a distant kindness of the sort that any woman would give a troubled child.

She never mentioned Ciaran's name or opened the door of his room.

Two days later, the police called on Dinah to tell her that her brother's body had washed up on the Jersey shore. She took the news with a grim coldness that must have surprised them. There was no word of Ciaran, though Duvi and Mendel looked at half a dozen John Does in the City Morgue.

A few days after that, Mendel took Daniel home to Helen. Then Dinah closed the shop and she and Mendel took Rachel to Uncle Shoe's farm in Connecticut.

Part Six

Stay me with flagons, comfort me with apples; for I am sick of love.

The Song of Solomon, 2:5

CHAPTER FORTY FIVE

Changed altogether

The Gustafino boys were going deep sea fishing. *Rain or shine* they had said to each other as they loaded up *The Rosalie* with their brand new fishing rods and a bucket of stinking gills and fish heads from the restaurant. *What's a little extra water?* they had laughed as, before dawn, they stowed bread, cheese and salami, and two jugs of Uncle Renzo's special brew, below.

But less than twenty minutes after they set out, Sal Gustafino, at the helm, was convinced that today was not going to be the day they tackled the Atlantic Ocean after all. The rain showed no sign of easing and the weather was altogether filthy. Sal's cheap yellow oilskins let water in all over the place. His armpits were wet, his neck was getting chapped and the rivulets coursing down his trousers were soaking his socks. They were still on the East River; they hadn't even come close to any real water yet, but his cousins, Polly and Freddo, were both hanging over the stern puking their guts into the wake.

Sal had worked at the Brooklyn Navy Yard before he joined the family business. Even though he only cooked in the civilian mess, everybody figured he knew the most about boats. So they made him captain. Now he made a captain's decision. They would have to forget about chasing cod fish, blue and sea bass, south of Long Island. Instead, they'd stick close to Brooklyn and slip into the shelter of Sheepshead Bay. The day wouldn't be a total loss. Plenty of flounder in Sheepshead Bay.

He wondered how he was going to break this disappointing news to his cousins. This was no ordinary fishing trip. The three Gustafinos had been planning it for years; ever since Uncle Renzo said that if they fixed her up, they could use *The Rosalie* whenever they wanted.

They had put two years of their spare time and most of their cash, spare and not so spare, to the task. Polly, who was good with motors, restored the engine and the generator. Freddo spruced up the hull, the deck and the tiny cabin. Sal supervised.

She was ready in June, all twenty-two feet of her ship shape and shiny. She even had running lights to go out in the dark. But so far, they had ventured no further than the mouth of Newtown Creek, just to get the hang of handling her. Back in Palermo, Uncle Renzo had not been known as a sharp dealer for nothing. After all their hard work, it had still taken most of the summer to talk him into giving them time off from the spaghetti house together. As it was, they had to be back in Greenpoint by three-thirty to get ready for the supper crowd.

"Some sailors, you guys," Sal shouted. "We ain't even gone under the Brooklyn Bridge yet."

Over the noisy grind of the engine, he could just about hear their replies, strangled grunts and fresh bouts of retching. Then Polly started yelling. "Christ almighty. Turn the boat around!"

Sal began to laugh. They might not be so disappointed after all. "Hey, whatsa matter you? Nobody never died from being seasick."

"Turn it around! Turn it around!"

"Whatsa matter? You okay? Somebody go overboard?"

He looked over his shoulder. Freddo and Polly were waving and pointing into the darkness behind them.

"Did you see that?" Freddo shouted. "Turn the boat around. We gotta get a closer look. Christ...Are you deaf? Didn't you hear it?"

"This ain't no sightseeing tour...Anyway, you're supposed to say 'Come about'."

"Yeah, yeah, whatever. Just do it moron. And get the flashlight, the big one. Somebody just fell off the Williamsburg Bridge!"

Flying falling holding tight to something someone the thunder of waves breaking and tumbling over and over over and over over and over in the lonely silent down down dark

I am so cold oh mother of god and I am I am

Who watches me what slippery fingers touch me pull me and bony faces calling toothless mouths full of names I cannot hear names I do not know do not remember

Promise me Say that you promise

My shirt against my face a shroud of linen   and from my pockets things of no importance slip away slip up and away to where *Always when you go on the water Say that you promise* I will I do I am

They call to me   names that were mine but are not   home that was home but is not and Lord I am so cold

A circle of light full and white   moon not moon   a bar of moonlight cutting through the dark to rest on gold *Come home*   but in its moonsilver a packet of linen unfolding unfolding above me spreading a web of light *that you will wear it in your pocket always when you go on the water Always Say that you promise* promise promise   that will not rest rest rest rest for I am am am

I am the promise   I am   I am the promise   unbroken   that will not that will not rest without I

Oh!

Below him, the treasure glittered from the algae thick dark and called to him by name. For one, lung splitting second, Ciaran hesitated. But it was of the sea now and he could not be. Because he was promised. He kicked his powerful legs. One of his shoes came free. He was startled to feel water flow through and around his toes. Wriggling his other foot free, he reached for the sparkling web that was spreading above him, freed from the linen packet as its blue ribbon floated away. Fierce pain flamed across his chest. He ignored it. He had promised her he would keep it always and while he was living, for as long or as little as that might be, his word would not fail. He struggled to grab hold of the filmy veil suspended between himself and the circle of light that was a dancing moon, sailing back and forth across the ceiling of the sea. His hand broke the surface. Somebody grabbed it.

The Rosalie's engines laboured to hold the little boat in place against the tide. All three Gustafino boys stared at the motionless man, sprawled belly down, his face in the puddle he had choked and vomited onto the deck. He had cried out once, in pain, when Polly leaned on his back to push the water from his lungs. Then he passed out.

Irresistible curiosity had led them to search the water under the bridge. They had never expected to haul in a living man. Freddo nearly fainted when the fellow's hand came up into the beam of the flashlight. The import of their reflexive rescue was just beginning to dawn on them.

"So now what we gonna do?" Sal said.

"We gotta go ashore someplace and call the cops or an ambulance or something," Freddo said.

"Yeah...so much for fishing trips."

"Why? We turn him over to somebody and then we go. How long could it take?"

"The rest of the day, maybe."

"Whaddya talking about? It's nothin' to do with us."

"Yeah? You think maybe the cops are gonna say, 'Thanks a lot boys. Have a good catch.'? Use your brains. They're gonna wanna know where we found him, what we saw. Hours it'll take."

"But we didn't see nothin'. Only that he jumped off the bridge."

"You know for sure he jumped? You don't know. What if somebody threw him off? What if the somebody what threw him off thinks we seen more than we seen?"

"Geez, I didn't think of that."

"Nobody never thinks of nothin' except me. .Any way you look at it, we get involved, the day is shot."

They passed around a jug of Uncle Renzo's special brew. Polly, who had handled the man more than the others, who had felt his breath and his one agonised cry through his fingertips, felt responsible.

"So whaddya saying, Sal?" he said. "We can't just dump him back. The guy is alive. We gotta do something."

"Yeah, I know." Sal took another swig from the jug and considered the options. "We could leave him somewhere," he said, "you know, where somebody'll find him. Like over by the Navy Yard. They got guards there all the time, all over the place."

Polly and Freddo looked doubtful.

"He ain't bleeding or nothing," Sal said. "He'll be okay...I guess."

"What if nobody finds him for a couple of hours?" Freddo said. "He could die...I don't know Sal. I mean, maybe this is like a test or something."

"A test?"

"You know...from the guy upstairs."

"Whadda you nuts?"

"Well, how come we just happen to be right there when this guy hits the water? You tell me. And alive. You think that happens every day? Whaddya

448

think the odds are that happening, just like that? You telling me things don't happen 'cause maybe they're s'posed to?"

Sal scowled.

"You think He ain't watching us all the time...to see what we get up to?" Freddo rubbed his St. Christopher medal. "You think he don't know what..."

"Awright, awright. Since when did you become St. Francis of Assisi?"

"I'm just saying..."

"Yeah, and I'm just thinking." While he was thinking, Sal had turned the boat toward the Brooklyn Navy Yard. Finally, he spoke. "Look, here's the plan. We go in, without lights, to one of them piers that's got steps down to them floating docks at the bottom...So we leave him on the dock, and, after, we make a lotta noise. We don't take off until we see somebody coming down the steps. We don't got no lights on; they can't see the name on the boat. By the time they get to the dock, we're on our way to Sheepshead Bay and they're too busy with *this* guy to worry about us. That make you happy, Monsignor?"

"Yeah...awright. Whaddya mean, Sheepshead Bay?"

∞

Light. Dark. Noise. Pain. Lifting hands and people shouting. *What is your name? Do you know where you are? Do you know how you got here?* When he breathed, it hurt. When he tried to move his head, it hurt. When he thought of her somewhere, frightened, crying, it hurt.

Engines and sirens and slamming doors. A corridor of green sea ice and flying globes of light. Angels with crisp white wings instead of haloes. Dreamless dark.

Someone pried open his eye, pulling him into pain and blinding light. A man with a mirror for a hat shone a light at him. *What is your name? Can you hear me? You've had a bad knock on the head. Do you understand me?* He tried to tell them, to say her name, but they did not seem to hear him. The man with a mirror for a hat said words that made no sense. *Concussion. Ribs. You're doing fine, Ray.* Was she there, dressed in light, with crisp white wings where a halo should be? Turning and turning, writing circles in the dew. Her eyes sad, hungry; bigger and bigger and bigger until there was nothing but their darkness. Nothing... darkness...nothing.

Through half closed lids, he watched a woman dressed in white, wearing a cap of starched white lace, hang a bottle upside down on a pole beside him. He was not certain how long he had been watching her adjust sheets, plump pillows. She didn't seem to notice that he was watching, busy as she was talking to somebody he couldn't see without turning his head, somebody named Ray. "I'll just straighten these blankets so you'll be more comfortable, Ray ...You're doing just fine, Ray ... Another bottle already? What a hungry fellow you are Ray..." His head was too heavy for turning, just at the moment.

Drowsily, and with slightly amused curiosity, he remembered he had taken this woman, or could be another dressed just the same, for an angel. When was that? She attached a brown rubber tube to the bottle. He felt her lift an arm, vaguely aware that it was his own. While she fiddled with something that had to do with the brown rubber tube and the arm, he remained limp. It was pleasant enough to be handled so gently by the soft hands of a woman. Then she touched something hard, sticking into the soft place beneath his elbow. The protest of an angry bruise stung him full awake.

"Ach!"

The woman jumped. "Well hello, Ray," she said. "How long have you been back with us?"

He tried to speak but his tongue was thick and gluey.

"Here, this will help." She put a bent glass drinking straw into his mouth. "Just a little, not too much."

With the water, he sipped feeling back into his tongue and lips. The woman smiled. "Better?"

"Mmm hmm...Why do you call me Ray?"

"I'm sorry, I don't mean to be familiar. But we don't know your last name."

He let her puzzling answer pass. "Is it a hospital I am in? I am livin' then?"

"I should hope so. You may be confused now. Don't worry it will pass. You've been asleep for quite a while."

"I have?" It seemed to Ciaran that he had been deep in pain and confusion only moments before. "How long?"

"The doctor will want to have a look at you. He'll be pleased you're awake." She turned to go.

"But wait...I...," he tried to sit up and discovered that, besides being dizzy, he was stiff and bound around the middle.

"Easy does it," the nurse said. "One step at a time." She helped him to sit, stacking up the pillows and adjusting a mechanical device behind the bed. "You broke some ribs. Doctor Miller will be around soon. You can ask him whatever you like."

"Do they, does Rachel know that I am here?"

"Is she your wife?"

It was easier to nod assent than to explain.

"She must be very worried about you. Does she have a telephone?"

Again, he nodded.

"After the doctor sees you, we'll call her up. All right?" She turned and left.

For the first time since he had opened his eyes, Ciaran took a proper look around. It was a ward he was in, long and sickly green, with double doors at either end and beds lining the walls. He could scarce count how many. Fifty at least. Could be more. Doctors, nurses, visitors and attendants of one sort and another milled about, wheeling trolleys, seeing to the sick and filling the high ceilinged space with whispers and groans. Dusty bands of daylight poured down from windows that were too high for any sort of view. The whole place reeked of disinfectant, urine and boiled carrots.

The strongest smell came from the bed beside him where a fellow was attacking a plate of greyish food. Ciaran must have been staring, for after a moment the fellow seemed to feel the need to speak.

"Yeah, I know, it's pretty disgusting. But what can you do? So, Rip Van Winkle, how you doin'?"

Why was everybody calling him names that were not his? "Who?"

"You know, that guy that fell asleep for twenty years; grew a long beard and everything, just like you. Bet if he snored like you, somebody woulda woke him up a whole lot sooner."

Ciaran touched his face. He had not gone without shaving since the three week crossing, so long ago it was in another life. Now he felt two weeks growth at least. Maybe more.

"Do you know how long I have been sleepin'?"

"No idea Mac. I only been here a coupla days myself...broken leg."

"Ah...What place is this, then? Bellevue I suppose?"

"Bellevue? You musta been in pretty bad shape even before you got slammed. We're in Brooklyn, pal. This here's King's County."

Brooklyn? How ever did he come to be there?

451

"Have you maybe seen somebody come to visit me, or ask after me at all?"

"Like I said, I only been here a coupla days...The cops come every day. And a guy from the immigration, yesterday. You some kinda gangster or something? They waitin' to send you back to wherever you come from?"

Ciaran's mind was too full of his own questions to answer anybody else's. Why had she not come looking for him? He remembered the sound of Schmuel's gun going off. Sure and it was over their heads. Harmless, into the sky. But what if it were not that way at all? What if she had come to grief. Or the boy. And had he killed the fellow? He could scarce breathe for the rush of panic. He had to get out of this place.

He swung his feet over the side of the bed and tested his balance. He had to sit at once; shaking he was, like a wee'un, new to standing. He took a deep breath and tried again. Well hadn't he felt wobbly, the like of this, for drink, or worse and all, more than once in his life? He had managed to stay upright then and he would manage it now.

"Hey Mac, take it easy. I didn't mean you no offence or nothing."

"There is none taken. Only I mean to stretch my legs for a bit of a while. Where do they put your clothes in this place?"

The man pointed to the metal bedside cabinet. Inside, Ciaran found his trousers and shirt, but no shoes. No matter. He pulled the tapes off his bruised inner arm and freed himself from the rubber tube with its short metal needle. A few drops of dark blood sprang to the centre of the bruise. Finding nothing with which to stop it, he tore a piece off the bottom of his unhemmed hospital gown and tied it round. As he slipped into his clothes, he stared in wonder at his bare, now unwebbed, toes that looked like they belonged to another. "Changed altogether," he muttered, thinking all the while that could be *that* was no matter and all.

Around the ward, busy people engaged themselves in their tasks. No one paid him any mind. He had only to walk through the doors and leave. Now, before the police came asking after him again. Or the immigration. He must find his way back to East Broadway. To home. To Rachel. Slowly, and as casually as his agitated state would allow, he made for the doors opposite the direction in which the nurse had vanished.

"Hey fella..."

He froze, his hand on the brass push plate. An orderly addressed him.

"...if you're looking for the john it's down on the next landing."

Not trusting himself to speak, Ciaran nodded and pushed through.

Five minutes later he was a free man, sticking his thumb out toward the sparse traffic of a Brooklyn morning. His pockets were empty and his feet were bare.

The shop was locked. He pounded on the boards that covered the smashed hall doorway but no one came. His racing brain guessing at disasters, Ciaran slid to down onto the milkbox beside the door and sat back against the shuttered shop to gather his strength. He had crossed the Brooklyn Bridge in the back of a builder's pick-up truck. He was tired and cold. How did it get to be autumn, so sudden like? He was hungry too and now, with the smells of turpentine and paint on his clothes mingling with pungent spoiled milk, he thought he might faint. Milk? Shifting to the ground, he opened the box and gagged at the stink. The box was made to hold six bottles but he counted at least ten, the newer deliveries laid on their sides atop the standing quarts. The first two he opened were too repellent to taste. A third was at the point of turning but was just palatable.

People passed in the street. No one bothered about a barefoot man, sitting on the ground drinking milk from a bottle. No one stopped to ask him his troubles and he was grateful, for what at all could he say who didn't even know the day of the week?

He waited for the milk to settle on his uneasy stomach. Then he made his way to Pier 25 and Mendel's warehouse on the docks.

CHAPTER FORTY SIX

The Harvest

Desperate October. The sun burned hard but vain through steely cataract skies. Around the little house, trees flamed, red and yellow defiance of inevitable winter. Cold crisped the edges of shortening days and only in the apple shed, where Uncle Shoe made cider from windfallen fruit, did the promise of renewal linger in summer nurtured scent.

For three weeks, Ciaran had been doing harvest work, a visitor and helper only. Once, the place had made him safe, had welcomed him with wholeness and a home feeling, solid and familiar. Now the feeling came and went, skittish and tentative, holding him at arm's length from the life he thought he had found. As did she.

The others had tried to prepare him, to tell him she had changed. After the tears and greetings, after they had pieced together their half-known histories of missing weeks and wondered at the restoration of a friendship snatched from death, Mendel phoned the farm but no one would let him speak to her.

"Not now," Shoe said. "You'll come. You'll see."

Then, though he had been desperate to leave at once, Mendel insisted they stop first at East Broadway to find him shoes and warmer clothes and food. In the parlour, the mirror was covered with a cloth, a hasty gesture of mourning. Mendel pulled it off. Ciaran snatched up his fiddle but found no comfort, clutching it all the way to Connecticut, while Mendel talked.

"She's different, far away, like when she was little."

Sure if she had become like a child, Mendel would have said so clear, straight off. Sensing there was more, Ciaran waited.

"You know, my father...he has a temper."

"Aye, she has said. And sure the man must hold his anger hard, for all this while he hasn't never spoke to her nor seen her at all."

"I don't think she cares."

"Is it the truth? I think it seems so, only."

"Well maybe, maybe not. All of us, when we were kids and he would be angry, we were all afraid of him. Even Duvi, with that smart mouth he's got on him. Even him. But not Rachel. Never. When he would be yelling and banging his fist on the table, or waving his finger at Mama, it was like Rachel would go away...someplace else. And then, she would come out with things that...that..." Mendel sighed. "How can I explain this?" he said. "Sometimes she would say things that made no sense. Or made too much sense, for a child to say, if you see what I mean. It used to scare my mother. So now, this is how she is, all the time...with all of us. She doesn't ask about Daniel. She never said your name, since...since...you know. And all the time she talks about Bubbie Ruchel. My grandmother. Bubbie Ruchel says this, Bubbie Ruchel says that..."

"Could be, she has fond memories that give her comfort. I talk of my Grand Da Donal much the same."

"Rachel never knew Bubbie Ruchel. She died before Rachel was born, Ciaran. I don't know, maybe she wouldn't even know you."

He could not say for certain whether she knew him or not. She seemed pleased to see him, in the mild sort of way that lonely people and old folk are glad of visitors to distract them from their sorrowful way of living. Nothing more. And though he ached to wrap his arms around her, to lift her up and bury his face in her hair, he had promised Mendel and Shoe he would wait for her to come to him. She didn't.

Shoe counselled patience. "Some shock it was, for all of us. But for Rucheleh, to see for herself, with her own eyes *nisht du gedacht*. And right before the wedding. Who knows what's going on in that head of hers now? So, you'll stay, pick apples. I'll teach you to work the cider press. She'll get used to you again. We all will."

Shoe's eyes, brimming with emotion, brought Bertie to mind so that Ciaran, too, came close to tears. Then Shoes slapped Ciaran on the shoulder and laughed. "If God wanted a tragedy," he said, "he wouldn't have made such a miracle that you should have a head as hard as a rock."

Ciaran would have been willing to do as Uncle Shoe said. Mother of God, he would have courted her all over again with songs and stories and moonlight walks along the shore. If not for what Dinah hinted, sure wouldn't he have been willing to wait all of his days just to feel her hand, full of trust, in his?

The night before she went, with Mendel, back to the city, Dinah invited him to walk after supper. She didn't say what it was that was on her mind until they were well clear of the house.

"There's something you should know," she said. "I haven't told the others because...well I can't be sure of it, but you have to know."

They had arrived at the stone wall that separated Shoe's orchard from the beach. Dinah had fallen silent. She had her back to him and was looking out over the Sound. "What is it," Ciaran asked. "What is it that you are wanting to say."

"You will stay with Rachel, no matter what, won't you."

"Aye, of course I will, why would you even ask me such a thing?"

"Because," Dinah said, without turning to face him, "I think she is in a family way."

He didn't speak at once. How could he with such a confusion of feelings, happiness and worry and frustration all fighting for his voice? Could be, in the dark, Dinah didn't see his distress of joy. She spoke again, slowly. "Do you understand what I'm saying, Ciaran? I think she's carrying your child."

"Ach, sure and I do, Dinah. And isn't it a grand miracle of a thing." He put his arms round her and lifted her right off the ground. At last the words came spilling out of him, unstoppable as tears. "A grand thing that you are telling me...Oh...a grand thing...grand...I will look after them, Dinah, her and the babe and Daniel too. You know that I will."

"I only pray to God that she'll let you."

Waiting all his days was not a choice anymore. Dinah was right. He could see it in the tight pulled stitches along the sides of her dresses, in the way she hiked the waists up high, for comfort. And yet, she was withering away. For she ate almost nothing at all. Her eyes, that had once frightened him with their still depth, darted about, nervous and preoccupied, peering out from shadowed hollows over sunken cheeks. Blue veins traced visible paths along the backs of her hands that were become like wee birds' claws. Could be she didn't know or care that life was growing inside of her, but it was devouring her all the same.

The wonder of it was, she was willing enough to work beside him. Right now she was waiting while he gathered windfall apples for the press. Forever, was a fine promise for stories, he thought, as he carried a bushel up through the orchard, but in the end, stories was just stories. Despite Shoe's advice, he must force her to come back. And soon.

The sound of machinery emerged from the shed. She had started grinding apples to make the mash that they would spread in frames and stack between felt blankets in the press. She was hard on it and did not see him watching from the doorway. His weeks of treading carefully had brought her no closer. Instinctively, he wanted to take her up and shake her awake. Maybe they were wrong, the others. Could be he shoulda done it from the start. There was only one thing certain; he could not bear to look at her so frail and distracted any more.

He would not.

Leaving the basket behind, he strode up to the house. Shoe was washing pots. Between them, the two men had enough bachelor years behind them to know well enough how to fend for themselves. Ciaran examined the contents of the icebox.

"Already you're hungry? We just had breakfast."

"No," Ciaran said. "She is."

Shoe raised his eyebrows but said nothing.

Armed with a glass of milk, a banana and a piece of boiled beef, Ciaran marched to the shed.

He wasted no time with pleasantries. "Here," he commanded. "Eat this."

"What? But I'm not hungry."

"It is no matter. There is hard work to be doing and you are wasting away for want of food. Eat it."

"But I..."

"*Eat!*"

To his amazement, she sat on the edge of a crate and, while he towered over her, sipped some milk and nibbled at the banana.

"All right?" she said.

"Aye, for now. When we go up to the house at lunch time, you will eat again, a proper meal."

"Why?"

"Why? What kinda daft question is that?"

"I mean, why do you care whether I eat or not?"

"Ach, look at yourself, woman. There was little enough to you to begin with. You are after turning yourself into one of them wraiths that haunt the glens with this foolishness."

At any other time, the brief, dark look she aimed his way would have shivered him through. But he was having none of this no more. Enough was enough.

They went to work, herself ladling the sticky brown pulp in the frames and him stacking them. The air was thick with sweetness.

"It is a fine smell. Do you not think so?"

She didn't answer. After a few minutes she rested her ladle on the side of the barrel. "It doesn't matter, you know," she said.

"What doesn't matter?"

"All of this...It's only dreams... that turn and turn again. You don't have to be sad or afraid. Dreams can't hurt you."

Now he had decided not to wait, he had also decided not to indulge such nonsense. His own anger surprised him so he took a breath to master himself. "I am not a dream," he said. "I am real. I am a..."

"Don't, I..."

He ignored her interruption and pressed on. "I am real and I am a man that loves you, Rachel. Daniel, your frightened wee boy that you have not even asked after is real and needing of his Mam. And him that is growing inside you, he is real too."

She didn't move. Her startled face, crossed with confusion, filled him with regret for his outburst. And what at all was he thinking of to talk to her of the child? Did she even know of it in the state that she was in? He was suddenly exhausted. He leaned against the cider press. "Ach, Rachel," he sighed. "I am not a dream. I am a man. And I am tired. And I am wanting to come home."

He watched her take up the ladle and spoon apple pulp from the barrel into the frames. Ah, what had he done with his impatience? Had he frightened her even deeper and farther away? For a while longer they worked together in silence.

But, when she looked up at him at last there was recognition in her calm, steady eyes; recognition and, for the first time in months, a kind of unveiled warmth.

"*She* maybe," she said.

"What are you saying?" She didn't answer but he thought he detected the hint of a smile playing across her face and heard the whisper of a laugh. She turned back to her work as a cloud of apple scent enveloped them both.

Acknowledgements

This book was a long time in the making. I would like to thank these friends, colleagues and experts without whose help it would not have been written:

Author Catherine Charley for introducing me to Rathlin Island and for sharing family recollections of summers at The Manor; Janet Mattes for years of unflagging support, editorial suggestions, tireless proof reading and friendship; my editor Larry O'Connor for his light suggestions that made a world of difference; Ulster storyteller Liz Weir for sharing selkie stories and Rathlin contacts; Rathlin storyteller Jim McFaul for his tales of Paddy the climber and memorable hours sharing island stories over Jamesons and endless cups of Irish coffee; Linda Ballard, folklorist at the Ulster Folk and Transport Museum for her knowledge of early twentieth century Rathlin customs and speech; my late grandmothers for the memories that inspired the story and added the textures of life in early twentieth century New York City; the New York City Department of Transport for history and engineering expertise about the Williamsburg Bridge; fellow writers and UEA workshop members for support and critiques, and, last but not least the late Malcolm Bradbury for his generosity and encouragement.

About the Author

Ferne Arfin earned a degree in journalism, speech and drama at Syracuse University in New York and worked as a journalist, copywriter and actress before doing the MA in Creative Writing at the University of East Anglia. She works as a travel writer and lives in London with Lulu, a feisty and well-travelled West Highland terrier.